ESSAYS OF
MICHEL DE MONTAIGNE

Essays of
MICHEL DE
Montaigne

TRANSLATED BY Charles Cotton

SELECTED AND ILLUSTRATED BY

Salvador Dali

DOUBLEDAY & COMPANY, INC.

Garden City, New York

CONTENTS

TO THE READER

READER, *thou hast here an honest book; it doth at the outset forewarn thee that, in contriving the same, I have proposed to myself no other than a domestic and private end: I have had no consideration at all either to thy service or to my glory. My powers are not capable of any such design. I have dedicated it to the particular commodity of my kinsfolk and friends, so that, having lost me (which they must do shortly), they may therein recover some traits of my conditions and humors, and by that means preserve more whole, and more life-like, the knowledge they had of me. Had my intention been to seek the world's favor, I should surely have adorned myself with borrowed beauties: I desire therein to be viewed as I appear in mine own genuine, simple, and ordinary manner, without study and artifice: for it is myself I paint. My defects are therein to be read to the life, and my imperfections and my natural form, so far as public reverence hath permitted me. If I had lived among those nations, which (they say) yet dwell under the sweet liberty of nature's primitive laws, I assure thee I would most willingly have painted myself quite fully and quite naked. Thus, reader, myself am the matter of my book: there's no reason thou shouldst employ thy leisure about so frivolous and vain a subject. Therefore, farewell.*

From Montaigne, the 12th June, 1580.

ESSAYS OF
MICHEL DE MONTAIGNE

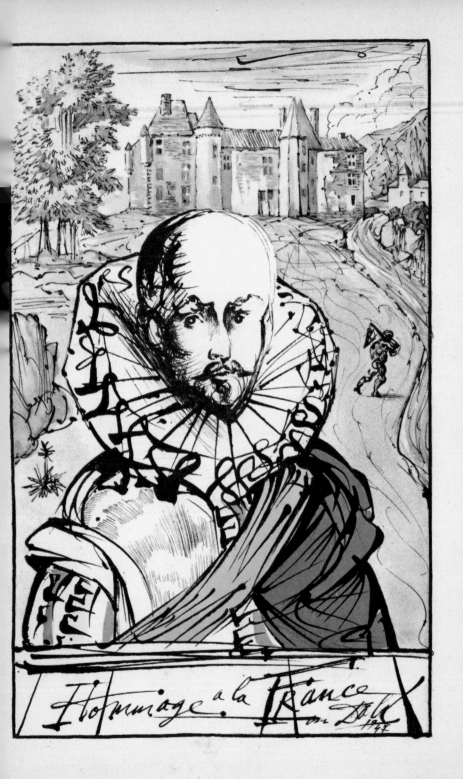

Hommage à la France on Dalí 1947

I

OF CUSTOM, AND THAT WE SHOULD NOT

EASILY CHANGE A LAW RECEIVED

HE SEEMS to have had a right and true apprehension of the power of custom, who first invented the story of a country-woman who, having accustomed herself to play with and carry a young calf in her arms, and daily continuing to do so as it grew up, obtained this by custom, that, when grown to be a great ox, she was still able to bear it. For, in truth, custom is a violent and treacherous schoolmistress. She, by little and little, slily and unperceived, slips in the foot of her authority, but having by this gentle and humble beginning, with the benefit of time, fixed and established it, she then unmasks a furious and tyrannic countenance, against which we have no more the courage or the power so much as to lift up our eyes. We see her, at every turn, forcing and violating the rules of nature: *"Usus efficacissimus rerum omnium magister."* I refer to her Plato's cave in his Republic, and the physicians, who so often submit the reasons of their art to her authority; as the story of that king, who by custom brought his stomach to that pass, as to live by poison, and the maid that Albertus reports to have lived upon spiders. In that new world of the Indies, there were found great nations, and in very differing climates, who were of the same diet, made provision of them, and fed them for their tables; as also, they did grasshoppers, mice, lizards, and bats; and in a time of scarcity of such delicacies, a toad was sold for six crowns, all which they cook, and dish up with several sauces. There were also others found, to whom our diet, and the flesh we eat, were venomous and

[1]

mortal. *"Consuetudinis magna vis est: pernoctant venatores in nive: in montibus uri se patiuutur: pugiles cœstibus contusi, ne ingemiscunt quidem."*

These strange examples will not appear so strange if we consider what we have ordinary experience of, how much custom stupefies our senses. We need not go to what is reported of the people about the cataracts of the Nile; and what philosophers believe of the music of the spheres, that the bodies of those circles being solid and smooth, and coming to touch and rub upon one another, cannot fail of creating a marvelous harmony, the changes and cadences of which cause the revolutions and dances of the stars; but that the hearing sense of all creatures here below, being universally, like that of the Egyptians, deafened, and stupefied with the continual noise, cannot, how great soever, perceive it. Smiths, millers, pewterers, forgemen and armorers could never be able to live in the perpetual noise of their own trades, did it strike their ears with the same violence that it does ours.

My perfumed doublet gratifies my own smelling at first; but after I have worn it three days together, 'tis only pleasing to the bystanders. This is yet more strange, that custom, notwithstanding long intermissions and intervals, should yet have the power to unite and establish the effect of its impressions upon our senses, as is manifest in such as live near unto steeples and the frequent noise of the bells. I myself lie at home in a tower, where every morning and evening a very great bell rings out the *Ave Maria:* the noise shakes my very tower, and at first seemed insupportable to me; but I am so used to it, that I hear it without any manner of offense, and often without awaking at it.

Plato reprehending a boy for playing at nuts, "Thou reprovest me," says the boy, "for a very little thing." "Custom," replied Plato, "is no little thing." I find that our greatest vices derive their first propensity from our most tender infancy, and that our principal education depends upon the nurse. Mothers are mightily pleased to see a child writhe off the neck of a chicken, or to please itself with hurting a dog or a cat; and such wise fathers there are in the world, who look upon it as a notable mark of a martial spirit, when

[2]

they hear a son miscall, or see him domineer over a poor peasant, or a lackey, that dares not reply, nor turn again; and a great sign of wit, when they see him cheat and overreach his playfellow by some malicious treachery and deceit. Yet these are the true seeds and roots of cruelty, tyranny, and treason; they bud and put out there, and afterward shoot up vigorously, and grow to prodigious bulk, cultivated by custom. And it is a very dangerous mistake to excuse these vile inclinations upon the tenderness of their age, and the triviality of the subject; first, it is nature that speaks, whose declaration is then more sincere, and inward thoughts more undisguised, as it is more weak and young; secondly, the deformity of cozenage does not consist nor depend upon the difference between crowns and pins; but I rather hold it more just to conclude thus: why should he not cozen in crowns since he does it in pins, than as they do, who say they only play for pins, they would not do it if it were for money? Children should carefully be instructed to abhor vices for their own contexture; and the natural deformity of those vices ought so to be represented to them, that they may not only avoid them in their actions, but especially so to abominate them in their hearts, that the very thought, should be hateful to them, with what mask soever they may be disguised.

I know very well, for what concerns myself, that from having been brought up in my childhood to a plain and straightforward way of dealing, and from having had an aversion to all manner of juggling and foul play in my childish sports and recreations (and, indeed, it is to be noted, that the plays of children are not performed in play, but are to be judged in them as their most serious actions), there is no game so small wherein from my own bosom naturally, and without study or endeavor, I have not an extreme aversion for deceit. I shuffle and cut and make as much clatter with the cards, and keep as strict account for farthings, as it were for double pistoles; when winning or losing against my wife and daughter, 'tis indifferent to me, as when I play in good earnest with others, for round sums. At all times, and in all places, my own eyes are sufficient to look to my fingers; I am not so narrowly watched by any other, neither is there any I have more respect to.

[3]

I saw the other day, at my own house, a little fellow, a native of Nantes, born without arms, who has so well taught his feet to perform the services his hands should have done him, that truly these have half forgotten their natural office; and, indeed, the fellow calls them his hands; with them he cuts anything, charges and discharges a pistol, threads a needle, sews, writes, puts off his hat, combs his head, plays at cards and dice, and all this with as much dexterity as any other could do who had more, and more proper, limbs to assist him. The money I gave him—for he gains his living by showing these feats—he took in his foot, as we do in our hand. I have seen another who, being yet a boy, flourished a two-handed sword, and, if I may so say, handled a halberd with the mere motions of his neck and shoulders for want of hands; tossed them into the air, and caught them again, darted a dagger, and cracked a whip as well as any coachman in France.

But the effects of custom are much more manifest in the strange impressions she imprints in our minds, where she meets with less resistance. What has she not the power to impose upon our judgments and beliefs? Is there any so fantastic opinion (omitting the gross impostures of religions, with which we see so many great nations, and so many understanding men, so strangely besotted; for this being beyond the reach of human reason, any error is more excusable in such as are not endued, through the divine bounty, with an extraordinary illumination from above), but, of other opinions, are there any so extravagant, that she has not planted and established for laws in those parts of the world upon which she has been pleased to exercise her power? And therefore that ancient exclamation was exceeding just: "*Non pudet physicum, id est speculatorem venatoremque naturæ, ab animis consuetudine imbutis quærere testimonium veritatis?*"

I do believe, that no so absurd or ridiculous fancy can enter into human imagination, that does not meet with some example of public practice, and that, consequently, our reason does not ground and back up. There are people, among whom it is the fashion to turn their backs upon him they salute, and never look upon the man they intend to honor. There is a place, where, whenever the king spits,

the greatest ladies of his court put out their hands to receive it; and another nation, where the most eminent persons about him stoop to take up his ordure in a linen cloth. Let us here steal room to insert a story.

A French gentleman was always wont to blow his nose with his fingers (a thing very much against our fashion), and he justifying himself for so doing, and he was a man famous for pleasant repartees, he asked me, what privilege this filthy excrement had, that we must carry about us a fine handkerchief to receive it, and, which was more, afterward to lap it carefully up and carry it all day about in our pockets, which, he said, could not but be much more nauseous and offensive, than to see it thrown away, as we did all other evacuations. I found that what he said was not altogether without reason, and by being frequently in his company, that slovenly action of his was at last grown familiar to me; which nevertheless we make a face at, when we hear it reported of another country. Miracles appear to be so, according to our ignorance of nature, and not according to the essence of nature: the continually being accustomed to anything, blinds the eye of our judgment. Barbarians are no more a wonder to us, than we are to them; nor with any more reason, as every one would confess if after having traveled over those remote examples, men could settle themselves to reflect upon, and rightly to confer them with their own. Human reason is a tincture almost equally infused into all our opinions and manners, of what form soever they are; infinite in matter, infinite in diversity. But I return to my subject.

There are peoples, where, his wife and children excepted, no one speaks to the king but through a tube. In one and the same nation, the virgins discover those parts that modesty should persuade them to hide, and the married women carefully cover and conceal them. To which, this custom, in another place, has some relation, where chastity, but in marriage, is of no esteem, for unmarried women may prostitute themselves to as many as they please, and being got with child, may lawfully take physic, in the sight of every one, to destroy their fruit. And, in another place, if a tradesman marry, all of the same condition, who are invited to the wedding, lie

with the bride before him; and the greater number of them there is, the greater is her honor, and the opinion of her ability and strength: if an officer marry, 'tis the same, the same with a laborer, or one of mean condition, but then, it belongs to the lord of the place to perform that office; and yet a severe loyalty during marriage is afterward strictly enjoined. There are places where brothels of young men are kept for the pleasure of women; where the wives go to war as well as the husbands, and not only share in the dangers of battle, but, moreover, in the honors of command. Others, where they wear rings not only through their noses, lips, cheeks, and on their toes, but also weighty gimmals of gold thrust through their paps and buttocks; where, in eating, they wipe their fingers upon their thighs, genitories, and the soles of their feet: where children are excluded, and brothers and nephews only inherit; and elsewhere, nephews only, saving in the succession of the prince: where, for the regulation of community in goods and estates, observed in the country, certain sovereign magistrates have committed to them the universal charge and overseeing of the agriculture, and distribution of the fruits, according to the necessity of every one: where they lament the death of children, and feast at the decease of old men; where they lie ten or twelve in a bed, men and their wives together: where women, whose husbands come to violent ends, may marry again, and others not: where the condition of women is looked upon with such contempt, that they kill all the native females, and buy wives of their neighbors to supply their use; where husbands may repudiate their wives without showing any cause, but wives cannot part from their husbands, for what cause soever; where husbands may sell their wives in case of sterility; where they boil the bodies of their dead, and afterward pound them to a pulp, which they mix with their wine, and drink it; where the most coveted sepulture is to be eaten with dogs, and elsewhere by birds; where they believe the souls of the blessed live in all manner of liberty, in delightful fields, furnished with all sorts of delicacies, and that it is these souls, repeating the words we utter, which we call echo; where they fight in the water, and shoot their arrows with the most mortal aim, swimming; where, for a sign of subjection, they lift up their shoul-

ders, and hang down their heads; where they put off their shoes when they enter the king's palace; where the eunuchs, who take charge of the sacred women, have, moreover, their lips and noses cut off, that they may not be loved; where the priests put out their own eyes, to be better acquainted with their demons, and the better to receive their oracles; where every one makes to himself a deity of what he likes best; the hunter of a lion or a fox, the fisher of some fish; idols of every human action or passion; in which place, the sun, the moon, and the earth are the principal deities, and the form of taking an oath is, to touch the earth, looking up to heaven; where both flesh and fish is eaten raw; where the greatest oath they take is, to swear by the name of some dead person of reputation, laying their hand upon his tomb; where the new year's gift the king sends every year to the princes, his vassals, is fire, which being brought, all the old fire is put out, and the neighboring people are bound to fetch the new, every one for themselves, upon pain of high treason; where, when the king, to betake himself wholly to devotion, retires from his administration (which often falls out), his next successor is obliged to do the same, and the right of the kingdom devolves to the third in succession; where they vary the form of government, according to the seeming necessity of affairs; depose the king when they think good, substituting certain elders to govern in his stead, and sometimes transferring it into the hands of the commonalty; where men and women are both circumcised and also baptized; where the soldier, who in one or several engagements, has been so fortunate as to present seven of the enemies' heads to the king, is made noble: where they live in that rare and unsociable opinion of the mortality of the soul; where the women are delivered without pain or fear: where the women wear copper leggings upon both legs, and if a louse bite them, are bound in magnanimity to bite them again, and dare not marry, till first they have made their king a tender of their virginity, if he please to accept it: where the or- dinary way of salutation is by putting a finger down to the earth, and then pointing it up toward heaven: where men carry burdens upon their heads, and women on their shoulders; where the women make water standing, and the men squatting: where they send their

[7]

blood in token of friendship, and offer incense to the men they
would honor, like gods: where, not only to the fourth, but in any
other remote degree, kindred are not permitted to marry: where the
children are four years at nurse, and often twelve; in which place,
also, it is accounted mortal to give the child suck the first day after
it is born: where the correction of the male children is peculiarly
designed to the fathers, and to the mothers of the girls; the punishment being to hang them by the heels in the smoke: where they cir-
cumcise the women: where they eat all sorts of herbs, without other
scruple than of the badness of the smell: where all things are open
—the finest houses, furnished in the richest manner, without doors,
windows, trunks, or chests to lock, a thief being there punished
double what they are in other places: where they crack lice with
their teeth like monkeys, and abhor to see them killed with one's
nails: where in all their lives they neither cut their hair nor pare
their nails; and, in another place, pare those of the right hand only,
letting the left grow for ornament and bravery: where they suffer
the hair on the right side to grow as long as it will, and shave the
other; and in the neighboring provinces, some let their hair grow
long before, and some behind, shaving close the rest: where parents
let out their children, and husbands their wives, to their guests to
hire: where a man may get his own mother with child and fathers
make use of their own daughters or sons, without scandal: where
at their solemn feasts they interchangeably lend their children to
one another, without any consideration of nearness of blood. In
one place, men feed upon human flesh; in another, 'tis reputed a
pious office for a man to kill his father at a certain age; elsewhere,
the fathers dispose of their children, while yet in their mothers'
wombs, some to be preserved and carefully brought up, and others
to be abandoned or made away. Elsewhere the old husbands lend
their wives to young men; and in another place they are in common,
without offense; in one place particularly, the women take it for
a mark of honor to have as many gay fringed tassels at the bottom
of their garment, as they have lain with several men. Moreover,
has not custom made a republic of women separately by themselves? has it not put arms into their hands, and made them raise

armies and fight battles? And does she not, by her own precept, instruct the most ignorant vulgar, and make them perfect in things
which all the philosophy in the world could never beat into the
heads of the wisest men? For we know entire nations, where death
was not only despised, but entertained with the greatest triumph;
where children of seven years old suffered themselves to be whipped
to death, without changing countenance; where riches were in such
contempt, that the meanest citizen would not have deigned to stoop
to take up a purse of crowns. And we know regions, very fruitful
in all manner of provisions, where, notwithstanding, the most ordinary diet, and that they are most pleased with, is only bread,
cresses, and water. Did not custom, moreover, work that miracle in
Chios that, in seven hundred years, it was never known that ever
maid or wife committed any act to the prejudice of her honor.

To conclude; there is nothing, in my opinion, that she does not,
or may not do; and, therefore, with very good reason it is, that
Pindar calls her the queen, and empress of the world. He that was
seen to beat his father, and reproved for so doing, made answer,
that it was the custom of their family: that, in like manner his father
had beaten his grandfather, his grandfather his great-grandfather,
"And this," says he, pointing to his son, "when he comes to my age,
shall beat me." And the father, whom the son dragged and hauled
along the streets, commanded him to stop at a certain door, for he
himself, he said, had dragged his father no farther, that being the
utmost limit of the hereditary outrage the sons used to practice
upon the fathers in their family. It is as much by custom as infirmity, says Aristotle, that women tear their hair, bite their nails, and
eats coals and earth, and, more by custom than nature, that men
abuse themselves with one another.

The laws of conscience, which we pretend to be derived from
nature, proceed from custom; every one, having an inward veneration for the opinions and manners approved and received among
his own people, cannot, without very great reluctance, depart from
them, nor apply himself to them without applause. In times past,
when those of Crete would curse any one, they prayed the gods to
engage him in some ill custom. But the principal effect of its power

[9]

is, so to seize and ensnare us, that it is hardly in us to disengage ourselves from its gripe, or so to come to ourselves, as to consider of and to weigh the things it enjoins. To say the truth, by reason that we suck it in with our milk, and that the face of the world presents itself in this posture to our first sight, it seems as if we were born upon condition to follow on this track; and the common fancies that we find in repute everywhere about us, and infused into our minds with the seed of our fathers, appear to be the most universal and genuine: from whence it comes to pass, that whatever is off the hinges of custom, is believed to be also off the hinges of reason; how unreasonably, for the most part, God knows.

If, as we who study ourselves, have learned to do, every one who hears a good sentence, would immediately consider how it does any way touch his own private concern, every one would find that it was not so much a good saying, as a severe lash to the ordinary stupidity of his own judgment; but men receive the precepts and admonitions of truth, as directed to the common sort, and never to themselves; and instead of applying them to their own manners, do only very ignorantly and unprofitably commit them to memory. But let us return to the empire of custom.

Such people as have been bred up to liberty, and subject to no other dominion but the authority of their own will, look upon all other form of government as monstrous and contrary to nature. Those who are inured to monarchy do the same; and what opportunity soever fortune presents them with to change, even then, when with the greatest difficulties they have disengaged themselves from one master, that was troublesome and grievous to them, they presently run, with the same difficulties, to create another; being unable to take into hatred subjection itself.

'Tis by the mediation of custom, that every one is content with the place where he is planted by nature; and the Highlanders of Scotland no more pant after Touraine, than the Scythians after Thessaly. Darius asking certain Greeks what they would take to assume the custom of the Indians, of eating the dead bodies of their fathers (for that was their use, believing they could not give them a better, nor more noble sepulture, than to bury them in their

own bodies), they made answer, that nothing in the world should hire them to do it; but having also tried to persuade the Indians to leave their custom, and, after the Greek manner, to burn the bodies of their fathers, they conceived a still greater horror at the

notion. Every one does the same, for use veils from us the true aspect of things.

"Nil adeo magnum, nec tam mirabile quidquam
Principio, quod non minuant mirarier omnes
Paullatim."

Taking upon me once to justify something in use among us, and that was received with absolute authority for a great many leagues round about us, and not content, as men commonly do, to establish it only by force of law and example, but inquiring still farther into its origin, I found the foundation so weak, that I who made it my business to confirm others, was very near being dissatisfied myself. 'Tis by this receipt that Plato undertakes to cure the unnatural and

preposterous loves of his time, as one which he esteems of sovereign virtue; namely, that the public opinion condemns them; that the poets, and all other sorts of writers, relate horrible stories of them; a recipe, by virtue of which the most beautiful daughters no more allure their father's lust; nor brothers, of the finest shape and fashion, their sisters' desire; the very fables of Thyestes, Œdipus, and Macareus, having with the harmony of their song, infused this wholesome opinion and belief into the tender brains of children. Chastity is, in truth, a great and shining virtue, and of which the utility is sufficiently known; but to treat of it, and to set it off in its true value, according to nature, is as hard as 'tis easy to do so according to custom, laws, and precepts. The fundamental and universal reasons are of very obscure and difficult research, and our masters either lightly pass them over, or not daring so much as to touch them, precipitate themselves into the liberty and protection of custom, there puffing themselves out and triumphing to their heart's content: such as will not suffer themselves to be withdrawn from this original source, do yet commit a greater error, and subject themselves to wild opinions; witness Chrysippus who, in so many of his writings, has strewed the little account he made of incestuous conjunctions, committed with how near relations soever.

Whoever would disengage himself from this violent prejudice of custom, would find several things received with absolute and undoubting opinion, that have no other support than the hoary head and riveled face of ancient usage. But the mask taken off, and things being referred to the decision of truth and reason, he will find his judgment as it were altogether overthrown, and yet restored to a much more sure estate. For example, I shall ask him, what can be more strange than to see a people obliged to obey laws they never understood; bound in all their domestic affairs, as marriages, donations, wills, sales and purchases to rules they cannot possibly know, being neither written nor published in their own language, and of which they are of necessity to purchase both the interpretation and the use? Not according to the ingenious opinion of Isocrates, who counseled his king to make the traffics and negotiations

of his subjects, free, frank, and of profit to them, and their quarrels and disputes burdensome, and laden with heavy impositions and penalties; but, by a prodigious opinion, to make sale of reason itself, and to give to laws a course of merchandise. I think myself obliged to fortune that, as our historians report, it was a Gascon gentleman, a countryman of mine, who first opposed Charlemagne, when he attempted to impose upon us Latin and imperial laws.

What can be more savage, than to see a nation where, by lawful custom, the office of a judge is bought and sold, where judgments are paid for with ready money, and where justice may legitimately be denied to him that has not wherewithal to pay; a merchandise in so great repute, as in a government to create a fourth estate of wrangling lawyers, to add to the three ancient ones of the church, nobility and people; which fourth estate, having the laws in their own hands, and sovereign power over men's lives and fortunes, makes another body separate from nobility: whence it comes to pass, that there are double laws, those of honor and those of justice, in many things altogether opposite one to another; the nobles as rigorously condemning a lie taken, as the other do a lie revenged: by the law of arms, he shall be degraded from all nobility and honor who puts up with an affront; and by the civil law, he who vindicates his reputation by revenge incurs a capital punishment; he who applies himself to the law for reparation of an offense none to his honor, disgraces himself; and he who does not, is censured and punished by the law. Yet of these two so different things, both of them referring to one head, the one has the charge of peace, the other of war; these have the profit, these the honor; those the wisdom, these the virtue; those the word, these the action; those justice, these valor; those reason, these force; those the long robe, these the short: divided between them.

For what concerns indifferent things, as clothes, who is there seeking to bring them back to their true use, which is the body's service and convenience, and upon which their original grace and fitness depend; for the most fantastic, in my opinion, that can be imagined, I will instance among others, our flat caps, that long tail of velvet that hangs down from our women's heads, with its party-

colored trappings; and that vain and futile model of a member we cannot in modesty so much as name, which nevertheless we make show and parade of in public. These considerations, notwithstanding, will not prevail upon any understanding man to decline the common mode; but, on the contrary, methinks, all singular and particular fashions are rather marks of folly and vain affectation, than of sound reason, and that a wise man ought, within, to withdraw and retire his soul from the crowd, and there keep it at liberty and in power to judge freely of things; but, as to externals, absolutely to follow and conform himself to the fashion of the time. Public society has nothing to do with our thoughts, but the rest, as our actions, our labors, our fortunes, and our lives, we are to lend and abandon them to its service, and to the common opinion; as did that good and great Socrates who refused to preserve his life by a disobedience to the magistrate, though a very wicked and unjust one: for it is the rule of rules, the general law of laws, that every one observe those of the place wherein he lives.

Νόμοις ἔπεσθαι τοῖσιν ἐγχωρίοις καλόν.

And now to another point. It is a very great doubt, whether any so manifest benefit can accrue from the alteration of a law received, let it be what it will, as there is danger and inconvenience in altering it; forasmuch as government is a structure composed of divers parts and members joined and united together, with so strict connection, that it is impossible to stir so much as one brick or stone, but the whole body will be sensible of it. The legislator of the Thurians ordained, that whosoever would go about either to abolish an old law, or to establish a new, should present himself with a halter about his neck to the people to the end, that if the innovation he would introduce should not be approved by every one, he might immediately be hanged; and he of the Lacedæmonians employed his life, to obtain from his citizens a faithful promise, that none of his laws should be violated. The Ephorus who so rudely cut the two strings that Phrynis had added to music, never stood to examine whether that addition made better harmony, or that by its means the instrument was more full and complete; it was enough for him to

condemn the invention, that it was a novelty, and an alteration of the old fashion. Which also is the meaning of the old rusty sword carried before the magistracy of Marseilles.

For my own part, I have a great aversion from novelty, what face or what pretense soever it may carry along with it, and have reason, having been an eyewitness of the great evils it has produced. For those for which for so many years have lain so heavy upon us, it is not wholly accountable; but one may say, with color enough, that it has accidentally produced and begotten the mischiefs and ruin that have since happened, both without and against it; it, principally, we are to accuse for these disorders.

> "Heu! patior telis vulnera facta meis."

They who give the first shock to a state, are almost naturally the first overwhelmed in its ruin; the fruits of public commotion are seldom enjoyed by him who was the first motor; he beats and disturbs the water for another's net. The unity and contexture of this monarchy, of this grand edifice, having been ripped and torn in her old age, by this thing called innovation, has since laid open a rent, and given sufficient admittance to such injuries: the royal majesty with greater difficulty declines from the summit to the middle, then it falls and tumbles headlong from the middle to the bottom. But if the inventors do the greater mischief, the imitators are more vicious, to follow examples of which they have felt and punished both the horror and the offense. And if there can be any degree of honor in ill-doing, these last must yield to the others the glory of contriving, and the courage of making the first attempt. All sorts of new disorders easily draw, from this primitive and ever-flowing fountain, examples and precedents to trouble and discompose our government; we read in our very laws, made for the remedy of this first evil, the beginning and pretenses of all sorts of wicked enterprises; and that befals us, which Thucydides said of the civil wars of his time, that, in favor of public vices, they gave them new and more plausible names for their excuse, sweetening and disguising their true titles; which must be done, forsooth, to reform our conscience and belief: *"honesta oratio est;"* but the

best pretence for innovation is of very dangerous consequence: *"adeo nihil motum ex antiquo probabile est."* And freely to speak my thoughts, it argues a strange self-love and great presumption to be so fond of one's own opinions, that a public peace must be overthrown to establish them, and to introduce so many inevitable mischiefs, and so dreadful a corruption of manners, as a civil war and the mutations of state consequent to it, always bring in their train, and to introduce them, in a thing of so high concern, into the bowels of one's own country. Can there be worse husbandry than to set up so many certain and knowing vices against errors that are only contested and disputable? And are there any worse sorts of vices than those committed against a man's own conscience, and the natural light of his own reason? The senate, upon the dispute between it and the people about the administration of their religion, was bold enough to return this evasion for current pay: *"Ad deos id magis, quam ad se, pertinere: ipsos visuros, ne sacra sua polluantur;"* according to what the oracle answered to those of Delphos who, fearing to be invaded by the Persians, in the Median war, inquired of Apollo, how they should dispose of the holy treasure of his temple; whether they should hide, or remove it to some other place? He returned them answer, that they should stir nothing from thence, and only take care of themselves, for he was sufficient to look to what belonged to him.

The Christian religion has all the marks of the utmost utility and justice: but none more manifest than the severe injunction it lays indifferently upon all to yield absolute obedience to the civil magistrate, and to maintain and defend the laws. Of which, what a wonderful example has the divine wisdom left us, that, to establish the salvation of mankind, and to conduct His glorious victory over death and sin, would do it after no other way, but at the mercy of our ordinary forms of justice, subjecting the progress and issue of so high and so salutiferous an effect, to the blindness and injustice of our customs and observances; sacrificing the innocent blood of so many of His elect, and so long a loss of so many years, to the maturing of this inestimable fruit? There is a vast difference between the case of one who follows the forms and laws of his

country, and of another who will undertake to regulate and change them; of whom the first pleads simplicity, obedience, and example for his excuse, who, whatever he shall do, it cannot be imputed to malice; 'tis at the worst but misfortune: *"Quis est enim, quem non moveat clarissimis monumentis testata consignataque antiquisas?"* besides what Isocrates says, that defect is nearer allied to moderation than excess: the other is a much more ruffling gamester; for whosoever shall take upon him to choose and alter, usurps the authority of judging, and should look well about him, and make it his business to discern clearly the defect of what he would abolish, and the virtue of what he is about to introduce.

This so vulgar consideration, is that which settled me in my station, and kept even my most extravagant and ungoverned youth under the rein, so as not to burden my shoulders with so great a weight, as to render myself responsible for a science of that importance, and in this to dare what in my better and more mature judgment I durst not do in the most easy and indifferent things I had been instructed in, and wherein the temerity of judging is of no consequence at all; it seeming to me very unjust to go about to subject public and established customs and institutions to the weakness and instability of a private and particular fancy (for private reason has but a private jurisdiction), and to attempt that upon the divine, which no government will endure a man should do, upon the civil laws; with which, though human reason has much more commerce than with the other, yet are they sovereignly judged by their own proper judges, and the extreme sufficiency serves only to expound and set forth the law and custom received, and neither to wrest it, nor to introduce anything of innovation. If, sometimes, the divine providence has gone beyond the rules to which it has necessarily bound and obliged us men, it is not to give us any dispensation to do the same; those are master strokes of the divine hand, which we are not to imitate, but to admire, and extraordinary examples, marks of express and particular purposes, of the nature of miracles, presented before us for manifestations of its almightiness, equally above both our rules and force, which it would be folly and impiety to attempt to represent and imitate; and that we

ought not to follow, but to contemplate with the greatest reverence: acts of his personage, and not for us. Cotta very opportunely declares: *"Quum de religione agitur, Ti. Coruncanium, P. Scipionem, P. Scævolam pontifices maximos, non Zenonem, aut Cleanthem, aut Chrysippum, sequor."* God knows in the present quarrel of our civil war, where there are a hundred articles to dash out and to put in, great and very considerable, how many there are who can truly boast they have exactly and perfectly weighed and understood the grounds and reasons of the one and the other party; 'tis a number, if they make any number, that would be able to give us very little disturbance. But what becomes of all the rest, under what ensigns do they march, in what quarter do they lie? Theirs have the same effect with other weak and ill-applied medicines; they have only set the humors they would purge more violently in work, stirred and exasperated by the conflict, and left them still behind. The potion was too weak to purge, but strong enough to weaken us; so that it does not work, but we keep it still in our bodies, and reap nothing from the operation but intestine gripes and dolors.

So it is, nevertheless, that Fortune, still reserving her authority in defiance of whatever we are able to do or say, sometimes presents us with a necessity so urgent, that 'tis requisite the laws should a little yield and give way; and when one opposes the increase of an innovation that thus intrudes itself by violence, to keep a man's self in so doing in all places and in all things within bounds and rules against those who have the power, and to whom all things are lawful that may any way serve to advance their design, who have no other law nor rule but what serves best to their own purpose, 'tis a dangerous obligation and an intolerable inequality:

"Aditum nocendi perfido præstat fides,"

forasmuch as the ordinary discipline of a healthful state does not provide against these extraordinary accidents; it presupposes a body that supports itself in its principal members and offices, and a common consent to its obedience and observation. A legitimate proceeding is cold, heavy, and constrained, and not fit to make head

[18]

against a headstrong and unbridled proceeding. 'Tis known to be, to this day, cast in the dish of those two great men, Octavius and Cato, in the two civil wars of Sylla and Cæsar, that they would rather suffer their country to undergo the last extremities, than relieve their fellow-citizens at the expense of its laws, or be guilty of any innovation; for, in truth, in these last necessities, where there is no other remedy, it would, peradventure, be more discreetly done to stoop and yield a little to receive the blow, than, by opposing without possibility of doing good, to give occasion to violence to trample all under foot; and better to make the laws do what they can when they cannot do what they would. After this manner did he who suspended them for four-and-twenty hours, and he who, for once, shifted a day in the calendar, and that other who of the month of June made a second of May. The Lacedæmonians themselves, who were so religious observers of the laws of their country, being straitened by one of their own edicts, by which it was expressly forbidden to choose the same man twice to be admiral; and on the other side, their affairs necessarily requiring that Lysander should again take upon him that command, they made one Aratus admiral, 'tis true, but withal, Lysander went superintendent of the navy; and, by the same subtlety, one of their ambassadors being sent to the Athenians to obtain the revocation of some decree, and Pericles remonstrating to him, that it was forbidden to take away the tablet wherein a law had once been engrossed, he advised him to turn it only; that being not forbidden; and Plutarch commends Philopœmen, that being born to command, he knew how to do it, not only according to the laws but also to overrule even the laws themselves, when the public necessity so required.

II

OF THE EDUCATION OF CHILDREN

To Madame Diane de Foix, Comtesse de Gurson.

I NEVER yet saw that father, but let his son be never so decrepit or deformed, would not, notwithstanding, own him: not, nevertheless, if he were not totally besotted, and blinded with his paternal affection, that he did not well enough discern his defects: but that with all defaults, he was still his. Just so, I see better than any other, that all I write here are but the idle reveries of a man that has only nibbled upon the outward crust of sciences in his nonage, and only retained a general and formless image of them; who has got a little snatch of everything, and nothing of the whole, *à la Françoise*. For I know, in general, that there is such a thing as physic, as jurisprudence; four parts in mathematics, and, roughly, what all these aim and point at; and peradventure, I yet know farther, what sciences in general pretend unto, in order to the service of our life: but to dive farther than that, and to have cudgeled my brains in the study of Aristotle, the monarch of all modern learning, or particularly addicted myself to any one science, I have never done it; neither is there any one art of which I am able to draw the first lineaments and dead color; insomuch that there is not a boy of the lowest form in a school, that may not pretend to be wiser than I, who am not able to examine him in his first lesson, which, if I am at any time forced upon, I am necessitated, in my own defense, to ask him, unaptly enough, some universal questions, such as may serve to try his natural understanding; a lesson as strange and unknown to him, as his is to me.

I never seriously settled myself to the reading any book of solid learning but Plutarch and Seneca; and there, like the Danaides, I eternally fill, and it as constantly runs out; something of which drops upon this paper, but little or nothing stays with me. History is my particular game as to matter of reading, or else poetry, for which I have particular kindness and esteem: for, as Cleanthes said, as the voice, forced through the narrow passage of a trumpet, comes out more forcible and shrill; so, methinks, a sentence pressed within the harmony of verse, darts out more briskly upon the understanding, and strikes my ear and apprehension with a smarter and more pleasing effect. As to the natural parts I have, of which this is the essay, I find them to bow under the burden; my fancy and judgment do but grope in the dark, tripping and stumbling in the way, and when I have gone as far as I can, I am in no degree satisfied; I discover still a new and greater extent of land before me, with a troubled and imperfect sight and wrapped up in clouds, that I am not able to penetrate. And taking upon me to write indifferently of whatever comes into my head, and therein making use of nothing but my own proper and natural means, if it befall me, as ofttimes it does, accidentally to meet in any good author, the same heads and commonplaces upon which I have attempted to write (as I did but just now in Plutarch's "Discourse of the Force of Imagination"), to see myself so weak and so forlorn, so heavy and so flat, in comparison of those better writers, I at once pity or despise myself. Yet do I please myself with this, that my opinions have often the honor and good fortune to jump with theirs, and that I go in the same path, though at a very great distance, and can say, "Ah, that is so." I am farther satisfied to find, that I have a quality, which every one is not blessed withal, which is, to discern the vast difference between them and me; and notwithstanding all that, suffer my own inventions, low and feeble as they are, to run on in their career, without mending or plastering up the defects that this comparison has laid open to my own view. And, in plain truth, a man had need of a good strong back to keep pace with these people. The indiscreet scribblers of our times, who among their laborious nothings, insert whole sections and pages

out of ancient authors, with a design, by that means, to illustrate their own writings, do quite contrary; for this infinite dissimilitude of ornaments renders the complexion of their own compositions so sallow and deformed, that they lose much more than they get.

The philosophers, Chrysippus and Epicurus, were in this of two quite contrary humors: the first not only in his books mixed passages and sayings of other authors, but entire pieces, and, in one, the whole "Medea" of Euripides; which gave Apollodorus occasion to say, that should a man pick out of his writings all that was none of his, he would leave him nothing but blank paper: whereas the latter, quite contrary, in three hundred volumes that he left behind him, has not so much as any one quotation.

I happened the other day upon this piece of fortune; I was reading a French book, where after I had a long time run dreaming over a great many words, so dull, so insipid, so void of all wit or common sense, that indeed they were only French words; after a long and tedious travel, I came at last to meet with a piece that was lofty, rich, and elevated to the very clouds; of which, had I found either the declivity easy or the ascent gradual, there had been some excuse; but it was so perpendicular a precipice, and so wholly cut off from the rest of the work, that, by the six first words, I found myself flying into the other world, and thence discovered the vale whence I came so deep and low, that I have never had since the heart to descend into it any more. If I should set out one of my discourses with such rich spoils as these, it would but too evidently manifest the imperfection of my own writing. To reprehend the fault in others that I am guilty of myself, appears to me no more unreasonable, than to condemn, as I often do, those of others in myself: they are to be everywhere reproved, and ought to have no sanctuary allowed them. I know very well how audaciously I myself, at every turn, attempt to equal myself to my thefts, and to make my style go hand in hand with them, not without a temerarious hope of deceiving the eyes of my reader from discerning the difference; but withal, it is as much by the benefit of my application, that I hope to do it, as by that of my invention or any force of my own. Besides, I do not offer to contend with the whole body

of these champions, nor hand to hand with any one of them: 'tis only by flights and little light attempts that I engage them; I do not grapple with them, but try their strength only, and never engage so far as I make a show to do. If I could hold them in play, I were a brave fellow; for I never attack them, but where they are most sinewy and strong. To cover a man's self (as I have seen some do) with another man's armor, so as not to discover so much as his fingers' ends; to carry on a design (as it is not hard for a man that has anything of a scholar in him, in an ordinary subject to do) under old inventions, patched up here and there with his own trumpery, and then to endeavor to conceal the theft, and to make it pass for his own, is first injustice and meanness of spirit in those who do it, who having nothing in them of their own fit to procure them a reputation, endeavor to do it by attempting to impose things upon the world in their own name, which they have no manner of title to; and, next, a ridiculous folly to content themselves with acquiring the ignorant approbation of the vulgar by such a pitiful cheat, at the price at the same time of degrading themselves in the eyes of men of understanding, who turn up their noses at all this borrowed incrustation, yet whose praise alone is worth the having. For my own part, there is nothing I would not sooner do than that, neither have I said so much of others, but to get a better opportunity to explain myself. Nor in this do I glance at the composers of centos, who declare themselves for such; of which sort of writers I have in my time known many very ingenious, and particularly one under the name of Capilupus, besides the ancients. These are really men of wit, and that make it appear they are so, both by that and other ways of writing; as for example, Lipsius, in that learned and laborious contexture of his politics.

But, be it how it will, and how inconsiderable soever these essays of mine may be, I will say I never intended to conceal them, no more than my old bald grizzled pate before them, where the painter has presented you not with a perfect face, but with mine. For these are my own particular opinions and fancies, and I deliver them as only what I myself believe, and not for what is to be believed by others. I have no other end in this writing, but only to discover

myself, who, also, shall, peradventure, be another thing tomorrow, if I chance to meet any new instruction to change me. I have no authority to be believed, neither do I desire it, being too conscious of my own inerudition to be able to instruct others.

A friend of mine, then, having read the preceding chapter, the other day told me, that I should a little farther have extended my discourse on the education of children. Now, madame, if I had any sufficiency in this subject, I could not possibly better employ it, than to present my best instructions to the little gentleman that threatens you shortly with a happy birth (for you are too generous to begin otherwise than with a male); for having had so great a hand in the treaty of your marriage, I have a certain particular right and interest in the greatness and prosperity of the issue that shall spring from it; besides that, your having had the best of my services so long in possession, sufficiently obliges me to desire the honor and advantage of all wherein you shall be concerned. But, in truth, all I understand as to that particular is only this, that the greatest and most important difficulty of human science is the education of children. For as in agriculture, the husbandry that is to precede planting, as also planting itself, is certain, plain, and well known; but after that which is planted comes to life, there is a great deal more to be done, more art to be used, more care to be taken, and much more difficulty to cultivate and bring it to perfection; so it is with men; it is no hard matter to get children; but after they are born, then begins the trouble, solicitude, and care rightly to train, principle, and bring them up. The symptoms of their inclinations in that tender age are so obscure, and the promises so uncertain and fallacious, that it is very hard to establish any solid judgment or conjecture upon them. Look at Cimon, for example, and Themistocles, and a thousand others, who very much deceived the expectation men had of them. Cubs of bears and puppies readily discover their natural inclination; but men, so soon as ever they are grown up, applying themselves to certain habits, engaging themselves in certain opinions, and conforming themselves to particular laws and customs, easily alter, or at least disguise, their true and real disposition; and yet it is hard to force the propension of nature.

[24]

Whence it comes to pass, that for not having chosen the right course, we often take very great pains, and consume a good part of our time in training up children to things, for which, by their natural constitution, they are totally unfit. In this difficulty, nevertheless, I am clearly of opinion, that they ought to be elemented in the best and most advantageous studies, without taking too much notice of, or being too superstitious in those light prognostics they give of themselves in their tender years, and to which Plato, in his Republic, gives, methinks, too much authority.

Madame, science, is a very great ornament, and a thing of marvelous use, especially in persons raised to that degree of fortune in which you are. And, in truth, in persons of mean and low condition, it cannot perform its true and genuine office, being naturally more prompt to assist in the conduct of war, in the government of peoples, in negotiating the leagues and friendships of princes and foreign nations, than in forming a syllogism in logic, in pleading a process in law, or in prescribing a dose of pills in physic. Wherefore, madame, believing you will not omit this so necessary feature in the education of your children, who yourself have tasted its sweetness, and are of a learned extraction (for we yet have the writings of the ancient Counts of Foix, from whom my lord, your husband, and yourself, are both of you descended, and Monsieur de Candale, your uncle, every day obliges the world with others, which will extend the knowledge of this quality in your family for so many succeeding ages), I will, upon this occasion, presume to acquaint your ladyship, with one particular fancy of my own, contrary to the common method, which is all I am able to contribute to your service in this affair.

The charge of the tutor you shall provide for your son, upon the choice of whom depends the whole success of his education, has several other great and considerable parts and duties required in so important a trust, besides that of which I am about to speak: these, however, I shall not mention, as being unable to add anything of moment to the common rules: and in this, wherein I take upon me to advise, he may follow it so far only as it shall appear advisable.

For a boy of quality then, who pretends to letters not upon the account of profit (for so mean an object as that is unworthy of the grace and favor of the Muses, and moreover, in it a man directs his service to and depends upon others), nor so much for outward ornament, as for his own proper and peculiar use, and to furnish and enrich himself within, having rather a desire to come out an accomplished cavalier than a mere scholar or learned man; for such a one, I say, I would, also, have his friends solicitous to find him out a tutor, who has rather a well-made than a well-filled head; seeking, indeed, both the one and the other, but rather of the two to prefer manners and judgment to mere learning, and that this man should exercise his charge after a new method.

'Tis the custom of pedagogues to be eternally thundering in their pupil's ears, as they were pouring into a funnel, while the business of the pupil is only to repeat what the others have said: now I would have a tutor to correct this error, and, that at the very first, he should, according to the capacity he has to deal with, put it to the test, permitting his pupil himself to taste things, and of himself to discern and choose them, sometimes opening the way to him, and sometimes leaving him to open it for himself; that is, I would not have him alone to invent and speak, but that he should also hear his pupil speak in turn. Socrates, and since him Arcesilaus, made first their scholars speak, and then they spoke to them. *"Obest plerumque iis, qui discere volunt, auctoritas eorum, qui docent."* It is good to make him, like a young horse, trot before him that he may judge of his going and how much he is to abate of his own speed, to accommodate himself to the vigor and capacity of the other. For want of which due proportion we spoil all; which also to know how to adjust, and to keep within an exact and due measure, is one of the hardest things I know, and 'tis the effect of a high and well-tempered soul to know how to condescend to such puerile motions and to govern and direct them. I walk firmer and more secure up hill than down.

Such as, according to our common way of teaching, undertake, with one and the same lesson, and the same measure of direction, to instruct several boys of differing and unequal capacities, are

infinitely mistaken; and 'tis no wonder, if in a whole multitude of scholars, there are not found above two or three who bring away any good account of their time and discipline. Let the master not only examine him about the grammatical construction of the bare words of his lesson, but about the sense and substance of them, and let him judge of the profit he has made, not by the testimony of his memory, but by that of his life. Let him make him put what he has learned into a hundred several forms, and accommodate it to so many several subjects, to see if he yet rightly comprehends it, and has made it his own, taking instruction of his progress by the pedagogic institutions of Plato. 'Tis a sign of crudity and indigestion to disgorge what we eat in the same condition it was swallowed; the stomach has not performed its office unless it have altered the form and condition of what was committed to it to concoct. Our minds work only upon trust, when bound and compelled to follow the appetite of another's fancy, enslaved and captivated under the authority of another's instruction; we have been so subjected to the trammel, that we have no free, nor natural pace of our own; our own vigor and liberty are extinct and gone: *"Nunquam tutelæ suæ fiunt."*

I was privately carried at Pisa to see a very honest man, but so great an Aristotelian, that his most usual thesis was: "That the touchstone and square of all solid imagination, and of all truth, was an absolute conformity to Aristotle's doctrine; and that all besides was nothing but inanity and chimera; for that he had seen all, and said all." A position, that for having been a little too injuriously and broadly interpreted, brought him once and long kept him in great danger of the Inquisition at Rome.

Let him make him examine and thoroughly sift everything he reads, and lodge nothing in his fancy upon simple authority and upon trust. Aristotle's principles will then be no more principles to him, than those of Epicurus and the Stoics: let this diversity of opinions be propounded to, and laid before him; he will himself choose, if he be able; if not, he will remain in doubt.

"Che, non men che saper, dubbiar m' aggrata,"

[27]

for, if he embrace the opinions of Xenophon and Plato, by his own reason, they will no more be theirs, but become his own. Who follows another, follows nothing, finds nothing, nay, is inquisitive after nothing. *"Non sumus sub rege; sibi quisque se vindicet."* Let him at least, know that he knows. It will be necessary that he imbibe their knowledge, not that he be corrupted with their precepts; and no matter if he forgot where he had his learning, provided he know how to apply it to his own use. Truth and reason are common to every one, and are no more his who spake them first, than his who speaks them after: 'tis no more according to Plato, than according to me, since both he and I equally see and understand them. Bees cull their several sweets from this flower and that blossom, here and there where they find them, but themselves afterward make the honey, which is all and purely their own, and no more thyme and marjoram: so the several fragments he borrows from others, he will transform and shuffle together to compile a work that shall be absolutely his own; that is to say, his judgment: his instruction, labor and study, tend to nothing else but to form that. He is not obliged to discover whence he got the materials that have assisted him, but only to produce what he has himself done with them. Men that live upon pillage and borrowing, expose their purchases and buildings to every one's view: but do not proclaim how they came by the money. We do not see the fees and perquisites of a gentleman of the long robe; but we see the alliances wherewith he fortifies himself and his family, and the titles and honors he has obtained for him and his. No man divulges his revenue; or at least, which way it comes in: but every one publishes his acquisitions. The advantages of our study are to become better and more wise. 'Tis, says Epicharmus, the understanding that sees and hears, 'tis the understanding that improves everything, that orders everything, and that acts, rules, and reigns: all other faculties are blind, and deaf, and without soul. And certainly we render it timorous and servile, in not allowing it the liberty and privilege to do anything of itself. Whoever asked his pupil what he thought of grammar or rhetoric, and of such and such a sentence of Cicero? Our masters stick them, full feathered, in our memories, and there establish

them like oracles, of which the letters and syllables are of the substance of the thing. To know by rote, is no knowledge, and signifies no more but only to retain what one has intrusted to our memory. That which a man rightly knows and understands, he is the free disposer of at his own full liberty, without any regard to the author from whence he had it or fumbling over the leaves of his book. A mere bookish learning is a poor, paltry learning; it may serve for ornament, but there is yet no foundation for any superstructure to be built upon it, according to the opinion of Plato, who says that constancy, faith, and sincerity, are the true philosophy, and the other sciences, that are directed to other ends, mere adulterate paint. I could wish that Paluel or Pompey, those two noted dancers of my time, could have taught us to cut capers, by only seeing them do it, without stirring from our places, as these men pretend to inform the understanding, without ever setting it to work; or that we could learn to ride, handle a pike, touch a lute, or sing, without the trouble of practice, as these attempt to make us judge and speak well, without exercising us in judging or speaking. Now in this initiation of our studies and in their progress, whatsoever presents itself before us is book sufficient; a roguish trick of a page, a sottish mistake of a servant, a jest at the table, are so many new subjects.

And for this reason, conversation with men is of very great use and travel into foreign countries; not to bring back (as most of our young monsieurs do) an account only of how many paces Santa Rotonda is in circuit; or of the richness of Signora Livia's petticoats; or, as some others, how much Nero's face, in a statue in such an old ruin, is longer and broader than that made for him on some medal; but to be able chiefly to give an account of the humors, manners, customs and laws of those nations where he has been, and that we may whet and sharpen our wits by rubbing them against those of others. I would that a boy should be sent abroad very young, and first, so as to kill two birds with one stone, into those neighboring nations whose language is most differing from our own, and to which, if it be not formed betimes, the tongue will grow too stiff to bend.

And also 'tis the general opinion of all, that a child should not be brought up in his mother's lap. Mothers are too tender, and their natural affection is apt to make the most discreet of them all so overfond, that they can neither find in their hearts to give them due correction for the faults they commit, nor suffer them to be inured to hardships and hazards, as they ought to be. They will not endure to see them return all dust and sweat from their exercise, to drink cold drink when they are hot, nor see them mount an unruly horse, nor take a foil in hand against a rude fencer, or so much as to discharge a carbine. And yet there is no remedy; whoever will breed a boy to be good for anything when he comes to be a man, must by no means spare him when young, and must very often transgress the rules of physic:

> "Vitamque sub dio, et trepidis agat
> In rebus."

It is not enough to fortify his soul: you are also to make his sinews strong; for the soul will be oppressed if not assisted by the members, and would have too hard a task to discharge two offices alone. I know very well, to my cost, how much mine groans under the burden, from being accommodated with a body so tender and indisposed, as eternally leans and presses upon her; and often in my reading perceive that our masters, in their writings, make examples pass for magnanimity and fortitude of mind, which really are rather toughness of skin and hardness of bones; for I have seen men, women, and children, naturally born of so hard and insensible a constitution of body, that a sound cudgeling has been less to them than a flirt with a finger would have been to me, and that would neither cry out, wince, nor shrink, for a good swinging beating; and when wrestlers counterfeit the philosophers in patience, 'tis rather strength of nerves than stoutness of heart. Now to be inured to undergo labor, is to be accustomed to endure pain: "*labor callum obducit dolori.*" A boy is to be broken into the toil and roughness of exercise, so as to be trained up to the pain and suffering of dislocations, cholics, cauteries, and even imprisonment and the rack itself; for he may come, by misfortune, to be reduced to the worst of these,

which (as this world goes) is sometimes inflicted on the good as well as the bad. As for proof, in our present civil war whoever draws his sword against the laws, threatens the honestest men with the whip and the halter.

And, moreover, by living at home, the authority of this governor, which ought to be sovereign over the boy he has received into his charge, is often checked and hindered by the presence of parents; to which may also be added, that the respect the whole family pay him, as their master's son, and the knowledge he has of the estate and greatness he is heir to, are, in my opinion, no small inconveniences in these tender years.

And yet, even in this conversing with men I spoke of but now, I have observed this vice, that instead of gathering observations from others, we make it our whole business to lay ourselves upon them, and are more concerned how to expose and set out our own commodities, than how to increase our stock by acquiring new. Silence, therefore, and modesty are very advantageous qualities in conversation. One should, therefore, train up this boy to be sparing and a husband of his knowledge when he has acquired it; and to forbear taking exceptions at or reproving every idle saying or ridiculous story that is said or told in his presence; for it is a very unbecoming rudeness to carp at everything that is not agreeable to our own palate. Let him be satisfied with correcting himself, and not seem to condemn everything in another he would not do himself, nor dispute it as against common customs. *"Licet sapere sine pompa, sine invidia."* Let him avoid these vain and uncivil images of authority, this childish ambition of coveting to appear better bred and more accomplished, than he really will, by such carriage, discover himself to be. And, as if opportunities of interrupting and reprehending were not to be omitted, to desire thence to derive the reputation of something more than ordinary. For as it becomes none but great poets to make use of the poetical license, so it is intolerable for any but men of great and illustrious souls to assume privilege above the authority of custom; *"si quid Socrates aut Aristippus contra morem et consuetudinem fecerunt, idem sibi ne arbitretur licere: magnis enim illi et divinis bonis hanc licentiam*

assequebantur." Let him be instructed not to engage in discourse or dispute but with a champion worthy of him, and, even there, not to make use of all the little subtleties that may seem pat for his purpose, but only such arguments as may best serve him. Let him be taught to be curious in the election and choice of his reasons, to abominate impertinence, and, consequently, to affect brevity; but, above all, let him be lessoned to acquiesce and submit to truth so soon as ever he shall discover it, whether in his opponent's argument, or upon better consideration of his own; for he shall never be preferred to the chair for a mere clatter of words and syllogisms, and is no further engaged to any argument whatever, than as he shall in his own judgment approve it: nor yet is arguing a trade, where the liberty of recantation and getting off upon better thoughts, are to be sold for ready money: *"neque, ut omnia, quæ præscripta et imperata sint, defendat, necessitate ulla cogitur."*

If his governor be of my humor, he will form his will to be a very good and loyal subject to his prince, very affectionate to his person, and very stout in his quarrel; but withal he will cool in him the desire of having any other tie to his service than public duty. Besides several other inconveniences that are inconsistent with the liberty every honest man ought to have, a man's judgment, being bribed and prepossessed by these particular obligations, is either blinded and less free to exercise its function, or is blemished with ingratitude and indiscretion. A man that is purely a courtier, can neither have power nor will to speak or think otherwise than favorably and well of a master, who, among so many millions of other subjects, has picked out him with his own hand to nourish and advance; this favor, and the profit flowing from it, must needs, and not without some show of reason, corrupt his freedom and dazzle him; and we commonly see these people speak in another kind of phrase than is ordinarily spoken by others of the same nation, though what they say in that courtly language is not much to be believed.

Let his conscience and virtue be eminently manifest in his speaking, and have only reason for their guide. Make him understand, that to acknowledge the error he shall discover in his own argument,

though only found out by himself, is an effect of judgment and sincerity, which are the principal things he is to seek after; that
obstinacy and contention are common qualities, most appearing in
mean souls; that to revise and correct himself, to forsake an unjust
argument in the height and heat of dispute, are rare, great, and
philosophical qualities. Let him be advised; being in company, to
have his eye and ear in every corner, for I find that the places of
greatest honor are commonly seized upon by men that have least in
them, and that the greatest fortunes are seldom accompanied with
the ablest parts. I have been present when, while they at the upper
end of the chamber have only been commending the beauty of the
arras, or the flavor of the wine, many things that have been very
finely said at the lower end of the table have been lost or thrown
away. Let him examine every man's talent; a peasant, a bricklayer,
a passenger: one may learn something from every one of these in
their several capacities, and something will be picked out of their
discourse whereof some use may be made at one time or another;
nay, even the folly and impertinence of others will contribute to his
instruction. By observing the graces and manners of all he sees, he
will create to himself an emulation of the good, and a contempt of
the bad.

Let an honest curiosity be suggested to his fancy of being inquisitive after everything; whatever there is singular and rare near the
place where he is, let him go and see it; a fine house, a noble fountain, an eminent man, the place where a battle has been anciently
fought, the passages of Cæsar and Charlemagne:

> "Quæ tellus sit lenta gelu, quæ putris ab æstu,
> Ventus in Italiam quis bene vela ferat."

Let him inquire into the manners, revenues and alliances of
princes, things in themselves very pleasant to learn, and very useful
to know.

In this conversing with men, I mean also, and principally, those
who only live in the records of history; he shall, by reading those
books, converse with the great and heroic souls of the best ages. 'Tis
an idle and vain study to those who make it by so doing it after

a negligent manner, but to those who do it with care and observation, 'tis a study of inestimable fruit and value; and the only study, as Plato reports, that the Lacedæmonians reserved to themselves. What profit shall he not reap as to the business of men, by reading the lives of Plutarch? But, withal, let my governor remember to what end his instructions are principally directed, and that he do not so much imprint in his pupil's memory the date of the ruin of Carthage, as the manners of Hannibal and Scipio; nor so much where Marcellus died, as why it was unworthy of his duty that he died there. Let him not teach him so much the narrative parts of history as to judge them; the reading of them, in my opinion, is a thing that of all others we apply ourselves unto with the most differing measure. I have read a hundred things in Livy that another has not, or not taken notice of at least; and Plutarch has read a hundred more there than ever I could find, or than, peradventure, that author ever wrote; to some it is merely a grammar study, to others the very anatomy of philosophy, by which the most abstruse parts of our human nature penetrate. There are in Plutarch many long discourses very worthy to be carefully read and observed, for he is, in my opinion, of all others the greatest master in that kind of writing; but there are a thousand others which he has only touched and glanced upon, where he only points with his finger to direct us which way we may go if we will, and contents himself sometimes with giving only one brisk hit in the nicest article of the question, whence we are to grope out the rest. As, for example, where he says that the inhabitants of Asia came to be vassals to one only, for not having been able to pronounce one syllable, which is No. Which saying of his gave perhaps matter and occasion to La Boetie to write his "Voluntary Servitude." Only to see him pick out a light action in a man's life, or a mere word that does not seem to amount even to that, is itself a whole discourse. 'Tis to our prejudice that men of understanding should so immoderately affect brevity; no doubt their reputation is the better by it, but in the meantime we are the worse. Plutarch had rather we should applaud his judgment than commend his knowledge, and had rather leave us with an appetite to read more, than glutted with that we have already read.

He knew very well, that a man may say too much even upon the best subjects, and that Alexandridas justly reproached him who made very good but too long speeches to the Ephori, when he said: "Oh stranger! thou speakest the things thou shouldst speak, but not as thou shouldst speak them." Such as have lean and spare bodies stuff themselves out with clothes; so they who are defective in matter, endeavor to make amends with words.

Human understanding is marvelously enlightened by daily conversation with men, for we are, otherwise, compressed and heaped up in ourselves, and have our sight limited to the length of our own noses. One asking Socrates of what country he was, he did not make answer, of Athens, but of the world; he whose imagination was fuller and wider, embraced the whole world for his country, and extended his society and friendship to all mankind; not as we do, who look no further than our feet. When the vines of my village are nipped with the frost, my parish priest presently concludes, that the indignation of God is gone out against all the human race, and that the cannibals have already got the pip. Who is it, that seeing the havoc of these civil wars of ours, does not cry out, that the machine of the world is near dissolution, and that the day of judgment is at hand; without considering, that many worse things have been seen, and that, in the meantime, people are very merry in a thousand other parts of the earth for all this? For my part, considering the license and impunity that always attend such commotions, I wonder they are so moderate, and that there is no more mischief done. To him who feels the hailstones patter about his ears, the whole hemisphere appears to be in storm and tempest; like the ridiculous Savoyard, who said very gravely, that if that simple king of France could have managed his fortune as he should have done, he might in time have come to have been steward of the household to the duke his master: the fellow could not, in his shallow imagination, conceive that there could be anything greater than a duke of Savoy. And, in truth, we are all of us, insensibly, in this error, an error of a very great weight and very pernicious consequence. But whoever shall represent to his fancy, as in a picture, that great image of our mother Nature, in her full majesty

and luster, whoever in her face shall read so general and so constant a variety, whoever shall observe himself in that figure, and not himself but a whole kingdom, no bigger than the least touch or prick of a pencil in comparison of the whole, that man alone is able to value things according to their true estimate and grandeur.

This great world which some do yet multiply as several species under one genus, is the mirror wherein we are to behold ourselves, to be able to know ourselves as we ought to do in the true bias. In short, I would have this to be the book my young gentleman should study with the most attention. So many humors, so many sects, so many judgments, opinions, laws and customs, teach us to judge aright of our own, and inform our understanding to discover its imperfection and natural infirmity, which is no trivial speculation. So many mutations of states and kingdoms, and so many turns and revolutions of public fortune, will make us wise enough to make no great wonder of our own. So many great names, so many famous victories and conquests drowned and swallowed in oblivion, render our hopes ridiculous of eternizing our names by the taking of half-a-score of light horse, or a henroost, which only derives its memory from its ruin. The pride and arrogance of so many foreign pomps and ceremonies, the tumorous majesty of so many courts and grandeurs, accustom and fortify our sight without astonishment or winking to behold the lustre of our own; so many millions of men, buried before us, encourage us not to fear to go seek such good company in the other world: and so of all the rest. Pythagoras was wont to say, that our life resembles the great and populous assembly of the Olympic games, wherein some exercise the body, that they may carry away the glory of the prize; others bring merchandise to sell for profit; there are, also, some (and those none of the worst sort) who pursue no other advantage than only to look on, and consider how and why everything is done, and to be spectators of the lives of other men, thereby the better to judge of and regulate their own.

To examples may fitly be applied all the profitable discourses of philosophy, to which all human actions, as to their best rule, ought to be especially directed: a scholar shall be taught to know—

"Quid fas optare, quid asper
Utile nummus habet; patriæ carisque propinquis
Quantum elargiri deceat; quem te Deus esse
Jussit, et humana qua parte locatus es in re;
Quid sumus, aut quidnam victuri gignimur,"

what it is to know, and what to be ignorant; what ought to be the end
and design of study; what valor, temperance and justice are; the
difference between ambition and avarice, servitude and subjection,
license and liberty; by what token a man may know true and solid
contentment; how far death, affliction, and disgrace are to be
apprehended:

"Et quo quemque modo fugiatque feratque laborem;"

by what secret springs we move, and the reason of our various
agitations and irresolutions: for, methinks, the first doctrine with
which one should season his understanding, ought to be that which
regulates his manners and his sense; that teaches him to know himself, and how both well to die and well to live. Among the liberal
sciences, let us begin with that which makes us free; not that they
do not all serve in some measure to the instruction and use of life,
as all other things in some sort also do; but let us make choice of
that which directly and professedly serves to that end. If we are
once able to restrain the offices of human life within their just and
natural limits, we shall find that most of the sciences in use are of
no great use to us, and even in those that are, that there are many
very unnecessary cavities and dilatations which we had better let
alone, and following Socrates' direction, limit the course of our
studies to those things only where is a true and real utility:

"Sapere aude,
Incipe; vivendi recte vui prorogat horam,
Rusticus exspectat, dum defluat amnis; at ille
Labitur et labetur in omne volubilis œvum."

'Tis a great foolery to teach our children—

"Quid moveant Pisces, animosaque signa Leonis,
Lotus et Hesperia quid Capricornus aqua,"

the knowledge of the stars and the motion of the eighth sphere, before their own.

"Τί Πλειαδεσσι καμοί;
Τί δ' α'στράσιν Βοωτεω;"

Anaximenes writing to Pythagoras, "To what purpose," said he, "should I trouble myself in searching out the secrets of the stars, having death or slavery continually before my eyes?" for the kings of Persia were at that time preparing to invade his country. Every one ought to say thus, "Being assaulted, as I am by ambition, avarice, temerity, superstition, and having within so many other enemies of life, shall I go cudgel my brains about the world's revolutions?"

After having taught him what will make him more wise and good, you may then entertain him with the elements of logic, physics, geometry, rhetoric, and the science which he shall then himself most incline to, his judgment being beforehand formed and fit to choose, he will quickly make his own. The way of instructing him ought to be sometimes by discourse, and sometimes by reading, sometimes his governor shall put the author himself, which he shall think most proper for him, into his hands, and sometimes only the marrow and substance of it; and if himself be not conversant enough in books to turn to all the fine discourses the books contain for his purpose, there may some man of learning be joined to him, that upon every occasion shall supply him with what he stands in need of, to furnish it to his pupil. And who can doubt, but that this way of teaching is much more easy and natural than that of Gaza, in which the precepts are so intricate, and so harsh, and the words so vain, lean, and insignificant, that there is no hold to be taken of them, nothing that quickens and elevates the wit and fancy, whereas here the mind has what to feed upon and to digest. This fruit, therefore, is not only without comparison, much more fair and beautiful; but will also be much more early ripe.

'Tis a thousand pities that matters should be at such a pass in this age of ours, that philosophy, even with men of understanding, should be looked upon as a vain and fantastic name, a thing of no use, no value, either in opinion or effect, of which I think those ergotisms and petty sophistries, by prepossessing the avenues to it,

are the cause. And people are much to blame to represent it to
children for a thing of so difficult access, and with such a frowning,
grim, and formidable aspect. Who is it that has disguised it thus,
with this false, pale, and ghostly countenance? There is nothing
more airy, more gay, more frolic, and I had like to have said, more
wanton. She preaches nothing but feasting and jollity; a melancholic anxious look shows that she does not inhabit there. Demetrius the grammarian finding in the temple of Delphos a knot of
philosophers set chatting together, said to them, "Either I am much
deceived, or by your cheerful and pleasant countenances, you are
engaged in no very deep discourse." To which one of them,
Heracleon the Megarean, replied: " 'Tis for such as are puzzled
about inquiring whether the future tense of the verb $\beta\acute{a}\lambda\lambda\omega$ be spelt
with a double λ or that hunt after the derivation of the compara-
tives $\chi\epsilon\acute{\iota}\rho o\nu$ and $\beta\acute{\epsilon}\lambda\tau\iota o\nu$, and the superlatives $\chi\epsilon\acute{\iota}\rho\iota\sigma\tau o\nu$ and $\beta\acute{\epsilon}\lambda\tau\iota\sigma\tau o\nu$,
to knit their brows while discoursing of their science, but as to
philosophical discourses, they always divert and cheer up those
that entertain them, and never deject them or make them sad."

> "Deprendas animi tormenta latentis in ægro
> Corpore; deprendas et gaudia; sumit utrumque
> Inde habitum facies."

The soul that lodges philosophy, ought to be of such a constitution of health, as to render the body in like manner healthful too;
she ought to make her tranquillity and satisfaction shine so as to
appear without, and her contentment ought to fashion the outward
behavior to her own mold, and consequently to fortify it with a
graceful confidence, an active and joyous carriage, and a serene
and contented countenance. The most manifest sign of wisdom
is a continual cheerfulness; her state is like that of things in the
regions above the moon, always clear and serene. 'Tis Baroco and
Baralipton that render their disciples so dirty and ill-favored, and
not she; they do not so much as know her but by hearsay. What! It
is she that calms and appeases the storms and tempests of the soul,
and who teaches famine and fevers to laugh and sing; and that, not
by certain imaginary epicycles, but by natural and manifest
reasons. She has virtue for her end; which is not, as the schoolmen

say, situate upon the summit of a perpendicular, rugged, inaccessible precipice: such as have approached her find her, quite on the contrary, to be seated in a fair, fruitful, and flourishing plain, from whence she easily discovers all things below; to which place any one may, however, arrive, if he know but the way, through shady, green, and sweetly flourishing avenues, by a pleasant, easy, and smooth descent, like that of the celestial vault. 'Tis for not having frequented this supreme, this beautiful, triumphant, and amiable, this equally delicious and courageous virtue, this so professed and implacable enemy to anxiety, sorrow, fear, and constraint, who, having nature for her guide, has fortune and pleasure for her companions, that they have gone, according to their own weak imaginations and created this ridiculous, this sorrowful, querulous, despiteful, threatening, terrible image of it to themselves and others, and placed it upon a rock apart, among thorns and brambles, and made of it a hobgoblin to affright people.

But the governor that I would have, that is such a one as knows it to be his duty to possess his pupil with as much or more affection than reverence to virtue, will be able to inform him, that the poets have evermore accommodated themselves to the public humor, and make him sensible, that the gods have planted more toil and sweat in the avenues of the cabinets of Venus than in those of Minerva. And when he shall once find him begin to apprehend, and shall represent to him a Bradamante or an Angelica for a mistress, a natural, active, generous, and not a viragoish, but a manly beauty, in comparison of a soft, delicate, artificial, simpering, and affected form; the one in the habit of a heroic youth, wearing a glittering helmet, the other tricked up in curls and ribbons like a wanton minx; he will then look upon his own affection as brave and masculine, when he shall choose quite contrary to that effeminate shepherd of Phrygia.

Such a tutor will make a pupil digest this new lesson, that the height and value of true virtue consists in the facility, utility, and pleasure of its exercise; so far from difficulty, that boys, as well as men, and the innocent as well as the subtle, may make it their own: it is by order, and not by force, that it is to be acquired. Socrates,

her first minion, is so averse to all manner of violence, as totally to throw it aside, to slip into the more natural facility of her own progress: 'tis the nursing mother of all human pleasures, who in rendering them just, renders them also pure and permanent; in moderating them, keeps them in breath and appetite; in interdicting those which she herself refuses, whets our desire to those that she allows; and, like a kind and liberal mother, abundantly allows all that nature requires, even to satiety, if not to lassitude: unless we mean to say, that the regimen which stops the toper before he has drunk himself drunk, the glutton before he has eaten to a surfeit, and the lecher before he has got the pox, is an enemy to pleasure. If the ordinary fortune fail, she does without it, and forms another, wholly her own, not so fickle and unsteady as the other. She can be rich, be potent and wise, and knows how to lie upon soft perfumed beds: she loves life, beauty, glory, and health; but her proper and peculiar office is to know how to regulate the use of all these good things, and how to lose them without concern: an office much more noble than troublesome, and without which the whole course of life is unnatural, turbulent, and deformed, and there it is indeed, that men may justly represent those monsters upon rocks and precipices.

If this pupil shall happen to be of so contrary a disposition, that he had rather hear a tale of a tub than the true narrative of some noble expedition or some wise and learned discourse; who at the beat of drum, that excites the youthful ardor of his companions, leaves that to follow another that calls to a morris or the bears; who would not wish, and find it more delightful and more excellent, to return all dust and sweat victorious from a battle, than from tennis or from a ball, with the prize of those exercises; I see no other remedy, but that he be bound prentice in some good town to learn to make minced pies, though he were the son of a duke; according to Plato's precept, that children are to be placed out and disposed of, not according to the wealth, qualities, or condition of the father, but according to the faculties and the capacity of their own souls.

Since philosophy is that which instructs us to live and that in-

fancy has there its lessons as well as other ages, why is it not communicated to children betimes?

"Udum et molle lutum est; nunc, nunc properandus, et acri Fingendus sine fine rota."

They begin to teach us to live when we have almost done living. A hundred students have got the pox before they have come to read Aristotle's lecture on temperance. Cicero said, that though he should live two men's ages, he should never find leisure to study the lyric poets; and I find these sophisters yet more deplorably unprofitable. The boy we would breed has a great deal less time to spare; he owes but the first fifteen or sixteen years of his life to education; the remainder is due to action. Let us, therefore, employ that short time in necessary instruction. Away with the thorny subtleties of dialectics, they are abuses, things by which our lives can never be amended: take the plain philosophical discourses, learn how rightly to choose, and then rightly to apply them; they

are more easy to be understood than one of Bocaccio's novels; a child from nurse is much more capable of them, than of learning to read or to write. Philosophy has discourses proper for childhood, as well as for the decrepit age of men.

I am of Plutarch's mind, that Aristotle did not so much trouble his great disciple with the knack of forming syllogisms, or with the elements of geometry, as with infusing into him good precepts concerning valor, prowess, magnanimity, temperance, and the contempt of fear; and with this ammunition, sent him, while yet a boy, with no more than thirty thousand foot, four thousand horse, and but forty-two thousand crowns, to subjugate the empire of the whole earth. For the other arts and sciences, he says, Alexander highly indeed commended their excellence and charm, and had them in very great honor and esteem, but not ravished with them to that degree, as to be tempted to affect the practice of them in his own person.

"Petite hinc, juvenesque senesque,
Finem animo certum, miserisque viatica canis."

Epicurus, in the beginning of his letter to Meniceus, says, "That neither the youngest should refuse to philosophize, nor the oldest grow weary of it." Who does otherwise, seems tacitly to imply, that either the time of living happily is not yet come, or that it is already past. And yet, for all that, I would not have this pupil of ours imprisoned and made a slave to his book; nor would I have him given up to the morosity and melancholic humor of a sour, ill-natured pedant; I would not have his spirit cowed and subdued, by applying him to the rack, and tormenting him, as some do, fourteen or fifteen hours a day, and so make a pack-horse of him. Neither should I think it good, when, by reason of a solitary and melancholic complexion, he is discovered to be overmuch addicted to his book, to nourish that humor in him; for that renders him unfit for civil conversation, and diverts him from better employments. And how many have I seen in my time totally brutified by an immoderate thirst after knowledge? Carneades was so besotted with it, that he would not find time as so much as to comb his head or to pare his nails. Neither would I have his generous manners spoiled and

corrupted by the incivility and barbarism of those of another. The French wisdom was anciently turned into proverb: "early, but of no continuance." And, in truth, we yet see, that nothing can be more ingenious and pleasing than the children of France; but they ordinarily deceive the hope and expectation that have been conceived of them; and grown up to be men, have nothing extraordinary or worth taking notice of: I have heard men of good understanding say, these colleges of ours to which we send our young people (and of which we have but too many) make them such animals as they are.

But to our little monsieur, a closet, a garden, the table, his bed, solitude and company, morning and evening, all hours shall be the same, and all places to him a study; for philosophy, who, as the formatrix of judgment and manners, shall be his principal lesson, has that privilege to have a hand in everything. The orator Isocrates, being at a feast entreated to speak of his art, all the company were satisfied with and commended his answer: "It is not now a time," said he, "to do what I can do; and that which it is now time to do, I cannot do." For to make orations and rhetorical disputes in a company met together to laugh and make good cheer, had been very unseasonable and improper, and as much might have been said of all the other sciences. But as to what concerns philosophy, that part of it at least that treats of man, and of his offices and duties, it has been the common opinion of all wise men, that, out of respect to the sweetness of her conversation, she is ever to be admitted in all sports and entertainments. And Plato, having invited her to his feast, we see after how gentle and obliging a manner, accommodated both to time and place, she entertained the company, though in a discourse of the highest and most important nature.

> "Æque pauperibus prodest locupletibus æque;
> Et, neglecta, æque pueris senibusque nocebit."

By this method of instruction, my young pupil will be much more and better employed than his fellows of the college are. But as the steps we take in walking to and fro in a gallery, though three times as many, do not tire a man so much as those we employ in a formal

journey, so our lesson, as it were accidentally occurring, without any set obligation of time or place, and falling naturally into every action, will insensibly insinuate itself. By which means our very exercises and recreations, running, wrestling, music, dancing, hunting, riding, and fencing, will prove to be a good part of our study. I would have his outward fashion and mien, and the disposition of his limbs, formed at the same time with his mind. 'Tis not a soul, 'tis not a body that we are training up, but a man, and we ought not to divide him. And, as Plato says, we are not to fashion one without the other, but make them draw together like two horses harnessed to a coach. By which saying of his, does he not seem to allow more time for, and to take more care of, exercises for the body, and to hold that the mind, in a good proportion, does her business at the same time too?

As to the rest, this method of education ought to be carried on with a severe sweetness, quite contrary to the practice of our pedants, who, instead of tempting and alluring children to letters by apt and gentle ways, do in truth present nothing before them but rods and ferules, horror and cruelty. Away with this violence! away with this compulsion! than which, I certainly believe nothing more dulls and degenerates a well-descended nature. If you would have him apprehend shame and chastisement, do not harden him to them: inure him to heat and cold, to wind and sun, and to dangers that he ought to despise; wean him from all effeminacy and delicacy in clothes and lodging, eating and drinking; accustom him to everything, that he may not be a Sir Paris, a carpet-knight, but a sinewy, hardy, and vigorous young man. I have ever from a child to the age wherein I now am, been of this opinion, and am still constant to it. But among other things, the strict government of most of our colleges has evermore displeased me; peradventure, they might have erred less perniciously on the indulgent side. 'Tis a real house of correction of imprisoned youth. They are made debauched, by being punished before they are so. Do but come in when they are about their lesson, and you shall hear nothing but the outcries of boys under execution, with the thundering noise of their pedagogues drunk with fury. A very pretty way this, to tempt

these tender and timorous souls to love their book, with a furious countenance, and a rod in hand! A cursed and pernicious way of proceeding! Besides what Quintilian has very well observed, that this imperious authority is often attended by very dangerous consequences, and particularly our way of chastising. How much more decent would it be to see their classes strewed with green leaves and fine flowers, than with the bloody stumps of birch and willows? Were it left to my ordering, I should paint the school with the pictures of joy and gladness; Flora and the Graces, as the philosopher Speusippus did his. Where their profit is, let them there have their pleasure too. Such viands as are proper and wholesome for children, should be sweetened with sugar, and such as are dangerous to them, embittered with gall. 'Tis marvelous to see how solicitous Plato is in his Laws concerning the gayety and diversion of the youth of his city, and how much and often he enlarges upon their races, sports, songs, leaps, and dances: of which, he says, that antiquity has given the ordering and patronage particularly to the gods themselves, to Apollo, Minerva, and the Muses. He insists long upon, and is very particular in giving innumerable precepts for exercises; but as to the lettered sciences, says very little, and only seems particularly to recommend poetry upon the account of music.

All singularity in our manners and conditions is to be avoided as inconsistent with civil society. Who would not be astonished at so strange a constitution as that of Demophoon, steward to Alexander the Great, who sweated in the shade, and shivered in the sun? I have seen those who have run from the smell of a mellow apple with greater precipitation than from a harquebus shot, others afraid of a mouse; others vomit at the sight of cream; others ready to swoon at the making of a feather bed; Germanicus could neither endure the sight nor the crowing of a cock. I will not deny, but that there may, peradventure, be some occult cause and natural aversion in these cases; but, in my opinion, a man might conquer it, if he took it in time. Precept has in this wrought so effectually upon me, though not without some pains on my part, I confess, that beer excepted, my appetite accommodates itself indifferently to all sorts of diet.

Young bodies are supple; one should, therefore, in that age bend and ply them to all fashions and customs: and provided a man can contain the appetite and the will within their due limits, let a young man, in God's name, be rendered fit for all nations and all companies, even to debauchery and excess, if need be; that is, where he shall do it out of complacency to the customs of the place. Let him be able to do everything, but love to do nothing but what is good. The philosophers themselves do not justify Callisthenes for forfeiting the favor of his master Alexander the Great, by refusing to pledge him a cup of wine. Let him laugh, play, wench, with his prince; nay, I would have him, even in his debauches, too hard for the rest of the company, and to excel his companions in ability and vigor, and that he may not give over doing it, either through defect of power or knowledge how to do it, but for want of will. *"Multum interest, utrum peccare ali quis nolit, an nesciat."* I thought I passed a compliment upon a lord, as free from those excesses as any man in France, by asking him before a great deal of very good company, how many times in his life he had been drunk in Germany, in the time of his being there about his majesty's affairs; which he also took as it was intended, and made answer. "Three times;" and withal, told us the whole story of his debauches. I know some, who for want of this faculty, have found a great inconvenience in negotiating with that nation. I have often with great admiration reflected upon the wonderful constitution of Alcibiades, who so easily could transform himself to so various fashions without any prejudice to his health; one while outdoing the Persian pomp and luxury, and another, the Lacedæmonian austerity and frugality; as reformed in Sparta, as voluptuous in Ionia.

"Omnis Aristippum decuit color, et status, et res."

I would have my pupil to be such a one,

"Quem duplici panno patientia velat,
Mirabor, vitæ via si conversa decebit,
Personamque feret non inconcinnus utramque."

These are my lessons, and he who puts them in practice shall reap more advantage than he who has had them read to him only,

and so only knows them. If you see him, you hear him; if you hear him, you see him. God forbid, says one in Plato, that to philosophize were only to read a great many books, and to learn the arts. *"Hanc amplissimam omnium artium bene vivendi disciplinam, vita magis quam literis, persequuti sunt."* Leo, prince of the Phliasians, asking Heraclides Ponticus of what art or science he made profession; "I know," said he, "neither art nor science, but I am a philosopher." One reproaching Diogenes, that, being ignorant, he should pretend to philosophy: "I therefore," answered he, "pretend to it with so much the more reason." Hegesias entreated that he would read a certain book to him: "You are pleasant," said he; "you choose those figs that are true and natural, and not those that are painted; why do you not also choose exercises which are naturally true, rather than those written?"

The lad will not so much get his lesson by heart as he will practice it: he will repeat it in his actions. We shall discover if there be prudence in his exercises, if there be sincerity and justice in his deportment, if there be grace and judgment in his speaking; if there be constancy in his sickness; if there be modesty in his mirth, temperance in his pleasures, order in his domestic economy, indifference in his palate, whether what he eats or drinks be flesh or fish, wine or water. *"Qui disciplinam suam non ostentationem scientiæ, sed legem vitæ putet: quique obtemperet ipse sibi, et decretis pareat."* The conduct of our lives is the true mirror of our doctrine. Zeuxidamus, to one who asked him, why the Lacedæmonians did not commit their constitutions of chivalry to writing, and deliver them to their young men to read, made answer, that it was because they would inure them to action, and not amuse them with words. With such a one, after fifteen or sixteen years' study, compare one of our college Latinists, who has thrown away so much time in nothing but learning to speak. The world is nothing but babble; and I hardly ever yet saw that man who did not rather prate too much, than speak too little. And yet half of our age is embezzled this way: we are kept four or five years to learn words only, and to tack them together into clauses; as many more to form them into a long discourse, divided into four or five parts; and other

[48]

five years, at least, to learn succinctly to mix and interweave them after a subtle and intricate manner: let us leave all this to those who make a profession of it.

Going one day to Orleans, I met in the plain on this side Clery, two pedants traveling toward Bordeaux, about fifty paces distant from one another; and a good way further behind them, I discovered a troop of horse, with a gentleman at the head of them, who was the late Monsieur le Comte de la Rochefoucauld. One of my people inquired of the foremost of these dominies, who that gentleman was that came after him; he, having not seen the train that followed after, and thinking his companion was meant, pleasantly answered: "He is not a gentleman, he is a grammarian, and I am a logician." Now we who, quite contrary, do not here pretend to breed a grammarian or a logician, but a gentleman, let us leave them to throw away their time at their own fancy: our business lies elsewhere. Let but our pupil be well furnished with things, words will follow but too fast; he will pull them after him if they do not voluntarily follow. I have observed some to make excuses, that they cannot express themselves, and pretend to have their fancies full of a great many very fine things, which yet, for want of eloquence, they cannot utter; 'tis a mere shift, and nothing else. Will you know what I think of it? I think they are nothing but shadows of some imperfect images and conceptions that they know not what to make of within, nor consequently bring out: they do not yet themselves understand what they would be at, and if you but observe how they haggle and stammer upon the point of parturition, you will soon conclude, that their labor is not to delivery, but about conception, and that they are but licking their formless embryo. For my part, I hold, and Socrates commands it, that whoever has in his mind a sprightly and clear imagination, he will express it well enough in one kind of tongue or another, and, if he be dumb, by signs

"Verbaque prævisam rem non invita sequentur."

And as another as poetically says in his prose, "Quum res animum occupavere, verba ambiunt:" and this other, "Ipsæ res verbc

rapiunt." He knows nothing of ablative, conjunctive, substantive, or grammar, no more than his lackey, or a fishwife of the Petit Pont; and yet these will give you a bellyful of talk, if you will hear them, and peradventure shall trip as little in their language as the best masters of art in France. He knows no rhetoric, nor how in a preface to bribe the benevolence of the courteous reader; neither does he care to know it. Indeed all this fine decoration of painting is easily effaced by the luster of a simple and blunt truth: these fine flourishes serve only to amuse the vulgar of themselves incapable of more solid and nutritive diet, as Aper very evidently demonstrates in Tacitus. The ambassadors of Samos, prepared with a long and elegant oration, came to Cleomenes, king of Sparta, to incite him to a war against the tyrant Polycrates; who, after he had heard their harangue with great gravity and patience, gave them this answer: "As to the exordium, I remember it not, nor consequently the middle of your speech; and for what concerns your conclusion, I will not do what you desire:" a very pretty answer this methinks, and a pack of learned orators most sweetly graveled. And what did the other man say? The Athenians were to choose one of two architects for a very great building they had designed; of these, the first, a pert affected fellow, offered this service in a long premeditated discourse upon the subject of the work in hand, and by his oratory inclined the voices of the people in his favor; but the other in three words: "Oh, Athenians, what this man says, I will do." When Cicero was in the height and heat of an eloquent harangue, many were struck with admiration; but Cato only laughed, saying: "We have a pleasant consul." Let it go before, or come after, a good sentence or a thing well said, is always in season; if it either suit well with what went before, nor has much coherence with what follows after, it is good in itself. I am none of those who think that good rhyme makes a good poem. Let him make short long, and long short if he will, 'tis no great matter; if there be invention, and that the wit and judgment have well performed their offices, I will say, here's a good poet, but an ill rhymer.

"Emunctæ naris, durus componere versus."

[50]

Let a man, says Horace, divest his work of all method and measure,

"Tempora certa modosque, et, quod prius ordine verbum est,
Posterius facias, præponens ultima primis
Invenias etiam disjecti membra poetæ,"

he will never the more lose himself for that; the very pieces will be fine by themselves. Menander's answer had this meaning, who being reproved by a friend, the time drawing on at which he had promised a comedy, that he had not yet fallen in hand with it: "It is made, and ready," said he, "all but the verses." Having contrived the subject, and disposed the scenes in his fancy, he took little care for the rest. Since Ronsard and Du Bellay have given reputation to our French poesy, every little dabbler, for aught I see, swells his words as high, and makes his cadences very near as harmonious as they. *"Plus sonat, quam valet."* For the vulgar, there were never so many poetasters as now; but though they find it no hard matter to imitate their rhyme, they yet fall infinitely short of imitating the rich descriptions of the one, and the delicate invention of the other of these masters.

But what will become of our young gentleman, if he be attacked with the sophistic subtlety of some syllogism? "A Westphalia ham makes a man drink, drink quenches thirst; therefore, a Westphalia ham quenches thirst." Why, let him laugh at it; it will be more discretion to do so, than to go about to answer it: or let him borrow this pleasant evasion from Aristippus: "Why should I trouble myself to untie that, which, bound as it is, gives me so much trouble?" One offering at this dialectic juggling against Cleanthes, Chrysippus took him short, saying, "Reserve these baubles to play with children, and do not by such fooleries divert the serious thoughts of a man of years." If these ridiculous subtleties, *"contorta et aculeata sophismata,"* as Cicero calls them, are designed to possess him with an untruth, they are dangerous; but if they signify no more than only to make him laugh, I do not see why a man need to be fortified against them. There are some so ridiculous, as to go a mile out of their way to hook in a fine word: *"Aut qui non verba rebus aptant, sed res extrinsecus arcessunt, quibus verba conveniant."* And as

another says, *"Qui alicujus verbi decore placentis, vocentur ad id, quod non proposuerant scribere."* I for my part rather bring in a fine sentence by head and shoulder to fit my purpose, than divert my designs to hunt after a sentence. On the contrary words are to serve, and to follow a man's purpose; and let Gascon come in play where French will not do. I would have things so excelling, and so wholly possessing the imagination of him that hears, that he should have something else to do, than to think of words. The way of speaking that I love, is natural and plain, the same in writing as in speaking, and a sinewy and muscular way of expressing a man's self, short and pithy, not so elegant and artificial as prompt and vehement:

"Hæc demum sapiet dictio, quæ feriet;"

rather hard than wearisome; free from affectation; irregular, incontinuous, and bold; where every piece makes up an entire body; not like a pedant, a preacher, or a pleader, but rather a soldier-like style, as Suetonius calls that of Julius Cæsar; and yet I see no reason why he should call it so. I have ever been ready to imitate the negligent garb, which is yet observable among the young men of our time, to wear my cloak on one shoulder, my cap on one side, a stocking in disorder, which seems to express a kind of haughty disdain of these exotic ornaments, and a contempt of the artificial; but I find this negligence of much better use in the form of speaking. All affectation, particularly in the French gayety and freedom, is ungraceful in a courtier, and in a monarchy every gentleman ought to be fashioned according to the court model; for which reason, an easy and natural negligence does well. I no more like a web where the knots and seams are to be seen, than a fine figure, so delicate, that a man may tell all the bones and veins. *"Quæ veritati operam dat oratio, incomposita sit et simplex." "Quis accurate loquitur, nisi qui vult putide loqui?"* That eloquence prejudices the subject it would advance, that wholly attracts us to itself. And as in our outward habit, 'tis a ridiculous effeminacy to distinguish ourselves by a particular and unusual garb or fashion; so in language, to study new phrases, and to affect words that are not of cur-

rent use, proceeds from a puerile and scholastic ambition. May I be bound to speak no other language than what is spoken in the market places of Paris! Aristophanes the grammarian was quite out, when he reprehended Epicurus for his plain way of delivering himself, and the design of his oratory, which was only perspicuity of speech. The imitation of words, by its own facility, immediately disperses itself through a whole people; but the imitation of inventing and fitly applying those words, is of a slower progress. The generality of readers, for having found a like robe, very mistakenly imagine they have the same body and inside too, whereas force and sinews are never to be borrowed; the gloss and outward ornament, that is, words and elocution, may. Most of those I converse with, speak the same language I here write; but whether they think the same thoughts I cannot say. The Athenians, says Plato, study fullness and elegancy of speaking; the Lacedæmonians affect brevity, and those of Crete to aim more at the fecundity of conception than the fertility of speech; and these are the best. Zeno used to say, that he had two sorts of disciples, one that he called φιλολόγους, curious to learn things, and these were his favorites; the other, λογοφίλους, that cared for nothing but words. Not that fine speaking is not a very good and commendable quality; but not so excellent and so necessary as some would make it; and I am scandalized that our whole life should be spent in nothing else. I would first understand my own language, and that of my neighbors with whom most of my business and conversation lies.

No doubt but Greek and Latin are very great ornaments, and of very great use, but we buy them too dear. I will here discover one way, which has been experimented in my own person, by which they are to be had better cheap, and such may make use of it as will. My late father having made the most precise inquiry that any man could possibly make among men of the greatest learning and judgment, of an exact method of education, was by them cautioned of this inconvenience then in use, and made to believe, that the tedious time we applied to the learning of the tongues of them who had them for nothing, was the sole cause we could not arrive to the grandeur of soul and perfection of knowledge, of the ancient

Greeks and Romans. I do not, however, believe that to be the only cause. However, the expedient my father found out for this was, that in my infancy, and before I began to speak, he committed me to the care of a German, who since died a famous physician in France, totally ignorant of our language, but very fluent, and a great critic in Latin. This man, whom he had fetched out of his own country, and whom he entertained with a very great salary for this only end, had me continually with him: to him there were also joined two others, of inferior learning, to attend me, and to relieve him; who all of them spoke to me in no other language but Latin. As to the rest of his family, it was an inviolable rule, that neither himself, nor my mother, man nor maid, should speak anything in my company, but such Latin words as every one had learned only to gabble with me. It is not to be imagined how great an advantage this proved to the whole family; my father and my mother by this means learned Latin enough to understand it perfectly well, and to speak it to such a degree as was sufficient for any necessary use; as also those of the servants did who were most frequently with me. In short, we Latined it at such a rate, that it overflowed to all the neighboring villages, where there yet remain, that have established themselves by custom, several Latin appellations of artisans and their tools. As for what concerns myself, I was above six years of age before I understood either French or Perigordin, any more than Arabic; and without art, book, grammar, or precept, whipping, or the expense of a tear, I had, by that time, learned to speak as pure Latin as my master himself, for I had no means of mixing it up with any other. If, for example, they were to give me a theme after the college fashion, they gave it to others in French, but to me they were to give it in bad Latin, to turn it into that which was good. And Nicholas Grouchy, who wrote a book "De Comitiis Romanorum," William Guerente, who wrote a comment upon Aristotle; George Buchanan, that great Scotch poet; and Mark Antony Muret (whom both France and Italy have acknowledged for the best orator of his time), my domestic tutors, have all of them often told me, that I had in my infancy, that language so very fluent and ready, that they were afraid to enter into discourse with me. And

particularly Buchanan, whom I since saw attending the late Mare-
schal de Brissac, then told me, that he was about to write a treatise
of education, the example of which he intended to take from mine,
for he was then tutor to that Count de Brissac who afterward proved
so valiant and so brave a gentleman.

As to Greek, of which I have but a mere smattering, my father
also designed to have it taught me by a devise, but a new one, and
by way of sport; tossing our declensions to and fro, after the manner of those who, by certain games at tables and chess, learn geometry and arithmetic. For he, among other rules, had been advised to
make me relish science and duty by an unforced will, and of my
own voluntary motion, and to educate my soul in all liberty and
delight, without any severity or constraint; which he was an ob-
server of to such a degree, even of superstition, if I may say so,
that some being of opinion that it troubles and disturbs the brains of
children suddenly to wake them in the morning, and to snatch them
violently and over-hastily from sleep (wherein they are much more
profoundly involved than we), he caused me to be wakened by the
sound of some musical instrument, and was never unprovided of
a musician for that purpose. By this example you may judge of the
rest, this alone being sufficient to recommend both the prudence and
the affection of so good a father, who is not to be blamed if he did
not reap fruits answerable to so exquisite a culture. Of this, two
things were the cause: first, a sterile and improper soil; for, though
I was of a strong and healthful constitution, and of a disposition
tolerably sweet and tractable, yet I was, withal, so heavy, idle, and
indisposed, that they could not rouse me from my sloth, not even to
get me out to play. What I saw, I saw clearly enough, and under this
heavy complexion nourished a bold imagination, and opinions
above my age. I had a slow wit, that would go no faster than it was
led; a tardy understanding, a languishing invention, and above all,
incredible defect of memory; so that, it is no wonder, if from all
these nothing considerable could be extracted. Secondly, like those,
who, impatient of a long and steady cure, submit to all sorts of
prescriptions and recipes, the good man being extremely timorous

[55]

of any way failing in a thing he had so wholly set his heart upon, suffered himself at last to be overruled by the common opinions; which always follow their leader as a flight of cranes, and complying with the method of the time, having no more those persons he had brought out of Italy, and who had given him the first model of education, about him, he sent me at six years of age to the College of Guienne, at that time the best and most flourishing in France. And there it was not possible to add anything to the care he had to provide me the most able tutors, with all other circumstances of education, reserving also several particular rules contrary to the college practice; but so it was, that with all these precautions it was a college still. My Latin immediately grew corrupt, of which also by discontinuance I have since lost all manner of use; so that this new way of education served me to no other end, than only at my first coming to prefer me to the first forms; for at thirteen years old, that I came out of the college, I had run through my whole course (as they call it), and, in truth, without any manner of advantage, that I can honestly brag of, in all this time.

The first thing that gave me any taste for books, was the pleasure I took in reading the fables of Ovid's Metamorphoses, and with them I was so taken, that being but seven or eight years old, I would steal from all other diversions to read them, both by reason that this was my own natural language, the easiest book that I was acquainted with, and for the subject, the most accommodated to the capacity of my age: for, as for Lancelot of the Lake, Amadis of Gaul, Huon of Bordeaux, and such trumpery, which children are most delighted with, I had never so much as heard their names, no more than I yet know what they contain; so exact was the discipline wherein I was brought up. But this was enough to make me neglect the other lessons that were prescribed me; and here it was infinitely to my advantage, to have to do with an understanding tutor, who very well knew discreetly to connive at this and other truantries of the same nature; for by this means I ran through Virgil's Æneid, and then Terence, and then Plautus, and then some Italian comedies, allured by the sweetness of the subject; whereas had he been so foolish as to have taken me off this diversion, I do really believe,

I had brought nothing away from the college but a hatred of books, as almost all our young gentlemen do. But he carried himself very discreetly in that business, seeming to take no notice, and allowing me only such time as I could steal from my other regular studies, which whetted my appetite to devour those books. For the chief things my father expected from their endeavors to whom he had delivered me for education, were affability and good humor; and, to say the truth, my manners had no other vice but sloth and want of mettle. The fear was not that I should do ill, but that I should do nothing; nobody prognosticated that I should be wicked, but only useless; they foresaw idleness, but no malice; and I find it falls out accordingly. The complaints I hear of myself are these: "He is idle, cold in the offices of friendship and relation, and in those of the public, too particular, too disdainful." But the most injurious do not say, "Why has he taken such a thing? Why has he not paid such a one?" but, "Why does he part with nothing? Why does he not give?" And I should take it for a favor that men would expect from me no greater effects of supererogation than these. But they are unjust to exact from me what I do not owe, far more rigorously than they require from others that which they do owe. In condemning me to it, they efface the gratification of the action, and deprive me of the gratitude that would be my due for it; whereas the active well-doing ought to be of so much the greater value from my hands, by how much I have never been passive that way at all. I can the more freely dispose of my fortune the more it is mine, and of myself the more I am my own. Nevertheless, if I were good at setting out my own actions, I could, peradventure, very well repel these reproaches, and could give some to understand, that they are not so much offended, that I do not enough, as that I am able to do a great deal more than I do.

Yet for all this heavy disposition of mine, my mind, when retired into itself, was not altogether without strong movements, solid and clear judgments about those objects it could comprehend, and could also, without any helps, digest them; but, among other things, I do really believe, it had been totally impossible to have made it to submit by violence and force. Shall I here acquaint you

with one faculty of my youth? I had great assurance of countenance, and flexibility of voice and gesture, in applying myself to
any part I undertook to act: for before—

"Alter ab undecimo tum me vix ceperat annus,"

I played the chief parts in the Latin tragedies of Buchanan, Guerente, and Muret, that were presented in our college of Guienne with
great dignity; now Andreas Goveanus, our principal, as in all
other parts of his charge, was, without comparison, the best of that
employment in France; and I was looked upon as one of the best
actors. 'Tis an exercise that I do not disapprove in young people
of condition; and I have since seen our princes, after the example
of some of the ancients, in person handsomely and commendably
perform these exercises; it was even allowed to persons of quality
to make a profession of it in Greece. "*Aristoni tragico actori rem
aperit: huic et genus et fortuna houesta erant: nec ars, quia nihil
tale apud Græcos pudori est, ea deformabat.*" Nay, I have always
taxed those with impertinence who condemn these entertainments,
and with injustice those who refuse to admit such comedians as are
worth seeing into our good towns, and grudge the people that public
diversion. Well-governed corporations take care to assemble their
citizens, not only to the solemn duties of devotion, but also to sports
and spectacles. They find society and friendship augmented by it;
and, besides, can there possibly be allowed a more orderly and
regular diversion than what is performed in the sight of every one,
and, very often, in the presence of the supreme magistrate himself?
And I, for my part, should think it reasonable, that the prince
should sometimes gratify his people at his own expense, out of
paternal goodness and affection; and that in populous cities there
should be theaters erected for such entertainments, if but to divert
them from worse and private actions.

To return to my subject, there is nothing like alluring the appetite and affections; otherwise you make nothing but so many asses
laden with books; by dint of the lash, you give them their pocketful
of learning to keep; whereas, to do well, you should not only lodge
it with them, but make them espouse it.

III

THAT FORTUNE IS OFTENTIMES OBSERVED
TO ACT BY THE RULES OF REASON

THE INCONSTANCY and various motions of fortune may reasonably make us expect she would present us with all sorts of
faces. Can there be a more express act of justice than this? The
Duke of Valentinois having resolved to poison Adrian, Cardinal
of Corneto, with whom Pope Alexander VI., his father and himself,
were to sup in the Vatican, he sent before a bottle of poisoned wine,
and withal, strict order to the butler to keep it very safe. The pope
being come before his son, and calling for drink, the butler supposing this wine had not been so strictly recommended to his care, but
only upon the account of its excellency, presented it forthwith to
the pope, and the duke himself coming in presently after, and being
confident they had not meddled with his bottle, took also his cup;
so that the father died immediately upon the spot, and the son,
after having been long tormented with sickness, was reserved to
another and a worse fortune.

Sometimes she seems to play upon us, just in the nick of an
affair: Monsieur d'Estrée, at that time ensign to Monsieur de Ven-
dôme, and Monsieur de Licques, lieutenant in the company of the
Duc d'Ascot, being both pretenders to the Sieur de Fouquerolles'
sister, though of several parties (as it oft falls out among frontier
neighbors), the Sieur de Licques carried her; but on the same day
he was married, and which was worse, before he went to bed to his
wife, the bridegroom having a mind to break a lance in honor of his
new bride, went out to skirmish near St. Omer, where the Sieur

d'Estrée, proving the stronger, took him prisoner, and the more to illustrate his victory, the lady herself was fain—

"Conjugis ante coacta novi dimittere collum,
Quam veniens una atque altera rursus hyems
Noctibus in longis avidum saturasset amorem"

—to request him of courtesy, to deliver up his prisoner to her, as he accordingly did, the gentlemen of France never denying anything to ladies.

Does she not seem to be an artist here? Constantine the son of Helen, founded the empire of Constantinople, and so many ages after, Constantine, the son of Helen, put an end to it. Sometimes she is pleased to emulate our miracles: we are told, that King Clovis besieging Angoulême, the walls fell down of themselves by divine favor: and Bouchet has it from some author, that King Robert having sat down before a city, and being stolen away from the siege to go keep the feast of St. Aignan at Orleans, as he was in devotion at a certain part of the mass, the walls of the beleaguered city, without any manner of violence, fell down with a sudden ruin. But she did quite contrary in our Milan war; for Captain Rense laying siege for us to the city Arona, and having carried a mine under a great part of the wall, the mine being sprung, the wall was lifted from its base, but dropped down again nevertheless, whole and entire, and so exactly upon its foundation, that the besieged suffered no inconvenience by that attempt.

Sometimes she plays the physician. Jason of Pheres being given over by the physicians, by reason of an imposthume in his breast, having a mind to rid himself of his pain, by death at least, threw himself in a battle desperately into the thickest of the enemy, where he was so fortunately wounded quite through the body, that the imposthume broke and he was perfectly cured. Did she not also excel painter Protogenes in his art? who having finished the picture of a dog quite tired and out of breath, in all the other parts excellently well to his own liking, but not being able to express, as he would, the slaver and foam that should come out of its mouth, vexed and angry at his work, he took his sponge, which by cleaning his pencils had

imbibed several sorts of colors, and threw it in a rage against the picture, with an attempt utterly to deface it; when fortune guiding the sponge to hit just upon the mouth of the dog, it there performed what all his art was not able to do. Does she not sometimes direct our counsels and correct them? Isabel, queen of England, having to sail from Zealand unto her own kingdom, with an army, in favor of her son, against her husband, had been lost, had she come into the port she intended, being there laid wait for by the enemy; but fortune, against her will, threw her into another haven, where she landed in safety. And that man of old who, throwing a stone at a dog, hit and killed his mother-in-law, had he not reason to pronounce this verse,

Ταντόματον ἡμῶν χαλλίω βουλευεται;

Icetes had contracted with two soldiers to kill Timoleon at Adrana in Sicily. These villains took their time to do it when he was assisting at a sacrifice, and thrusting into the crowd, as they were making signs to one another, that now was a fit time to do their business, in steps a third, who with a sword takes one of them full drive over the pate, lays him dead upon the place and runs away, which the other seeing, and concluding himself discovered and lost, runs to the altar and begs for mercy, promising to discover the whole truth, which as he was doing, and laying open the full conspiracy, behold the third man, who being apprehended, was, as a murderer, thrust and hauled by the people through the press, toward Timoleon, and the other most eminent persons of the assembly, before whom being brought, he cries out for pardon, pleading that he had justly slain his father's murderer; which he, also, proving upon the spot, by sufficient witnesses, whom his good fortune very opportunely supplied him withal, that his father was really killed in the city of the Leontines, by that very man on whom he had taken his revenge, he was presently awarded ten Attic minæ, for having had the good fortune, by designing to revenge the death of his father, to preserve the life of the common father of Sicily. Fortune, truly, in her conduct surpasses all the rules of human prudence.

But to conclude: is there not a direct application of her favor,

bounty, and piety manifestly discovered in this action? Ignatius the father and Ignatius the son, being proscribed by the triumvirs of Rome, resolved upon this generous act of mutual kindness, to fall by the hands of one another, and by that means to frustrate and defeat the cruelty of the tyrants; and accordingly, with their swords drawn, ran full drive upon one another, where fortune so guided the points, that they made two equally mortal wounds, affording withal so much honor to so brave a friendship, as to leave them just strength enough to draw out their bloody swords, that they might have liberty to embrace one another in this dying condition, with so close and hearty an embrace, that the executioners cut off both their heads at once, leaving the bodies still fast linked together in this noble bond, and their wounds joined mouth to mouth, affectionately sucking in the last blood and remainder of the lives of each other.

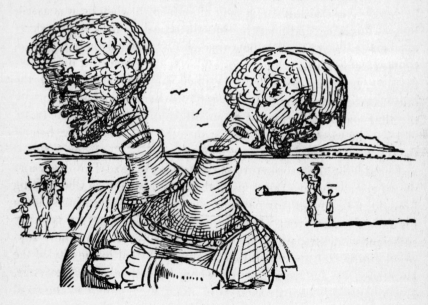

IV

OF CANNIBALS

WHEN King Pyrrhus invaded Italy, having viewed and considered the order of the army the Romans sent out to meet him: "I know not," said he, "what kind of barbarians," (for so the Greeks called all other nations) "these may be; but the disposition of this army, that I see, has nothing of barbarism in it." As much said the Greeks of that which Flaminius brought into their country; and Philip, beholding from an eminence the order and distribution of the Roman camp formed in his kingdom by Publius Sulpicius Galba, spake to the same effect. By which it appears how cautious men ought to be of taking things upon trust from vulgar opinion, and that we are to judge by the eye of reason, and not from common report.

I long had a man in my house that lived ten or twelve years in the New World, discovered in these latter days, and in that part of it where Villegaignon landed, which he called Antarctic France. This discovery of so vast a country seems to be of very great consideration. I cannot be sure, that hereafter there may not be another, so many wiser men than we having been deceived in this. I am afraid our eyes are bigger than our bellies, and that we have more curiosity than capacity; for we grasp at all, but catch nothing but wind.

Plato brings in Solon, telling a story that he had heard from the priests of Sais in Egypt, that of old, and before the Deluge, there was a great island called Atlantis, situate directly at the mouth of

[63]

the Straits of Gibraltar, which contained more countries than both
Africa and Asia put together; and that the kings of that country,
who not only possessed that isle, but extended their dominion so
far into the continent that they had a country of Africa as far as
Egypt, and extending in Europe to Tuscany, attempted to encroach
even upon Asia, and to subjugate all the nations that border upon
the Mediterranean Sea, as far as the Black Sea; and to that effect
overran all Spain, the Gauls, and Italy, so far as to penetrate into
Greece, where the Athenians stopped them: but that sometime after,
both the Athenians, and they and their island, were swallowed by
the Flood.

It is very likely that this extreme irruption and inundation of
water made wonderful changes and alterations in the habitations
of the earth, as 'tis said that the sea then divided Sicily from Italy—

> "Hæc loca, vi quondam, et vasta convulsa ruina,
>   Dissiluisse ferunt, quum protenus utraque tellus
>   Una foret."

—Cyprus from Syria, the isle of Negropont from the continent of
Bœotia, and elsewhere united lands that were separate before, by
filling up the channel between them with sand and mud:

> "Sterilisque diu palus, aptaque remis,
>   Vicinas urbes alit, et grave sentit aratrum."

But there is no great appearance that this isle was this New World
so lately discovered: for that almost touched upon Spain, and it
were an incredible effect of an inundation, to have tumbled back so
prodigious a mass, above twelve hundred leagues: besides that our
modern navigators have already almost discovered it to be no island,
but *terra firma*, and continent with the East Indies on the one side,
and with the lands under the two poles on the other side; or, if it be
separate from them, it is by so narrow a strait and channel, that it
none the more deserves the name of an island for that.

It should seem, that in this great body, there are two sorts of
motions, the one natural, and the other febrific, as there are in ours.
When I consider the impression that our river of Dordoigne has
made in my time, on the right bank of its descent, and that in

twenty years it has gained so much, and undermined the foundations of so many houses, I perceive it to be an extraordinary agitation: for had it always followed this course, or were hereafter to do it, the aspect of the world would be totally changed. But rivers alter their course, sometimes beating against the one side, and sometimes the other, and sometimes quietly keeping the channel. I do not speak of sudden inundations, the causes of which everybody understands. In Medoc, by the seashore, the Sieur d'Arsac, my brother, sees an estate he had there, buried under the sands which the sea vomits before it: where the tops of some houses are yet to be seen, and where his rents and domains are converted into pitiful barren pasturage. The inhabitants of this place affirm, that of late years the sea has driven so vehemently upon them, that they have lost above four leagues of land. These sands are her harbingers: and we now see great heaps of moving sand, that march half a league before her, and occupy the land.

The other testimony from antiquity, to which some would apply this discovery of the New World, is in Aristotle; at least, if that little book of unheard-of miracles be his. He there tells us, that certain Carthaginians, having crossed the Atlantic Sea without the Straits of Gibraltar, and sailed a very long time, discovered at last a great and fruitful island, all covered over with wood, and watered with several broad and deep rivers; far remote from all *terra-firma*, and that they, and others after them, allured by the goodness and fertility of the soil, went thither with their wives and children, and began to plant a colony. But the senate of Carthage perceiving their people by little and little to diminish, issued out an express prohibition, that none, upon pain of death, should transport themselves thither; and also drove out these new inhabitants; fearing, 'tis said, lest in process of time they should so multiply as to supplant themselves and ruin their state. But this relation of Aristotle no more agrees with our new-found lands than the other.

This man that I had was a plain ignorant fellow, and therefore the more likely to tell truth: for your better bred sort of men are much more curious in their observation, 'tis true, and discover a great deal more, but then they gloss upon it, and to give the greater

weight to what they deliver and allure your belief, they cannot forbear a little to alter the story; they never represent things to you simply as they are, but rather as they appeared to them, or as they would have them appear to you, and to gain the reputation of men of judgment, and the better to induce your faith, are willing to help out the business with something more than is really true, of their own invention. Now, in this case, we should either have a man of irreproachable veracity, or so simple that he has not wherewithal to contrive, and to give a color of truth to false relations, and who can have no ends in forging an untruth. Such a one was mine; and besides, he has at divers times brought to me several seamen and merchants who at the same time went the same voyage. I shall therefore content myself with his information, without inquiring what the cosmographers say to the business. We should have topographers to trace out to us the particular places where they have been; but for having had this advantage over us, to have seen the Holy Land, they would have the privilege, forsooth, to tell us stories of all the other parts of the world besides. I would have every one write what he knows, and as much as he knows, but no more; and that not in this only, but in all other subjects; for such a person may have some particular knowledge and experience of the nature of such a river, or such a fountain, who, as to other things, knows no more than what everybody does, and yet to keep a clutter with this little pittance of his, will undertake to write the whole body of physics: a vice from which great inconveniences derive their original.

Now, to return to my subject, I find that there is nothing barbarous and savage in this nation, by anything that I can gather, excepting, that every one gives the title of barbarism to everything that is not in use in his own country. As, indeed, we have no other level of truth and reason, than the example and idea of the opinions and customs of the place wherein we live: there is always the perfect religion, there the perfect government, there the most exact and accomplished usage of all things. They are savages at the same rate that we say fruit are wild, which nature produces of herself and by her own ordinary progress; whereas in truth, we ought rather

to call those wild, whose natures we have changed by our artifice, and diverted from the common order. In those, the genuine, most useful and natural virtues and properties are vigorous and sprightly, which we have helped to degenerate in these, by accommodating them to the pleasure of our own corrupted palate. And yet for all this our taste confesses a flavor and delicacy, excellent even to emulation of the best of ours, in several fruits wherein those countries abound without art or culture. Neither is it reasonable that art should gain the pre-eminence of our great and powerful mother nature. We have so surcharged her with the additional ornaments and graces we have added to the beauty and riches of her own works by our inventions, that we have almost smothered her; yet in other places, where she shines in her own purity and proper luster, she marvelously baffles and disgraces all our vain and frivolous attempts.

> "Et veniunt hederæ sponte sua melius;
> Surgit et in solis formosior arbutus antris;
> Et volucres nulla dulcius arte canunt."

Our utmost endeavors cannot arrive at so much as to imitate the nest of the least of birds, its contexture, beauty, and convenience: not so much as the web of a poor spider.

All things, says Plato, are produced either by nature, by fortune, or by art; the greatest and most beautiful by the one or the other of the former, the least and the most imperfect by the last.

These nations then seem to me to be so far barbarous, as having received but very little form and fashion from art and human invention, and consequently to be not much remote from their original simplicity. The laws of nature, however, govern them still, not as yet much vitiated with any mixture of ours: but 'tis in such purity, that I am sometimes troubled we were not sooner acquainted with these people, and that they were not discovered in those better times, when there were men much more able to judge of them than we are. I am sorry that Lycurgus and Plato had no knowledge of them: for to my apprehension, what we now see in those nations, does not only surpass all the pictures with which the poets have

adorned the golden age, and all their inventions in feigning a happy state of man, but, moreover, the fancy and even the wish and desire of philosophy itself; so native and so pure a simplicity, as we by experience see to be in them, could never enter into their imagination, nor could they ever believe that human society could have been maintained with so little artifice and human patchwork. I should tell Plato, that it is a nation wherein there is no manner of traffic, no knowledge of letters, no science of numbers, no name of magistrate or political superiority; no use of service, riches or poverty, no contracts, no successions, no dividends, no properties, no employments, but those of leisure, no respect of kindred, but common, no clothing, no agriculture, no metal, no use of corn or wine; the very words that signify lying, treachery, dissimulation, avarice, envy, detraction, pardon, never heard of. How much would he find his imaginary republic short of his perfection? *"Viri a diis recentes."*

"Hos natura modos primum dedit."

As to the rest, they live in a country very pleasant and temperate, so that, as my witnesses inform me, 'tis rare to hear of a sick person, and they moreover assure me, that they never saw any of the natives, either paralytic, blear-eyed, toothless, or crooked with age. The situation of their country is along the seashore, enclosed on the other side toward the land, with great and high mountains, having about a hundred leagues in breadth between. They have great store of fish and flesh, that have no resemblance to those of ours: which they eat without any other cookery, than plain boiling, roasting and broiling. The first that rode a horse thither, though in several other voyages he had contracted an acquaintance and familiarity with them, put them into so terrible a fright, with his centaur appearance, that they killed him with their arrows before they could come to discover who he was. Their buildings are very long, and of capacity to hold two or three hundred people, made of the barks of tall trees, reared with one end upon the ground, and leaning to and supporting one another, at the top, like some of our barns, of which the coverings hang down to the very ground,

and serves for the side walls. They have wood so hard, that they cut with it, and make their swords of it, and their grills of it to broil their meat. Their beds are of cotton, hung swinging from the roof, like our easman's hammocks, every man his own, for the wives lie apart from their husbands. They rise with the sun, and so soon as they are up, eat for all day, for they have no more meals but that: they do not then drink, as Suidas reports of some other people of the East that never drank at their meals; but drink very often all day after, and sometimes to a rousing pitch. Their drink is made of a certain root, and is of the color of our claret, and they never drink it but lukewarm. It will not keep above two or three days; it has a somewhat sharp, brisk taste, is nothing heady, but very comfortable to the stomach; laxative to strangers, but a very pleasant beverage to such as are accustomed to it. They make use, instead of bread, of a certain white compound, like Coriander comfits; I have tasted of it; the taste is sweet and a little flat. The whole day is spent in dancing. Their young men go a-hunting after wild beasts with bows and arrows; one part of their women are employed in preparing their drink the while, which is their chief employment. One of their old men, in the morning before they fall to eating, preaches to the whole family, walking from the one end of the house to the other, and several times repeating the same sentence, till he has finished the round, for their houses are at least a hundred yards long. Valor toward their enemies and love toward their wives, are the two heads of his discourse, never failing in the close, to put them in mind, that 'tis their wives who provide them their drink warm and well seasoned. The fashion of their beds, ropes, swords, and of the wooden bracelets they tie about their wrists, when they go to fight, and of the great canes, bored hollow at one end, by the sound of which they keep the cadence of their dances, are to be seen in several places, and among others, at my house. They shave all over, and much more neatly than we, without other razor than one of wood or stone. They believe in the immortality of the soul, and that those who have merited well of the gods, are lodged in that part of heaven where the sun rises, and the accursed in the west.

They have I know not what kind of priests and prophets, who very rarely present themselves to the people, having their abode in the mountains. At their arrival, there is a great feast, and solemn assembly of many villages: each house, as I have described, makes a village, and they are about a French league distant from one another. This prophet declaims to them in public, exhorting them to virtue and their duty: but all their ethics are comprised in these two

articles, resolution in war, and affection to their wives. He also prophesies to them events to come, and the issues they are to expect from their enterprises, and prompts them to or diverts them from war: but let him look to't; for if he fail in his divination, and anything happen otherwise than he has foretold, he is cut into a thousand pieces, if he be caught, and condemned for a false prophet: for that reason, if any of them has been mistaken, he is no more heard of.

Divination is a gift of God, and therefore to abuse it, ought to

be a punishable imposture. Among the Scythians, where their
diviners failed in the promised effect, they were laid, bound hand
and foot, upon carts loaded with furze and bavins, and drawn by
oxen, on which they were burned to death. Such as only meddle
with things subject to the conduct of human capacity, are excusable in doing the best they can: but those other fellows that
come to delude us with assurances of an extraordinary faculty,
beyond our understanding, ought they not to be punished, when
they do not make good the effect of their promise, and for the
temerity of their imposture?

They have continual war with the nations that live further within
the mainland, beyond their mountains, to which they go naked, and
without other arms than their bows and wooden swords, fashioned at one end like the heads of our javelins. The obstinacy of
their battles is wonderful, and they never end without great effu-
sion of blood: for as to running away, they know not what it is.
Every one for a trophy brings home the head of an enemy he has
killed, which he fixes over the door of his house. After having a
long time treated their prisoners very well, and given them all the
regales they can think of, he to whom the prisoner belongs, invites
a great assembly of his friends. They being come, he ties a rope to
one of the arms of the prisoner, of which, at a distance, out of his
reach, he holds the one end himself, and gives to the friend he loves
best the other arm to hold after the same manner; which being
done, they two, in the presence of all the assembly, despatch him
with their swords. After that they roast him, eat him among them,
and send some chops to their absent friends. They do not do this,
as some think, for nourishment, as the Scythians anciently did, but
as a representation of an extreme revenge; as will appear by this:
that having observed the Portuguese, who were in league with their
enemies, to inflict another sort of death upon any of them they took
prisoners, which was to set them up to the girdle in the earth, to
shoot at the remaining part till it was stuck full of arrows, and then
to hang them, they thought those people of the other world (as being
men who had sown the knowledge of a great many vices among their
neighbors, and who were much greater masters in all sorts of mis-

chief than they) did not exercise this sort of revenge without a meaning, and that it must needs be more painful than theirs, they began to leave their old way, and to follow this. I am not sorry that we should here take notice of the barbarous horror of so cruel an action, but that, seeing so clearly into their faults, we should be so blind to our own. I conceive there is more barbarity in eating a man alive, than when he is dead; in tearing a body limb from limb by racks and torments, that is yet in perfect sense; in roasting it by degrees; in causing it to be bitten and worried by dogs and swine (as we have not only read, but lately seen, not among inveterate and mortal enemies, but among neighbors and fellow-citizens, and, which is worse, under color of piety and religion), than to roast and eat him after he is dead.

Chrysippus and Zeno, the two heads of the Stoic sect, were of opinion that there was no hurt in making use of our dead carcasses, in what way soever for our necessity, and in feeding upon them too; as our own ancestors, who being besieged by Cæsar in the city of Alexia, resolved to sustain the famine of the siege with the bodies of their old men, women, and other persons who were incapable of bearing arms.

> "Vascones, ut fama est, alimentis talibus usi
> Produxere animas."

And the physicians make no bones of employing it to all sorts of use, either to apply it outwardly; or to give it inwardly for the health of the patient. But there never was any opinion so irregular, as to excuse treachery, disloyalty, tyranny, and cruelty, which are our familiar vices. We may then call these people barbarous, in respect to the rules of reason: but not in respect to ourselves, who in all sorts of barbarity exceed them. Their wars are throughout noble and generous, and carry as much excuse and fair pretense, as that human malady is capable of; having with them no other foundation than the sole jealousy of valor. Their disputes are not for the conquest of new lands, for these they already possess are so fruitful by nature, as to supply them without labor or concern, with all things necessary, in such abundance that they have no need

to enlarge their borders. And they are moreover, happy in this, that they only covet so much as their natural necessities require: all beyond that, is superfluous to them: men of the same age call one another generally brothers, those who are younger, children; and the old men are fathers to all. These leave to their heirs in common the full possession of goods, without any manner of division, or other title than what nature bestows upon her creatures, in bringing them into the world. If their neighbors pass over the mountains to assault them, and obtain a victory, all the victors gain by it is glory only, and the advantage of having proved themselves the better in valor and virtue: for they never meddle with the goods of the conquered, but presently return into their own country, where they have no want of anything necessary, nor of this greatest of all goods, to know happily how to enjoy their condition and to be content. And those in turn do the same; they demand of their prisoners no other ransom, than acknowledgment that they are overcome: but there is not one found in an age, who will not rather choose to die than make such a confession, or either by word or look, recede from the entire grandeur of an invincible courage. There is not a man among them who had not rather be killed and eaten, than so much as to open his mouth to entreat he may not. They use them with all liberality and freedom, to the end their lives may be so much the dearer to them; but frequently entertain them with menaces of their approaching death, of the torments they are to suffer, of the preparations making in order to it, of the mangling their limbs, and of the feast that is to be made, where their carcass is to be the only dish. All which they do, to no other end, but only to extort some gentle or submissive word from them, or to frighten them so as to make them run away, to obtain this advantage that they were terrified, and that their constancy was shaken; and indeed, if rightly taken, it is in this point only that a true victory consists.

> "Victoria nulla est,
> Quam quæ confessos animo quoque subjugat hostes."

The Hungarians, a very warlike people, never pretend further than to reduce the enemy to their discretion; for having forced this

confession from them, they let them go without injury or ransom, excepting, at the most, to make them engage their word never to bear arms against them again. We have sufficient advantages over our enemies that are borrowed and not truly our own; it is the quality of a porter, and no effect of virtue, to have stronger arms and legs; it is a dead and corporeal quality to set in array; 'tis a turn of fortune to make our enemy stumble, or to dazzle him with the light of the sun; 'tis a trick of science and art, and that may happen in a mean base fellow, to be a good fencer. The estimate and value of a man consist in the heart and in the will: there his true honor lies. Valor is stability, not of legs and arms, but of the courage and the soul; it does not lie in the goodness of our horse or our arms: but in our own. He that falls obstinate in his courage—*"Si succiderit, de genu pugnat"*—he who, for any danger of imminent death, abates nothing of his assurance; who, dying, yet darts at his enemy a fierce and disdainful look, is overcome not by us, but by fortune; he is killed, not conquered; the most valiant are sometimes the most unfortunate. There are defeats more triumphant than victories. Never could those four sister victories, the fairest the sun ever beheld, of Salamis, Platæa, Mycale, and Sicily, venture to oppose all their united glories, to the single glory of the discomfiture of King Leonidas and his men, at the pass of Thermopylæ. Whoever ran with a more glorious desire and greater ambition, to the winning, than Captain Iscolas to the certain loss of a battle? Who could have found out a more subtle invention to secure his safety, than he did to assure his destruction? He was set to defend a certain pass of Peloponnesus against the Arcadians, which, considering the nature of the place and the inequality of forces, finding it utterly impossible for him to do, and seeing that all who were presented to the enemy, must certainly be left upon the place; and on the other side, reputing it unworthy of his own virtue and magnanimity and of the Lacedæmonian name to fail in any part of his duty, he chose a mean between these two extremes after this manner; the youngest and most active of his men, he preserved for the service and defense of their country, and sent them back; and with the rest, whose loss would be of less consideration, he

resolved to make good the pass, and with the death of them, to make the enemy buy their entry as dear as possibly he could; as it fell out, for being presently environed on all sides by the Arcadians, after having made a great slaughter of the enemy, he and his were all cut in pieces. Is there any trophy dedicated to the conquerors, which was not much more due to these who were overcome? The part that true conquering is to play, lies in the encounter, not in the coming off; and the honor of valor consists in fighting, not in subduing.

But to return to my story: these prisoners are so far from discovering the least weakness, for all the terrors that can be represented to them that, on the contrary, during the two or three months they are kept, they always appear with a cheerful countenance; importune their masters to make haste to bring them to the test, defy, rail at them, and reproach them with cowardice, and the number of battles they have lost against those of their country. I have a song made by one of these prisoners, wherein he bids them "come all, and dine upon him, and welcome, for they shall withal eat their own fathers and grandfathers, whose flesh has served to feed and nourish him. These muscles," says he, "this flesh and these veins, are your own: poor silly souls as you are, you little think that the substance of your ancestors' limbs is here yet; notice what you eat, and you will find in it the taste of your own flesh:" in which song there is to be observed an invention that nothing relishes of the barbarian. Those that paint these people dying after this manner, represent the prisoner spitting in the faces of his executioners and making wry mouths at them. And 'tis most certain, that to the very last gasp, they never cease to brave and defy them both in word and gesture. In plain truth, these men are very savage in comparison of us; of necessity, they must either be absolutely so or else we are savages; for there is a vast difference between their manners and ours.

The men there have several wives, and so much the greater number, by how much they have the greater reputation for valor. And it is one very remarkable feature in their marriages, that the same jealousy our wives have to hinder and divert us from the friendship and familiarity of other women, those employ to promote their

husbands' desires, and to procure them many spouses; for being above all things solicitous of their husbands' honor, 'tis their chiefest care to seek out, and to bring in the most companions they can, forasmuch as it is a testimony of the husband's virtue. Most of our ladies will cry out, that 'tis monstrous; whereas in truth, it is not so; but a truly matrimonial virtue, and of the highest form. In the Bible, Sarah, with Leah and Rachel, the two wives of Jacob, gave the most beautiful of their handmaids to their husbands; Livia preferred the passions of Augustus to her own interest; and the wife of King Deiotarus, Stratonice, did not only give up a fair young maid that served her to her husband's embraces, but moreover carefully brought up the children he had by her, and assisted them in the succession to their father's crown.

And that it may not be supposed, that all this is done by a simple and servile obligation to their common practice, or by any authoritative impression of their ancient custom, without judgment or reasoning and from having a soul so stupid, that it cannot contrive what else to do, I must here give you some touches of their sufficiency in point of understanding. Besides what I repeated to you before, which was one of their songs of war, I have another, a love-song, that begins thus: "Stay, adder, stay, that by thy pattern my sister may draw the fashion and work of a rich ribbon, that I may present to my beloved, by which means thy beauty and the excellent order of thy scales shall forever be preferred before all other serpents." Wherein the first couplet, "Stay, adder," etc., makes the burden of the song. Now I have conversed enough with poetry to judge thus much: that not only, there is nothing of barbarous in this invention, but, moreover, that it is perfectly Anacreontic. To which may be added, that their language is soft, of a pleasing accent, and something bordering upon the Greek terminations.

Three of these people, not foreseeing how dear their knowledge of the corruptions of this part of the world will one day cost their happiness and repose, and that the effect of this commerce will be their ruin, as I presuppose it is in a very fair way (miserable men to suffer themselves to be deluded with desire of novelty and to have left the serenity of their own heaven, to come so far to gaze

at ours!) were at Rouen at the time that the late King Charles IX. was there. The king himself talked to them a good while, and they were made to see our fashions, our pomp, and the form of a great city. After which, some one asked their opinion, and would know of them, what of all the things they had seen, they found most to be admired? To which they made answer, three things, of which I have forgotten the third, and am troubled at it, but two I yet remember. They said, that in the first place they thought it very strange, that so many tall men wearing beards, strong, and well armed, who were about the king ('tis like they meant the Swiss of his guard) should submit to obey a child, and that they did not rather choose out one among themselves to command. Secondly (they have a way of speaking in their language, to call men the half of one another), that they had observed, that there were among us men full and crammed with all manner of commodities, while, in the meantime, their halves were begging at their doors, lean, and half-starved with hunger and poverty; and they thought it strange that these necessitous halves were able to suffer so great an inequality and injustice, and that they did not take the others by the throats, or set fire to their houses.

I talked to one of them a great while together, but I had so ill an interpreter, and one who was so perplexed by his own ignorance to apprehend my meaning, that I could get nothing out of him of any moment. Asking him, what advantage he reaped from the superiority he had among his own people (for he was a captain, and our mariners called him king), he told me: to march at the head of them to war. Demanding of him further, how many men he had to follow him? he showed me a space of ground, to signify as many as could march in such a compass, which might be four or five thousand men; and putting the question to him, whether or no his authority expired with the war? he told me this remained: that when he went to visit the villages of his dependence, they plained him paths through the thick of their woods, by which he might pass at his ease. All this does not sound very ill, and the last was not at all amiss, for they wear no breeches.

V

OF WAR-HORSES, OR DESTRIERS

I HERE have become a grammarian, I who never learned any language but by rote, and who do not yet know adjectives, conjunction, or ablative. I think I have read that the Romans had a sort of horses, by them called *funales* or *dextrarios*, which were either led horses, or horses laid on at several stages to be taken fresh upon occasion, and thence it is that we call our horses of service *destriers*; and our romances commonly use the phrase of *adestrer* for *accompagner*, to accompany. They also called those that were trained in such sort, that running full speed, side by side, without bridle or saddle, the Roman gentlemen armed at all pieces, would shift and throw ourselves from one to the other, *desultorios equos*. The Numidian men-at-arms had always a led horse in one hand, besides that they rode upon, to change in the heat of battle: *"quibus, desultorum in modum, binos trahentibus, equos, interacerrimam sæpe pugnam, in recentem equum, ex fesso, armatis transultare mos erat: tanta velocitas ipsis, tamque docile equorum genus."* There are many horses trained to help their riders so as to run upon any one that appears with a drawn sword, to fall both with mouth and heels upon any that front or oppose them: but it often happens that they do more harm to their friends than to their enemies; and moreover, you cannot lose them from their hold, to reduce them again into order, when they are once engaged and grappled, by which means you remain at the mercy of their quarrel. It happened very ill to Artybius, general of the Persian army,

fighting, man to man, with Onesilus, king of Salamis, to be mounted upon a horse trained after this manner, it being the occasion of his death, the squire of Onesilus cleaving the horse down with a scythe, between the shoulders as it was reared up upon his master. And what the Italians report that in the battle of Fornova King Charles' horse, with kicks and plunges, disengaged his master from the enemy that pressed upon him, without which he had been slain, sounds like a very great chance, if it be true. The Mamalukes make their boast that they have the most ready horses of any cavalry in the world; that by nature and custom they were taught to know and distinguish the enemy, and to fall foul upon him with mouth and heels, according to a word or sign given; as also to gather up with their teeth darts and lances scattered upon the field, and present them to their riders, on the word of command. 'Tis said, both of Cæsar and Pompey, that among their other excellent qualities they were both very good horsemen, and particularly of Cæsar, that in his youth, being mounted on the bare back, without saddle or bridle, he could make the horse run, stop, and turn, and perform all its airs, with his hands behind him. As nature designed to make of this person and of Alexander, two miracles of military art, so one would say she had done her utmost to arm them after an extraordinary manner: for every one knows that Alexander's horse, Bucephalus, had a head inclining to the shape of a bull; that he would suffer himself to be mounted and governed by none but his master, and that he was so honored after his death as to have a city erected to his name. Cæsar had also one which had forefeet like those of a man, his hoofs being divided in the form of fingers, which likewise was not to be ridden by any but Cæsar himself, who after his death, dedicated his statue to the goddess Venus.

I do not willingly alight when I am once on horseback, for it is the place where, whether well or sick, I find myself most at ease. Plato recommends it for health, as also Pliny says it is good for the stomach and the joints. Let us go further into this matter since here we are.

We read in Xenophon a law forbidding any one who was master of a horse to travel on foot. Trogus and Justin say that the Parthians

were wont to perform all offices and ceremonies, not only in war but also all affairs whether public or private, make bargains, confer, entertain, take the air, and all on horseback; and that the greatest distinction between freemen and slaves among them was that the one rode on horseback and the other went on foot, an institution of which King Cyrus was the founder.

There are several examples in the Roman history (and Suetonius more particularly observes it of Cæsar) of captains who, on pressing occasions, commanded their cavalry to alight, both by that means to take from them all hopes of flight, as also for the advantage they hoped in this sort of fight. *"Quo haud dubie superat Romanus,"* says Livy. And so the first thing they did to prevent the mutinies and insurrections of nations of late conquest was to take from them their arms and horses, and therefore it is that we so often meet in Cæsar: *"arma proferri, jumenta produci, obsides dari jubet."* The Grand Signior to this day suffers not a Christian or a Jew to keep a horse of his own throughout his empire.

Our ancestors, and especially at the time they had war with the English, in all their greatest engagements and pitched battles fought for the most part on foot, that they might have nothing but their own force, courage, and constancy to trust to in a quarrel of so great concern as life and honor. You stake (whatever Chrysanthes in Xenophon says to the contrary) your valor and your fortune upon that of your horse; his wounds or death bring your person into the same danger; his fear or fury shall make you reputed rash or cowardly; if he have an ill mouth, or will not answer to the spur, your honor must answer for it. And, therefore, I do not think it strange that those battles were more firm and furious than those that are fought on horseback:

> "Cædebant pariter, pariterque ruebant
> Victores victique; neque his fuga nota, neque illis."

Their battles were much better disputed. Nowadays there are nothing but routs: *"primus clamor atque impetus rem decernit."* And the means we choose to make use of in so great a hazard should be as much as possible at our own command: wherefore I

should advise to choose weapons of the shortest sort, and such of which we are able to give the best account. A man may repose more confidence in a sword he holds in his hand than in a bullet he discharges out of a pistol, wherein there must be a concurrence of several circumstances to make it perform its office, the powder, the stone, and the wheel: if any of which fail it endangers your fortune. A man himself strikes much surer than the air can direct his blow.

> "Et, quo ferre velint, permittere vulnera ventis;
> Ensis habet vires; et gens quæcumque virorum est,
> Bella gerit gladiis."

But of that weapon I shall speak more fully when I come to compare the arms of the ancients with those of modern use; only, by the way, the astonishment of the ear abated, which every one grows familiar with in a short time, I look upon it as a weapon of very little execution, and hope we shall one day lay it aside. That missile weapon which the Italians formerly made use of both with fire and by sling was much more terrible: they called a certain kind of javelin, armed at the point with an iron three feet long, that it might pierce through and through an armed man, Phalarica, which they sometimes in the field darted by hand, sometimes from several sorts of engines for the defense of beleaguered places; the shaft being rolled round with flax, wax, rosin, oil, and other combustible matter, took fire in its flight, and lighting upon the body of a man or his target, took away all the use of arms and limbs. And yet, coming to close fight, I should think they would also damage the assailant, and that the camp being as it were planted with these flaming truncheons, would produce a common inconvenience to the whole crowd.

> "Magnum stridens contorta Phalarica venit,
> Fulminis acta modo."

They had moreover, other devices which custom made them perfect in (which seem incredible to us who have not seen them), by which they supplied the effects of our powder and shot. They darted their spears with so great force as ofttimes to transfix two targets and

two armed men at once, and pin them together. Neither was the effect of their slings, less certain of execution or of shorter carriage:

"*Saxis globosis . . . funda, mare apertum incessentes . . . coronas modici circuli, magno ex intervallo loci, assueti trajicere, non capita modo hostium vulnerabant, sed quem locum destinassent.*"

These pieces of battery had not only the execution of but the thunder of our cannon also:

"*Ad ictus mœnium cum terribili sonitu editos, pavor et trepidatio cepit.*"

The Gauls, our kinsmen in Asia, abominated these treacherous missile arms, it being their use to fight, with greater bravery, hand to hand.

"*Non tam patentibus plagis moventur . . . ubi latior quam altior plaga est, etiam gloriosius se pugnare putant: iidem quum aculeus sagittœ aut glandis abditœ introrsus tenui vulnere in speciem urit . . . tum in rabiem et pudorem tam parvœ perimentis pestis versi, prosternunt corpora humi.*"

A pretty description of something very like a harquebus-shot. The ten thousand Greeks in their long and famous retreat met with a nation who very much galled them with great and strong bows, carrying arrows so long, that, taking them up, one might return them back like a dart, and with them pierce a buckler and an armed man through and through. The engines that Dionysius invented at Syracuse to shoot vast massy darts and stones of a prodigious greatness, with so great impetuosity and at so great a distance, came very near to our modern inventions.

But in this discourse of horses and horsemanship, we are not to forget the pleasant posture of one Maistre Pierre Pol, a doctor of divinity, upon his mule, whom Monstrelet reports always to have ridden aside through the streets of Paris like a woman. He says also, elsewhere, that the Gascons had terrible horses, that would wheel in their full speed, which the French, Picards, Flemings and Brabanters looked upon as a miracle, "having never seen the like before," which are his very words.

Cæsar speaking of the Suabians: "in the charges **they** make on

horseback," says he, "they often throw themselves off to fight on foot, having taught their horses not to stir in the meantime from the place, to which they presently run again upon occasion; and according to their custom, nothing is so unmanly and so base as to use saddles or pads, and they despise such as make use of those conveniences: insomuch that, being but a very few in number, they fear not to attack a great many." That which I have formerly wondered at, to see a horse made to perform all his airs with a switch only and the reins upon his neck, was common with the Massilians, who rode their horses without saddle or bridle.

> "Et gens, quæ nudo residens Massylia dorso,
> Ora levi flectit, frænorum nescia, virga."

> "Et Numidæ infræni cingunt."

"Equi sine frœnis, deformis ipse cursus, rigida cervice, et extento capite currentium."

King Alphonso, he who first instituted the Order of the Band or Scarf in Spain, among other rules of the order, gave them this, that they should never ride mule or mulet, upon penalty of a mark of silver; this I had lately out of Guevara's Letters, whoever gave these the title of Golden Epistles, had another kind of opinion of them than I have. The courtier says, that till his time it was a disgrace to a gentleman to ride on one of these creatures: but the Abyssinians, on the contrary, the nearer they are to the person of Prester John, love to be mounted upon large mules, for the greatest dignity and grandeur.

Xenophon tells us, that the Assyrians were fain to keep their horses fettered in the stable, they were so fierce and vicious; and that it required so much time to loose and harness them, that to avoid any disorder this tedious preparation might bring upon them in case of surprise, they never sat down in their camp till it was first well fortified with ditches and ramparts. His Cyrus, who was so great a master in all manner of horse service, kept his horses to their due work, and never suffered them to have anything to eat till first they had earned it by the sweat of some kind of exercise. The Scythians when in the field and in scarcity of provisions used to let

their horses' blood which they drank, and sustained themselves by that diet:

"Venit et epoto Sarmata pastus equo."

Those of Crete, being besieged by Metellus, were in so great necessity for drink that they were fain to quench their thirst with their horses' urine.

To show how much cheaper the Turkish armies support themselves than our European forces, 'tis said, that besides the soldiers drink nothing but water and eat nothing but rice and salt flesh pulverized (of which every one may easily carry about with him a month's provision) they know how to feed upon the blood of their horses as well as the Muscovite and Tartar, and salt it for their use.

These new-discovered people of the Indies when the Spaniards first landed among them, had so great an opinion both of the men and horses, that they looked upon the first as gods and the other as animals ennobled above their nature; insomuch that after they were subdued, coming to the men to sue for peace and pardon, and to bring them gold and provisions, they failed not to offer of the same to the horses, with the same kind of harangue to them they had made to the others: interpreting their neighing for a language of truce and friendship.

In the other Indies, to ride upon an elephant was the first and royal place of honor; the second to ride in a coach with four horses; the third to ride upon a camel; and the last and least honor to be carried or drawn by one horse only. Some one of our late writers tells us that he has been in countries in those parts, where they ride upon oxen with pads, stirrups, and bridles, and very much at their ease.

Quintus Fabius Maximus Rutilianus, in a battle with the Samnites, seeing his horse, after three or four charges, had failed of breaking into the enemy's battalion, took this course, to make them unbridle all their horses and spur their hardest, so that having nothing to check their career, they might through weapons and men open the way to his foot, who by that means gave them a bloody defeat. The same command was given by Quintus Fulvius Flaccus

against the Celtiberians: *"Id quum majore vi equorum facietis, si effrœnatos in hostes equos immittis; quod sœpe Romanos equites cum laude fecisse sua, memoriœ proditum est . . . detractisque frœnis, bis ultro citroque cum magna strage hostium, infractis omnibus hastis, transcurrerunt."*

The duke of Muscovy was anciently obliged to pay this reverence to the Tartars, that when they sent an embassy to him he went out to meet them on foot, and presented them with a goblet of mares' milk (a beverage of greatest esteem among them), and if, in drinking, a drop fell by chance upon their horse's mane, he was bound to lick it off with his tongue. The army that Bajazet had sent into Russia was overwhelmed with so dreadful a tempest of snow, that to shelter and preserve themselves from the cold, many killed and embowelled their horses, to creep into their bellies and enjoy the benefit of that vital heat. Bajazet, after that furious battle wherein he was overthrown by Tamerlane, was in a hopeful way of securing his own person by the fleetness of an Arabian mare he had under him, had he not been constrained to let her drink her fill at the ford of a river in his way, which rendered her so heavy and indisposed, that he was afterward easily overtaken by those that pursued him. They say indeed, that to let a horse stale takes him off his mettle, but, as to drinking, I should rather have thought it would refresh her.

Crœsus, marching his army through certain waste lands near Sardis, met with an infinite number of serpents, which the horses devoured with great appetite, and which Herodotus says was a prodigy of ominous portent to his affairs.

We call a horse *cheval entire*, that has his mane and ears entire, and no other will pass muster. The Lacedæmonians, having defeated the Athenians in Sicily, returning triumphant from the victory into the city of Syracuse, among other insolences, caused all the horses they had taken to be shorn and led in triumph. Alexander fought with a nation called Dahæ, whose discipline it was to march two and two together armed on one horse, to the war; and being in fight one of them alighted, and so they fought on horseback and on foot, one after another by turns.

I do not think that for graceful riding any nation in the world excels the French. A good horseman, according to our way of speaking, seems rather to have respect to the courage of the man than address in riding. Of all that ever I saw, the most knowing in that art, who had the best seat and the best method in breaking horses, was Monsieur de Carnavalet, who served our King Henry II.

I have seen a man ride with both his feet upon the saddle, take off his saddle, and at his return take it up again and replace it, riding all the while full speed; having galloped over a cap, make at it very good shots backward with his bow; take up anything from the ground, setting one foot on the ground and the other in the stirrup: with twenty other ape's tricks, which he got his living by.

There has been seen in my time at Constantinople two men upon one horse, who, in the height of its speed, would throw themselves off and into the saddle again by turn; and one who bridled and saddled his horse with nothing but his teeth; another who between two horses, one foot upon one saddle and the other upon the other, carrying another man upon his shoulders, would ride full career, the other standing bolt upright upon him and making very good shots with his bow; several who would ride full speed with their heels upward, and their heads upon the saddle between several scimitars, with the points upward, fixed in the harness. When I was a boy, the prince of Sulmona, riding a rough horse at Naples to all his airs, held reals under his knees and toes, as if they had been nailed there, to show the firmness of his seat.

VI

OF DEMOCRITUS AND HERACLITUS

THE judgment is an utensil proper for all subjects, and will have an oar in everything: which is the reason, that in these essays I take hold of all occasions where, though it happen to be a subject I do not very well understand, I try however, sounding it at a distance, and finding it too deep for my stature, I keep me on the shore; and this knowledge that a man can proceed no further, is one effect of its virtue, yea, one of those of which it is most proud. One while in an idle and frivolous subject, I try to find out matter whereof to compose a body, and then to prop and support it; another while, I employ it in a noble subject, one that has been tossed and tumbled by a thousand hands, wherein a man can scarce possibly introduce anything of his own, the way being so beaten on every side that he must of necessity walk in the steps of another: in such a case, 'tis the work of the judgment to take the way that seems best, and of a thousand paths, to determine that this or that is the best. I leave the choice of my arguments to fortune, and take that she first presents to me; they are all alike to me, I never design to go through any of them; for I never see all of anything: neither do they who so largely promise to show it to others. Of a hundred members and faces that everything has, I take one, one while to look it over only, another while to ripple up the skin, and sometimes to pinch it to the bones: I give a stab, not so wide but as deep as I can, and am for the most part tempted to take it in hand by some new light I discover in it. Did I know myself less, I might

perhaps venture to handle something or other to the bottom, and to be deceived in my own inability; but sprinkling here one word and there another, patterns cut from several pieces and scattered without design and without engaging myself too far, I am not responsible for them, or obliged to keep close to my subject, without varying at my own liberty and pleasure, and giving up myself to doubt and uncertainty, and to my own govering method, ignorance.

All motion discovers us: the very same soul of Cæsar, that made itself so conspicuous in marshaling and commanding the battle of Pharsalia, was also seen as solicitous and busy in the softer affairs of love and leisure. A man makes a judgment of a horse, not only by seeing him when he is showing off his paces, but by his very walk, nay, and by seeing him stand in the stable.

Among the functions of the soul, there are some of a lower and meaner form; he who does not see her in those inferior offices as well as in those of nobler note, never fully discovers her; and, peradventure, she is best shown where she moves her simpler pace. The winds of passions take most hold of her in her highest flights; and the rather by reason that she wholly applies herself to, and exercises her whole virtue upon, every particular subject, and never handles more than one thing at a time, and that not according to it, but according to herself. Things in respect to themselves have, peradventure, their weight, measures and conditions; but when we once take them into us, the soul forms them as she pleases. Death is terrible to Cicero, coveted by Cato, indifferent to Socrates. Health, conscience, authority, knowledge, riches, beauty, and their contraries, all strip themselves at their entering into us, and receive a new robe, and of another fashion, from the soul; and of what color, brown, bright, green, dark, and of what quality, sharp, sweet, deep, or superficial, as best pleases each of them, for they are not agreed upon any common standard of forms, rules, or proceedings; every one is a queen in her own dominions. Let us, therefore, no more excuse ourselves upon the external qualities of things; it belongs to us to give ourselves an account of them. Our good or ill has no other dependence but on ourselves. 'Tis there that our offer-

ings and our vows are due, and not to fortune: she has no power over our manners; on the contrary, they draw and make her follow in their train, and cast her in their own mold. Why should not I judge of Alexander at table, ranting and drinking at the prodigious rate he sometimes used to do? Or, if he played at chess? what string of his soul was not touched by this idle and childish game? I hate and avoid it, because it is not play enough, that it is too grave and serious a diversion, and I am ashamed to lay out as much thought and study upon it as would serve to much better uses. He did not more pump his brains about his glorious expedition into the Indies, nor than another in unraveling a passage upon which depends the safety of mankind. To what a degree does this ridiculous diversion molest the soul, when all her faculties are summoned together upon this trivial account! and how fair an opportunity she herein gives every one to know and to make a right judgment of himself? I do not more thoroughly sift myself in any other posture than this: what passion are we exempted from in it? Anger, spite, malice, impatience, and a vehement desire of getting the better in a concern wherein it were more excusable to be ambitious of being overcome; for to be eminent, to excel above the common rate in frivolous things, nowise befits a man of honor. What I say in this example may be said in all others. Every particle, every employment of man manifests him equally with any other.

Democritus and Heraclitus were two philosophers, of whom the first, finding human condition ridiculous and vain, never appeared abroad but with a jeering and laughing countenance; whereas Heraclitus commiserating that same condition of ours, appeared always with a sorrowful look, and tears in his eyes:

> "Alter
> Ridebat, quoties a limine moverat unum
> Protuleratque pedem; flebat contrarius alter."

I am clearly for the first humor: not because it is more pleasant to laugh than to weep, but because it expresses more contempt and condemnation than the other, and I think we can never be despised according to our full desert. Compassion and bewailing seem to

imply some esteem of and value for the thing bemoaned; whereas the things we laugh at are by that expressed to be of no moment. I do not think that we are so unhappy as we are vain, or have in us so much malice as folly; we are not so full of mischief as inanity; nor so miserable as we are vile and mean. And therefore Diogenes, who passed away his time in rolling himself in his tub, and made nothing of the great Alexander esteeming us no better than flies, or bladders puffed up with wind, was a sharper and more penetrating, and, consequently in my opinion, a juster judge than Timon, surnamed the Man-hater; for what a man hates he lays to heart. This last was an enemy to all mankind, who passionately desired our ruin, and avoided our conversation as dangerous, proceeding from wicked and depraved natures: the other valued us so little that we could neither trouble nor infect him by our example; and left us to herd one with another, not out of fear, but from contempt of our society: concluding us as incapable of doing good as ill.

Of the same strain was Statilius' answer, when Brutus courted him into the conspiracy against Cæsar; he was satisfied that the enterprise was just, but he did not think mankind worthy of a wise man's concern; according to the doctrine of Hegesias, who said, that a wise man ought to do nothing but for himself, forasmuch as he only was worthy of it: and to the saying of Theodorus, that it was not reasonable a wise man should hazard himself for his country, and endanger wisdom for a company of fools. Our condition is as ridiculous as risible.

VII

OF AGE

I CANNOT allow of the way in which we settle for ourselves the duration of our life. I see that the sages contract it very much in comparison of the common opinion: "What," said the younger Cato to those who would stay his hand from killing himself, "am I now of an age to be reproached that I go out of the world too soon?" And yet he was but eight-and-forty years old. He thought that to be a mature and advanced age, considering how few arrive unto it. And such as, soothing their thoughts with I know not what course of nature, promise to themselves some years beyond it, could they be privileged from the infinite number of accidents to which we are by a natural subjection exposed, they might have some reason so to do. What an idle conceit is it to expect to die of a decay of strength, which is the effect of extremest age, and to propose to ourselves no shorter lease of life than that, considering it is a kind of death of all others the most rare and very seldom seen? We call that only a natural death; as if it were contrary to nature to see a man break his neck with a fall, be drowned in shipwreck, be snatched away with a pleurisy or the plague, and as if our ordinary condition did not expose us to these inconveniences. Let us no longer flatter ourselves with these fine words; we ought rather, peradventure, to call that natural, which is general, common, and universal.

To die of old age is a death rare, extraordinary, and singular, and therefore, so much less natural than the others 'tis the last and extremest sort of dying: and the more remote, the less to be hoped

for. It is indeed, the bourn beyond which we are not to pass, and which the law of nature has set as a limit, not to be exceeded: but it is, withal, a privilege she is rarely seen to give us to last till then. 'Tis a lease she only signs by particular favor, and it may, be to one only in the space of two or three ages, and then with a pass to boot, to carry him through all the traverses and difficulties she has strewed in the way of this long career. And therefore my opinion is, that when once forty years we should consider it as an age to which very few arrive. For seeing that men do not usually proceed so far, it is a sign that we are pretty well advanced; and since we have exceeded the ordinary bounds, which is the just measure of life, we ought not to expect to go much further; having escaped so many precipices of death whereinto we have seen so many other men fall, we should acknowledge that so extraordinary a fortune as that which has hitherto rescued us from those eminent perils, and kept us alive beyond the ordinary term of living, is not likely to continue long.

'Tis a fault in our very laws to maintain this error: these say that a man is not capable of managing his own estate till he be five-and-twenty years old, whereas he will have much ado to manage his life so long. Augustus cut off five years from the ancient Roman standard, and declared, that thirty years old was sufficient for a judge. Servius Tullius superseded the knights of above seven-and-forty years of age from the fatigues of war; Augustus dismissed them at forty-five; though methinks it seems a little unreasonable that men should be sent to the fireside till five-and-fifty or sixty years of age. I should be of opinion that our vocation and employment should be as far as possible extended for the public good: I find the fault on the other side, that they do not employ us early enough. This emperor was arbiter of the whole world at nineteen, and yet would have a man to be thirty before he could be fit to determine a dispute about a gutter.

For my part, I believe our souls are adult at twenty as much as they are ever like to be, and as capable then as ever. A soul that has not by that time given evident earnest of its force and virtue will never after come to proof. The natural qualities and virtues

produce what they have of vigorous and fine, within that term or never.

> "Si l'espine nou picque quand nai
> A pene que picque jamai,"

as they say in Dauphiné.

Of all the great human actions I ever heard or read of, of what sort soever, I have observed, both in former ages and our own, more were performed before the age of thirty than after; and this ofttimes in the very lives of the same men. May I not confidently instance in those of Hannibal and his great concurrent Scipio? The better half of their lives they lived upon the glory they had acquired in their youth; great men after, 'tis true, in comparison of others; but by no means in comparison of themselves. As to my own particular, I do certainly believe that since that age, both my understanding and my constitution have rather decayed than improved, and retired rather than advanced. 'Tis possible, that with those who make the best use of their time, knowledge and experience may increase with their years; but vivacity, promptitude, steadiness, and other pieces of us, of much greater importance, and much more essentially our own, languish and decay.

> "Ubi jam validis quassatum est viribus ævi
> Corpus, et obtusis ceciderunt viribus artus,
> Claudicat ingenium, delirat linquaque, mensque."

Sometimes the body first submits to age, sometimes the mind; and I have seen enough who have got a weakness in their brains before either in their legs or stomach; and by how much the more it is a disease of no great pain to the sufferer, and of obscure symptoms, so much greater is the danger. For this reason it is that I complain of our laws, not that they keep us too long to our work, but that they set us to work too late. For the frailty of life considered, and to how many ordinary and natural rocks it is exposed, one ought not to give up so large a portion of it to childhood, idleness and apprenticeship.

VIII

OF DRUNKENNESS

THE world is nothing but variety and dissemblance: vices are all alike, as they are vices, and peradventure the Stoic understand them so; but although they are equally vices, yet they are not at all equal vices; and he who has transgressed the ordinary bounds of a hundred paces,

"Quos ultra, citraque nequit consistere rectum,"

should not be in a worse condition than he that has advanced but ten, is not to be believed; or that sacrilege is not worse than stealing a cabbage:

"Nec vincet ratio hoc, tantumdem ut peccet, idemque,
  Qui teneros caules alieni fregerit horti,
  Et qui nocturnus divum sacua legerit."

There is in this as great diversity is in anything whatever. The confounding of the order and measure of sins is dangerous: murderers, traitors, and tyrants get too much by it, and it is not reasonable they should flatter their consciences, because another man is idle, lascivious, or not assiduous at his devotion. Every one lays weight upon the sin of his companions, but lightens his own. Our very instructors themselves rank them sometimes, in my opinion, very ill. As Socrates said that the principal office of wisdom was to distinguish good from evil, we, the best of whom are vicious, ought also to say the same of the science of distinguishing between vice and vice, without which, and that very exactly performed,

the virtuous and the wicked will remain confounded and unrecognized.

Now, among the rest, drunkenness seems to me to be a gross and brutish vice. The soul has greater part in the rest, and there are some vices that have something, if a man may so say, of generous in them; there are vices wherein there is a mixture of knowledge, diligence, valor, prudence, dexterity and address; this one is totally corporeal and earthly. And the rudest nation this day in Europe is that alone where it is in fashion. Other vices discompose the understanding: this totally overthrows it and renders the body stupid.

> "Cum vini vis penetravit . . .
> Consequitur gravitas membrorum, præpediuntur
> Crura vacillanti, tardescit lingua, madet mens,
> Nant oculi; clamor, singultus, jurgia, gliscunt."

The worst state of man is that wherein he loses the knowledge and government of himself. And 'tis said, among other things upon this subject, that, as the must fermenting in a vessel, works up to the top whatever it has in the bottom, so wine, in those who have drunk beyond measure, vents the most inward secrets.

> "Tu sapientium
> Curas et arcanum jocoso
> Consilium retegis Lyæo."

Josephus tells us that by giving an ambassador the enemy had sent to him his full dose of liquor, he wormed out his secrets. And yet, Augustus, committing the most inward secrets of his affairs to Lucius Piso, who conquered Thrace, never found him faulty in the least, no more than Tiberius did Cossus, with whom he intrusted his whole counsels, though we know they were both so given to drink that they have often been fain to carry both the one and the other drunk out of the senate.

> "Hesterno inflatum venas, de more, Lyæo."

And the design of killing Cæsar was as safely communicated to Cimber, though he would often be drunk, as to Cassius, who drank

nothing but water. We see our Germans, when drunk as the devil, know their post, remember the word, and keep to their ranks:

> "Nec facilis victoria de madidis, et
> Blæsis, atque mero titubantibus."

I could not have believed there had been so profound, senseless, and dead a degree of drunkenness had I not read in history that Attalus, having, to put a notable affront upon him, invited to supper the same Pausanias, who upon the very same occasion afterward killed Philip of Macedon, a king who by his excellent qualities gave sufficient testimony of his education in the house and company of Epaminondas, made him drink to such a pitch that he could after abandon his beauty, as of a hedge strumpet, to the muleteers and servants of the basest office in the house. And I have been further told by a lady whom I highly honor and esteem, that near Bordeaux and about Castres where she lives, a country woman, a widow of chaste repute, perceiving in herself the first symptoms of breeding, innocently told her neighbors that if she had a husband she should think herself with child; but the causes of suspicion every day more and more increasing, and at last growing up to a manifest proof, the poor woman was reduced to the necessity of causing it to be proclaimed in her parish church, that whoever had done that deed and would frankly confess it, she did not only promise to forgive, but moreover to marry him, if he liked the motion; whereupon a young fellow that served her in the quality of a laborer, encouraged by this proclamation, declared that he had one holiday found her, having taken too much of the bottle, so fast asleep by the chimney and in so indecent a posture, that he could conveniently do his business without waking her; and they yet live together man and wife.

It is true that antiquity has not much decried this vice; the writings even of several philosophers speak very tenderly of it, and even among the Stoics there are some who advise folks to give themselves sometimes the liberty to drink, nay, to drunkenness, to refresh the soul.

> "Hoc quoque virtutum quondam certamine, magnum
> Socratem palmam promeruisse ferunt."

[97]

That censor and reprover of others, Cato, was reproached that he was a hard drinker.

"Narratur et prisci Catonis
Sæpe mero caluisse virtus."

Cyrus, that so renowned king, among the other qualities by which he claimed to be preferred before his brother Artaxerxes, urged this excellence, that he could drink a great deal more than he. And in the best governed nations this trial of skill in drinking is very much in use. I have heard Silvius, an excellent physician of Paris, say that lest the digestive faculties of the stomach should grow idle, it were not amiss once a month to rouse them by this excess, and to spur them lest they should grow dull and rusty; and one author tells us that the Persians used to consult about their most important affairs after being well warmed with wine.

My taste and constitution are greater enemies to this vice than I am; for besides that I easily submit my belief to the authority of ancient opinions, I look upon it indeed as an unmanly and stupid vice, but less malicious and hurtful than the others, which, almost all, more directly jostle public society. And if we cannot please ourselves but it must cost us something, as they hold, I find this vice costs a man's conscience less than the others, besides that it is of no difficult preparation, nor hard to be found, a consideration not altogether to be despised. A man well advanced both in dignity and age, among three principal commodities that he said remained to him of life, reckoned to me this for one, and where would a man more justly find it than among the natural conveniences? But he did not take it right, for delicacy and the curious choice of wines is therein to be avoided. If you found your pleasure upon drinking of the best, you condemn yourself to the penance of drinking of the worst. Your taste must be more indifferent and free; so delicate a palate is not required to make a good toper. The Germans drink almost indifferently of all wines with delight: their business is to pour down and not to taste; and it's so much the better for them; their pleasure is so much the more plentiful and nearer at hand. Secondly, to drink, after the French fashion, but at two meals, and

then very moderately, is to be too sparing of the favors of the god. There is more time and constancy required than so. The ancients spent whole nights in this exercise, and ofttimes added the day following to eke it out, and therefore we are to take greater liberty and stick closer to our work. I have seen a great lord of my time, a man of high enterprise and famous success, that without setting himself to it, and after his ordinary rate of drinking at meals, drank not much less than five quarts of wine, and at his going away appeared but too wise and discreet, to the detriment of our affairs. The pleasure we hold in esteem for the course of our lives ought to have a greater share of our time dedicated to it; we should, like shop-boys and laborers, refuse no occasion nor omit any opportunity of drinking, and always have it in our minds. Methinks we every day abridge and curtail the use of wine, and that the after breakfasts, dinner snatches, and collations I used to see in my father's house, when I was a boy, were more usual and frequent then than now.

Is it that we pretend to a reformation? Truly, no; but it may be we are more addicted to Venus than our fathers were. They are two exercises that thwart and hinder one another in their vigor. Lechery weakens our stomach on the one side, and on the other, sobriety renders us more spruce and amorous for the exercise of love.

'Tis not to be imagined what strange stories I have heard my father tell of the chastity of that age wherein he lived. It was for him to say it, being both by art and nature cut out and finished for the service of ladies. He spoke well and little; ever mixing his language with some illustration out of authors most in use, especially in Spanish. Marcus Aurelius was very frequent in his mouth. His behavior was grave, humble, and very modest; he was very solicitous of neatness and propriety both in his person and clothes, whether on horseback or afoot; he was monstrously punctual of his word; and of a conscience and religion generally tending rather toward superstition than otherwise. For a man of little stature, very strong, well proportioned, and well knit; of a pleasing countenance, inclining to brown, and very adroit in all noble exercises. I have

yet in the house to be seen canes poured full of lead, with which they say he exercised his arms for throwing the bar or the stone, or in fencing; and shoes with leaden soles to make him lighter for running or leaping. Of his vaulting he has left little miracles behind him; I have seen him when past three score laugh at our exercises, and throw himself in his furred gown into the saddle, make the tour of a table upon his thumbs, and scarce ever mount the stairs into his chamber without taking three or four steps at a time. But as to what I was speaking of before, he said there was scarce one woman of quality of ill fame in a whole province: he would tell of strange privacies, and some of them his own, with virtuous women, free from any manner of suspicion of ill; and for his own part solemnly swore he was a virgin at his marriage; and yet it was after a long practice of arms beyond the mountains, of which wars he left us a journal under his own hand, wherein he has given a precise account from point to point of all passages, both relating to the public and to himself. And he was, moreover, married at a well advanced maturity, in the year 1528, the three-and-thirtieth year of his age, upon his way home from Italy. But let us return to our bottle.

The incommodities of old age, that stand in need of some refreshment and support, might with reason beget in me a desire of this faculty, it being as it were the last pleasure the course of years deprives us of. The natural heat, say the good-fellows, first seats itself in the feet: that concerns infancy; thence it mounts into the middle region, where it makes a long abode and produces, in my opinion, the sole true pleasures of human life; all other pleasures in comparison sleep; toward the end, like a vapor that still mounts upward, it arrives at the throat, where it makes its final residence, and concludes the progress. I do not, nevertheless, understand how a man can extend the pleasure of drinking beyond thirst, and forge in his imagination an appetite artificial and against nature; my stomach would not proceed so far; it has enough to do to deal with what it takes in for its necessity. My constitution is not to care for drink but as following eating and washing down my meat, and for that reason my last draught is always the greatest. And seeing that

in old age we have our palate furred with phlegms or depraved by some other ill constitution, the wine tastes better to us as the pores are cleaner washed and laid more open. At least, I seldom taste the first glass well. Anacharsis wondered that the Greeks drank in greater glasses toward the end of a meal than at the beginning;

which was, I suppose, for the same reason the Germans do the same, who then begin the battle of drink.

Plato forbids children wine till eighteen years of age, and to get drunk till forty; but, after forty, gives them leave to please themselves, and to mix a little liberally in their feasts the influence of Dionysos, that good deity who restores to younger men their gayety, and to old men their youth; who mollifies the passions of the soul, as iron is softened by fire; and in his laws allows such merry meetings, provided they have a discreet chief to govern and keep them

in order, as good and of great utility; drunkenness being, he says, a true and certain trial of every one's nature, and, withal, fit to inspire old men with mettle to divert themselves in dancing and music; things of great use, and that they dare not attempt when sober. He, moreover, says that wine is able to supply the soul with temperance and the body with health. Nevertheless, these restrictions, in part borrowed from the Carthaginians, please him: that men forbear excesses in the expeditions of war; that every judge and magistrate abstain from it when about the administrations of his place or the consultations of the public affairs; that the day is not to be employed with it, that being a time due to other occupations, nor the night on which a man intends to get children.

'Tis said that the philosopher Stilpo, when oppressed with age, purposely hastened his end by drinking pure wine. The same thing, but not designed by him, dispatched also the philosopher Arcesilaus.

But, 'tis an old and pleasant question, whether the soul of a wise man can be overcome by the strength of wine?

"Si munitæ adhibet vim sapientiæ."

To what vanity does the good opinion we have of ourselves push us? The most regular and most perfect soul in the world has but too much to do to keep itself upright, and from being overthrown by its own weakness. There is not one of a thousand that is right and settled so much as one minute in a whole life, and that may not very well doubt, whether according to her natural condition she ever can be; but to join constancy to it is her utmost perfection; I mean when nothing should jostle and discompose her, which a thousand accidents may do. 'Tis to much purpose that the great poet Lucretius keeps such a clatter with his philosophy, when, behold! he goes mad with a love philter. Is it to be imagined that an apoplexy will not stun Socrates as well as a porter? Some men have forgotten their own names by the violence of a disease; and a slight wound has turned the judgment of others topsey-turvey. Let him be as wise as he will, after all he is but a man; and than that

what is there more frail, more miserable, or more nothing? Wisdom does not force our natural dispositions.

> "Sudores itaque, et pallorem exsistere toto
> Corpore, et infringi linguam, vocemque aboriri,
> Caligare oculos, sonere aures, succidere artus,
> Denique concidere, ex animi terrore, videmus:"

he must shut his eyes against the blow that threatens him; he must tremble upon the margin of a precipice, like a child; nature having reserved these light marks of her authority, not to be forced by our reason and the stoic virtue, to teach man his mortality and our weakness; he turns pale with fear, red with shame, and groans with the cholic, if not with desperate outcry, at least with hoarse and broken voice:

> "Humani a se nihil alienum putet."

The poets, that feign all things at pleasure, dare not acquit their greatest heroes of tears:

> "Sic fatur lacrymans, classique immittit habenas."

'Tis sufficient for a man to curb and moderate his inclinations, for totally to suppress them is not in him to do. Even our great Plutarch, that excellent and perfect judge of human actions, when he sees Brutus and Torquatus kill their children, begins to doubt whether virtue could proceed so far, and to question whether these persons had not rather been stimulated by some other passion. All actions exceeding the ordinary bounds are liable to sinister interpretation, forasmuch as our liking no more holds with what is above than with what is below it.

Let us leave that other sect, that sets up an express profession of scornful superiority; but when even in that sect, reputed the most quiet and gentle, we hear these rhodomontades of Metrodorus: *"Occupavi te, Fortuna, atque cepi: omnesque aditus tuos interclusi ut ad me aspirare non possess;"* when Anaxarchus, by command of Nicocreon the tyrant of Cyprus, was put into a stone mortar, and laid upon with mauls of iron, ceases not to say, "Strike, batter, break, 'tis not Anaxarchus, 'tis but his sheath that you pound and

bray so;" when we hear our martyrs cry out to the tyrant in the middle of the flame: "This side is roasted enough, fall to and eat, it is enough done; fall to work with the other;" when we hear the child in Josephus torn piece-meal with pincers, defying Antiochus, and crying out with a constant and assured voice: "Tyrant, thou losest thy labor, I am still at ease; where is the pain, where are the torments with which thou didst so threaten me? Is this all thou canst do? My constancy torments thee more than thy cruelty does me. Oh, pitiful coward, thou faintest, and I grow stronger; make me complain, make me bend, make me yield if thou canst; encourage thy guards, cheer up thy executioners; see, see they faint, and can do no more; arm them, flesh them anew, spur them up;" truly, a man must confess that there is some frenzy, some fury, how holy soever, that at that time possesses those souls. When we come to these Stoical sallies: "I had rather be mad than voluptuous," a saying of Antisthenes; Μανείην μᾶλλον, ἢ ἡσθείην. When Sextius tells us, "he had rather be fettered with affliction than pleasure;" when Epicurus takes upon him to play with his gout, and, refusing health and ease, defies all torments, and despising the lesser pains, as disdaining to contend with them, he covets and calls out for others sharper, more violent, and more worthy of him;

> "Spumantemque dari, pecora inter inertia, votis
> Optat aprum, aut fulvum descendere monte leonem."

who but must conclude that these are wild sallies pushed on by a courage that has broken loose from its place? Our soul cannot from her own seat reach so high; 'tis necessary she must leave it, raise herself up, and, taking the bridle in her teeth, transport her man so far that he shall afterward himself be astonished at what he has done; as, in war the heat of battle impels generous soldiers to perform things of so infinite danger, as afterward, recollecting them they themselves are the first to wonder at; as it also fares with the poets, who are often rapt with admiration of their own writings, and know not where again to find the track through which they performed so fine a career; which also is in them called fury and rapture. And as Plato says, 'tis no purpose for a sober-minded man

to knock at the door of poesy: so Aristotle says that no excellent soul is exempt from a mixture of madness; and he has reason to call all transports, how commendable soever, that surpass our own judgment and understanding, madness; forasmuch as wisdom is a regular government of the soul, which is carried on with measure and proportion, and for which she is to herself responsible. Plato argues thus, that the faculty of the prophesying is so far above us, that we must be out of ourselves when we meddle with it, and our prudence must either be obstructed by sleep or sickness, or lifted from her place by some celestial rapture.

IX

OF GLORY

THERE is the name and the thing; the name is a voice which denotes and signifies the thing; the name is no part of the thing, nor of the substance; 'tis a foreign piece joined to the thing, and outside it.

God, who is all fullness in Himself and the height of all perfection, cannot augment or add anything to Himself within; but His name may be augmented and increased by the blessing and praise we attribute to His exterior works: which praise seeing we cannot incorporate it in Him, forasmuch as He can have no accession of good, we attribute to His name, which is the part out of Him that is nearest to us. Thus is it that to God alone glory and honor appertain; and there is nothing so remote from reason as that we should go in quest of it for ourselves; for, being indigent and necessitous within, our essence being imperfect, and having continual need of amelioration, 'tis to that we ought to employ all our endeavor. We are all hollow and empty; 'tis not with wind and voice that we are to fill ourselves; we want a more solid substance to repair us: a man starving with hunger would be very simple to seek rather to provide himself with a gay garment than with a good meal: we are to look after that whereof we have most need. As we have it in our ordinary prayers, *"Gloria in excelsis Deo, et in terra pax hominibus."* We are in want of beauty, health, wisdom, virtue, and such like essential qualities: exterior ornaments should be looked after when we have made provision for necessary things. Divinity treats

[106]

amply and more pertinently of this subject, but I am not much versed in it.

Chrysippus and Diogenes were the earliest and firmest advocates of the contempt of glory; and maintained that among all pleasures, there was none more dangerous nor more to be avoided, than that which proceeds from the approbation of others. And, in truth, experience makes us sensible of many very hurtful treasons in it. There is nothing that so poisons princes as flattery, nor anything whereby wicked men more easily obtain credit and favor with them; nor panderism so apt and so usually made use of to corrupt the chastity of women as to wheedle and entertain them with their own praises. The first charm the Syrens made use of to allure Ulysses is of this nature:

"Deça vers nous, deça, otres-louable Ulysse,
    Et le plus grand honneur dont la Grece fleurisse."

These philosophers said, that all the glory of the world was not worth an understanding man's holding out his finger to obtain it:

"Gloria quantalibet quid erit, si gloria tantum est?"

I say for it alone; for it often brings several commodities along with it, for which it may justly be desired: it acquires us good will, and renders us less subject and exposed to insult and offense from others, and the like. It was also one of the principal doctrines of Epicurus; for this precept of his sect, conceal thy life, that forbids men to encumber themselves with public negotiations and offices, also necessarily presupposes a contempt of glory, which is the world's approbation of those actions we produce in public. He that bids us conceal ourselves, and to have no other concern but for ourselves, and who will not have us known to others, would much less have us honored and glorified; and so advises Idomeneus not in any sort to regulate his actions by the common reputation or opinion, except so as to avoid the other accidental inconveniences that the contempt of men might bring upon him.

Those discourses are, in my opinion, very true and rational; but we are, I know not how, double in ourselves, which is the cause

that what we believe we do not believe, and cannot disengage ourselves from what we condemn. Let us see the last and dying words
of Epicurus; they are grand, and worthy of such a philosopher, and
yet they carry some touches of the recommendation of his name
and of that humor he had decried by his precepts. Here is a letter
that he dictated a little before his last gasp:

"EPICURUS to HERMACHUS, greeting.
"While I was passing over the happy and last day of my life, I
write this, but at the same time, afflicted with such pain in my
bladder and bowels that nothing can be greater, but it was recompensed with the pleasure the remembrance of my inventions and
doctrines brought to my soul. Now, as the affection thou hast ever
from thy infancy borne toward me and philosophy requires, take
upon thee the protection of Metrodorus' children."

This is the letter. And that which makes me interpret that the
pleasure he says he had in his soul concerning his inventions, has
some reference to the reputation he hoped for thence after his
death, is the manner of his will in which he gives order that Amyno-
machus and Timocrates, his heirs should, every January, defray
the expense of the celebration of his birthday as Hermachus should
appoint: and also the expense that should be made the twentieth of
every moon in entertaining the philosophers, his friends, who
should assemble in honor of the memory of him and of Metrodorus.
Carneades was head of the contrary opinion, and maintained
that glory was to be desired for itself, even as we embrace our
posthumous issue for themselves, having no knowledge nor enjoyment of them. This opinion has not failed to be the more universally
followed, as those commonly are that are most suitable to our inclinations. Aristotle gives it the first place among external goods;
and avoids, as too extreme vices, the immoderate either seeking or
evading it. I believe that, if we had the books Cicero wrote upon
this subject, we should there find pretty stories; for he was so possessed with this passion, that, if he had dared, I think he could
willingly have fallen into the excess that others did, that virtue

itself was not to be coveted, but upon the account of the honor that always attends it:

> "Paulum sepultæ distat inertiæ
> Celata virtus:"

which is an opinion so false, that I am vexed it could ever enter into the understanding of a man that was honored with the name of philosopher.

If this were true, men need not be virtuous but in public; and we should be no further concerned to keep the operations of the soul, which is the true seat of virtue, regular and in order, than as they are to arrive at the knowledge of others. Is there no more in it, then, but only slyly and with circumspection to do ill? "If thou knowest," says Carneades, "of a serpent lurking in a place where, without suspicion, a person is going to sit down, by whose death thou expectest an advantage, thou dost ill if thou dost not give him caution of his danger; and so much the more because the action is to be known by none but thyself." If we do not take up of ourselves the rule of well-doing, if impunity pass with us for justice, to how many sorts of wickedness shall we every day abandon ourselves? I do not find what Sextus Peduceus did, in faithfully restoring the treasure that C. Plotius had committed to his sole secrecy and trust, a thing that I had often done myself so commendable, as I should think it an execrable baseness had we done otherwise; and I think it of good use in our days to recall the example of P. Sextilius Rufus, whom Cicero accuses to have entered upon an inheritance contrary to his conscience, not only not against law, but even by the determination of the laws themselves; and M. Crassus and Q. Hortensius, who, by reason of their authority and power, having been called in by a stranger to share in the succession of a forged will, that so he might secure his own part, satisfied themselves with having no hand in the forgery, and refused not to make their advantage and to come in for a share: secure enough, if they could shroud themselves from accusations, witnesses, and the cognizance of the laws: *"Meminerint Deum se habere testem, id est (ut ego arbitror) mentem suam."*

Virtue is a very vain and frivolous thing, if it derive its recommendation from glory; and 'tis to no purpose that we endeavor to give it a station by itself, and separate it from fortune; for what is more accidental than reputation? *"Profecto fortuna in omni re dominatur: ea res cunctas ex libidine magis, quam ex vero, celebrat, obscuratque."* So to order it that actions may be known and seen is purely the work of fortune; 'tis chance that helps us to glory, according to its own temerity. I have often seen her go before merit, and often very much outstrip it. He who first likened glory to a shadow did better than he was aware of; they are both of them things pre-eminently vain: glory also, like a shadow, goes sometimes before the body, and sometimes in length infinitely exceeds it. They who instruct gentlemen only to employ their valor for the obtaining of honor, *"quasi non sit honestum, quod nobilitatum non sit;"* what do they intend by that but to instruct them never to hazard themselves if they are not seen, and to observe well if there be witnesses present who may carry news of their valor, whereas a thousand occasions of well-doing present themselves which cannot be taken notice of? How many brave individual actions are buried in the crowd of a battle? Whoever shall take upon him to watch another's behavior in such a confusion is not very busy himself, and the testimony he shall give of his companion's deportment will be evidence against himself. *"Vera et sapiens animi magnitudo, honestum illud, quod maxime naturam sequitur, in factis positum, non in gloria, judicat."*

All the glory that I pretend to derive from my life is that I have lived in it quiet; in quiet, not according to Metrodorus, or Arcesilaus, or Aristippus, but according to myself. For seeing philosophy has not been able to find out any way to tranquillity that is good in common, let every one seek it in particular.

To what do Cæsar and Alexander owe the infinite grandeur of their renown but to fortune? How many men has she extinguished in the beginning of their progress, of whom we have no knowledge, who brought as much courage to the work as they, if their adverse hap had not cut them off in the first sally of their arms? Among so many and so great dangers I do not remember I have anywhere

read that Cæsar was ever wounded; a thousand have fallen in less dangers than the least of those he went through. An infinite number of brave actions must be performed without witness and lost, before one turns to account. A man is not always on the top of a breach, or at the head of an army, in the sight of his general, as upon a scaffold; a man is often surprised between the hedge and the ditch; he must run the hazard of his life against a henroost; he must dislodge four rascally musketeers out of a barn; he must prick out single from his party, and alone make some attempts, according as necessity will have it. And whoever will observe will, I believe, find it experimentally true, that occasions of the least luster are ever the most dangerous; and that in the wars of our own times there have more brave men been lost in occasions of little moment, and in the dispute about some little paltry fort, than in places of greatest importance, and where their valor might have been more honorably employed.

Who thinks his death unworthy of him if he do not fall in some signal occasion, instead of illustrating his death willfully obscures his life, suffering in the meantime many very just occasions of hazarding himself to slip out of his hands; and every just one is illustrious enough, every man's conscience being a sufficient trumpet to him. *"Gloria nostra est testimonium conscientiæ nostræ."* He who is only a good man that men may know it, and that he may be the better esteemed when 'tis known: who will not do well but upon condition that his virtue may be known to men: is one from whom much service is not to be expected.

> "Credo ch 'el resto di quel verno cose
> Facesse degne di tenerne conto;
> Ma fur sin da quel tempo sì nascose,
> Che non e colpa mia s' or 'non le conto:
> Perche Orlando a far l 'opre virtuose,
> Più ch' a narrale poi, sempre era pronto;
> Nè mai fu alcuno de' suoi fatti espresso,
> Se non quando ebbe i testimoni appresso."

A man must go to the war upon the account of duty, and expect the recompense that never fails brave and worthy actions, how

private soever, or even virtuous thoughts—the satisfaction that a well-disposed conscience receives in itself in doing well. A man must be valiant for himself, and upon account of the advantage it is to him to have his courage seated in a firm and secure place against the assaults of fortune:

> "Virtus, repulsæ nescia sordidæ
> Intaminatis fulget honoribus:
> Nec sumit, aut ponit secures
> Arbitrio popularis auræ."

It is not for outward show that the soul is to play its part, but for ourselves within, where no eyes can pierce but our own; there she defends us from the fear of death, of pain, of shame itself; there she arms us against the loss of our children, friends, and fortunes; and when opportunity presents itself, she leads us on to the hazards of war, *"non emolumento aliquo, sed ipsius honestatis decore."* This profit is of much greater advantage, and more worthy to be coveted and hoped for, than honor and glory, which are no other than a favorable judgment given of us.

A dozen men must be called out of a whole nation to judge about an acre of land; and the judgment of our inclinations and actions, the most difficult and most important matter that is, we refer to the voice and determination of the rabble, the mother of ignorance, injustice, and inconstancy. Is it reasonable that the life of a wise man should depend upon the judgment of fools? *"An quidquom stultius, quam, quos singulos contemnas, eos aliquid putare, esse universos?"* He that makes it his business to please them, will have enough to do and never have done; 'tis a mark that can never be aimed at or hit: *"Nil tam incestimabile est, quam animi multitudinis."* Demetrius pleasantly said of the voice of the people, that he made no more account of that which came from above than of that which came from below. Cicero says more: *"Ego hoc judico, si quando turpe non sit, tamen non esse non turpe, quum id à multitudine laudatur."* No art, no activity of wit, could conduct our steps so as to follow so wandering and so irregular a guide; in this windy confusion of the noise of vulgar reports and opinions that drive

us on, no way worth anything can be chosen. Let us not propose to ourselves so floating and wavering an end; let us follow constantly after reason; let the public approbation follow us there, if it will; and as it wholly depends upon fortune, we have no reason sooner to expect it by any other way than that. Even though I would not follow the right way because it is right, I should, however, follow it as having experimentally found that, at the end of the reckoning, 'tis commonly the most happy and of greatest utility: *"Dedit hoc providentia hominicus munus, ut honesta magis juvarent."* The mariner of old said thus to Neptune, in a great tempest: "Oh God, thou mayest save me if thou wilt, and if thou wilt, thou mayest destroy me; but, however, I will steer my rudder true. I have seen in my time a thousand men supple, mongrel, ambiguous, whom no one doubted to be more worldy wise than I, destroy themselves, where I have saved myself:

"Risi successu posse carere dolos."

Paulus Æmilius, going on the glorious expedition of Macedonia, above all things charged the people of Rome not to speak of his actions during his absence. Oh, the license of judgments is a great disturbance to great affairs! forasmuch as every one has not the firmness of Fabius against common, adverse, and injurious tongues, who rather suffered his authority to be dissected by the vain fancies of men, than to do less well in his charge with a favorable reputation and the popular applause.

There is I know not what natural sweetness in hearing one's self commended; but we are a great deal too fond of it:

"Laudari haud metuam, neque enim mihi cornea fibra est:
  Sed recti finemque, extremumque esse recuso,
  Euge tuum, et belle."

I care not so much what I am in the opinion of others, as what I am in my own; I would be rich of myself, and not by borrowing. Strangers see nothing but events and outward appearances; everybody can set a good face on the matter, when they have trembling and terror within; they do not see my heart, they see but my

countenance. 'Tis with good reason that men decry the hypocrisy that is in war; for what is more easy to an old soldier than to shift in a time of danger, and to counterfeit the brave when he has no more heart than a chicken? There are so many ways to avoid hazarding a man's own person, that we have deceived the world a thousand times before we come to be engaged in a real danger: and even then, finding ourselves in an inevitable necessity of doing something, we can make shift for that time to conceal our apprehensions by setting a good face on the business, though the heart beats within; and whoever had the use of the Platonic ring, which renders those invisible that wear it, if turned inward toward the palm of the hand, a great many would very often hide themselves when they ought most to appear, and would repent being placed in so honorable a post, when necessity must make them bold.

"Falsus honor juvat, et mendax infamia terret
Quem, nisi mendosum et mendacem?"

Thus we see how all the judgments that are founded upon external appearances, are marvelously uncertain and doubtful; and that there is no so certain testimony as every one is to himself. In these, how many soldier's boys are companions of our glory? he who stands firm in an open trench, what does he in that more than fifty poor pioneers who open to him the way and cover it with their own bodies for fivepence a day pay, do before him?

"Non si quid turbida Roma
Elevet, accedas; examenque improbum in illa
Castiges trutina: nec te quæsiveris extra."

The dispersing and scattering our names into many mouths, we call making them more great; we will have them there well received, and that this increase turn to their advantage, which is all that can be excusable in this design. But the excess of this disease proceeds so far that many covet to have a name, be it what it will. Trogus Pompeius says of Herostratus, and Titus Livius of Manlius Capitolinus, that they were more ambitious of a great reputation than of a good one. This is very common; we are more solicitous

that men speak of us, than how they speak: and it is enough for us
that our names are often mentioned, be it after what manner it will.
It should seem that to be known, is in some sort to have a man's
life and its duration in others' keeping. I, for my part, hold that
I am not, but in myself; and of that other life of mine which lies in
the knowledge of my friends, to consider it naked and simply in
itself, I know very well that I am sensible of no fruit nor enjoyment
from it but by the vanity of a fantastic opinion; and when I shall
be dead, I shall be still and much less sensible of it; and shall,
withal, absolutely lose the use of those real advantages that sometimes accidentally follow it. I shall have no more handle whereby
to take hold of reputation, neither shall it have any whereby to
take hold of or to cleave to me; for to expect that my name should
be advanced by it, in the first place, I have no name that is enough
my own; of two that I have, one is common to all my race, and,
indeed, to others also; there are two families at Paris and Mont-
pellier, whose surname is Montaigne, another in Brittany, and one
in Xaintonge, De La Montaigne. The transposition of one syllable
only would suffice so to ravel our affairs that I shall share in their
glory, and they, peradventure, shall partake of my shame: and,
moreover, my ancestors have formerly been surnamed Eyquem, a
name wherein a family well known in England is at this day concerned. As to my other name, every one may take it that will, and
so, perhaps, I may honor a porter in my own stead. And, besides,
though I had a particular distinction by myself, what can it distinguish when I am no more? Can it point out and favor inanity?

> "Nunc levior cippus non imprimit ossa.
> Laudat posteritas; nunc non e manibus illis,
> Nunc non e tumulo, fortunataque favilla,
> Nascuntur violæ:"

but of this I have spoken elsewhere. As to what remains, in a great
battle where ten thousand men are maimed or killed, there are not
fifteen who are taken notice of; it must be some very eminent greatness, or some consequence of great importance that fortune has
added to it, that signalizes a private action, not of a harquebuser

[115]

only, but of a great captain; for to kill a man, or two, or ten: to expose a man's self bravely to the utmost peril of death, is, indeed, something in every one of us, because we there hazard all; but for the world's concern, they are things so ordinary, and so many of them are every day seen, and there must of necessity be so many of the same kind to produce any notable effect, that we cannot expect any particular renown from it:

"Casus multis hic cognitus, ac jam
Tritus, et e medio fortunæ ductus acervo."

Of so many thousands of valiant men who have died within these fifteen hundred years in France with their swords in their hands, not a hundred have come to our knowledge. The memory, not of the commanders only, but of battles and victories, is buried and gone; the fortunes of above half of the world, for want of a record, stir not from their place, and vanish without duration. If I had unknown events in my possession, I should think with great ease to out-do those that are recorded, in all sorts of examples. Is it not strange that even of the Greeks and Romans, with so many writers and witnesses, and so many rare and noble exploits, so few are arrived at our knowledge?

"Ad nos vix tenuis famæ perlabitur aura."

It will be much if a hundred years hence, it be remembered in gross that in our times there were civil wars in France. The Lacedæmonians, entering into battle, sacrificed to the Muses, to the end that their actions might be well and worthily written, looking upon it as a divine and no common favor, that brave acts should find witnesses that could give them life and memory. Do we expect that at every musket shot we receive, and at every hazard we run, there must be a register ready to record it? and, besides, a hundred registers may enrol them whose commentaries will not last above three days, and will never come to the sight of any one. We have not the thousandth part of ancient writings; 'tis fortune that gives them a shorter or longer life, according to her favor; and 'tis

permissible to doubt whether those we have be not the worst, not having seen the rest. Men do not write histories of things of so little moment: a man must have been general in the conquest of an empire or a kingdom; he must have won two-and-fifty set battles, and always the weaker in number, as Cæsar did: ten thousand brave fellows and many great captains lost their lives valiantly in his service, whose names lasted no longer than their wives and children lived:

"Quos fama obscura recondit."

Even those we see behave themselves the best, three months or three years after they have been knocked on the head, are no more spoken of than if they had never been. Whoever will justly consider, and with due proportion, of what kind of men and of what sort of actions the glory sustains itself in the records of history, will find that there are very few actions and very few persons of our times who can there pretend any right. How many worthy men have we known to survive their own reputation, who have seen and suffered the honor and glory most justly acquired in their youth, extinguished in their own presence? And for three years of this fantastic and imaginary life we must go and throw away our true and essential life, and engage ourselves in a perpetual death! The sages propose to themselves a nobler and more just end in so important an enterprise: "*Recte facti, fecisse merces est: officii fructus, ipsum officium est.*" It were, peradventure, excusable in a painter or other artisan, or in a rhetorician or a grammarian, to endeavor to raise himself a name by his works; but the actions of virtue are too noble in themselves to seek any other reward than from their own value, and especially to seek it in the vanity of human judgments.

If this false opinion, nevertheless, be of such use to the public as to keep men in their duty; if the people are thereby stirred up to virtue; if princes are touched to see the world bless the memory of Trajan, and abominate that of Nero; if it moves them to see the name of that great beast, once so terrible and feared, so freely cursed and reviled by every schoolboy, let it by all means increase, and be as much as possible nursed up and cherished among us; and

Plato, bending his whole endeavor to make his citizens virtuous, also advises them not to despise the good repute and esteem of the people; and says it falls out, by a certain divine inspiration, that even the wicked themselves ofttimes, as well by word as opinion, can rightly distinguish the virtuous from the wicked. This person and his tutor are both marvelous and bold artificers everywhere to add divine operations and revelations where human force is wanting. *"Ut tragici poetæ confugiunt ad deum, cum explicare argumenti exitum non possunt:"* and, peradventure, for this reason it was that Timon, railing at him called him the great forger of miracles. Seeing that men by their insufficiency, cannot pay themselves well enough with current money, let the counterfeit be superadded. 'Tis a way that has been practiced by all the legislators; and there is no government that has not some mixture either of ceremonial vanity or of false opinion, that serves for a curb to keep the people in their duty. 'Tis for this that most of them have their originals and beginnings fabulous, and enriched with supernatural mysteries; 'tis this that has given credit to bastard religions, and caused them to be countenanced by men of understanding; and for this, that Numa and Sertorius, to possess their men with a better opinion of them, fed them with this foppery; one, that the nymph Egeria, the other that his white hind, brought them all their counsels from the gods. And the authority that Numa gave to his laws, under the title of the patronage of this goddess, Zoroaster, legislator of the Bactrians and Persians, gave to his under the name of the god Oromazis; Trismegistus, legislator of the Egyptians, under that of Mercury; Xamolxis, legislator of the Scythians, under that of Vesta; Charandas, legislator of the Chalcidians, under that of Saturn; Minos, legislator of the Candiots, under that of Jupiter: Lycurgus, legislator of the Lacedæmonians, under that of Apollo; and Draco and Solon, legislators of the Athenians, under that of Minerva. And every government has a god at the head of it; the others falsely, that truly, which Moses set over the Jews at their departure out of Egypt. The religion of the Bedouins, as the Sire de Joinville reports, among other things, enjoined a belief that the soul of him among them who died for his prince, went into another

body more happy, more beautiful, and more robust than the former, by which means they much more willingly ventured their lives:

> "In ferrum mens prona viris, animæque capaces
> Mortis, et ignavum est redituræ parcere vitæ."

This is a very comfortable belief, however erroneous. Every nation has many such examples of its own; but this subject would require a treatise by itself.

To add one word more to my former discourse, I would advise the ladies no longer to call that honor which is but their duty; *"Ut enim consuetudo loquitur, id solum dicitur honestum, quod est populari fama gloriosum;"* their duty is the mark, their honor but the outward rind. Neither would I advise them to give this excuse for payment of their denial: for I presuppose that their intentions, their desire, and will, which are things wherein their honor is not at all concerned, forasmuch as nothing thereof appears without, are much better regulated than the effects:

> "Quæ, quia non liceat, non sacit, illa facit:"

The offense, both toward God and in the conscience, would be as great to desire as to do it: and, besides, they are actions so private and secret of themselves, as would be easily enough kept from the knowledge of others, wherein the honor consists, if they had not another respect to their duty, and the affection they bear to chastity, for itself. Every woman of honor will much rather choose to lose her honor, than to hurt her conscience.

X

OF PRESUMPTION

THERE is another sort of glory, which is the having too good an opinion of our own worth. 'Tis an inconsiderate affection with which we flatter ourselves, and that represents us to ourselves other than we truly are; like the passion of love, and that lends beauties and graces to the object, and makes those who are caught by it, with a depraved and corrupt judgment, consider the thing which they love other and more perfect than it is.

I would not, nevertheless, for fear of failing on this side, that a man should not know himself aright, or think himself less than he is; the judgment ought in all things to maintain its rights; 'tis all the reason in the world he should discern in himself, as well as in others, what truth sets before him; if it be Cæsar, let him boldly think himself the greatest captain in the world. We are nothing but ceremony; ceremony carries us away, and we leave the substance of things; we hold by the branches, and quit the trunk and the body; we have taught the ladies to blush when they hear that but named which they are not at all afraid to do; we dare not call our members by their right names, yet are not afraid to employ them in all sorts of debauchery; ceremony forbids us to express by words things that are lawful and natural, and we obey it; reason forbids us to do things unlawful and ill, and nobody obeys it. I find myself here fettered by the laws of ceremony; for it neither permits a man to speak well of himself, nor ill; we will leave it there for this time.

They whom fortune (call it good or ill) has made to pass their

lives in some eminent degree, may by their public actions manifest what they are; but they whom she has only employed in the crowd, and of whom nobody will say a word unless they speak themselves, are to be excused if they take the boldness to speak of themselves to such as are interested to know them; by the example of Lucilius,

> "Ille velut fidis arcana sodalibus olim
> Credebat libris, neque si male cesserat, usquam
> Decurrens alio, neque si bene: quo fit, ut omnis,
> Votiva pateat veluti descripta tabella
> Vita senis;"

he always committed to paper his actions and thoughts, and there portrayed himself such as he found himself to be; *"Nec id Rutilio et Scauro citra fidem, aut obtrectationi fuit."*

I remember, then, that from my infancy there was observed in me I know not what kind of carriage and behavior, that seemed to relish of pride and arrogance. I will say this, by the way, that it is not unreasonable to suppose that we have qualities and inclinations so much our own, and so incorporate in us, that we have not the means to feel and recognize them; and of such natural inclinations the body will retain a certain bent, without our knowledge or consent. It was an affectation conformable with his beauty, that made Alexander carry his head on one side, and caused Alcibiades to lisp; Julius Cæsar scratched his head with one finger, which is the fashion of a man full of troublesome thoughts; and Cicero, as I remember, was wont to pucker up his nose, a sign of a man given to scoffing; such motions as these may imperceptibly happen in us. There are other artificial ones which I meddle not with, as salutations and congees, by which men acquire, for the most part unjustly, the reputation of being humble and courteous; one may be humble out of pride. I am prodigal enough of my hat, especially in summer, and never am so saluted but that I pay it again from persons of what quality soever, unless they be in my own service. I should make it my request to some princes whom I know, that they would be more sparing of that ceremony, and bestow that courtesy where it is more due; for being so indiscreetly and indifferently conferred on all, it is thrown away to no purpose; if it be without respect of persons, it loses its effect. Among irregular deportment, let us not forget that haughty one of the Emperor Constantius, who always in public held his head upright and stiff, without bending or turning on either side, not so much as to look upon those who saluted him on one side, planting his body in a rigid immovable posture, without suffering it to yield to the motion of his coach, not daring so much as to spit, blow his nose, or wipe his face before people. I know not whether the gestures that were observed in me were of this first quality, and whether I had really any occult propension to this vice, as it might well be; and I cannot

be responsible for the motions of the body; but as to the motions of the soul, I must here confess what I think of the matter.

This glory consists of two parts; the one in setting too great a value upon ourselves, and the other in setting too little a value

upon others. As to the one, methinks these considerations ought, in the first place, to be of some force; I feel myself importuned by an error of the soul that displeases me, both as it is unjust, and still more as it is troublesome; I attempt to correct it, but I cannot root it out: and this is, that I lessen the just value of things that I possess,

and overvalue things, because they are foreign, absent, and none of mine; this humor spreads very far. As the prerogative of the authority makes husbands look upon their own wives with a vicious disdain, and many fathers their children; so I, between two equal merits should always be swayed against my own; not so much that the jealousy of my advancement and bettering troubles my judgment, and hinders me from satisfying myself, as that of itself possession begets a contempt of what it holds and rules. Foreign governments, manners, and languages, insinuate themselves into my esteem; and I am sensible that Latin allures me by the favor of its dignity to value it above its due, as it does with children, and the common sort of people: the domestic government, house, horse, of my neighbor, though no better than my own, I prize above my own, because they are not mine. Besides that I am very ignorant in my own affairs, I am struck by the assurance that every one has of himself: whereas, there is scarcely anything that I am sure I know, or that I dare be responsible to myself that I can do: I have not my means of doing anything in condition and ready, and am only instructed therein after the effect; as doubtful of my own force as I am of another's. Whence it comes to pass that if I happen to do anything commendable, I attribute it more to my fortune than industry, forasmuch as I design everything by chance and in fear. I have this, also, in general, that of all the opinions antiquity has held of men in gross, I most willingly embrace and adhere to those that most contemn and undervalue us, and most push us to naught; methinks, philosophy has never so fair a game to play as when it falls upon our vanity and presumption; when it most lays open our irresolution, weakness, and ignorance. I look upon the too good opinion that man has of himself to be the nursing mother of all the most false opinions, both public and private. Those people who ride astride upon the epicycle of Mercury, who see so far into the heavens, are worse to me than a tooth-drawer that comes to draw my teeth; for in my study, the subject of which is man, finding so great a variety of judgments, so profound a labyrinth of difficulties, one upon another, so great diversity and uncertainty, even in the school of wisdom itself, you may judge, seeing these people could

not resolve upon the knowledge of themselves and their own condition, which is continually before their eyes, and within them, seeing they do not know how that moves, which they themselves move, nor how to give us a description of the springs they themselves govern and make use of, how can I believe them about the ebbing and flow-

ing of the Nile. The curiosity of knowing things has been given to man for a scourge, says the holy Scripture.

But to return to what concerns myself; I think it would be very difficult for any other man to have a meaner opinion of himself; nay, for any other to have a meaner opinion of me than I have of myself: I look upon myself as one of the common sort, saving in

this, that I have no better an opinion of myself; guilty of the meanest and most popular defects, but not disowning or excusing them; and I do not value myself upon any other account than because I know my own value. If there be any vanity in the case, 'tis superficially infused into me by the treachery of my complexion, and has no body that my judgment can discern; I am sprinkled, but not dyed. For in truth, as to the effects of the mind, there is no part of me, be it what it will, with which I am satisfied; and the approbation of others makes me not think the better of myself. My judgment is tender and nice, especially in things that concern myself; I ever repudiate myself, and feel myself float and waver by reason of my weakness. I have nothing of my own that satisfies my judgment. My sight is clear and regular enough, but, at working, it is apt to dazzle; as I most manifestly find in poetry: I love it infinitely, and am able to give a tolerable judgment of other men's works; but, in good earnest, when I apply myself to it, I play the child, and am not able to endure myself. A man may play the fool in everything else, but not in poetry;

> "Mediocribus esse poetis
> Non dii, non homines, non concessere columnæ."

I would to God this sentence was written over the doors of all our printers, to forbid the entrance of so many rhymesters!

> "Verum
> Nihil securius est malo poeta."

Why have not we such people? Dionysius the father valued himself upon nothing so much as his poetry; at the Olympic games, with chariots surpassing all the others in magnificence, he sent also poets and musicians to present his verses, with tent and pavilions royally gilt and hung with tapestry. When his verses came to be recited, the excellence of the delivery at first attracted the attention of the people; but when they afterwards came to poise the meanness of the composition, they first entered into disdain, and continuing to nettle their judgments, presently proceeded to fury, and ran to pull down and tear to pieces all his pavilions: and, that his chariots

neither performed anything to purpose in the race, and that the ship which brought back his people failed of making Sicily, and was by the tempest driven and wrecked upon the coast of Tarentum, they certainly believed was through the anger of the gods, incensed, as they themselves were, against that paltry poem; and even the mariners who escaped from the wreck seconded this opinion of the people: to which also the oracle that foretold his death seemed to subscribe; which was, "that Dionysius should be near his end, when he should have overcome those who were better than himself," which he interpreted of the Carthaginians, who surpassed him in power; and having war with them, often declined the victory, not to incur the sense of this prediction, but he understood it ill; for the god indicated the time of the advantage, that by favor and injustice he obtained at Athens over the tragic poets, better than himself, having caused his own play called the Leneians to be acted in emulation; presently after which victory he died, and partly of the excessive joy he conceived at the success.

What I find tolerable of mine, is not so really and in itself, but in comparison of other worse things, that I see well enough received. I envy the happiness of those who can please and hug themselves in what they do; for 'tis an easy thing to be so pleased, because a man extracts that pleasure from himself, especially if he be constant in his self-conceit. I know a poet, against whom the intelligent and the ignorant, abroad and at home, both heaven and earth exclaim that he has but very little notion of it; and yet for all that he has never a whit the worse opinion of himself; but is always falling upon some new piece, always contriving some new invention, and still persists in his opinion, by so much the more obstinately, as it only concerns him to maintain it.

My works are so far from pleasing me, that as often as I review them, they disgust me:

> "Cum relego, scripsisse pudet; quia plurima cerno,
> Me quoque, qui feci, judice, digna lini."

I have always an idea in my soul, and a sort of disturbed image which presents me as in a dream with a better form than that I have

[127]

made use of; but I cannot catch it nor fit it to my purpose; and even that idea is but of the meaner sort. Hence I conclude that the productions of those great and rich souls of former times are very much beyond the utmost stretch of my imagination or my wish: their writings do not only satisfy and fill me, but they astound me, and ravish me with admiration; I judge of their beauty; I see it, if not to the utmost, yet so far at least as 'tis possible for me to

aspire. Whatever I undertake, I owe a sacrifice to the Graces, as
Plutarch says of some one, to conciliate their favor;

> "Si quid enim placet,
> Si quid dulce hominum sensibus influit,
> Debentur lepidis omnia Gratiis."

They abandon me throughout; all I write is rude; polish and beauty
are wanting: I cannot set things off to any advantage; my handling
adds nothing to the matter; for which reason I must have it forcible,
very full, and that has luster of its own. If I pitch upon subjects
that are popular and gay, 'tis to follow my own inclination, who
do not affect a grave and ceremonious wisdom, as the world does;
and to make myself more sprightly, but not my style more wanton,
which would rather have them grave and severe; at least, if I may
call that a style, which is an inform and irregular way of speaking,
a popular jargon, a proceeding without definition, division, conclusion, perplexed like that Amafanius and Rabirius. I can neither
please nor delight, nor even tickle my readers: the best story in the
world is spoiled by my handling, and becomes flat; I cannot speak
but in rough earnest, and am totally unprovided of that facility
which I observe in many of my acquaintance, of entertaining the
first comers and keeping a whole company in breath, or taking up
the ear of a prince with all sorts of discourse without wearying
themselves: they never want matter by reason of the faculty and
grace they have in taking hold of the first thing that starts up, and
accommodating it to the humor and capacity of those with whom
they have to do. Princes do not much affect solid discourses, nor I
to tell stories. The first and easiest reasons, which are commonly
the best taken, I know not how to employ: I am an ill orator to the
common sort. I am apt of everything to say the extremest that I
know. Cicero is of opinion that in treatises of philosophy the exordium is the hardest part; if this be true, I am wise in sticking to
the conclusion. And yet we are to know how to wind the string to
all notes, and the sharpest is that which is the most seldom touched.
There is at least as much perfection in elevating an empty as in
supporting a weighty thing. A man must sometimes superficially

handle things, and sometimes push them home. I know very well that most men keep themselves in this lower form from not conceiving things otherwise than by this outward bark; but I likewise know that the greatest masters, and Xenophon and Plato are often seen to stoop to this low and popular manner of speaking and treating of things, but supporting it with graces which never fail them.

Further, my language has nothing in it that is facile and polished; 'tis rough, free, and irregular, and as such pleases, if not my judgment, at all events my inclination, but I very well perceive that I sometimes give myself too much rein, and that by endeavoring to avoid art and affectation I fall into the other inconvenience:

> "Brevis esse laboro,
> Obscurus fio."

Plato says, that the long or the short are not properties that either take away or give value to language. Should I attempt to follow the other more moderate, united, and regular style, I should never attain to it; and though the short round periods of Sallust best suit with my humor, yet I find Cæsar much grander and harder to imitate; and though my inclination would rather prompt me to imitate Seneca's way of writing, yet I do, nevertheless, more esteem that of Plutarch. Both in doing and speaking I simply follow my own natural way; whence, peradventure, it falls out that I am better at speaking than writing. Motion and action animate words, especially in those who lay about them briskly, as I do, and grow hot. The comportment, the countenance, the voice, the robe, the place, will set off some things that of themselves would appear no better than prating. Massalla complains in Tacitus of the straightness of some garments in his time, and of the fashion of the benches where the orators were to declaim, that were a disadvantage to their eloquence.

My French tongue is corrupted, both in the pronunciation and otherwise, by the barbarism of my country. I never saw a man who was a native of any of the provinces on his side of the kingdom who had not a twang of his place of birth, and that was not offensive

to ears that were purely French. And yet it is not that I am so perfect in my Perigordin: for I can no more speak it than High Dutch, nor do I much care. 'Tis a language (as the rest about me on every side, of Poitou, Xaintonge, Angoumousin, Limosin, Auvergne), a poor, drawling, scurvy language. There is, indeed, above us toward the mountains a sort of Gascon spoken, that I am mightily taken with: blunt, brief, significant, and in truth a more manly and military language than any other I am acquainted with, as sinewy, powerful, and pertinent as the French is graceful, neat, and luxuriant.

As to the Latin, which was given me for my mother tongue, I have, by discontinuance, lost the use of speaking it, and, indeed, of writing it too, wherein I formerly had a particular reputation, by which you may see how inconsiderable I am on that side.

Beauty is a thing of great recommendation in the correspondence among men; 'tis the first means of acquiring the favor and good liking of one another, and no man is so barbarous and morose as not to perceive himself in some sort struck with its attraction. The body has a great share in our being, has an eminent place there, and therefore its structure and composition are of very just consideration. They who go about to disunite and separate our two principal parts from one another are to blame; we must, on the contrary, reunite and rejoin them. We must command the soul not to withdraw and entertain itself apart, not to despise and abandon the body (neither can she do it but by some apish counterfeit), but to unite herself close to it, to embrace, cherish, assist, govern, and advise it, and to bring it back and set it into the true way when it wanders; in sum, to espouse and be a husband to it, so that their effects may not appear to be diverse and contrary, but uniform and concurring. Christians have a particular instruction concerning this connection, for they know that the Divine justice embraces this society and juncture of body and soul, even to the making the body capable of eternal rewards; and that God has an eye to the whole man's ways, and will that he receive entire chastisement or reward according to his demerits or merits. The sect of the Peripatetics, of all sects the most sociable, attribute to wisdom this sole care

equally to provide for the good of these two associate parts: and the other sects, in not sufficiently applying themselves to the consideration of this mixture, show themselves to be divided, one for the body and the other for the soul, with equal error, and to have lost sight of their subject, which is Man, and their guide, which they generally confess to be Nature. The first distinction that ever was among men, and the first consideration that gave some pre-eminence over others, 'tis likely was the advantage of beauty:

"Agros divisere atque dedere
Pro facie cujusque, et viribus, ingenaque;
Nam facies multum valuit, viresque vigebant."

Now I am of something lower than the middle stature, a defect that not only borders upon deformity, but carries withal a great deal of inconvenience along with it, especially for those who are in office and command; for the authority which a graceful presence and a majestic mien beget, is wanting. C. Marius did not willingly enlist any soldiers who were not six feet high. The courtier has, indeed, reason to desire a moderate stature in the gentlemen he is setting forth, rather than any other, and to reject all strangeness that should make him be pointed at. But if I were to choose whether this medium must be rather below than above the common standard, I would not have it so in a soldier. Little men, says Aristotle, are pretty but not handsome; and greatness of soul is discovered in a great body, as beauty is in a conspicuous stature: the Ethiopians and Indians, says he, in choosing their kings and magistrates, had regard to the beauty and stature of their persons. They had reason; for it creates respect in those who follow them, and is a terror to the enemy to see a leader of a brave and goodly stature march at the head of a battalion.

"Ipse inter primos præstanti corpore Turnus
Vertitur, arma tenens, et toto vertice supra est."

Our holy and heavenly king, of whom every circumstance is most carefully and with the greatest religion and reverence to be observed, has not himself rejected bodily recommendation, "*Speciosus forma præ filiis hominum.*" And Plato, together with tem-

perance and fortitude, requires beauty in the conservators of his republic. It would vex you that a man should apply himself to you among your servants to inquire where monsieur is, and that you should only have the remainder of the compliment of the hat that is made to your barber or your secretary; as it happened to poor Philopœmen, who arriving the first of all his company at an inn where he was expected, the hostess who knew him not, and saw him an unsightly fellow, employed him to go help her maids a little to draw water, and make a fire against Philopœmen's coming: the gentlemen of his train arriving presently after, and surprised to see him busy in this fine employment, for he failed not to obey his landlady's command, asked him what he was doing there. "I am," said he, "paying the penalty of my ugliness." The other beauties belong to women; the beauty of stature is the only beauty of men. Where there is a contemptible stature, neither the largeness and roundness of the forehead, nor the whiteness and sweetness of the eyes, nor the moderate proportion of the nose, nor the littleness of the ears and mouth, nor the evenness and whiteness of the teeth, nor the thickness of a well-set brown beard, shining like the husk of a chestnut, nor curled hair, nor the just proportion of the head, nor a fresh complexion, nor a pleasing air of a face, nor a body without any offensive scent, nor the just proportion of limbs, can make a handsome man. I am, as to the rest, strong and well knit; my face is not puffed, but full, and my complexion between jovial and melancholic, moderately sanguine and hot,

"Unde rigent setis mihi crura, et pectora villis;"

my health vigorous and sprightly, even to a well advanced age, and rarely troubled with sickness. Such I was, for I do not now make any account of myself, now that I am engaged in the avenues of old age, being already past forty:

"Minutatim vires et robur adultum
Frangit, et in partem pejorem liquitur ætas:"

what shall be from this time forward, will be but a half-being, and no more me. I every day escape and steal away from myself:

"Singula de nobis anni prædantur euntes:"

[133]

Agility and address I never had, and yet am the son of a very active and sprightly father, who continued to be so to an extreme old age. I have scarce known any man of his condition, his equal in all bodily exercises: as I have seldom met with any who have not excelled me, except in running, at which I was pretty good. In music or singing, for which I have a very unfit voice, or to play on any sort of instrument, they could never teach me anything. In dancing, tennis, or wrestling, I could never arrive to more than an ordinary pitch; in swimming, fencing, vaulting, and leaping, to none at all. My hands are so clumsy that I cannot even write so as to read it myself, so that I had rather do what I have scribbled over again, than take upon me the trouble to make it out. I do not read much better than I write, and feel that I weary my auditors: otherwise, not a bad clerk. I cannot decently fold up a letter, nor could ever make a pen, or carve at table worth a pin, nor saddle a horse, nor carry a hawk and fly her, nor hunt the dogs, nor lure a hawk, nor speak to a horse. In fine, my bodily qualities are very well suited to those of my soul; there is nothing sprightly, only a full and firm vigor: I am patient enough of labor and pains, but it is only when I go voluntary to work, and only so long as my own desire prompts me to it,

"Molliter austerum studio fallente laborem:"

otherwise, if I am not allured with some pleasure, or have other guide than my own pure and free inclination, I am good for nothing: for I am of a humor that, life and health excepted, there is nothing for which I will bite my nails, and that I will purchase at the price of torment of mind and constraint:

"Tanti mihi non sit opaci
Omnis arena Tagi, quodque in mare volvitur aurum."

Extremely idle, extremely given up to my own inclination both by nature and art, I would as willingly lend a man my blood as my pains. I have a soul free and entirely its own, and accustomed to guide itself after its own fashion; having hitherto never had either

master or governor imposed upon me; I have walked as far as I would, and at the pace that best pleased myself; that is it that has rendered me unfit for the service of others, and has made me of no use to any one but myself.

Nor was there any need of forcing my heavy and lazy disposition; for being born to such a fortune as I had reason to be contented with (a reason, nevertheless, that a thousand others of my acquaintance would have rather made use of for a plank upon which to pass over in search of higher fortune, to tumult and disquiet), and with as much intelligence as I required, I sought for no more, and also got no more:

"Non agimur tumidis velis Aquilone secundo,
Non tamen adversis ætatem ducimus Austris;
Viribus, ingenio, specie, virtute, loco, re,
Extremi primorum, extremis usque priores."

I had only need of what was sufficient to content me: which nevertheless is a government of soul, to take it right, equally difficult in all sorts of conditions, and that, of custom, we see more easily found in want than in abundance: forasmuch, peradventure, as according to the course of our other passions, the desire of riches is more sharpened by their use than by the need of them: and the virtue of moderation more rare than that of patience: and I never had anything to desire, but happily to enjoy the estate that God by His bounty had put into my hands. I have never known anything of trouble, and have had little to do in anything but the management of my own affairs: or, if I have, it has been upon condition to do it at my own leisure and after my own method; committed to my trust by such as had a confidence in me, who did not importune me, and who knew my humor; for good horsemen will make shift to get service out of a rusty and broken-winded jade.

Even my infancy was trained up after a gentle and free manner, and exempt from any rigorous subjection. All this has helped me to a complexion delicate and incapable of solicitude, even to that degree that I love to have my losses and the disorders wherein I am concerned, concealed from me. In the account of my expenses, I

put down what my negligence costs me in feeding and maintaining it;

"Hæc nempe supersunt
Quæ dominum fallunt, quæ prosunt furibus."

I love not to know what I have, that I may be less sensible of my loss; I entreat those who serve me, where affection and integrity are absent, to deceive me with something like a decent appearance. For want of constancy enough to support the shock of adverse accidents to which we are subject, and of patience seriously to apply myself to the management of my affairs, I nourish as much as I can this in myself, wholly leaving all to fortune "to take all things at the worst, and to resolve to bear that worst with temper and patience;" that is the only thing I aim at, and to which I apply my whole meditation. In a danger, I do not so much consider how I shall escape it, as of how little importance it is, whether I escape it or no; should I be left dead upon the place, what matter? Not being able to govern events, I govern myself, and apply myself to them, if they will not apply themselves to me. I have no great art to evade, escape from or force fortune, and by prudence to guide and incline things to my own bias. I have still less patience to undergo the troublesome and painful care therein required; and the most uneasy condition for me is to be suspended on urgent occasions, and to be agitated between hope and fear.

Deliberation, even in things of lightest moment, is very troublesome to me; and I find my mind more put to it to undergo the various tumblings and tossings of doubt and consultation, than to set up its rest and to acquiesce in whatever shall happen after the die is thrown. Few passions break my sleep, but of deliberations, the least will do it. As in roads, I preferably avoid those that are sloping and slippery, and put myself into the beaten track how dirty or deep soever, where I can fall no lower, and there seek my safety; so I love misfortunes that are purely so, that do not torment and teaze me with the uncertainty of their growing better; but that at the first push plunge me directly into the worst that can be expected:

"Dubia plus torquent mala."

In events, I carry myself like a man; in the conduct, like a child. The fear of the fall more fevers me than the fall itself. The game is not worth the candle. The covetous man fares worse with his passion than the poor, and the jealous man than the cuckold; and a man ofttimes loses more by defending his vineyard than if he gave it up. The lowest walk is the safest; 'tis the seat of constancy; you have there need of no one but yourself; 'tis there founded and wholly stands upon its own basis. Has not this example of a gentleman very well known, some air of philosophy in it? He married, being well advanced in years, having spent his youth in good fellowship, a great talker and a great jeerer, calling to mind how much the subject of cuckoldry had given him occasion to talk and scoff at others. To prevent them from paying him in his own coin he married a wife from a place where any one may have flesh for his money; "Good-morrow strumpet;" "good-morrow, cuckold;" and there was not anything wherewith he more commonly and openly entertained those who came to see him, than with this design of his, by which he stopped the private chattering of mockers, and blunted all the point from this reproach.

As to ambition, which is neighbor, or rather daughter to presumption, fortune, to advance me, must have come and taken me by the hand; for to trouble myself for an uncertain hope, and to have submitted myself to all the difficulties that accompany those who endeavor to bring themselves into credit in the beginning of their progress, I could never have done it:

"Spem pretio non emo:"

I apply myself to what I see and to what I have in my hand, and go not very far from the shore;

"Alter remus aquas, alter tibi radat arenas:"

and besides, a man rarely arrives to these advancements but in first hazarding what he has of his own; and I am of opinion, that if a man have sufficient to maintain him in the condition wherein he was born and brought up, 'tis a great folly to hazard that upon

the uncertainty of augmenting it. He to whom fortune has denied whereon to set his foot, and to settle a quiet and composed way of living, is to be excused if he venture what he has, because, happen what will, necessity puts him upon shifting for himself:

"Capienda rebus in malis præceps via est:"

and I rather excuse a younger brother for exposing what his friends have left him to the courtesy of fortune, than him with whom the honor of his family is entrusted, who cannot be necessitous but by his own fault. I have found a much shorter and more easy way, by the advice of the good friends I had in my younger days, to free myself from any such ambition, and to sit still;

"Cui sit conditio dulcis sine pulvere palmæ;"

judging rightly enough of my own strength, that it was not capable of any great matters; and calling to mind the saying of the late Chancellor Olivier, that the French were like monkeys that swarm up a tree from branch to branch, and never stop till they come to the highest, and there show their breech.

"Turpe est, quod nequeas, capiti committere pondus,
Et pressum inflexo mox dare terga genu."

I should find the best qualities I have useless in this age; the facility of my manners would have been called weakness and negligence; my faith and conscience, scrupulosity and superstition; my liberty and freedom would have been reputed troublesome, inconsiderate, and rash. Ill luck is good for something. It is good to be born in a very depraved age; for so, in comparison of others, you shall be reputed virtuous cheaply; he who in our days is but a parricide and a sacrilegious person, is an honest man and a man of honor:

"Nunc, si depositum non inficiatur amicus,
Si reddat veterem cum tota ærugine follem,
Prodigiosa fides, et Tuscis digna libellis,
Quæque coronata lustrari debeat agna:"

and never was time or place wherein princes might propose to themselves more assured or greater rewards for virtue and justice. The first who shall make it his business to get himself into favor and esteem by those ways, I am much deceived if he do not and by the best title outstrip his competitors: force and violence can do something, but not always all. We see merchants, country justices, and artisans, go cheek by jowl with the best gentry in valor and military knowledge: they perform honorable actions, both in public engagements and private quarrels; they fight duels, they defend towns in our present wars; a prince stifles his special recommendation, renown, in this crowd; let him shine bright in humanity, truth, loyalty, temperance, and especially in justice; marks rare, unknown, and exiled; 'tis by no other means but by the sole good will of the people that he can do his business; and no other qualities can attract their good will like those, as being of the greatest utility to them: *"Nil est tam populare, quam bonitas."*

By this standard, I had been great and rare, just as I find myself now pigmy and vulgar by the standard of some past ages, wherein, if no other better qualities concurred, it was ordinary and common to see a man moderate in his revenges, gentle in resenting injuries, religious of his word, neither double nor supple, nor accommodating his faith to the will of others, or the turns of the times: I would rather see all affairs go to wreck and ruin than falsify my faith to secure them. For as to this new virtue of feigning and dissimulation, which is now in so great credit, I mortally hate it; and of all vices find none that evidences so much baseness and meanness of spirit. 'Tis a cowardly and servile humor to hide and disguise a man's self under a visor, and not to dare to show himself what he is; 'tis by this our servants are trained up to treachery; being brought up to speak what is not true, they make no conscience of a lie. A generous heart ought not to belie its own thoughts; it will make itself seen within; all there is good, or at least, human. Aristotle reputes it the office of magnanimity openly and professedly to love and hate; to judge and speak with all freedom; and not to value the approbation or dislike of others in comparison of truth. Apollonius said, it was for slaves to lie, and for freemen to

speak truth: 'tis the chief and fundamental part of virtue; we must love it for itself. He who speaks truth because he is obliged so to do, and because it serves him, and who is not afraid to lie when it signifies nothing to anybody, is not sufficiently true. My soul naturally abominates lying, and hates the very thought of it. I have an inward shame and a sharp remorse, if sometimes a lie escape me; as sometimes it does, being surprised by occasions that allow me no premeditation. A man must not always tell all, for that were folly: but what a man says should be what he thinks, otherwise 'tis knavery. I do not know what advantage men pretend to by eternally counterfeiting and dissembling, if not, never to be believed when they speak the truth; it may once or twice pass with men; but to profess the concealing their thought, and to brag, as some of our princes have done, that they would burn their shirts if they knew their true intentions, which was a saying of the ancient Metellus of Macedon; and that they who know not how to dissemble know not how to rule, is to give warning to all who have anything to do with them, that all they say is nothing but lying and deceit: *"Quo quis versuitior et callidior est, hoc invisior et suspectior, detracta opinione probitatis:"* it were a great simplicity in any one to lay any stress either on the countenance or word of a man, who has put on a resolution to be always another thing without than he is within, as Tiberius did; and I cannot conceive what part such persons can have in conversation with men, seeing they produce nothing that is received as true: whoever is disloyal to truth, is the same to falsehood also.

Those of our time, who have considered in the establishment of the duty of a prince, the good of his affairs only, and have preferred that to the care of his faith and conscience, might have something to say to a prince whose affairs fortune had put into such a posture that he might forever establish them by only once breaking his word: but it will not go so; they often buy in the same market; they make more than one peace and enter into more than one treaty in their lives. Gain tempts to the first breach of faith, and almost always presents itself, as in all other ill acts, sacrileges, murders, rebellions, treasons, as being undertaken for some kind of advan-

tage; but this first gain has infinite mischievous consequences, throwing this prince out of all correspondence and negotiation, by this example of infidelity. Soliman, of the Ottoman race, a race not very solicitous of keeping their words or compacts, when, in my infancy he made his army land at Otranto, being informed that Mercurino de' Gratinare, and the inhabitants of Castro were detained prisoners, after having surrendered the place, contrary to the articles of their capitulation, sent orders to have them set at liberty, saying that having other great enterprises in hand in those parts, the disloyalty, though it carried a show of present utility, would for the future bring on him a disrepute and distrust of infinite prejudice.

Now, for my part, I had rather be troublesome and indiscreet, than a flattterer and a dissembler. I confess that there may be some mixture of pride and obstinacy in keeping myself so upright and open as I do, without any consideration of others; and methinks I am a little too free, where I ought least to be so, and that I grow hot by the opposition of respect; and it may be also, that I suffer myself to follow the propension of my own nature for want of art; using the same liberty, speech and countenance toward great persons, that I bring with me from my own house: I am sensible how much it declines toward incivility and indiscretion: but, besides that I am so bred, I have not a wit supple enough to evade a sudden question and to escape by some evasion, nor to feign a truth, nor memory enough to retain it so feigned; nor, truly, assurance enough to maintain it, and so play the brave out of weakness. And therefore it is that I abandon myself to candor, always to speak as I think, both by complexion and design leaving the event to fortune. Aristippus was wont to say, that the principal benefit he had extracted from philosophy was that he spoke freely and openly to all.

Memory is a faculty of wonderful use, and without which the judgment can very hardly perform its office; for my part I have none at all. What any one will propound to me, he must do it piecemeal, for to answer a speech consisting of several heads I am not able. I could not receive a commission by word of mouth, without

a note book. And when I have a speech of consequence to make, if it be long, I am reduced to the miserable necessity of getting by heart word for word, what I am to say; I should otherwise have neither method nor assurance, being in fear that my memory would play me a slippery trick. But this way is no less difficult to me than the other; I must have three hours to learn three verses. And besides, in a work of a man's own, the liberty and authority of altering the order, of changing a word, incessantly varying the matter, makes it harder to stick in the memory of the author. The more I mistrust it the worse it is; it serves me best by chance; I must solicit it negligently; for if I press it, 'tis confused, and after it once begins to stagger, the more I sound it, the more it is perplexed; it serves me at its own hour, not at mine.

And the same defect I find in my memory, I find also in several other parts. I fly command, obligation, and constraint; that which I can otherwise naturally and easily do, if I impose it upon myself by an express and strict injunction, I cannot do it. Even the members of my body, which have a more particular jurisdiction of their own, sometimes refuse to obey me, if I enjoin them a necessary service at a certain hour. This tyrannical and compulsive appointment baffles them; they shrink up either through fear or spite, and fall into a trance. Being once in a place where it is looked upon as the greatest discourtesy imaginable not to pledge those who drink to you, though I had there all liberty allowed me, I tried to play the good fellow, out of respect to the ladies who were there, according to the custom of the country; but there was sport enough; for this threatening and preparation, that I was to force myself contrary to my custom and inclination, so stopped my throat that I could not swallow one drop, and was deprived of drinking so much as with my meat; I found myself gorged, and my thirst quenched by the quantity of drink that my imagination had swallowed. This effect is most manifest in such as have the most vehement and powerful imagination; but it is natural, notwithstanding, and there is no one who does not in some measure feel it. They offered an excellent archer, condemned to die, to save his life, if he would show some notable proof of his art, but he refused to try, fearing

lest the too great contention of his will should make him shoot wide, and that instead of saving his life, he should also lose the reputation he had got of being a good marksman. A man who thinks of something else, will not fail to take over and over again the same number and measure of steps, even to an inch, in the place where he walks; but if he make it his business to measure and count them, he will find that what he did by nature and accident, he cannot so exactly do by design.

My library, which is of the best sort of country libraries, is situated in a corner of my house; if anything comes into my head that I have a mind to look at or to write there, lest I should forget it in but going across the court, I am fain to commit it to the memory of some other. If I venture in speaking to digress never so little from my subject, I am infallibly lost, which is the reason that I keep myself, in discourse, strictly close. I am forced to call the men who serve me either by the names of their offices or their country; for names are very hard for me to remember. I can tell, indeed, that there are three syllables, that it has a harsh sound, and that it begins or ends with such a letter, but that's all: and if I should live long, I do not doubt but I should forget my own name, as some others have done. Messala Corvinus was two years without any trace of memory, which is also said of Georgius Trapezuntius. For my own interest, I often meditate what a kind of life theirs was, and if, without this faculty, I should have enough left to support me with any manner of ease; and prying narrowly into it, I fear that this privation, if absolute, destroys all the other functions of the soul:

"Plenus rimarum sum, hac atque illac perfluo."

It has befallen me more than once to forget the watchword I had three hours before given or received, and to forget where I had hidden my purse; whatever Cicero is pleased to say, I help myself to lose what I have a particular care to lock safe up. *"Memoria certe non modo Philosophiam, sed omnis vitæ usum, omnesque artes, una maxime continet."* Memory is the receptacle and case of science: and therefore mine being so treacherous, if I know little,

I cannot much complain. I know, in general, the names of the arts, and of what they treat, but nothing more. I turn over books; I do not study them. What I retain I no longer recognize as another's; 'tis only what my judgment has made its advantage of, the discourses and imaginations in which it has been instructed: the author, place, words, and other circumstances, I immediately forget; and I am so excellent at forgetting, that I no less forget my own writings and compositions than the rest. I am very often quoted to myself and am not aware of it. Whoever should inquire of me where I had the verses and examples that I have here huddled together, would puzzle me to tell him, and yet I have not borrowed them but from famous and known authors, not contenting myself that they were rich, if I, moreover, had them not from rich and honorable hands, where there is a concurrence of authority with reason. It is no great wonder if my book run the same fortune that other books do, and if my memory lose what I have written as well as what I have read, and what I give as well as what I receive.

Besides the defect of memory, I have others which very much contribute to my ignorance; I have a slow and heavy wit, the least cloud stops its progress, so that, for example, I never proposed to it any never so easy a riddle that it could find out; there is not the least idle subtlety that will not gravel me; in games, where wit is required, as chess, draughts, and the like, I understand no more than the common movements. I have a slow and perplexed apprehension, but what it once apprehends, it apprehends well, for the time it retains it. My sight is perfect, entire, and discovers at a very great distance, but is soon weary and heavy at work, which occasions that I cannot read long, but am forced to have one to read to me. The younger Pliny can inform such as has not experimented it themselves, what, and how important, an impediment this is to those who addict themselves to study.

There is no so wretched and coarse a soul, wherein some particular faculty is not seen to shine; no soul so buried in sloth and ignorance, but it will sally at one end or another; and how it comes to pass that a man blind and asleep to everything else, shall be found sprightly, clear, and excellent in some one particular effect, we

are to inquire of our masters: but the beautiful souls are they that are universal, open, and ready for all things; if not instructed, at least capable of being so; which I say to accuse my own; for whether it be through infirmity or negligence (and to neglect that which lies at our feet, which we have in our hands, and what nearest concerns the use of life, is far from my doctrine) there is not a soul in the world so awkward as mine, and so ignorant of many common things, and such as a man cannot without shame fail to know. I must give some examples.

I was born and bred up in the country, and among husbandmen; I have had business and husbandry in my own hands ever since my predecessors, who were lords of the estate I now enjoy, left me to succeed them; and yet I can neither cast accounts, nor reckon my counters; most of our current money I do not know, nor the difference between one grain and another, either growing or in the barn, if it be not too apparent; and scarcely can distinguish between the cabbage and lettuce in my garden. I do not so much as understand the names of the chief instruments of husbandry, nor the most ordinary elements of agriculture, which the very children know; much less the mechanic arts, traffic, merchandise, the variety and nature of fruits, wines and viands, nor how to make a hawk fly, nor to physic a horse or a dog. And, since I must publish my whole shame 'tis not above a month ago, that I was trapped in my ignorance of the use of leaven to make bread, or to what end it was to keep wine in the vat. They conjectured of old at Athens, an aptitude for the mathematics in him they saw ingeniously bavin up a burthen of brushwood. In earnest, they would draw a quite contrary conclusion from me, for give me the whole provision and necessaries of a kitchen, I should starve. By these features of my confession men may imagine others to my prejudice: but whatever I deliver myself to be, provided it be such as I really am, I have my end; neither will I make any excuse for committing to paper such mean and frivolous things as these; the meanness of the subject compels me to it. They may, if they please, accuse my project, but not my progress; so it is, that without anybody's needing to tell me, I sufficiently see of how little weight and value all this is, and the

folly of my design: 'tis enough that my judgment does not contradict itself, of which these are the essays:

> "Nasutus sis usque licet, sis denique nasus,
>   Quantum noleurit ferre rogatus Atlas;
> Et possis ipsum tu deridere Latinum,
>   Non potes in nugas dicere plura meas,
> Ipse ego quam dixi: quid dentem dente juvabit
>   Rodere? carne opus est, si satur esse velis.
> Ne perdas operam; qui se mirantur, in illos
>   Virus habe; nos hæc novimus esse nihil."

I am not obliged to refrain from uttering absurdities, provided I
am not deceived in them and know them to be such; and to trip
knowingly, is so ordinary with me, that I seldom do it otherwise,
and rarely trip by chance. 'Tis no great matter to add ridiculous
actions to the temerity of my humor, since I cannot ordinarily help
supplying it with those that are vicious.

I was present one day at Barleduc, when King Francis II., for a
memorial of René, king of Sicily, was presented with a portrait
he had drawn of himself; why is it not, in like manner, lawful for
every one to draw himself with a pen as he did with a crayon? I
will not therefore omit this blemish, though very unfit to be published, which is irresolution; a very great defect, and very incommodious in the negotiations of the affairs of the world; in doubtful
enterprises, I know not which to choose:

> "Ne si, ne no, nel cor mi suona intero."

I can maintain an opinion, but I cannot choose one. By reason
that in human things, to what sect soever we incline, many appearances present themselves that confirm us in it (and the philosopher
Chrysippus said, that he would of Zeno and Cleanthes, his masters,
learn their doctrines only; for, as to proofs and reasons, he should
find enough of his own), which way soever I turn, I still furnish
myself with causes, and likelihood enough to fix me there; which
makes me detain doubt and the liberty of choosing, till occasion
presses; and then, to confess the truth, I, for the most part, throw
the feather into the wind, as the saying is, and commit myself to

the mercy of fortune; a very light inclination and circumstance carries me along with it:

> "Dum in dubio est animus, paulo momento huc atque
> Illuc impellitur."

The uncertainty of my judgment is so equally balanced in most occurrences, that I could willingly refer it to be decided by the chance of a die: and I observe, with great consideration of our human infirmity, the examples that the divine history itself has left us of this custom of referring to fortune and chance the determination of election in doubtful things: "*Sors cecidit super Matthiam.*" Human reason is a two-edged and dangerous sword: observe in the hands of Socrates, her most intimate and familiar friend, how many several points it has. I am thus good for nothing but to follow and suffer myself to be easily carried away with the crowd; I have not confidence enough in my own strength to take upon me to command and lead; I am very glad to find the way beaten before me by others. If I must run the hazard of an uncertain choice, I am rather willing to have it under such a one as is more confident in his opinions than I am in mine, whose ground and foundation I find to be very slippery and unsure.

Yet, I do not easily change, by reason that I discern the same weakness in contrary opinions: "*Ipsa consuetudo assentiendi periculosa esse videtur, et lubrica;*" especially in political affairs, there is a large field open for changes and contestation:

> "Justa pari premitur veluti cum pondere libra,
> Prona, nec hac plus parte sedet, nec surgit ab illa."

Macchiavelli's writings, for example, were solid enough for the subject, yet were they easy enough to be controverted; and they who have taken up the cudgels against him, have left as great a facility of controverting theirs; there was never wanting in that kind of argument, replies and replies upon replies, and as infinite a contexture of debates, as our wrangling lawyers have extended in favor of long suits:

> "Cædimur, et totidem plagis consumimus hostem;"

the reasons having little other foundation than experience, and the variety of human events presenting us with infinite examples of all sorts of forms. An understanding person of our times says: That whoever would, in contradiction to our almanacs, write cold where they say hot, and wet where they say dry, and always put the contrary to what they foretell; if he were to lay a wager, he would not care which side he took, excepting where no uncertainty could fall out, as to promise excessive heats at Christmas, or extremity of cold at midsummer. I have the same opinion of these political controversies; be on which side you will, you have as fair a game to play as your adversary, provided you do not proceed so far as to jostle principles that are too manifest to be disputed. And yet, in my conceit, in public affairs, there is no government so ill, provided it be ancient and has been constant, that is not better than change and alteration. Our manners are infinitely corrupt, and wonderfully incline to the worse; of our laws and customs there are many that are barbarous and monstrous; nevertheless, by reason of the difficulty of reformation, and the danger of stirring things, if I could put something under to stop the wheel, and keep it where it is, I would do it with all my heart:

"Numquam adeo fœdis, adeoque pudendis
Utimur exemplis, ut non pejora supersint,"

The worst thing I find in our state is instability, and that our laws, no more than our clothes, cannot settle in any certain form. It is very easy to accuse a government of imperfection, for all mortal things are full of it: it is very easy to beget in a people a contempt of ancient observances; never any man undertook it but he did it; but to establish a better regimen in the stead of that which a man has overthrown, many who have attempted it have foundered. I very little consult my prudence in my conduct; I am willing to let it be guided by the public rule. Happy the people who do what they are commanded, better than they who command, without tormenting themselves as to the causes; who suffer themselves gently to roll after the celestial revolution! Obedience is never pure nor calm in him who reasons and disputes.

In fine, to return to myself: the only thing by which I esteem myself to be something, is that wherein never any man thought himself to be defective; my recommendation is vulgar and common, for who ever thought he wanted sense? It would be a proposition that would imply a contradiction in itself; 'tis a disease that never is where it is discerned; 'tis tenacious and strong, but what the first ray of the patient's sight nevertheless pierces through and disperses, as the beams of the sun do thick and obscure mists: to accuse one's self would be to excuse in this case, and to condemn, to absolve. There never was porter or the silliest girl, that did not think they had sense enough to do their business. We easily enough confess in others an advantage of courage, strength, experience, activity, and beauty; but an advantage in judgment we yield to none; and the reasons that proceed simply from the natural conclusions of others, we think, if we had but turned our thoughts that way, we should ourselves have found out as well as they. Knowledge, style, and such parts as we see in others' works, we are soon aware of, if they excel our own: but for the simple products of the understanding, every one thinks he could have found out the like in himself, and is hardly sensible of the weight and difficulty, if not (and then with much ado), in an extreme and incomparable distance. And whoever should be able clearly to discern the height of another's judgment, would be also able to raise his own to the same pitch. So that it is a sort of exercise, from which a man is to expect very little praise; a kind of composition of small repute. And, besides, for whom do you write? The learned, to whom the authority appertains of judging books, know no other value but that of learning, and allow of no other proceeding of wit but that of erudition and art: if you have mistaken one of the Scipios for another, what is all the rest you have to say worth? Whoever is ignorant of Aristotle, according to their rule, is in some sort ignorant of himself; vulgar souls cannot discern the grace and force of a lofty and delicate style. Now these two sorts of men take up the world. The third sort into whose hands you fall, of souls that are regular and strong of themselves, is so rare, that it justly has neither name

nor place among us; and 'tis so much time lost to aspire unto it, or to endeavor to please it.

'Tis commonly said that the justest portion nature has given us of her favors, is that of sense; for there is no one who is not contented with his share: is it not reason? whoever should see beyond that, would see beyond his sight. I think my opinions are good and sound, but who does not think the same of his own? One of the best proofs I have that mine are so, is the small esteem I have of myself; for had they not been very well assured, they would easily have suffered themselves to have been deceived by the peculiar affection I have to myself, as one that place it almost wholly in myself, and do not let much run out. All that others distribute among an infinite number of friends and acquaintance, to their glory and grandeur, I dedicate to the repose of my own mind and to myself; that which escapes thence is not properly by my direction:

"Mihi nempe valere et vivere doctus."

Now I find my opinions very bold and constant in condemning my own imperfection. And, to say the truth, 'tis a subject upon which I exercise my judgment, as much as upon any other. The world looks always opposite; I turn my sight inward, and there fix and employ it. I have no other business but myself, I am eternally meditating upon myself, considering and tasting myself. Other men's thoughts are ever wandering abroad, if they will but see it; they are still going forward;

"Nemo in sese tentat descendere;"

for my part, I circulate in myself. This capacity of trying the truth, whatever it be, in myself, and this free humor of not over easily subjecting my belief, I owe principally to myself; for the strongest and most general imaginations I have are those that, as a man may say, were born with me; they are natural and entirely my own. I produced them crude and simple, with a strong and bold production, but a little troubled and imperfect; I have since established and fortified them with the authority of others and the sound examples of the ancients, whom I have found of the same judgment; they

have given me faster hold, and a more manifest fruition and possession of that I had before embraced. The reputation that every one pretends to of vivacity and promptness of wit, I seek in regularity; the glory they pretend to from a striking and signal action, or some particular excellence, I claim from order, correspondence, and tranquillity of opinions and manners: *"Omnine si quidquam est decorum, nihil est profecto magis, quam æquabilitas universæ vitæ, tum singularum actionum, quam conservare non possis, si, aliorum naturam imitans omittas tuam."*

Here, then, you see to what degree I find myself guilty of this first part, that I said was the vice of presumption. As to the second, which consists in not having a sufficient esteem for others, I know not whether or no I can so well excuse myself; but whatever comes on't I am resolved to speak the truth. And whether, peradventure, it be that the continual frequentation I have had with the humors of the ancients, and the idea of those great souls of past ages, put me out of taste both with others and myself, or that, in truth, the age we live in produces but very indifferent things, yet so it is that I see nothing worthy of any great admiration. Neither, indeed, have I so great an intimacy with many men as is requisite to make a right judgement of them; and those with whom my condition makes me the most frequent, are, for the most part, men who have little care of the culture of the soul, but that look upon honor as the sum of all blessings, and valor as the height of all perfection.

What I see that is fine in others I very readily commend and esteem: nay, I often say more in their commendation than I think they really deserve, and give me myself so far leave to lie, for I cannot invent a false subject: my testimony is never wanting to my friends in what I conceive deserves praise, and where a foot is due I am willing to give them a foot and a half; but to attribute to them qualities that they have not, I cannot do it, nor openly defend their imperfections. Nay, I frankly give my very enemies their due testimony of honor; my affection alters, my judgment does not, and I never confound my animosity with other circumstances that are foreign to it; and I am so jealous of the liberty of my judgment that I can very hardly part with it for any passion

what ever. I do myself a greater injury in lying than I do him of whom I tell a lie. This commendable and generous custom is observed of the Persian nation, that they spoke of their mortal enemies and with whom they were at deadly war, as honorably and justly as their virtues deserved.

I know men enough that have several fine parts; one wit, another courage, another address, another conscience, another language, one, one science, another, another; but a generally great man, and who has all these brave parts together, or any one of them to such a degree of excellence that we should admire him or compare him with those we honor of times past, my fortune never brought me acquainted with; and the greatest I ever knew, I mean for the natural parts of the soul, was Etienne De la Boetie; his was a full soul indeed, and that had every way a beautiful aspect: a soul of the old stamp, and that had produced great effects had his fortune been so pleased, having added much to those great natural parts by learning and study.

But how it comes to pass I know not, and yet it is certainly so, there is as much vanity and weakness of judgment in those who profess the greatest abilities, who take upon them learned callings and bookish employments as in any other sort of men whatever; either because more is required and expected from them, and that common defects are excusable in them, or because the opinion they have of their own learning makes them more bold to expose and lay themselves too open, by which they lose and betray themselves. As an artificer more manifests his want of skill in a rich matter he has in hand, if he disgrace the work by ill handling and contrary to the rules required, than in a matter of less value; and men are more displeased at a disproportion in a statue of gold than in one of plaster; so do these when they advance things that in themselves and in their place would be good; for they make use of them without discretion, honoring their memories at the expense of their understandings, and making themselves ridiculous by honoring Cicero, Galen, Ulpian, and St. Jerome alike.

I willingly fall again into the discourse of the vanity of our education, the end of which is not to render us good and wise, but

learned, and she has obtained it. She has not taught us to follow and embrace virtue and prudence, but she has imprinted in us their derivation and etymology, we know how to decline virtue, if we know not how to love it: if we do not know what prudence is really and in effect, and by experience, we have it, however, by jargon and heart: we are not content to know the extraction, kindred, and alliances of our neighbors; we desire, moreover, to have them our friends and to establish a correspondence and intelligence with them; but this education of ours has taught us definitions, divisions, and partitions of virtue, as so many surnames and branches of a genealogy, without any further care of establishing any familiarity or intimacy between her and us. It has culled out for our initiatory instruction not such books as contain the soundest and truest opinions, but those that speak the best Greek and Latin, and by their fine words has instilled into our fancy the vainest humors of antiquity.

A good education alters the judgment and manners; as it happened to Polemon, a lewd and debauched young Greek, who going by chance to hear one of Xenocrates' lectures, did not only observe the eloquence and learning of the reader, and not only brought away the knowledge of some fine matter, but a more manifest and a more solid profit, which was the sudden change and reformation of his former life. Whoever found such an effect of our discipline?

> "Faciasne, quod olim
> Mutatus Polemon? ponas insignia morbi
> Fasciolas, cubital, focalia; potus ut ille
> Dicitur ex collo furtim carpsisse coronas,
> Postquam est impransi correptus voce magistri."

That seems to me to be the least contemptible condition of men, which by its plainness and simplicity is seated in the lowest degree, and invites us to a more regular course. I find the rude manners and language of country people commonly better suited to the rule and prescription of true philosophy, than those of our philosophers themselves: *"Plus sapit vulgus, quia tantum, quantum opus est, sapit."*

The most remarkable men, as I have judged by outward appear-

ance (for to judge of them according to my own method, I must penetrate a great deal deeper) for soldiers and military conduct, were the duke of Guise, who died at Orleans, and the late Marshal Strozzi; and for men of great ability and no common virtue, Olivier, and De l'Hospital, chancellors of France. Poetry, too, in my opinion, has flourished in this age of ours; we have abundance of very good artificers in the trade; D'Aurat, Beza, Buchanan, L'Hospital, Montdoré, Turnebus: as to the French poets, I believe they raised their art to the highest pitch to which it can ever arrive; and in those parts of it wherein Ronsard and du Bellay excel, I find them little inferior to the ancient perfection. Adrian Turnebus knew more, and what he did know, better than any man of his time, or long before him. The lives of the last duke of Alva, and of our Constable de Montmorency, were both of them great and noble, and that had many rare resemblances of fortune; but the beauty and glory of the death of the last, in the sight of Paris and of his king, in their service, against his nearest relations, at the head of an army through his conduct victorious, and by a sudden stroke, in so extreme old age, merits methinks to be recorded among the most remarkable events of our times. As also the constant goodness, sweetness of manners, and conscientious facility of Monsieur de la Noue, in so great an injustice of armed parties (the true school of treason, inhumanity, and robbery), wherein he always kept up the reputation of a great and experienced captain.

I have taken a delight to publish in several places the hopes I have of Marie de Gournay le Jars, my adopted daughter, and certainly beloved by me with more than a paternal love, and enveloped in my solitude and retirement as one of the best parts of my own being; I have no longer regard to anything in this world but her. And if a man may presage from her youth, her soul will one day be capable of very great things; and among others, of the perfection of that sacred friendship, to which we do not read that any of her sex could ever yet arrive; the sincerity and solidity of her manners are already sufficient for it, and her affection towards me more than superabundant, and such, in short, as that there is nothing more to be wished, if not that the apprehension she has of

my end, being now five and fifty years old, might not so much afflict her. The judgment she made of my first Essays, being a woman, so young, and in this age, and alone in her own country; and the famous vehemence wherewith she loved me, and desired my acquaintance solely from the esteem she had thence of me, before she ever saw my face, is an incident very worthy of consideration.

Other virtues have had little or no credit in this age; but valor is become popular by our civil wars; and in this, we have souls brave even to perfection, and in so great number that the choice is impossible to be made.

This is all of extraordinary and not common grandeur that has hitherto arrived at my knowledge.

XI

THAT WE TASTE NOTHING
PURE

THE imbecility of our condition is such that things cannot, in their natural simplicity and purity, fall into our use; the elements that we enjoy are changed, and so 'tis with metals; and gold must be debased with some other matter to fit it for our service. Neither has virtue, so simple as that which Aristo, Pyrrho, and also the Stoics, made the end of life; nor the Cyrenaic and Aristippic pleasure, been without mixture useful to it. Of the pleasure and goods that we enjoy, there is not one exempt from some mixture of ill and inconvenience:

> "Medio de fonte leporum,
> Surgit amari aliquid, quod in ipsis floribus angat."

Our extremest pleasure has some air of groaning and complaining in it; would you not say that it is dying of pain? Nay when we frame the image of it in its full excellence, we stuff it with sickly and painful epithets and qualities, languor, softness, feebleness, faintness, *morbidezza:* a great testimony of their consanguinity and consubstantiality. The most profound joy has more of severity than gayety in it. The highest and fullest contentment offers more of the grave than of the merry; *"Ipsa felicitas, se nisi temperat, premit."* Pleasure chews and grinds us; according to the old Greek verse, which says that the gods sell us all the goods they give us; that is to say, that they give us nothing pure and perfect, and that we do not purchase but at the price of some evil.

Labor and pleasure, very unlike in nature, associate, nevertheless, by I know not what natural conjunction. Socrates says, that
some god tried to mix in one mass and to confound pain and pleasure, but not being able to do it, he bethought him at least, to couple
them by the tail. Metrodorus said that in sorrow there is some
mixture of pleasure. I know not whether or no he intended anything else by that saying; but for my part, I am of opinion that
there is design, consent, and complacency in giving a man's self
up to melancholy. I say, that beside ambition, which may also have
a stroke in the business, there is some shadow of delight and delicacy which smiles upon and flatters us even in the very lap of
melancholy. Are there not some constitutions that feed upon it?

"Est quædam flere voluptas."

and one Attalus in Seneca says, that the memory of our lost friends
is as grateful to us, as bitterness in wine, when too old, is to the
palate—

"Minister vetuli, puer, Falerni
Inger' mi calices amaroires"

and as apples that have a sweet tartness.

Nature discovers this confusion to us; painters hold that the
same motions and screwings of the face that serve for weeping,
serve for laughter too; and indeed, before the one or the other be
finished, do but observe the painter's manner of handling, and you
will be in doubt to which of the two the design tends; and the
extreme of laughter does, at last bring tears. *"Nullum sine auctora-
mento malum est."*

When I imagine man abounding with all the conveniences that
are to be desired (let us put the case that all his members were
always seized with a pleasure like that of generation, in its most
excessive height) I feel him melting under the weight of his delight,
and see him utterly unable to support so pure, so continual, and so
universal a pleasure. Indeed, he is running away while he is there,
and naturally makes haste to escape as from a place where he cannot stand firm, and where he is afraid of sinking.

When I religiously confess myself to myself, I find that the best

virtue I have has in it some tincture of vice; and I am afraid that Plato, in his purest virtue (I, who am as sincere and loyal a lover of virtue of that stamp, as any other whatever) if he had listened and laid his ear close to himself, and he did so no doubt, would have heard some jarring sound of human mixture, but faint and only perceptible to himself. Man is wholly and throughout but patch and motley. Even the laws of justice themselves cannot subsist without mixture of injustice; insomuch that Plato says they undertake to cut off the hydra's head, who pretend to clear the law of all inconveniences. *"Omne magnum exemplum habet aliquid ex iniquo, quod contra singulos utilitate publica rependitur,"* says Tacitus.

It is likewise true, that for the use of life and the service of public commerce, there may be some excesses in the purity and perspicacity of our minds; that penetrating light has in it too much of subtlety and curiosity: we must a little stupefy and blunt them to render them more obedient to example and practice, and a little veil and obscure them, the better to proportion them to this dark and earthy life. And therefore common and less speculative souls are found to be more proper for and more successful in the management of affairs; and the elevated and exquisite opinions of philosophy unfit for business. This sharp vivacity of soul, and the supple and restless volubility attending it, disturb our negotiations. We are to manage human enterprises more superficially and roughly, and leave a great part to fortune; it is not necessary to examine affairs with so much subtlety and so deep: a man loses himself in the consideration of so many contrary lusters, and so many various forms; *"Volutantibus res inter se pugnantes, obtorpuerant . . . animi."*

'Tis what the ancients say of Simonides, that by reason his imagination suggested to him, upon the question King Hiero had put to him (to answer which he had had many days to meditate in), several sharp and subtle considerations, while he doubted which was the most likely, he totally despaired of the truth.

He who dives into and in his inquisition comprehends all circumstances and consequences, hinders his elections: a little engine

well handled is sufficient for executions, whether of less or greater weight. The best managers are those who can worst give account how they are so; while the greatest talkers, for the most part, do nothing to purpose: I know one of this sort of men, and a most excellent discourser upon all sorts of good husbandry, who has miserably let a hundred thousand livres yearly revenue slip through his hands; I know another who talks, who better advises than any man of his counsel, and there is not in the world a fairer show of soul and understanding than he has; nevertheless, when he comes to the test, his servants find him quite another thing; not to make any mention of his misfortunes.

XII

OF THUMBS

Tacitus reports, that among certain barbarian kings their manner was, when they would make a firm obligation, to join their right hands close to one another, and intertwist their thumbs; and when, by force of straining, the blood it appeared in the ends, they lightly pricked them with some sharp instrument, and mutually sucked them.

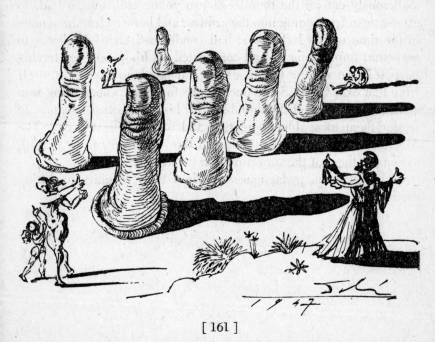

Physicians say, that the thumbs are the master fingers of the hand, and that their Latin etymology is derived from "pollere." The Greeks called them Ἀντιχειρ, as who should say, another hand. And it seems that the Latins also sometimes take it in this sense for the whole hand;

> "Sed nec vocibus excitata blandis,
> Molli pollice nec rogata, surgit."

It was at Rome a signification of favor to depress and turn in the thumbs:

> "Fautor utroque tuum laudabit pollice ludum:"

and of disfavor to elevate and thrust them outward:

> "Converso pollice vulgi,
> Quemlibet occidunt populariter."

The Romans exempted from war all such as were maimed in the thumbs, as having no more sufficient strength to hold their weapons. Augustus confiscated the strength of a Roman knight, who had maliciously cut off the thumbs of two young children he had, to excuse them from going into the armies: and before him, the senate, in the time of the Italic war, had condemned Caius Vatienus to perpetual imprisonment, and confiscated all his goods, for having purposely cut off the thumb of his left hand, to exempt himself from that expedition. Some one, I have forgotten who, having won a naval battle, cut off the thumbs of all his vanquished enemies, to render them incapable of fighting and of handling the oar. The Athenians also caused the thumbs of the Æginatans to be cut off, to deprive them of the superiority in the art of navigation.

In Lacedæmon, pedagogues chastised their scholars by biting their thumb.

XIII

OF THE RESEMBLANCE OF CHILDREN

TO THEIR FATHERS

THIS faggoting up of so many divers pieces is so done that I
never set pen to paper, but when I have too much idle time,
and never anywhere but at home; so that it is compiled after divers
interruptions and intervals, occasions keeping me sometimes many
months elsewhere. As to the rest I never correct my first by any
second conceptions; I, peradventure, may alter a word or so: but
'tis only to vary the phrase, and not to destroy my former meaning.
I have a mind to represent the progress of my humors, and that
every one may see each piece as it came from the forge. I could
wish I had begun sooner, and had taken more notice of the course
of my mutations. A servant of mine whom I employed to transcribe
for me, thought he had got a prize by stealing several pieces from
me, wherewith he was best pleased; but it is my comfort that he
will be no greater a gainer than I shall be a loser by the theft. I am
grown older by seven or eight years since I began; nor has it been
without some new acquisition: I have, in that time, by the liberality
of years, been acquainted with the stone: their commerce and long
converse do not well pass away without some such inconvenience.
I could have been glad that of other infirmities age has to present
long-lived men withal, it had chosen some one that would have been
more welcome to me, for it could not possibly have laid upon me
a disease, for which, even from my infancy, I have had so great a
horror; and it is, in truth, of all the accidents of old age, that of
which I have ever been most afraid. I have often thought with my-

self, that I went on too far; and that in so long a voyage I should at last run myself into some disadvantage; I perceived and have often enough declared, that it was time to depart, and that life should be cut off in the sound and living part, according to the

surgeon's rule in amputations; and that nature made him pay very strict usury, who did not in due time pay the principal. And yet I was so far from being ready, that in the eighteen months time or thereabout, that I have been in this uneasy condition, I have so inured myself to it as to be content to live on in it; and have found wherein to comfort myself, and to hope: so much are men enslaved

to their miserable being, that there is no condition so wretched they will not accept, provided they may live! Hear Mæcenas,

> "Debilem facito manu,
> Debilem pede, coxa,
> Lubricos quate dentes;
> Vita dum superest, bene est."

And Tamerlane, with a foolish humanity, palliated the fantastic cruelty he exercised upon lepers, when he put all he could hear of to death, to deliver them, as he pretended, from the painful life they lived. For there was not one of them who would not rather have undergone a triple leprosy than be deprived of his being. And Antisthenes the Stoic, being very sick, and crying out, "Who will deliver me from these evils?" Diogenes, who had come to visit him, "This," said he, presenting him a knife, "presently, if thou wilt." "I do not mean from my life," he replied, "but from my disease." The sufferings that only attack the mind, I am not so sensible of as most other men; and this partly out of judgment, for the world looks upon several things as dreadful or to be avoided at the expense of life, that are almost indifferent to me: partly, through a dull and insensible complexion I have in accidents which do not point blank hit me; and that insensibly I look upon as one of the best parts of my natural condition: but essential and corporeal pains I am very sensible of. And yet, having long since foreseen them, though with a sight weak and delicate and softened with the long and happy health and quiet that God has been pleased to give me the greatest part of my time, I had in my imagination fancied them so insupportable, that, in truth, I was more afraid than I have since found I had cause: by which I am still more fortified in this belief, that most of the faculties of the soul, as we employ them, more trouble the repose of life than they are any way useful to it.

I am in conflict with the worst, the most sudden, the most painful, the most mortal, and the most irremediable of all diseases; I have already had the trial of five or six very long and very painful fits; and yet I either flatter myself, or there is even in this state what is very well to be endured by a man who has his soul free from the

fear of death, and of the menaces, conclusions, and consequences which physic is ever thundering in our ears; but the effect even of pain itself is not so sharp and intolerable as to put a man of understanding into rage and despair. I have at least this advantage by my stone, that what I could not hitherto prevail upon myself to resolve upon, as to reconciling and acquainting myself with death, it will perfect; for the more it presses upon and importunes me, I shall be so much the less afraid to die. I had already gone so far as only to love life for life's sake, but my pain will dissolve this intelligence; and, God grant that in the end, should the sharpness of it be once greater than I shall be able to bear, it does not throw me into the other no less vicious extreme, to desire and wish to die!

"Summum nec metuas diem, nec optes:"

they are two passions to be feared, but the one has its remedy much nearer at hand than the other.

As to the rest, I have always found the precept, that so rigorously enjoins a resolute countenance and disdainful and indifferent comportment in the toleration of infirmities, to be merely ceremonial. Why should philosophy, which only has respect to life and effects, trouble itself about these external appearances? Let us leave that care to actors and masters of rhetoric, who set so great a value upon our gestures. Let her allow this vocal frailty to disease, if it be neither cordial nor stomachic, and permit the ordinary ways of expressing grief by sighs, sobs, palpitations, and turning pale, that nature has put out of our power; provided the courage be undaunted, and the tones not expressive of despair, let her be satisfied. What matter the wringing of our hands, if we do not wring our thoughts? She forms us for ourselves, not for others; to be, not to seem; let her be satisfied with governing our understanding which she has taken upon her the care of instructing; that, in the fury of the colic, she maintain the soul in a condition to know itself, and to follow its accustomed way, contending with, and enduring not meanly truckling, under pain; moved and heated, not subdued and conquered, in the contention; capable and discourse and other things, to a certain degree. In such extreme accidents, 'tis cruelty to

require so exact a composedness. 'Tis no great matter that we make a wry face, if the mind plays its part well; if the body find itself relieved by complaining, let it complain; if agitation ease it, let it tumble and toss at pleasure; if it seem to find the disease evaporate (as some physicians hold that it helps women in delivery) in making loud outcries, or if this do but divert its torments, let it roar as it will. Let us not command this voice to sally, but stop it not. Epicurus not only forgives his sage for crying out in torments, but advises him to it: *"Pugiles etiam, quum feriunt, in jactandis cœstibus ingemiscunt, quia profundenda voce omne corpus intenditur, venitque plaga vehementior."* We have enough to do to deal with the disease, without troubling ourselves with these superfluous rules.

Which I say in excuse of those whom we ordinarily see impatient in the assaults of this malady; for as to what concerns myself, I have passed it over hitherto with a little better countenance, and contented myself with groaning without roaring out; not, nevertheless, that I put any great constraint upon myself to maintain this exterior decorum, for I make little account of such an advantage; I allow herein as much as the pain requires; but either my pains are not so excessive, or I have more than ordinary patience. I complain, I confess, and am a little impatient in a very sharp fit, but I do not arrive to such a degree of despair as he who with

"Ejulatu, questu, gemitu, fremitibus
Resonando, multum flebiles voces refert:"

I try myself in the depth of my dolor, and have always found that I was in a capacity to speak, think, and give a rational answer as well as at any other time, but not so firmly, being troubled and interrupted by the pain. When I am looked upon by my visitors to be in the greatest torment, and that they therefore forbear to trouble me, I often essay my own strength, and myself set some discourse on foot, the most remote I can contrive from my present condition. I can do anything upon a sudden endeavor, but it must not continue long. Oh, what pity 'tis I have not the faculty of that dreamer in Cicero, who dreaming he was lying with a wench, found

he had discharged his stone in the sheets! My pains strangely disappetite me that way. In the intervals from this excessive torment, when my ureters only languish without any great dolor, I presently feel myself in my wonted state, forasmuch as my soul takes no other alarm but what is sensible and corporal, which I certainly owe to the care I have had of preparing myself by meditation against such accidents:

> "Laborum
> Nulla mihi nova nunc facies inopinaque surgit;
> Omnia præcepi, atque animo mecum ante peregi."

I am, however, a little roughly handled for a learner, and with a sudden and sharp alteration, being fallen in an instant from a very easy and happy condition of life into the most uneasy and painful that can be imagined. For besides that it is a disease very much to be feared in itself, it begins with me after a more sharp and severe manner than it is used to do with other men. My fits come so thick upon me that I am scarcely ever at ease; yet I have hitherto kept my mind so upright that, provided I can still continue it, I find myself in a much better condition of life than a thousand others, who have no fever nor other disease but what they create to themselves for want of meditation.

There is a certain sort of crafty humility that springs from presumption, as this, for example, that we confess our ignorance in many things, and are so courteous as to acknowledge that there are in the works of nature some qualities and conditions that are imperceptible to us, and of which our understanding cannot discover the means and causes; by this so honest and conscientious declaration we hope to obtain that people shall also believe us as to those that we say we do understand. We need not trouble ourselves to seek out foreign miracles and difficulties; methinks, among the things that we ordinarily see, there are such incomprehensible wonders as surpass all difficulties of miracles. What a wonderful thing it is that the drop of seed from which we are produced should carry in itself the impression not only of the bodily form, but even of the thoughts and inclinations of our fathers! Where can that drop of fluid matter contain that infinite number of

forms? and how can they carry on these resemblances with so temerarious and irregular a progress that the son shall be like his great-grandfather, the nephew like his uncle? In the family of Lepidus at Rome there were three, not successively but by intervals, who were born with the same eye covered with a cartilage. At Thebes there was a race that carried from their mother's womb the form of the head of a lance, and he who was not born so was looked upon as illegitimate. And Aristotle says that in a certain nation, where the women were in common, they assigned the children to their fathers by their resemblance.

'Tis to be believed that I derive this infirmity from my father, for he died wonderfully tormented with a great stone in his bladder, he was never sensible of his disease till the sixty-seventh year of his age; and before that had never felt any menace or symptoms of it, either in his reins, sides, or any other part, and had lived, till then, in a happy, vigorous state of health, little subject to infirmities, and he continued seven years after, in this disease, dragging on a very painful end of life. I was born above five and twenty years before his disease seized him, and in the time of his most flourishing and healthful state of body, his third child in order of birth, where could his propension to this malady lie lurking all that while? And he being then so far from the infirmity, how could that small part of his substance wherewith he made me, carry away so great an impression for its share? and how so concealed, that till five and forty years after, I did not begin to be sensible of it? being the only one to this hour, among so many brothers and sisters, and all by one mother, that was ever troubled with it. He that can satisfy me in this point, I will believe him in as many other miracles as he pleases; always provided that, as their manner is, he do not give me a doctrine much more intricate and fantastic than the thing itself for current pay.

Let the physicians a little excuse the liberty I take, for by this same infusion and fatal insinuation it is that I have received a hatred and contempt of their doctrine; the antipathy I have against their art is hereditary. My father lived threescore and fourteen years, my grandfather sixty-nine, my great grandfather almost fourscore

years, without ever tasting any sort of physic: and, with them, whatever was not ordinary diet, was instead of a drug. Physic is
grounded upon experience and examples: so is my opinion. And
is not this an express and very advantageous experience? I do not
know that they can find me in all their records three that were
born, bred and died under the same roof, who have lived so long
by their conduct. They must here of necessity confess, that if reason
be not, fortune at least is on my side, and with physicians, fortune
goes a great deal further than reason. Let them not take me now
at a disadvantage; let them not threaten me in the subdued condition wherein I now am; that were treachery. In truth, I have
enough the better of them by these domestic examples, that they
should rest satisfied. Human things are not usually so constant; it
has been two hundred years, save eighteen, that this trial has lasted,
for the first of them was born in the year 1402: 'tis now, indeed,
very good reason that this experience should begin to fail us. Let
them not, therefore, reproach me with the infirmities under which
I now suffer; is it not enough that I for my part have lived seven
and forty years in good health? though it should be the end of my
career, 'tis of the longer sort.

My ancestors had an aversion to physic by some occult and
natural instinct: for the very sight of a potion was loathsome to my
father. The Seigneur de Gaviac, my uncle by the father's side, a
churchman, and a valetudinary from his birth, and yet who made
that crazy life hold out to sixty-seven years, being once fallen into a
furious fever, it was ordered by the physicians he should be plainly
told that if he would not make use of help (for so they call that
which is very often quite contrary), he would infallibly be a dead
man. The good man, though terrified with this dreadful sentence,
yet replied, "I am then a dead man." But God soon after made the
prognostic false. The youngest of the brothers—there were four of
them—and by many years the youngest, the Sieur de Bussaguet,
was the only one of the family who made use of medicine, by reason
I suppose, of the commerce he had with the other arts, for he was
a councilor in the court of parliament, and it succeeded so ill with
him, that being in outward appearance, of the strongest constitu-

tion, he yet died before any of the rest, the Sieur de Saint Michel only excepted.

'Tis possible I may have derived this natural antipathy to physic from them; but had there been no other consideration in the case, I would have endeavored to have overcome it; for all these conditions that spring in us without reason, are vicious, 'tis a kind of disease that we should wrestle with. It may be I had naturally this propension; but I have supported and fortified it by arguments and reasons which have established in me the opinion I am of. For I also hate the consideration of refusing physic for the nauseous taste: I should hardly be of that humor, who hold health to be worth purchasing by all the most painful cauteries and incisions that can be applied. And with Epicurus, I conceive that pleasures are to be avoided, if greater pains be the consequence, and pains to be coveted, that will terminate in greater pleasures. Health is a precious thing, and the only one, in truth, meriting that a man should lay out, not only his time, sweat, labor and goods, but also his life itself to obtain it; forasmuch as, without it, life is wearisome and injurious to us: pleasure, wisdom, learning, and virtue, without it, wither away and vanish; and to the most labored and solid discourses that philosophy would imprint in us to the contrary, we need no more but oppose the image of Plato being struck with an epilepsy or apoplexy; and, in this presupposition, to defy him to call the rich faculties of his soul to his assistance. All means that conduce to health can neither be too painful nor too dear to me. But I have some other appearances that make me strangely suspect all this merchandise. I do not deny but that there may be some art in it, that there are not among so many works of nature, things proper for the conservation of health: that is most certain: I very well know there are some simples that moisten and others that dry; I experimentally know that radishes are windy, and senna-leaves purging; and several other such experiences I have, as that mutton nourishes me, and wine warms me: and Solon said "that eating was physic against the malady hunger." I do not disapprove the use we make of things the earth produces, nor doubt, in the least, of the power and fertility of nature, and of its application to our necessi-

ties: I very well see that pikes and swallows live by her laws; but I mistrust the inventions of our mind, our knowledge and art, to countenance which, we have abandoned nature and her rules, and wherein we keep no bounds nor moderation. As we call the piling up of the first laws that fall into our hands, justice, and their practice and dispensation very often foolish and very unjust; and as those who scoff at and accuse it, do not nevertheless, blame that noble virtue itself, but only condemn the abuse and profanation of that sacred title; so in physic I very much honor that glorious name, its propositions, its promises, so useful for the service of mankind, but the ordinances it foists upon us, between ourselves, I neither honor nor esteem.

In the first place, experience makes me dread it; for among all my acquaintance, I see no people so soon sick, and so long before they are well, as those who take much physic; their very health is altered and corrupted by their frequent prescriptions. Physicians are not content to deal only with the sick, but they will moreover corrupt health itself, for fear men should at any time escape their authority. Do they not, from a continual and perfect health, extract suspicion of some great sickness to ensue? I have been sick often enough, and have always found my sicknesses easy enough to be supported (though I have made trial of almost all sorts) and as short as those of any other, without their help, or without swallowing their ill-tasting doses. The health I have is full and free, without other rule or discipline than my own custom and pleasure. Every place serves me well enough to stay in, for I need no other conveniences, when I am sick, than what I must have when I am well. I never disturb myself that I have no physician, no apothecary, nor any other assistance, which I see most other sick men more afflicted at than they are with their disease. What! Do the doctors themselves show us more felicity and duration in their own lives, that may manifest to us some apparent effect of their skill?

There is not a nation in the world that has not been many ages without physic; and these the first ages, that is to say, the best and most happy; and the tenth part of the world knows nothing of it yet; many nations are ignorant of it to this day, where men live more

healthful and longer than we do here, and even among us the common people live well enough without it. The Romans were six hundred years before they received it; and after having made trial of it, banished it from their city at the instance of Cato the Censor, who made it appear how easy it was to live without it, having himself lived four score and five years, and kept his wife alive to an extreme old age, not without physic, but without a physician: for everything that we find to be healthful to life may be called physic. He kept his family in health, as Plutarch says, if I mistake not, with hare's milk; as Pliny reports, that the Arcadians cured all manner of diseases with that of a cow; and Herodotus says, the Lybians generally enjoy rare health, by a custom they have, after their children are arrived to four years of age, to burn and cauterize the veins of their head and temples, by which means they cut off all defluxions of rheum for their whole lives. And the country people of our province make use of nothing, in all sorts of distempers, but the strongest wine they can get, mixed with a great deal of saffron and spice, and always with the same success.

And to say the truth, of all this diversity and confusion of prescriptions, what other end and effect is there after all, but to purge the belly? which a thousand ordinary simples will do as well; and I do not know whether such evacuations be so much to our advantage as they pretend, and whether nature does not require a residence of her excrements to a certain proportion, as wine does of its lees to keep it alive: you often see healthful men fall into vomitings and fluxes of the belly by some extrinsic accident, and make a great evacuation of excrements, without any preceding need, or any following benefit, but rather with hurt to their constitution. 'Tis from the great Plato, that I lately learned, that of three sorts of motions which are natural to us, purging is the worst, and that no man unless he be a fool, ought to take anything to that purpose but in the extremest necessity. Men disturb and irritate the disease by contrary oppositions; it must be the way of living that must gently dissolve, and bring it to its end. The violent gripings and contest between the drug and the disease, are ever to our loss, since the combat is fought within ourselves, and that the drug is an

assistant not to be trusted, being in its own nature an enemy to our health and by trouble having only access into our condition. Let it alone a little; the general order of things that takes care of fleas and moles, also takes care of men, if they will have the same patience that fleas and moles have, to leave it to itself. 'Tis to much purpose we cry out *"Bihore,"* 'tis a way to make us hoarse, but not to hasten the matter. 'Tis a proud and uncompassionate order; our fears, our despair displease and stop it from, instead of inviting it to our relief; it owes its course to the disease, as well as to health; and will not suffer itself to be corrupted in favor of the one to the prejudice of the other's right, for it would then fall into disorder. Let us, in God's name follow it; it leads those that follow, and those who will not follow it, drags along, both their fury and physic together. Order a purge for your brain, it will there be much better employed than upon your stomach.

One asking a Lacedæmonian what had made him live so long, he made answer, "The ignorance of physic;" and so Emperor Adrian continually exclaimed as he was dying, that the crowd of physicians had killed him. A bad wrestler turned physician: "Courage," says Diogenes to him, "thou hast done well, for now thou wilt throw those who had formerly thrown thee." But they have this advantage, according to Nicocles, that the sun gives light to their success and the earth covers their failures. And besides, they have a very advantageous way of making use of all sorts of events; for what fortune, nature, or any other cause (of which the number is infinite), produces of good and healthful in us, it is the privilege of physic to attribute to itself; all the happy successes that happen to the patient, must be thence derived; the accidents that have cured me, and a thousand others, who do not employ physicians, physicians usurp to themselves: and as to ill accidents, they either absolutely disown them, in laying the fault upon the patient, by such frivolous reasons as they are never at a loss for; as "he lay with his arms out of bed," or "he was disturbed with the rattling of a coach:"

> "Rhedarum transitus arcto
> Vicorum inflexu;"

or "somebody had set open the casement," or "he had lain upon his left side;" or "he had some disagreeable fancies in his head;" in sum, a word, a dream, or a look, seems to them excuse sufficient wherewith to palliate their own errors; or, if they so please, they even make use of our growing worse, and do their business in this way which can never fail them; which is by buzzing us in the ear when the disease is more enflamed by their medicaments, that it had been much worse but for those remedies; he, whom from an ordinary cold they have thrown into a double tertian-ague, had but for them been in a continued fever. They do not much care what mischief they do, since it turns to their own profit. In earnest, they have reason to require a very favorable belief from their patients; and, indeed, it ought to be a very easy one, to swallow things so hard to be believed. Plato said very well, that physicians were the only men who might lie at pleasure, since our health depends upon the vanity and falsity of their promises.

Æsop, a most excellent author, and of whom few men discover all the graces, pleasantly represents to us the tyrannical authority physicians usurp over poor creatures, weakened and subdued by sickness and fear, when he tells us, that a sick person, being asked by his physician what operation he found of the potion he had given him: "I have sweated very much," says the sick man. "That's good," says the physician. Another time, having asked how he felt himself after his physic: "I have been very cold, and have had a great shivering upon me," said he. "That is good," replied the physician. After the third potion he asked him again how he did: "Why, I find myself swollen, and puffed up," said he, "as if I had a dropsy." "That is very well," said the physician. One of his servants coming presently after to inquire how he felt himself, "Truly, friend," said he, "with being too well I am about to die."

There was a more just law in Egypt, by which the physician, for the first three days, was to take charge of his patient; at the patient's own risk and cost: but those three days being past, it was to be at his own. For what reason is it, that their patron, Æscu-

lapius, should be struck with thunder for restoring Hippolitus from death to life,

> "Nam Pater omnipotens, aliquem indignatus ab umbris
> Mortalem infernis ad lumina surgere vitæ,
> Ipse repertorem medicinæ talis, et artis,
> Fulmine Phœbigenam Stygias detrusit ad undas;"

and his followers be pardoned, who send so many souls from life to death? A physician, boasting to Nicocles that his art was of great authority: "It is so, indeed," said Nicocles, "that can with impunity kill so many people."

As to what remains, had I been of their counsel, I would have rendered my discipline more sacred and mysterious; they begun well, but they have not ended so. It was a good beginning to make gods and demons the authors of their science, and to have used a peculiar way of speaking and writing, notwithstanding that philosophy concludes it folly to persuade a man to his own good by an unintelligible way: *"Ut si quis medicus imperet, ut sumat:"*

> "Terrigenam, herbigradam, domipotam, sanguina cassam."

It was a good rule in their art, and that accompanies all other vain, fantastic, and supernatural arts, that the patient's belief should prepossess them with good hope and assurance of their effects and operation: a rule they hold to that degree, as to maintain that the most inexpert and ignorant physician is more proper for a patient who has confidence in him, than the most learned and experienced, whom he is not so acquainted with. Nay, even the very choice of most of their drugs is in some sort mysterious and divine; the left foot of a tortoise, the urine of a lizard, the dung of an elephant, the liver of a mole, blood drawn from under the right wing of a white pigeon; and for us who have the stone (so scornfully they use us in our miseries) the excrement of rats beaten to powder, and such like trash and fooleries which rather carry a face of magical enchantment than of any solid science. I omit the odd number of their pills, the destination of certain days and feasts of the year, the superstition of gathering their simples at certain hours, and that so austere and very wise countenance and carriage

which Pliny himself so much derides. But they have, as I said, failed in that they have not added to this fine beginning, the making their meetings and consultations more religious and secret, where no profane person should have admission, no more than in the secret ceremonies of Æsculapius; for by the reason of this it falls out that their irresolution, the weakness of their arguments, divinations and foundations, the sharpness of their disputes, full of hatred, jealousy, and self-consideration, coming to be discovered by every one, a man must be marvelously blind not to see that he runs a very great hazard in their hands. Who ever saw one physician approve of another's prescription, without taking something away, or adding something to it? by which they sufficiently betray their tricks, and make it manifest to us that they therein more consider their own reputation, and consequently their profit, than their patient's interest. He was a much wiser man of their tribe, who of old gave it as a rule, that only one physician should undertake a sick person; for if he do nothing to purpose, one single man's default can bring no great scandal upon the art of medicine; and, on the contrary, the glory will be great, if he happen to have success; whereas, when there are many, they at every turn bring a disrepute upon their calling, forasmuch as they oftener do hurt than good. They ought to be satisfied with the perpetual disagreement which is found in the opinions of the principal masters and ancient authors of this science, which is only known to men well read, without discovering to the vulgar the controversies and various judgments which they still nourish and continue among themselves.

Will you have one example of the ancient controversy in physic? Herophilus lodges the original cause of all diseases in the humors; Erasistratus, in the blood of the arteries; Asclepiades, in the invisible atoms of the pores; Alcmæon, in the exuberance or defect of our bodily strength; Diocles, in the inequality of the elements of which the body is composed, and in the quality of the air we breathe; Strato, in the abundance, crudity, and corruption of the nourishment we take; and Hippocrates lodges it in the spirits. There is a certain friend of theirs, whom they know better than I, who declares upon this subject, "that the most important science in

practice among us, as that which is intrusted with our health and conservation, is, by ill luck, the most uncertain, the most perplexed, and agitated with the greatest mutations." There is no great danger in our mistaking the height of the sun, or the fraction of some astronomical computation: but here, where our whole being is concerned, 'tis not wisdom to abandon ourselves to the mercy of the agitation of so many contrary winds.

Before the Peloponnesian war, there was no great talk of this science. Hippocrates brought it into repute; whatever he established, Chrysippus overthrew; after that, Erasistratus, Aristotle's grandson, overthrew what Chrysippus had written; after these, the Empirics started up, who took a quite contrary way to the ancients in the management of this art; when the credit of these began a little to decay, Herophilus set another sort of practice on foot, which Asclepiades in turn stood up against, and overthrew; then, in their turn the opinions first of Themiso, and then of Musa, and after that those of Vectius Valens, a physician famous through the intelligence he had with Messalina, came in vogue; the empire of physic in Nero's time was established in Thessalus, who abolished and condemned all that had been held till his time; this man's doctrine was refuted by Crinas of Marseilles, who first brought all medicinal operations under the Ephemerides and motions of the stars, and reduced eating, sleeping, and drinking to hours that were most pleasing to Mercury, and the moon; his authority was soon after supplanted by Charinus, a physician of the same city of Marseilles; a man who not only controverted all the ancients methods of physic, but moreover the usage of hot baths, that had been generally, and for so many ages in common use; he made men bathe in cold water, even in winter, and plunged his sick patients in the natural waters of streams. No Roman till Pliny's time had ever vouchsafed to practice physic; that office was only performed by Greeks and foreigners, as 'tis now among us French, by those who sputter Latin; for, as a very great physician says, we do not easily accept the medicine we understand, no more than we do the drugs we ourselves gather. If the nations whence we fetch our guaiacum, sarsaparilla, and China wood, have physicians, how

great a value must we imagine, by the same recommendation of strangeness, rarity, and dear purchase, do they set upon our cabbage and parsley? for who would dare to contemn things so far fetched, and sought out at the hazard of so long and dangerous a voyage?

Since these ancient mutations in physic, there have been infinite others down to our own times, and, for the most part, mutations entire and universal, as those, for example, produced by Paracelsus, Fioravanti, and Argentier; for they, as I am told, not only alter one recipe, but the whole contexture and rules of the body of physic, accusing all others of ignorance and imposition who have practiced before them. At this rate, in what a condition the poor patient must be, I leave you to judge.

If we were even assured that, when they make a mistake that mistake of theirs would do us no harm, though it did us no good, it were a reasonable bargain to venture the making ourselves better without any danger of being made worse. Æsop tells a story, that one who had bought a Morisco slave, believing that his black complexion was accidental in him, and occasioned by the ill usage of his former master, caused him to enter into a course of physic, and with great care to be often bathed and purged: it happened that the Moor was nothing amended in his tawny complexion, but he wholly lost his former health. How often do we see physicians impute the death of their patients to one another? I remember that some years ago, there was an epidemical disease, very dangerous, and for the most part mortal, that raged in the towns about us: the storm being over which had swept away an infinite number of men, one of the most famous physicians of all the country, presently after published a book upon that subject, wherein, upon better thoughts, he confesses, that the letting blood in that disease was the principal cause of so many mishaps. Moreover, their authors hold that there is no physic that has not something hurtful in it. And if even those of the best operation in some measure offend us, what must those do that are totally misapplied? For my own part, though there were nothing else in the case, I am of opinion, that to those who loathe the taste of physic, it must needs be a dan-

[179]

gerous and prejudicial endeavor to force it down at so incommodious a time, and with so much aversion, and believe that it marvelously distempers a sick person at a time when he has so much need of repose. And moreover, if we but consider the occasions upon which they usually ground the cause of our diseases, they are so light and nice, that I thence conclude a very little error in the dispensation of their drugs may do a great deal of mischief. Now, if the mistake of a physician be so dangerous, we are in but a scurvy condition; for it is almost impossible but he must often fall into those mistakes: he had need of too many parts, considerations, and circumstances, rightly to level his design: he must know the sick person's complexion, his temperament, his humors, inclinations, actions, nay, his very thoughts and imaginations; he must be assured of the external circumstances, of the nature of the place, the quality of the air and season, the situation of the planets, and their influences: he must know in the disease, the causes, prognostics, affections, and critical days; in the drugs, the weight, the power of working, the country, figure, age, and dispensation, and he must know how rightly to proportion and mix them together, to beget a just and perfect symmetry; wherein if there be the least error, if among so many springs there be but any one out of order, 'tis enough to destroy us. God knows with how great difficulty most of these things are to be understood: for (for example) how shall a physician find out the true sign of the disease, every disease being capable of an infinite number of indications? How many doubts and controversies have they among themselves upon the interpretation of urines? otherwise, whence should the continual debates we see among them about the knowledge of the disease proceed? how could we excuse the error they so oft fall into, of taking fox for marten? In the diseases I have had, though there were ever so little difficulty in the case, I never found three of one opinion: which I instance, because I love to introduce examples wherein I am myself concerned.

A gentleman at Paris was lately cut for the stone by order of the physicians, in whose bladder, being accordingly so cut, there was found no more stone than in the palm of his hand; and, in the

same place, a bishop, who was my particular good friend, having been earnestly pressed by the majority of the physicians in town, whom he consulted, to suffer himself to be cut, to which also, upon their word, I used my interest in persuade him, when he was dead, and opened, it appeared that he had no malady but in the kidneys. They are least excusable for any error in this disease, by reason that it is in some sort palpable; and 'tis thence, that I conclude surgery to be much more certain, by reason that it sees and feels what it does, and so goes less upon conjecture; whereas the physicians have no *speculum matricis,* by which to examine our brains, lungs, and liver.

Even the very promises of physic are incredible in themselves; for, having to provide against divers and contrary accidents that often afflict us at one and the same time, and that have almost a necessary relation, as the heat of the liver, and the coldness of the stomach, they will needs persuade us, that of their ingredients one will heat the stomach, and the other will cool the liver; one has its commission to go directly to the kidneys, nay even to the bladder, without scattering its operations by the way, and is to retain its power and virtue through all those turns and meanders, even to the place to the service of which it is designed, by its own occult property; this will dry the brain; that will moisten the lungs. Of all this bundle of things having mixed up a potion, is it not a kind of madness to imagine or to hope that these differing virtues should separate themselves from one another in this mixture and confusion, to perform so many various errands? I should very much fear that they would either lose or change their tickets, and disturb one another's quarters. And who can imagine but that, in this liquid confusion, these faculties must corrupt, confound and spoil one another? And is not the danger still more, when the making up of this medicine is intrusted to the skill and fidelity of still another, to whose mercy we again abandon our lives?

As we have doublet and breeches makers, distinct trades, to clothe us, and are so much the better fitted, seeing that each of them meddles only with his own business, and has less to trouble his head with than the tailor who undertakes all; and as, in matter

of diet, great persons, for their better convenience and to the end they may be better served, have cooks for the different offices, this for soups and potages, that for roasting, instead of which if one cook should undertake the whole service, he could not so well perform it; so also as to the cure of our maladies. The Egyptians had reason to reject this general trade of physician; and to divide the profession: to each disease, to each part of the body, its particular workman; for that part was more properly and with less confusion cared for, seeing the person looked to nothing else. Ours are not aware that he who provides for all, provides for nothing; and that the entire government of this microcosm is more than they are able to undertake. While they were afraid of stopping a dysentery, lest they should put the patient into a fever, they killed me a friend, who was worth more than the whole pack of them put together. They counterpoise their own divinations with the present evils; and because they will not cure the brain to the prejudice of the stomach, they injure both with their dissentient and tumultuary drugs.

As to the variety and weakness of the rationale of this profession, they are more manifest in it than in any other art; aperitive medicines are proper for a man subject to the stone, by reason that opening and dilating the passages they helped forward the slimy matter whereof gravel and stone are engendered, and convey that downward which begins to harden and gather in the reins; aperitive things are dangerous for a man subject to the stone, by reason that, opening and dilating the passages, they help forward the matter proper to create the gravel toward the reins, which by their own propension being apt to seize it, 'tis not to be imagined but that a great deal of what has been conveyed thither must remain behind: moreover, if the medicine happen to meet with anything too large to be carried through all the narrow passages it must pass to be expelled, that obstruction, whatever it is, being stirred by these aperitive things and thrown into those narrow passages, coming to stop them, will occasion a certain and most painful death. They have the like uniformity in the counsels they give us for the regiment of life; it is good to make water often, for we experimentally see that in letting it lie long in the bladder we give it time to settle

the sediment which will concrete into a stone; it is good not to make water often; for the heavy excrements it carries along with it will not be voided without violence, as we see by experience that a torrent that runs with force washes the ground it rolls over much cleaner than the course of a slow and tardy stream; so, it is good to have often to do with women, for that opens the passages and helps to evacuate gravel; it is also very ill to have often to do with women, because it heats, tires, and weakens the reins. It is good to bathe frequently in hot water, forasmuch as that relaxes and mollifies the places where the gravel and stone lie; it is also ill by reason that this application of external heat helps the reins to bake, harden, and petrify the matter so disposed. For those who are taking baths it is most healthful to eat little at night, to the end that the waters they are to drink the next morning may have a better operation upon an empty stomach; on the other hand it is better to eat little at dinner, that it hinder not the operation of the waters, while it is not yet perfect, and not to oppress the stomach so soon after the other labor, but leave the office of digestion to the night, which will much better perform it than the day, when the body and soul are in perpetual moving and action. Thus do they juggle and cant in all their discourses at our expense; and they cannot give me one proposition against which I cannot erect a contrary of equal force. Let them, then, no longer exclaim against those who in this trouble of sickness suffer themselves to be gently guided by their own appetite and the advice of nature, and commit themselves to the common fortune.

I have seen in my travels almost all the famous baths of Christendom, and for some years past have begun to make use of them myself: for I look upon bathing as generally wholesome, and believe that we suffer no little inconveniences in our health by having left off the custom that was generally observed, in former times, almost by all nations, and is yet in many, of bathing every day; and I cannot imagine but that we are much the worse by having our limbs crusted and our pores stopped with dirt. And as to the drinking of them, fortune has in the first place rendered them not at all unacceptable to my taste; and secondly, they are

natural and simple, which at least carry no danger with them, though they may do us no good, of which the infinite crowd of people of all sorts and complexions who repair thither I take to be a sufficient warranty; and although I have not there observed any extraordinary and miraculous effects, but that on the contrary, having more narrowly than ordinary inquired into it, I have found all the reports of such operations that have been spread abroad in those places ill-grounded and false, and those that believe them (as people are willing to be gulled in what they desire) deceived in them, yet I have seldom known any who have been made worse by those waters, and a man cannot honestly deny but that they beget a better appetite, help digestion, and do in some sort revive us, if we do not go too late and in too weak a condition, which I would dissuade every one from doing. They have not the virtue to raise men from desperate and inveterate diseases, but they may help some light indisposition, or prevent some threatening alteration. He who does not bring along with him so much cheerfulness as to enjoy the pleasure of the company he will there meet, and of the walks and exercises to which the amenity of those places invite us, will doubtless lose the best and surest part of their effect. For this reason I have hitherto chosen to go to those of the most pleasant situation, where there was the best conveniency of lodging, provision, and company, as the baths of Bagnères in France, those of Plombieres, on the frontiers of Germany and Lorraine, those of Baden in Switzerland, those of Lucca in Tuscany, and especially those of Della Villa, which I have the most and at various seasons frequented.

Every nation has particular opinions touching their use, and particular rules and methods in using them; and all of them, according to what I have seen, almost with like effect. Drinking them is not at all received in Germany; the Germans bathe for all diseases, and will lie dabbling in the water almost from sun to sun; in Italy, where they drink nine days, they bathe at least thirty, and commonly drink the water mixed with some other drugs to make it work the better. Here we are ordered to walk to digest it; there we are kept in bed after taking it till it be wrought off, our stomachs

and feet having continually hot cloths applied to them all the while; and as the Germans have a particular practice generally to use cupping and scarification in the bath, so the Italians have their *doccie,* which are certain little streams of this hot water brought through pipes, and with these bathe an hour in the morning, and as much in the afternoon, for a month together, either the head, stomach, or any other part where the evil lies. There are infinite other varieties of customs in every country, or rather there is no manner of resemblance to one another. By this, you may see that this little part of physic to which I have only submitted, though the least depending upon art of all others, has yet a great share of the confusion and uncertainty everywhere else manifest in the profession.

The poets put what they would say with greater emphasis and grace; witness these two epigrams:

"Alcon hesterno signum Jovis attigit: ille,
Quamvis marmoreus, vim patitur medici.
Ecce hodie, jussus transferri, ex æde vetusta,
Effertur, quamvis sit Deus atque lapis:"

and the other:

"Lotus nobiscum est, hilaris cœnavit; et idem
Inventus mane est mortuus Andragoras.
Tam subitæ mortis causam, Faustine, requiris?
In somnis medicum viderat Hermocratem:"

upon which I will relate two stories.

The Baron de Caupene, in Chalosse, and I, have between us the advowson of a benefice of great extent, at the foot of our mountains; called Lahontan. It is with the inhabitants of this angle, as 'tis said of those of the Val d'Angrougne: they lived a peculiar sort of life, their fashions, clothes, and manners distinct from other people; ruled and governed by certain particular laws and usages, received from father to son, to which they submitted, without other constraint than the reverence to custom. This little state had continued from all antiquity in so happy a condition, that no

neighboring judge was ever put to the trouble of inquiring into their doings; no advocate was ever retained to give them counsel, no stranger ever called in to compose their differences; nor was ever any of them seen to go a-begging. They avoided all alliances and traffic with the outer world, that they might not corrupt the purity of their own government; till, as they say, one of them, in the memory of man having a mind spurred on with a noble ambition, took it into his head, to bring his name into credit and reputation, to make one of his sons something more than ordinary, and having put him to learn to write in a neighboring town, made him at last a brave village notary. This fellow, having acquired such dignity, began to disdain their ancient customs, and to buzz into the people's ears the pomp of the other parts of the nation; the first prank he played was to advise a friend of his, whom somebody had offended by sawing off the horns of one of his goats, to make his complaint to the royal judges thereabout, and so he went on from one to another, till he had spoiled and confounded all. In the tail of this corruption, they say, there happened another, and of worse consequence, by means of a physician, who falling in love with one of their daughters, had a mind to marry her and to live among them. This man first of all began to teach them the names of fevers, colds, and imposthumes; the seat of the heart, liver, and intestines, a science till then utterly unknown to them; and instead of garlic, with which they were wont to cure all manner of diseases how painful or extreme soever, he taught them, though it were but for a cough, or any little cold, to take strange mixtures, and began to make a trade not only of their health but of their lives. They swear till then they never perceived the evening air to be offensive to the head; that to drink, when they were hot, was hurtful, and that the winds of autumn were more unwholesome than those of spring; that, since this use of physic, they find themselves oppressed with a legion of unaccustomed diseases, and that they perceive a general decay in their ancient vigor, and their lives are cut shorter by the half. This is the first of my stories.

The other is, that before I was afflicted with the stone, hearing that the blood of a he-goat was with many in very great esteem,

and looked upon as a celestial manna rained down upon these latter ages for the good and preservation of the lives of men, and having heard it spoken of by men of understanding for an admirable drug, and of infallible operation; I, who have ever thought myself subject to all the accidents that can befall other men, had a mind, in my perfect health, to furnish myself with this miracle, and therefore gave order to have a goat fed at home according to the recipe: for he must be taken in the hottest month of all summer, and must only have aperitive herbs given him to eat, and white wine to drink. I came home by chance the very day he was to be killed; and some one came and told me, that the cook had found two or three great balls in his paunch, that rattled against one another among what he had eaten. I was curious to have all his entrails brought before me, where, having caused the skin that enclosed them to be cut, there tumbled out three great lumps, as light as sponges, so that they appeared to be hollow; but, as to the rest, hard and firm without, and spotted and mixed all over with various dead colors; one was perfectly round, and of the bigness of an ordinary ball; the other two something less, of an imperfect roundness, as seeming not to be arrived at their full growth. I find, by inquiry of people accustomed to open these animals, that it is a rare and unusual accident. 'Tis likely these are stones of the same nature with ours: and if so, it must needs be a very vain hope in those who have the stone, to extract their cure from the blood of a beast that was himself about to die of the same disease. For to say that the blood does not participate of this contagion, and does not thence alter its wonted virtue, it is rather to be believed than nothing is engendered in a body but by the conspiracy and communication of all the parts; the whole mass works together, though one part contributes more to the work than another, according to the diversity of operations: wherefore it is very likely that there was some petrifying quality in all the parts of this goat. It was not so much for fear of the future, and for myself, that I was curious in this experiment, but because it falls out in mine, as it does in many other families, that the women store up such little trumperies for the service of the people, using the same recipe in fifty several

diseases, and such a recipe as they will not take themselves, and yet triumph when they happen to be successful.

As to what remains I honor physicians, not according to the precept for their necessity (for to this passage may be opposed another of the prophet reproving King Asa for having recourse to a physician), but for themselves, having known many very good men of that profession, and most worthy to be beloved. I do not attack them; 'tis their art I inveigh against, and do not much blame them for making their advantage of our folly, for most men do the same. Many callings, both of greater and of less dignity than theirs, have no other foundation or support than public abuse. When I am sick I send for them if they be near, only to have their company, and pay them as others do. I give them leave to command me to keep myself warm, because I naturally love to do it, and to appoint leeks or lettuce for my broth; to order me white wine or claret; and so as to all other things, which are indifferent to my palate and custom. I know very well that I do nothing for them in so doing, because sharpness and strangeness are incidents of the very essence of physic. Lycurgus ordered wine for the sick Spartans: Why? because they abominated the drinking it when they were well; as a gentleman, a neighbor of mine, takes it as an excellent medicine in his fever, because naturally he mortally hates the taste of it. How many do we see among them of my humor, who despise taking physic themselves, are men of a liberal diet, and live a quite contrary sort of life to what they prescribe others? What is this but flatly to abuse our simplicity? for their own lives and health are no less dear to them than ours are to us, and consequently they would accommodate their practice to their rules, if they did not themselves know how false these are.

'Tis the fear of death and of pain, impatience of disease, and a violent and indiscreet desire of a present cure, that so blind us; 'tis pure cowardice that makes our belief so pliable and easy to be imposed upon: and yet most men do not so much believe as they acquiesce and permit; for I hear them find fault and complain as well as we; but they resolve at last, "What should I do then?" As if impatience were of itself a better remedy than patience. Is

there any one of those who have suffered themselves to be persuaded into this miserable subjection, who does not equally surrender himself to all sorts of impostures? who does not give up himself to the mercy of whoever has the impudence to promise him a cure? The Babylonians carried their sick into the public square; the physician was the people; every one who passed by, being in humanity and civility obliged to inquire of their condition, gave some advice according to his own experience. We do little better; there is not so simple a woman whose chatterings and drenches we do not make use of; and according to my humor, if I were to take physic, I would sooner choose to take theirs than any other, because at least, if they do no good, they will do no harm. What Homer and Plato said of the Egyptians, that they were all physicians, may be said of all nations; there is not a man among any of them who does not boast of some rare recipe, and who will not venture it upon his neighbor, if he will let him. I was the other day in company where some of my fraternity told us of a new sort of pills made up of a hundred and odd ingredients; it made us very merry, and was a singular consolation, for what rock could withstand so great a battery? And yet I hear from those who have made trial of it, that the least atom of gravel will not stir for't.

I cannot take my hand from the paper, before I have added a word or two more concerning the assurance they give us of the infallibility of their drugs, from the experiments they have made.

The greatest part, I should say above two-thirds, of the medicinal virtues, consist in the quintessence, or occult property of simples, of which we can have no other instruction than use and custom; for quintessence is no other than a quality of which we cannot by our reason find out the cause. In such proofs, those they pretend to have acquired by the inspiration of some demon, I am content to receive (for I meddle not with miracles); and also the proofs which are drawn from things that, upon some other account, often fall into use among us; as if in the wool, wherewith we are wont to clothe ourselves, there has accidentally some occult dessicative property been found out of curing kibed heels, or as if in the radish we eat for food, there has been found out some aperitive operation. Galen

reports, that a man happened to be cured of a leprosy by drinking wine out of a vessel into which a viper had crept by chance. In this example we find the means and a very likely guide and conduct to this experience, as we also do in those that physicians pretend to have been directed to by the example of some beasts. But in most of their other experiments wherein they affirm they have been conducted by fortune, and to have had no other guide than chance, I find the progress of this information incredible. Suppose man looking round about him upon the infinite number of things, plants, animals, metals; I do not know where he would begin his trial; and though his first fancy should fix him upon an elk's horn, wherein there must be a very pliant and easy belief, he will yet find himself as perplexed in his second operation. There are so many maladies and so many circumstances presented to him, that before he can attain the certainty of the point to which the perfection of his experience should arrive, human sense will be at the end of its lesson; and before he can, among this infinity of things, find out what this horn is; among so many diseases, what is epilepsy; the many complexions in a melancholy person; the many seasons in winter; the many nations in the French; the many ages in age; the many celestial mutations in the conjunction of Venus and Saturn; the many parts in man's body, nay, in a finger; and being, in all this, directed neither by argument, conjecture, example, nor divine inspirations, but merely by the sole motion of fortune, it must be by a perfectly artificial, regular, and methodical fortune. And after the cure is performed, how can he assure himself that it was not because the disease had arrived at its period or an effect of chance? or the operation of something else that he had eaten, drunk, or touched that day? or by virtue of his grandmother's prayers? And, moreover, had this experiment been perfect, how many times was it repeated, and this long beadroll of haps and concurrences strung anew by chance to conclude a certain rule? And when the rule is concluded, by whom, I pray you? Of so many millions, there are but three men who take upon them to record their experiments: must fortune needs just hit one of these? What if another, and a hundred others, have made contrary experiments? We might,

peradventure, have some light in this, were all the judgments and arguments of men known to us: but that three witnesses, three doctors, should lord it over all mankind, is against reason: it were necessary that human nature should have deputed and culled them out, and that they were declared our comptrollers by express letters of attorney.

"TO MADAME DE DURAS.

"MADAME:—The last time you honored me with a visit, you found me at work upon this chapter, and as these trifles may one day fall into your hands, I would also that they testify in how great honor the author will take any favor you shall please to show them. You will there find the same air and mien you have observed in his conversation; and though I could have borrowed some better or more favorable garb than my own, I would not have done it: for I require nothing more of these writings, but to present me to your memory such as I naturally am. The same conditions and faculties you have been pleased to frequent and receive with much more honor and courtesy than they deserve, I would put together (but without alteration or change) in one solid body, that may peradventure continue some years, or some days, after I am gone; where you may find them again when you shall please to refresh your memory, without putting you to any greater trouble; neither are they worth it. I desire you should continue the favor of your friendship to me, by the same qualities by which it was acquired.

"I am not at all ambitious that any one should love and esteem me more dead than living. The humor of Tiberius is ridiculous, but yet common, who was more solicitous to extend his renown to posterity than to render himself acceptable to men of his own time. If I were one of those to whom the world could owe commendation, I would give out of it one-half to have the other in hand; let their praises come quick and crowding about me, more thick than long, more full than durable; and let them cease, in God's name, with my own knowledge of them, and when the sweet sound can no longer pierce my ears. It were an idle humor to essay, now that I am about to forsake the commerce of men, to offer myself to them by a new

recommendation. I make no account of the goods I could not employ in the service of my life. Such as I am, I will be elsewhere than in paper: my art and industry have been ever directed to render myself good for something; my studies, to teach me to do, and not to write. I have made it my whole business to frame my life: this has been my trade and my work; I am less a writer of books than anything else. I have coveted understanding for the service of my present and real conveniences, and not to lay up a stock for my posterity. He who has anything of value in him, let him make it appear in his conduct, in his ordinary discourses, in his courtships, and his quarrels: in play, in bed, at table, in the management of his affairs, in his economics. Those whom I see make good books in ill breeches, should first have mended their breeches, if they would have been ruled by me. Ask a Spartan, whether he had rather be a good orator or a good soldier; and if I was asked the same question, I would rather choose to be a good cook, had I not one already to serve me. Good God! Madame, how should I hate the reputation of being a pretty fellow at writing, and an ass and an inanity in everything else! Yet I had rather be a fool in anything than to have made so ill a choice wherein to employ my talent. And I am so far from expecting to gain any new reputation by these follies, that I shall think I come off pretty well if I lose nothing by them of that little I had before. For besides that this dead and mute painting will take from my natural being, it has no resemblance to my better condition, but is much lapsed from my former vigor and cheerfulness, growing faded and withered: I am toward the bottom of the barrel, which begins to taste of the lees.

"As to the rest, madame, I should not have dared to make so bold with the mysteries of physic, considering the esteem that you and so many others have of it, had I not had encouragement from their own authors. I think there are of these among the old Latin writers but two, Pliny and Celsus: if these ever fall into your hands, you will find that they speak much more rudely of their art than I do: I but pinch it, they cut its throat. Pliny, among other things, twits them with this, that when they are at the end of their rope,

they have a pretty device to save themselves, by recommending their patients, whom they have teased and tormented with their drugs and diets to no purpose, some to vows and miracles, others to the hot baths. (Be not angry, madame; he speaks not of those in our parts, which are under the protection of your house, and all Gramontins.) They have a third way of saving their own credit, of ridding their hands of us and securing themselves from the reproaches we might cast in their teeth of our little amendment, when they have had us so long in their hands that they have not one more invention left wherewith to amuse us, which is, to send us to the better air of some other country. This, madame, is enough: I hope you will give me leave to return to my discourse, from which I have so far digressed, the better to divert you."

It was, I think, Pericles, who being asked how he did: "you may judge," says he, "by these," showing some little scrolls of parchment he had tied about his neck and arms. By which he would infer, that he must needs be very sick when he was reduced to a necessity of having recourse to such idle and vain fopperies, and of suffering himself to be so equipped. I dare not promise but that I may one day be so much a fool as to commit my life and death to the mercy and government of physicians; I may fall into such a frenzy; I dare not be responsible for my future constancy; but then, if any one ask me how I do, I may also answer, as Pericles did, "You may judge by this," showing my hand clutching six drachms of opium. It will be a very evident sign of a violent sickness: my judgment will be very much out of order; if once fear and impatience get such an advantage over me, it may very well be concluded that there is a dreadful fever in my mind.

I have taken the pains to plead this cause, which I understand indifferently, a little to back and support the natural aversion to drugs and the practice of physic, I have derived from my ancestors; to the end it may not be a mere stupid and inconsiderate aversion, but have a little more form; and also, that they who shall see me so obstinate in my resolution against all exhortations and menaces that shall be given me, when my infirmity shall press hardest upon

1947

me, may not think 'tis mere obstinacy in me; or any one so ill-natured, as to judge it to be any motive of glory; for it would be a strange ambition to seek to gain honor by an action my gardener or my groom can perform as well as I. Certainly, I have not a heart too tumorous and windy, that I should exchange so solid a pleasure as health, for an airy and imaginary pleasure: glory, even that of the four sons of Aymon, is too dear bought by a man of my humor, if it cost him three swinging fits of the stone. Give me health, in God's name! Such as love physic, may also have good, great, and convincing considerations; I do not hate opinions contrary to my own; I am so far from being angry to see a discrepancy between mine and other men's judgments, and from rendering myself unfit for the society of men, from being of another sense and party than mine, that on the contrary (the most general way that nature has followed being variety, and more in souls than bodies, forasmuch as they are of a more supple substance, and more susceptible of forms) I find it much more rare to see our humors and designs jump and agree. And there never were, in the world, two opinions alike, no more than two hairs, or two grains; the most universal quality is diversity.

XIV

OF REPENTANCE

Others form man; I only report him: and represent a particular one, ill fashioned enough, and whom, if I had to model him anew, I should certainly make something else than what he is: but that's past recalling. Now, though the features of my picture alter and change, 'tis not, however, unlike: the world eternally turns round; all things therein are incessantly moving, the earth, the rocks of Caucasus, and the pyramids of Egypt, both by the public motion and their own. Even constancy itself is no other but a slower and more languishing motion. I cannot fix my object; 'tis always tottering and reeling by a natural giddiness: I take it as it is at the instant I consider it; I do not paint its being, I paint its passage; not a passing from one age to another, or, as the people say, from seven to seven years, but from day to day, from minute to minute. I must accommodate my history to the hour: I may presently change, not only by fortune, but also by intention. 'Tis a counterpart of various and changeable accidents, and of irresolute imaginations, and, as it falls out, sometimes contrary: whether it be that I am then another self, or that I take subjects by other circumstances and considerations: so it is, that I may peradventure contradict myself, but, as Demades said, I never contradict the truth. Could my soul once take footing, I would not essay but resolve: but it is always learning and making trial.

I propose a life ordinary and without lustre: 'tis all one; all moral philosophy may as well be applied to a common and private

life, as to one of richer composition: every man carries the entire form of human condition. Authors communicate themselves to the people by some especial and extrinsic mark; I, the first of any, by my universal being; as Michel de Montaigne, not as a grammarian, a poet, or a lawyer. If the world find fault that I speak too much of myself, I find fault that they do not so much as think of themselves. But is it reason, that being so particular in my way of living, I should pretend to recommend myself to the public knowledge? And is it also reason that I should produce to the world, where art and handling have so much credit and authority, crude and simple effects of nature, and of a weak nature to boot? Is it not to build a wall without stone or brick, or some such thing, to write books without learning and without art? The fancies of music are carried on by art; mine by chance. I have this, at least, according to discipline, that never any man treated of a subject he better understood and knew, than I what I have undertaken, and that in this I am the most understanding man alive: secondly, that never any man penetrated farther into his matter, nor better and more distinctly sifted the parts and sequences of it, nor ever more exactly and fully arrived at the end he proposed to himself. To perfect it, I need bring nothing but fidelity to the work; and that is there, and the most pure and sincere that is anywhere to be found. I speak truth, not so much as I would, but as much as I dare; and I dare a little the more, as I grow older; for, methinks, custom allows to age more liberty of prating, and more indiscretion of talking of a man's self. That cannot fall out here, which I often see elsewhere, that the work and the artificer contradict one another: "Can a man of such sober conversation have written so foolish a book?" Or "Do so learned writings proceed from a man of so weak conversation?" He who talks at a very ordinary rate, and writes rare matter, 'tis to say that his capacity is borrowed and not his own. A learned man is not learned in all things: but a sufficient man is sufficient throughout, even to ignorance itself; here my book and I go hand in hand together. Elsewhere men may commend or censure the work, without reference to the workman; here they cannot: who touches the one, touches the other. He who shall judge of it without knowing him,

will more wrong himself than me; he who does know him, gives me all the satisfaction I desire. I shall be happy beyond my desert, if I can obtain only thus much from the public approbation, as to make men of understanding perceive that I was capable of profiting by knowledge, had I had it; and that I deserved to have been assisted by a better memory.

Be pleased here to excuse what I often repeat, that I very rarely repent, and that my conscience is satisfied with itself, not as the conscience of an angel, or that of a horse, but as the conscience of a man, always adding this clause, not one of ceremony, but a true and real submission, that I speak inquiring and doubting, purely and simply referring myself to the common and accepted beliefs for the resolution. I do not teach, I only relate.

There is no vice that is absolutely a vice which does not offend, and that a sound judgment does not accuse; for there is in it so manifest a deformity and inconvenience, that, peradventure, they are in the right who say that it is chiefly begotten by stupidity and ignorance: so hard is it to imagine that a man can know without abhorring it. Malice sucks up the greatest part of its own venom, and poisons itself. Vice leaves repentance in the soul, like an ulcer in the flesh, which is always scratching and lacerating itself; for reason effaces all other grief and sorrows, but it begets that of repentance, which is so much the more grievous, by reason it springs within, as the cold and heat of fevers are more sharp than those that only strike upon the outward skin. I hold for vices (but every one according to its proportion), not only those which reason and nature condemn, but those also which the opinion of men, though false and erroneous, have made such, if authorized by law and custom.

There is likewise no virtue which does not rejoice a well-descended nature; there is a kind of, I know not what, congratulation in well doing that gives us an inward satisfaction, and a generous boldness that accompanies a good conscience: a soul daringly vicious may, peradventure, arm itself with security, but it cannot supply itself with this complacency and satisfaction. 'Tis no little satisfaction to feel a man's self preserved from the contagion of so

depraved an age, and to say to himself: "Whoever could penetrate into my soul would not there find me guilty either of the affliction or ruin of any one, or of revenge or envy, or any offense against the public laws, or of innovation or disturbance, or failure of my word; and though the license of the time permits and teaches every one so to do, yet have I not plundered any Frenchman's goods, or taken his money, and have lived upon what is my own, in war as well as in peace; neither have I set any man to work without paying him his hire." These testimonies of a good conscience please, and this natural rejoicing is very beneficial to us, and the only reward that we can never fail of.

To ground the recompense of virtuous actions upon the approbation of others is too uncertain and unsafe a foundation, especially in so corrupt and ignorant an age as this, wherein the good opinion of the vulgar is injurious: upon whom do you rely to show you what is recommendable? God defend me from being an honest man, according to the descriptions of honor I daily see every one make of himself. *"Quæ fuerant vitia, mores sunt."* Some of my friends have at times schooled and scolded me with great sincerity and plainness, either of their own voluntary motion, or by me entreated to it as to an office, which to a well-composed soul surpasses not only in utility, but in kindness all other offices of friendship: I have always received them with the most open arms, both of courtesy and acknowledgment; but, to say the truth, I have often found so much false measure, both in their reproaches and praises, that I had not done much amiss, rather to have done ill, than to have done well according to their notions. We, who live private lives, not exposed to any other view than our own, ought chiefly to have settled a pattern within ourselves by which to try our actions; and according to that, sometimes to encourage and sometimes to correct ourselves. I have my laws and my judicature to judge of myself, and apply myself more to these than to any other rules: I do, indeed, restrain my actions according to others; but extend them not by any other rule than my own. You yourself only know if you are cowardly and cruel, loyal and devout: others see you not, and only guess at you by uncertain conjectures, and do not

so much see your nature as your art; rely not therefore upon their opinions, but stick to your own: *"Tuo tibi judicio est utendum . . . Virtutis et vitiorum grave ipsius conscientiæ pondus est: qua sublata, jacent omnia."*

But the saying that repentance immediately follows the sin seems not to have respect to sin in its high estate, which is lodged in us as in its own proper habitation. One may disown and retract the vices that surprise us, and to which we are hurried by passions; but those which by a long habit are rooted in a strong and vigorous will are not subject to contradiction. Repentance is no other but a recanting of the will and an opposition to our fancies, which lead us which way they please. It makes this person disown his former virtue and continency:

> "Quæ mens est hodie, cur eadem non puero fuit?
> Vel cur his animis incolumes non redeunt genæ?"

'Tis an exact life that maintains itself in due order in private. Every one may juggle his part, and represent an honest man upon the stage: but within, and in his own bosom, where all may do as they list, where all is concealed, to be regular—there's the point. The next degree is to be so in his house, and in his ordinary actions, for which we are accountable to none, and where there is no study nor artifice. And therefore Bias, setting forth the excellent state of a private family, says: "of which the master is the same within, by his own virtue and temper, that he is abroad, for fear of the laws and report of men." And it was a worthy saying of Julius Drusus, to the masons who offered him, for three thousand crowns, to put his house in such a posture that his neighbours should no longer have the same inspection into it as before; "I will give you," said he, "six thousand to make it so that everybody may see into every room." 'Tis honorably recorded of Agesilaus, that he used in his journeys always to take up his lodgings in temples, to the end that the people and the gods themselves might pry into his most private actions. Such a one has been a miracle to the world, in whom neither his wife nor servant has ever seen anything so much as remarkable; few men have been admired by their own domestics; no one was ever a prophet, not merely in his own house, but in his

own country, says the experience of histories: 'tis the same in things of naught, and in this low example the image of a greater is to be seen. In my country of Gascony, they look upon it as a drollery to see me in print; the further off I am read from my own home, the better I am esteemed. I am fain to purchase printers in Guienne; elsewhere they purchase me. Upon this it is that they lay their foundation who conceal themselves present and living, to obtain a name when they are absent and dead. I had rather have a great deal less in hand, and do not expose myself to the world upon any other account than my present share; when I leave it I quit the rest. See this functionary whom the people escort in state, with wonder and applause, to his very door; he puts off the pageant with his robe, and falls so much the lower by how much he was higher exalted: in himself within, all is tumult and degraded. And though all should be regular there, it will require a vivid and well-chosen judgment to perceive it in these low and private actions; to which may be added, that order is a dull, somber virtue. To enter a breach, conduct an embassy, govern a people, are actions of renown: to reprehend, laugh, sell, pay, love, hate, and gently and justly converse with a man's own family, and with himself; not to relax, not to give a man's self the lie is more rare and hard, and less remarkable. By which means, retired lives, whatever is said to the contrary, undergo duties of as great or greater difficulty than the others do; and private men, says Aristotle, serve virtue more painfully and highly, than those in authority do: we prepare ourselves for eminent occasions, more out of glory than conscience. The shortest way to arrive at glory, would be to do that for conscience which we do for glory: and the virtue of Alexander appears to me of much less vigor in his great theater, than that of Socrates in his mean and obscure employment. I can easily conceive Socrates in the place of Alexander, but Alexander in that of Socrates, I cannot. Who shall ask the one what he can do, he will answer, "Subdue the world:" and who shall put the same question to the other, he will say, "Carry on human life conformably with its natural condition;" a much more general, weighty, and legitimate science than the other.

The virtue of the soul does not consist in flying high, but in walking orderly; its grandeur does not exercise itself in grandeur, but in mediocrity. As they who judge and try us within, make no great account of the luster of our public actions, and see they are only streaks and rays of clear water springing from a slimy and muddy bottom: so, likewise, they who judge of us by this gallant outward appearance, in like manner conclude of our internal constitution; and cannot couple common faculties, and like their own, with the other faculties that astonish them, and are so far out of their sight. Therefore it is, that we give such savage forms to demons: and who does not give Tamerlane great eyebrows, wide nostrils, a dreadful visage, and a prodigious stature, according to the imagination he has conceived by the report of his name? Had any one formerly brought me to Erasmus, I should hardly have believed but that all was adage and apothegm he spoke to his man or his hostess. We much more aptly imagine an artisan upon his closestool, or upon his wife, than a great president venerable by his port and sufficiency: we fancy that they, from their high tribunals, will not abase themselves so much as to live. As vicious souls are often incited by some foreign impulse to do well, so are virtuous souls to do ill; they are therefore to be judged by their settled state, when they are at home, whenever that may be; and, at all events, when they are nearer repose, and in their native station.

Natural inclinations are much assisted and fortified by education: but they seldom alter and overcome their institution: a thousand natures of my time have escaped toward virtue or vice, through a quite contrary discipline;

> "Sic ubi desuetæ silvis in carcere clausæ
> Mansuevere feræ, et vultus posuere minaces,
> Atque hominem didicere pati, si torrida parvus
> Venit in ora cruor, redeunt rabiesque furorque,
> Admonitæque tument gustato sanguine fauces;
> Fervet, et a trepido vix abstinet ira magistro;"

these original qualities are not to be rooted out; they may be covered and concealed. The Latin tongue is as it were natural to me; I understand it better than French; but I have not been used

[202]

to speak it, nor hardly to write it these forty years. Yet, upon extreme and sudden emotions which I have fallen into twice or thrice in my life, and once, seeing my father in perfect health fall upon me in a swoon, I have always uttered my first outcries and ejaculations in Latin; nature starting up, and forcibly expressing itself, in spite of so long a discontinuation; and this example is said of many others.

They who in my time have attempted to correct the manners of the world by new opinions, reform seeming vices, but the essential vices they leave as they were, if indeed, they do not augment them; and augmentation is, therein, to be feared; we defer all other well doing upon the account of these external reformations, of less cost and greater show, and thereby expiate cheaply, for the other natural consubstantial and intestine vices. Look a little into our experience: there is no man, if he listen to himself, who does not in himself discover a particular and governing form of his own, that jostles his education, and wrestles with the tempest of passions that are contrary to it. For my part, I seldom find myself agitated with surprises; I always find myself in my place, as heavy and unwieldy bodies do; if I am not at home, I am always near at hand; my dissipations do not transport me very far, there is nothing strange nor extreme in the case; and yet I have sound and vigorous turns.

The true condemnation, and which touches the common practice of men, is, that their very retirement itself is full of filth and corruption; the idea of their reformation composed; their repentance sick and faulty, very nearly as much as their sin. Some, either from having been linked to vice by a natural propension, or long practice, cannot see its deformity. Others (of which constitution I am) do indeed feel the weight of vice, but they counterbalance it with pleasure, or some other occasion; and suffer, and lend themselves to it, for a certain price, but viciously and basely. Yet there might, haply, be imagined so vast a disproportion of measure, where with justice the pleasure might excuse the sin, as we say of utility; not only if accidental, and out of sin, as in thefts, but the very exercise of sin, as in the enjoyment of women, where the temptation is violent, and 'tis said, sometimes not to be overcome.

Being the other day at Armaignac, on the estate of a kinsman of mine, I there saw a country fellow who was by every one nick-named the thief. He thus related the story of his life; that being born a beggar, and finding that he should not be able, so as to be clear of indigence, to get his living by the sweat of his brow, he resolved to turn thief, and by means of his strength of body, had exercised this trade all the time of his youth in great security; for he ever made his harvest and vintage in other men's grounds, but a great way off, and in so great quantities, that it was not to be imagined one man could have carried away so much in one night upon his shoulders; and, moreover, was careful equally to divide and distribute the mischief he did, that the loss was of less impor-tance to every particular man. He is now grown old, and rich for a man of his condition, thanks to his trade, which he openly con-fesses to every one. And to make his peace with God, he says, that he is daily ready by good offices to make satisfaction to the succes-sors of those he has robbed, and if he do not finish (for to do it all at once he is not able) he will then leave it in charge to his heirs to perform the rest, proportionably to the wrong he himself only knows he has done to each. By this description, true or false, this man looks upon theft as a dishonest action, and hates it, but less than poverty, and simply repents; but to the extent he has thus recompensed, he repents not. This is not that habit which incor-porates us into vice, and conforms even our understanding itself to it; nor is it that impetuous whirlwind that by gusts troubles and blinds our souls and for the time precipitates us, judgment and all, into the power of vice.

I customarily do what I do thoroughly and make but one step on't; I have rarely any movement that hides itself and steals away from my reason, and that does not proceed in the matter by the consent of all my faculties, without division or intestine sedition; my judgment is to have all the blame or all the praise; and the blame it once has, it has always; for almost from my infancy it has ever been one; the same inclination, the same turn, the same force; and as to universal opinions, I fixed myself from my child-hood in the place where I resolved to stick. There are some sins

that are impetuous, prompt, and sudden; let us set them aside; but in these other sins so often repeated, deliberated, and contrived, whether sins of complexion or sins of profession and vocation, I cannot conceive that they should have so long been settled in the same resolution, unless the reason and conscience of him who has them, be constant to have them; and the repentance he boasts to be inspired with on a sudden, is very hard for me to imagine or form. I follow not the opinion of the Pythagorean sect, "that men take up a new soul when they repair to the images of the gods to receive their oracles," unless he mean that it must needs be extrinsic, new, and lent for the time; our own showing so little sign of purification and cleanness, fit for such an office.

They act quite contrary to the stoical precepts, who do indeed, command us to correct the imperfections and vices we know ourselves guilty of, but forbid us therefore to disturb the repose of our souls; these make us believe that they have great grief and remorse within; but of amendment, correction, or interruption, they make nothing appear. It cannot be a cure if the malady be not wholly discharged; if repentance were laid upon the scale of the balance, it would weigh down sin. I find no quality so easy to counterfeit as devotion, if men do not conform their manners and life to the profession; its essence is abstruse and occult; the appearances easy and ostentatious.

For my own part, I may desire in general to be other than I am; I may condemn and dislike my whole form, and beg of Almighty God for an entire reformation, and that He will please to pardon my natural infirmity: but I ought not to call this repentance, methinks, no more, than the being dissatisfied that I am not an angel or Cato. My actions are regular, and conformable with what I am, and to my condition; I can do no better; and repentance does not properly touch things that are not in our power; sorrow does. I imagine an infinite number of natures more elevated and regular than mine; and yet I do not for all that improve my faculties, no more than my arm or will grow more strong and vigorous for conceiving those of another to be so. If to conceive and wish a nobler way of acting than that we have, should produce a repentance of

our own, we must then repent us of our most innocent actions, forasmuch as we may well suppose that in a more excellent nature they would have been carried on with greater dignity and perfection; and we would that ours were so. When I reflect upon the deportments of my youth, with that of my old age, I find that I have commonly behaved myself with equal order in both, according to what I understand: this is all that my resistance can do. I do not flatter myself; in the same circumstances I should do the same things. It is not a patch, but rather an universal tincture, with which I am stained. I know no repentance, superficial, half-way and ceremonious; it must sting me all over before I can call it so, and must prick my bowels as deeply and universally as God sees into me.

As to business, many excellent opportunities have escaped me for want of good management; and yet my deliberations were sound enough, according to the occurrences presented to me: 'tis their way to choose always the easiest and safest course. I find that, in my former resolves, I have proceeded with discretion, according to my own rule, and according to the state of the subject proposed, and should do the same a thousand years hence in like occasions; I do not consider what it is now, but what it was then, when I deliberated on it: the force of all counsel consists in the time; occasions and things eternally shift and change. I have in my life committed some important errors, not for want of good understanding, but for want of good luck. There are secret, and not to be foreseen, parts in matters we have in hand, especially in the nature of men; mute conditions, that make no show, unknown sometimes even to the possessors themselves, that spring and start up by incidental occasions; if my prudence could not penetrate into nor foresee them, I blame it not: 'tis commissioned no further than its own limits; if the event be too hard for me, and take the side I have refused, there is no remedy; I do not blame myself, I accuse my fortune, and not my work; this cannot be called repentance.

Phocion, having given the Athenians an advice that was not followed, and the affair nevertheless succeeding contrary to his opinion, some one said to him; "Well, Phocion, art thou content that matters go so well?" "I am very well content," replied he, "that

this has happened so well, but I do not repent that I counseled the other." When any of my friends address themselves to me for advice, I give it candidly and clearly, without sticking, as almost all other men do, at the hazard of the thing's falling out contrary to my opinion, and that I may be reproached for my counsel; I am very indifferent as to that, for the fault will be theirs for having consulted me, and I could not refuse them that office.

I, for my own part, can rarely blame any one but myself for my oversights and misfortunes, for indeed I seldom solicit the advice of another, if not by honor of ceremony, or excepting where I stand in need of information, special science, or as to matter of fact. But in things wherein I stand in need of nothing but judgment, other men's reasons may serve to fortify my own, but have little power to dissuade me; I hear them all with civility and patience: but to my recollection, I never made use of any but my own. With me, they are but flies and atoms, that confound and distract my will; I lay no great stress upon my opinions; but I lay as little upon those of others, and fortune rewards me accordingly: if I receive but little advice, I also give but little. I am seldom consulted, and still more seldom believed, and know no concern, either public or private, that has been mended or bettered by my advice. Even they whom fortune had in some sort tied to my direction, have more willingly suffered themselves to be governed by any other counsels than mine. And as a man who am as jealous of my repose as of my authority, I am better pleased that it should be so; in leaving me there, they humor what I profess, which is to settle and wholly contain myself within myself. I take a pleasure in being uninterested in other men's affairs, and disengaged from being their warranty, and responsible for what they do.

In all affairs that are past, be it how it will, I have very little regret; for this imagination puts me out of my pain, that they were so to fall out; they are in the great revolution of the world, and in the chain of stoical causes: your fancy cannot, by wish and imagination, move one tittle, but that the great current of things will not reverse both the past and the future.

As to the rest, I abominate that incidental repentance which old

age brings along with it. He, who said of old, that he was obliged to his age for having weaned him from pleasure, was of another opinion than I am; I can never think myself beholden to impotency, for any good it can do to me; *"Nec tam aversa unquam videbitur ab opere suo providentia, ut debilitas inter optima inventa sit."* Our appetites are rare in old age; a profound satiety seizes us after the act; in this I see nothing of conscience; chagrin and weakness imprint in us a drowsy and rheumatic virtue. We must not suffer ourselves to be so wholly carried away by natural alterations, as to suffer our judgments to be imposed upon by them. Youth and pleasure have not formerly so far prevailed with me, that I did not well enough discern the face of vice in pleasure; neither does the distaste that years have brought me, so far prevail with me now, that I cannot discern pleasure in vice. Now that I am no more in my flourishing age, I judge as well of these things as if I were. I, who narrowly and strictly examine it, find my reason the very same it was in my most licentious age, except, perhaps, that 'tis weaker and more decayed by being grown older; and I find that the pleasure it refuses me upon the account of my bodily health, it would no more refuse now, in consideration of the health of my soul, than at any time heretofore. I do not repute it the more valiant for not being able to combat; my temptations are so broken and mortified, that they are not worth its opposition; holding but out my hands, I repel them. Should one present the old concupiscence before it, I fear it would have less power to resist it than heretofore; I do not discern that in itself it judges anything otherwise now, than it formerly did, nor that it has acquired any new light: wherefore, if there be convalescence, 'tis an enchanted one. Miserable kind of remedy, to owe one's health to one's disease! 'Tis not that our misfortune should perform this office, but the good fortune of our judgment. I am not to be made to do anything by persecutions and afflictions, but to curse them: that is for people who cannot be roused but by a whip. My reason is much more free in prosperity, and much more distracted, and put to't to digest pains than pleasures: I see best in a clear sky; health admonishes me more cheerfully, and to better purpose, than sickness. I did all that in me lay to

reform and regulate myself from pleasures, at a time when I had health and vigor to enjoy them; I should be ashamed and envious, that the misery and misfortune of my old age should have credit over my good, healthful, sprightly, and vigorous years; and that men should estimate me, not by what I have been, but by what I have ceased to be.

In my opinion, 'tis the happy living, and not (as Antisthenes said) the happy dying, in which human felicity consists. I have not made it my business to make a monstrous addition of a philosopher's tail to the head and body of a libertine; nor would I have this wretched remainder give the lie to the pleasant, sound, and long part of my life: I would present myself uniformly throughout. Were I to live my life over again, I should live it just as I have lived it; I neither complain of the past, nor do I fear the future; and if I am not much deceived, I am the same within that I am without. 'Tis one main obligation I have to my fortune, that the succession of my bodily estate has been carried on according to the natural seasons; I have seen the grass, the blossom, and the fruit; and now see the withering; happily, however, because naturally. I bear the infirmities I have the better, because they came not till I had reason to expect them, and because also they make me with greater pleasure remember that long felicity of my past life. My wisdom may have been just the same in both ages; but it was more active, and of better grace while young and sprightly, than now it is when broken, peevish and uneasy. I repudiate, then, these casual and painful reformations. God must touch our hearts; our consciences must amend of themselves, by the aid of our reason, and not by the decay of our appetites; pleasure is, in itself, neither pale nor discolored, to be discerned by dim and decayed eyes.

We ought to love temperance for itself, and because God has commanded that and chastity; but that which we are reduced to by catarrhs, and for which I am indebted to the stone, is neither chastity nor temperance; a man cannot boast that he despises and resists pleasure, if he cannot see it, if he knows not what it is, and cannot discern its graces, its force, and most alluring beauties; I know both the one and the other, and may therefore the better say it.

But, methinks, our souls, in old age, are subject to more trouble-some maladies and imperfections than in youth; I said the same when young and when I was reproached with the want of a beard; and I say so now that my gray hairs give me some authority. We call the difficulty of our humors and the disrelish of present things wisdom; but, in truth, we do not so much forsake vices as we change them, and, in my opinion, for worse. Besides a foolish and feeble pride, an impertinent prating, froward and insociable humors, superstition, and a ridiculous desire of riches when we have lost the use of them, I find there more envy, injustice and malice. Age im-prints more wrinkles in the mind than it does on the face; and souls are never, or very rarely seen, that in growing old do not smell sour and musty. Man moves all together, both toward his perfec-tion and decay. In observing the wisdom of Socrates, and many circumstances of his condemnation, I should dare to believe, that he in some sort himself purposely, by collusion, contributed to it, seeing that, at the age of seventy years, he might fear to suffer the lofty motions of his mind to be cramped, and his wonted luster obscured. What strange metamorphoses do I see age every day make in many of my acquaintance! 'Tis a potent malady, and that naturally and imperceptibly steals into us; a vast provision of study and great precaution are required to evade the imperfections it loads us with, or at least, to weaken their progress. I find that, notwithstanding all my entrenchments, it gets foot by foot upon me; I make the best resistance I can, but I do not know to what at last it will reduce me. But fall out what will, I am content the world may know, when I am fallen, from what I fell.

XV

UPON SOME VERSES OF VIRGIL

B Y HOW much profitable thoughts are more full and solid, by
so much are they also more cumbersome and heavy: vice,
death, poverty, diseases, are grave and grievous subjects. A man
should have his soul instructed in the means to sustain and contend
with evils, and in the rules of living and believing well; and often
rouse it up, and exercise it in this noble study; but in an ordinary
soul it must be by intervals and with moderation; it will otherwise
grow besotted if continually intent upon it. I found it necessary,
when I was young, to put myself in mind and solicit myself to keep
me to my duty: gayety and health do not, they say, so well agree
with those grave and serious meditations; I am at present in another
state: the conditions of age but too much put me in mind, urge me
to wisdom, and preach to me. From the excess of sprightliness I am
fallen into that of severity, which is much more troublesome: and
for that reason I now and then suffer myself purposely a little to
run into disorder, and occupy my mind in wanton and youthful
thoughts, wherewith it diverts itself. I am of late but too reserved,
too heavy, and too ripe; years every day read to me lectures of
coldness and temperance. This body of mine avoids disorder, and
dreads it; 'tis now my body's turn to guide my mind toward reformation; it governs, in turn, and more rudely and imperiously than
the other; it lets me not an hour alone, sleeping or waking, but is
always preaching to me death, patience, and repentance. I now
defend myself from temperance, as I have formerly done from

pleasure; it draws me too much back, and even to stupidity. Now I will be master of myself, to all intent and purposes; wisdom has its excesses, and has no less need of moderation than folly. Therefore, lest I should wither, dry up, and overcharge myself with prudence, in the intervals and truces my infirmities allow me,

"Mens intenta suis ne siet usque malis."

I gently turn aside, and avert my eyes from the stormy and cloudy sky I have before me, which, thanks be to God I regard without fear, but not without meditation and study, and amuse myself in the remembrance of my better years:

"Animus quo perdidit, optat,
Atque in præterita se totus imagine versat."

Let childhood look forward, and age, backward; is not this the signification of Janus' double face? Let years haul me along if they will, but it shall be backward, as long as my eyes can discern the pleasant season expired, I shall now and then turn them that way; though it escape from my blood and veins, I shall not, however, root the image of it out of my memory:

"Hoc est
Vivere bis, vita posse priore frui."

Plato ordains that old men should be present at the exercises, dances, and sports of young people, that they may rejoice in others for the activity and beauty of body which is no more in themselves, and call to mind the grace and comeliness of that flourishing age; and wills that in these recreations the honor of the prize should be given to that young man who has most diverted the company. I was formerly wont to mark cloudy and gloomy days as extraordinary; these are now my ordinary days; the extraordinary are the clear and bright; I am ready to leap out of my skin for joy, as for an unwonted favor, when nothing happens me. Let me tickle myself, I cannot force a poor smile from this wretched body of mine; I am only merry in conceit and in dreaming, by artifice to divert the melancholy of age; but, in faith, it requires another remedy than

a dream. A weak contest of art against nature. 'Tis great folly to lengthen and anticipate human incommodities, as every one does; I had rather be a less while old than be old before I am really so. I seize on even the least occasions of pleasure I can meet. I know very well, by hearsay, several sorts of prudent pleasures, effectually so, and glorious to boot; but opinion has not power enough over me to give me an appetite to them. I covet not so much to have them magnanimous, magnificent, and pompous, as I do to have them sweet, facile and ready: *"A natura discedimus; populo nos damus, nullius rei bono auctori."* My philosophy is in action, in natural and present practice, very little in fancy; what if I have a mind to play at cob-nut or to whip a top!

> "Non ponebat enim rumores ante salutem."

Pleasure is a quality of very little ambition: it thinks itself rich enough of itself without any addition of repute; and is best pleased where most retired. A young man should be whipped who pretends to a taste in wine and sauces; there was nothing which, at that age, I less valued or knew; now I begin to learn; I am very much ashamed on't; but what should I do? I am more ashamed and vexed at the occasions that put me upon't. 'Tis for us to dote and trifle away the time, and for young men to stand upon their reputation and nice punctilios; they are going toward the world and the world's opinion; we are retiring from it: *"Sibi arma, sibi equos, sibi hastas, sibi clavam, sibi pilam, sibi natationes, et cursus habeant: nobis senibus ex lusionibus multis, talos relinquant et tesseras;"* the laws themselves send us home. I can do no less in favor of this wretched condition into which my age has thrown me, than furnish it with toys to play withal, as they do children; and, in truth, we become such. Both wisdom and folly will have enough to do to support and relieve me by alternate services in this calamity of age:

> "Misce stultitiam consiliis brevem."

I accordingly avoid the lightest punctures; and those that formerly would not have rippled the skin, now pierce me through and

through: my habit of body is now so naturally declining to ill:
"In fragili corpore, odiosa omnis offensio est;"

"Mensque pati durum sustinet ægra nihil."

I have ever been very susceptibly tender as to offenses; I am much
more tender now, and open throughout:

"Et minime vires frangere quassa valent."

My judgment restrains me from kicking against and murmuring
at the inconveniences that nature orders me to endure, but it does
not take away my feeling them: I, who have no other thing in my
aim but to live and be merry, would run from one end of the world
to the other to seek out one good year of pleasant and jocund tranquillity. A melancholic and dull tranquillity may be enough for
me, but it benumbs and stupefies me; I am not contented with it. If
there be any person, any knot of good company in country or city,
in France, or elsewhere, resident, or in motion, who can like my
humor, and whose humors I can like, let them but whistle and I
will run and furnish them with essays in flesh and bone.

Seeing it is the privilege of the mind to rescue itself from old age,
I advise mine to it with all the power I have; let it meanwhile continue green, and flourish if it can, like mistletoe upon a dead tree.
But I fear 'tis a traitor; it has contracted so strict a fraternity with
the body that it leaves me at every turn, to follow that in its need. I
wheedle and deal with it apart in vain; I try to much purpose to
wean it from this correspondence, to much effect quote to it Seneca
and Catullus, and represent to it beautiful ladies and royal
masques: if its companion have the stone, it seems to have it too;
even the faculties that are most peculiarly and properly its own
cannot then perform their functions, but manifestly appear stupefied and asleep; there is no sprightliness in its productions, if there
be not at the same time an equal proportion in the body too.

Our masters are to blame, that in searching out the causes of
the extraordinary emotions of the soul, besides attributing it to a
divine ecstasy, love, martial fierceness, poesy, wine, they have not
also attributed a part to health: a boiling, vigorous, full, and lazy

health, such as formerly the verdure of youth and security, by fits, supplied me withal; that fire of sprightliness and gayety darts into the mind flashes that are lively and bright beyond our natural light, and of all enthusiasms the most jovial, if not the most extravagant.

It is, then, no wonder if a contrary state stupefy and clog my spirit, and produce a contrary effect:

"Ad nullum consurgit opus, cum corpore languet;"

and yet would have me obliged to it for giving, as it wants to make out, much less consent to this stupidity, than is the ordinary case with men of my age. Let us, at least, while we have truce, drive away incommodities and difficulties from our commerce;

"Dum licet, obducta solvatur fronte senectus:"

"*Tetrica sunt amœnanda jocularibus.*" I love a gay and civil wisdom, and fly from all sourness and austerity of manners, all grumness of visage being suspected by me,

"Tristemque vultus tetrici arrogantiam:"

"Et habet tristis quoque turba cinædos."

I am very much of Plato's opinion, who says that facile or harsh humors are great indications of the good or ill disposition of the mind. Socrates had a constant countenance, but serene and smiling; not sourly constant, like the elder Crassus, whom no one ever saw laugh. Virtue is a pleasant and gay quality.

I know very well that few will quarrel with the license of my writings, who have not more to quarrel with in the license of their own thoughts: I conform myself well enough to their inclinations, but I offend their eyes. 'Tis a fine humor to strain the writings of Plato, to wrest his pretended intercourses with Phædo, Dion, Stella, and Archeanassa. "*Non pudeat dicere, quod non pudet sentire.*" I hate a froward and dismal spirit, that slips over all the pleasures of life and seizes and feeds upon misfortunes; like flies, that cannot stick to a smooth and polished body, but fix and repose themselves upon craggy and rough places; and like cupping-glasses, that only suck and attract bad blood.

As to the rest, I have enjoined myself to dare to say all that I dare to do; even thoughts that are not to be published, displease me; the worst of my actions and qualities do not appear to me so evil, as I find it evil and base not to dare to own them. Every one is wary and discreet in confession, but men ought to be so in action; the boldness of doing ill is in some sort compensated and restrained by the boldness of confessing it. Whoever will oblige himself to tell all, should oblige himself to do nothing that he must be forced to conceal. I wish that this excessive license of mine may draw men to freedom, above these timorous and mincing virtues, sprung from our imperfections; and that at the expense of my immoderation, I may reduce them to reason. A man must see and study his vice to correct it; they who conceal it from others, commonly conceal it from themselves; and do not think it close enough, if they themselves see it: they withdraw and disguise it from their own consciences: *"Quare vitia sua nemo confitetur? Quia etiam nunc in illis est; somnium narrare, vigilantis est."* The diseases of the body explain themselves by their increase; we find that to be the gout which we called a rheum or a strain; the diseases of the soul, the greater they are, keep themselves the most obscure; the most sick are the least sensible; therefore it is, that with an unrelenting hand, they must often, in full day, be taken to task, opened, and torn from the hollow of the heart. As in doing well, so in doing ill, the mere confession is sometimes satisfaction. Is there any deformity in doing amiss, that can excuse us from confessing ourselves? It is so great a pain to me to dissemble, that I evade the trust of another's secrets, wanting the courage to disavow my knowledge. I can keep silent; but deny I cannot without the greatest trouble and violence to myself imaginable: to be very secret, a man must be so by nature not by obligation. 'Tis little worth, in the service of a prince, to be secret, if a man be not a liar to boot. If he who asked Thales the Milesian, whether he ought solemnly to deny that he had committed adultery, had applied himself to me, I should have told him, that he ought not to do it; for I look upon lying as a worse fault than the other. Thales advised him quite contrary, bidding him swear, to shield the greater fault by the less: nevertheless, this counsel was

not so much an election, as a multiplication, of vice. Upon which, let us say this by-the-by, that we deal well with a man of conscience, when we propose to him some difficulty in counterpoise of the vice; but when we shut him up between two vices, he is put to a hard choice: as Origen was, either to idolatrize, or to suffer himself to be carnally abused by a great Ethiopian slave they brought to him. He submitted to the first condition, and wrongly people say. And yet those women of our times are not much out, according to their error, who protest they had rather burden their consciences with ten men than one mass.

If it be indiscretion so to publish one's errors, yet there is no great danger that it pass into example and custom; for Aristo said, that the winds men most fear, are those that lay them open. We must tuck up this ridiculous rag that hides our manners: they send their consciences to the stews, and keep a starched countenance: even traitors and assassins espouse the laws of ceremony and there fix their duty. So that neither can injustice complain of incivility nor malice of indiscretion. 'Tis pity but a bad man should be a fool to boot and that outward decency should palliate his vice: this rough-cast only appertains to a good and sound wall, that deserves to be preserved and whited.

In favor of the Huguenots, who condemn our auricular and private confession, I confess myself in public, religiously and purely: St. Augustin, Origen and Hippocrates, have published the errors of their opinions; I, moreover, of my manners. I am greedy of making myself known, and I care not to how many, provided it be truly; or to say better, I hunger for nothing, but I mortally hate to be mistaken by those who come to learn my name. He who does all things for honor and glory, what can he think to gain by showing himself to the world in a visor and by concealing his true being from the people? Praise a humpback for his stature, he has reason to take it for an affront; if you are a coward, and men commend you for your valor, is it of you they speak? They take you for another. I should like him as well, who glorifies himself in the compliments and congees that are made him as if he were master of the company, when he is one of the least of the train. Archelaus, king

of Macedon, walking along the street, somebody threw water on his head, which they who were with him said he ought to punish: "Ay but," said he, "whoever it was, he did not throw the water upon me, but upon him whom he took me to be." Socrates being told that people spoke ill of him, "Not at all," said he, "there is nothing in me of what they say." For my part, if any one should recommend me as a good pilot, as being very modest, or very chaste, I should owe him no thanks; and so, whoever should call me traitor, robber or drunkard, I should be as little concerned. They who do not rightly know themselves, may feed themselves with false approbations; not I, who see myself and who examine myself even to my very bowels, and who very well know what is my due. I am content to be less commended, provided I am better known. I may be reputed a wise man in such a sort of wisdom as I take to be folly. I am vexed that my Essays only serve the ladies for a common movable, a book to lay in the parlor window; this chapter shall prefer me to the closet. I love to traffic with them a little in private; public conversation is without favor and without savor. In farewells, we oftener than not heat our affections toward the things we take leave of; I take my last leave of the pleasures of this world; these are our last embraces.

But to come to my subject: what has rendered the act of generation, an act so natural, so necessary, and so just, a thing not to be spoken of without blushing and to be excluded from all serious and regular discourse? We boldly pronounce, kill, rob, betray, but the other we dare only to mutter between the teeth. Is it to say, the less we expend in words, we may pay so much the more in thinking? For it is certain that the words least in use, most seldom written, and best kept in, are the best and most generally known; no age, no manners, are ignorant of them, no more than the word bread: they imprint themselves in every one, without being expressed, without voice, and without figure; and the sex that most practices it, is bound to say least of it. 'Tis an act that we have placed in the franchise of silence, from which to take it is a crime, even to accuse and judge it; neither dare we reprehend it but by periphrasis and picture. A great favor to a criminal to be so execrable that justice

thinks it unjust to touch and see him; free and safe by the benefit
of the severity of his condemnation. Is it not here as in matter of
books, that sell better and become more public for being suppressed? For my part, I will take Aristotle at his word who says,
that "Bashfulness is an ornament to youth, but a reproach to old
age." These verses are preached in the ancient school, a school that
I much more adhere to than the modern: its virtues appear to me
to be greater and the vices less:

> "Ceux qui par trop fuyant Venus estrivent,
>   Faillent autant que ceulx qui trop la suyvent."

"Tu, dea, tu rerum naturam sola gubernas,
Nec sine te quicquam dias in luminis oras
Exoritur, neque fit lætum, nec amabile quicquam."

I know not who could set Pallas and the Muses at variance with Venus, and make them cold toward Love: but I see no deities so well met, or that are more indebted to one another. Who will deprive the Muses of amorous imaginations, will rob them of the best entertainment they have, and of the noblest matter of their work: and who will make Love lose the communication and service of poesy, will disarm him of his best weapons: by this means, they charge the god of familiarity and good will, and the protecting goddesses of humanity and justice, with the vice of ingratitude and unthankfulness. I have not been so long cashiered from the state and service of this god, that my memory is not still perfect in his force and value;

"Agnosco veteris vestigia flammæ;"

There are yet some remains of heat and emotion after the fever;

"Nec mihi deficiat calor hic, hiemantibus annis!"

Withered and drooping as I am, I feel yet some remains of that past ardor:

"Qual l'alto Egeo, perche Aquilone o Noto
Cessi, che tutto prima il volse e scosse,
Non's accheta egli pero; ma'l suono e'l moto
Ritien del l' onde anco agitate e grosse:"

but from what I understand of it, the force and power of this god are more lively and animated in the picture of poesy than in their own essence,

"Et versus digitos habet:"

it has, I know not what kind of air more amorous than love itself. Venus is not so beautiful, naked, alive, and panting, as she is here in Virgil:

"Dixerat; et niveis hinc atque hinc diva lacertis
Cunctantem amplexu molli fovet.   Ille repente
Accepit solitam flammam; notusque medullas
Intravit calor, et labefacta per ossa cucurrit:

> Non secus atque olim tonitru cum rupta corusco
> Ignea rima micans percurrit lumine nimbos.
> . . Ea verba loquutus,
> Optatos dedit amplexus; placidumque petivit
> Conjugis infusus gremio per membra soporem."

All that I find fault with in considering it is, that he has represented her a little too passionate for a married Venus; in this discreet kind of coupling, the appetite is not usually so wanton, but more grave and dull. Love hates that people should hold of any but itself, and goes but faintly to work in familiarities derived from any other title, as marriage is: alliance, dowry, therein sway by reason, as much or more than grace and beauty. Men do not marry for themselves, let them say what they will; they marry as much or more for their posterity and family; the custom and interest of marriage concern our race much more than us; and therefore it is, that I like to have a match carried on by a third hand rather than a man's own, and by another man's liking than that of the party himself; and how much is all this opposite to the conventions of love? And also it is a kind of incest to employ in this venerable and sacred alliance, the heat and extravagance of amorous license, as I think I have said elsewhere. A man, says Aristotle, must approach his wife with prudence and temperance, lest in dealing too lasciviously with her, the extreme pleasure make her exceed the bounds of reason. What he says upon the account of conscience, the physicians say upon the account of health: "that a pleasure excessively lascivious, voluptuous, and frequent, makes the seed too hot, and hinders conception:" 'tis said, elsewhere, that to a languishing congression, as this naturally is, to supply it with a due and fruitful heat, a man must do it but seldom, and by notable intermissions,

> "Quo rapiat sitiens Venerem, interiusque recondat."

I see no marriages where the conjugal intelligence sooner fails, than those that we contract upon the account of beauty and amorous desires; there should be more solid and constant foundation, and they should proceed with greater circumspection; this furious ardor is worth nothing.

They who think they honor marriage by joining love to it, do, methinks, like those who, to favor virtue, hold that nobility is nothing else but virtue. They are indeed things that have some relation to one another, but there is a great deal of difference; we should not so mix their names and titles; 'tis a wrong to them both, so to confound them. Nobility is a brave quality, and with good reason introduced; but forasmuch as 'tis a quality depending upon others, and may happen in a vicious person, in himself nothing, 'tis in estimate infinitely below virtue: 'tis a virtue, if it be one, that is artificial and apparent, depending upon time and fortune; various in form, according to the country; living and mortal; without birth, as the river Nile; genealogical and common; of succession and similitude; drawn by consequence, and a very weak one. Knowledge, strength, goodness, beauty, riches, and all other qualities, fall into communication and commerce, but this is consummated in itself, and of no use to the service of others. There was proposed to one of our kings the choice of two concurrents for the same command, of whom one was a gentleman, the other not; he ordered, that without respect to quality, they should choose him who had the most merit; but where the worth of the competitors should appear to be entirely equal, they should have respect to birth: this was justly to give it its rank. A young man unknown, coming to Antigonus to make suit for his father's command, a valiant man, lately dead: "Friend," said he, "in such preferments as these, I have not so much regard to the nobility of my soldiers as to their prowess." And, indeed, it ought not to go as it did with the officers of the kings of Sparta, trumpeters, fiddlers, cooks, the children of whom always succeeded to their places, how ignorant soever, and were preferred before the most experienced in the trade. They of Calicut make of nobles a sort of persons above human: they are interdicted marriage and all but warlike employments: they may have of concubines their fill, and the women as many lovers, without being jealous of one another; but 'tis a capital and irremissible crime to couple with a person of meaner condition than themselves; and they think themselves polluted, if they have but touched one in walking along; and supposing their nobility to be marvelously

interested and injured in it, kill such as only approach a little too near them: insomuch that the ignoble are obliged to cry out as they walk, like the gondoliers of Venice, at the turnings of streets for fear of jostling; and the nobles command them to step aside to what part they please: by which means these avoid what they repute a perpetual ignominy, and those certain death. No time, no favor of the prince, no office, or virtue, or riches, can ever prevail to make a plebeian become noble; to which this custom contributes, that marriages are interdicted between different trades; the daughter of a shoemaker is not permitted to marry a carpenter; and the parents are obliged to train up their children precisely in their own callings, and not put them to any other trade; by which means the distinction and continuance of their position is maintained.

A good marriage, if there be any such, rejects the company and conditions of love, and tries to represent those of friendship. 'Tis a sweet society of life, full of constancy, trust, and an infinite number of useful and solid services and mutual obligations; which any woman who has a right taste,

"Optato quam junxit lumine tæda."

would be loath to serve her husband in quality of a mistress. If she be lodged in his affection as a wife, she is more honorably and securely placed. When he purports to be in love with another, and works all he can to obtain his desire, let any one but ask him, on which he had rather a disgrace should fall, his wife or his mistress, which of their misfortunes would most afflict him, and to which of them he wishes the most grandeur, the answer to these questions is out of dispute in a sound marriage.

And that so few are observed to be happy, is a token of its price and value. If well formed and rightly taken, 'tis the best of all human societies; we cannot live without it, and yet we do nothing but decry it. It happens, as with cages, the birds without despair to get in, and those within despair of getting out. Socrates, being asked, whether it was more commodious to take a wife, or not; "Let a man take which course he will," said he, "he will be sure to repent." 'Tis a contract to which the common saying, *"Homo*

homini, aut deus, aut lupus," may very fitly be applied; there must
be a concurrence of many qualities in the construction. It is found
nowadays more convenient for simple and plebeian souls, where
delights, curiosity, and idleness do not so much disturb it; but
extravagant humors, such as mine, that hate all sorts of obligation
and restraint, are not so proper for it:

> "Et mihi dulce magis resoluto vivere collo."

Might I have had my own will, I would not have married Wisdom
herself, if she would have had me. But 'tis to much purpose to evade
it; the common custom and usance of life will have it so. The most
of my actions are guided by example, not by choice, and yet I did
not go to it of my own voluntary motion; I was led and drawn to
it by extrinsic occasions, for not only things that are incommodious
in themselves, but also things however ugly, vicious, and to be
avoided, may be rendered acceptable by some condition or accident; so unsteady and vain is all human resolution! and I was persuaded to it, when worse prepared, and less tractable than I am
at present, that I have tried what it is: and as great a libertine as I
am taken to be, I have in truth more strictly observed the laws of
marriage, than I either promised or expected. 'Tis in vain to kick,
when a man has once put on his fetters: a man must prudently manage his liberty; but having once submitted to obligation, he must
confine himself within the laws of common duty, at least, do what
he can toward it. They who engage in this contract, with a design
to carry themselves in it with hatred and contempt, do an unjust and
inconvenient thing; and the fine rule that I hear pass from hand to
hand among the women, as a sacred oracle,

> "Sers ton mary comme ton maistre,
> Et t'en garde comme d'un traistre,"

which is to say, comport thyself toward him with a dissembled,
inimical, and distrustful reverence (a cry of war and defiance), is
equally injurious and hard. I am too mild for such rugged designs;
to say the truth, I am not arrived to that perfection of ability and
refinement of wit, to confound reason with injustice, and to laugh
at all rule and order that does not please my palate; because I hate

1946

superstition, I do not presently run into the contrary extreme of irreligion. If a man does not always perform his duty, he ought at least to love and acknowledge it; 'tis treachery to marry without espousing.

Let us proceed.

Our poet represents a marriage happy in good intelligence, wherein nevertheless there is not much loyalty. Does he mean, that it is not impossible but a woman may give the reins to her own passion, and yield to the importunities of love, and yet reserve some duty toward marriage, and that it may be hurt, without being totally broken? A serving man may cheat his master, whom nevertheless he does not hate. Beauty, opportunity, and destiny (for destiny has also a hand in't),

> "Fatum est in partibus illis
> Quas sinus abscondit; nam, si tibi sidera cessent,
> Nil faciet longi mensura incognita nervi;"

have attached her to a stranger; though not so wholly, peradventure, but that she may have some remains of kindness for her husband. They are two designs, that have several paths leading to them, without being confounded with one another; a woman may yield to a man she would by no means have married, not only for the condition of his fortune, but for those also of his person. Few men have made a wife of a mistress, who have not repented it. And even in the other world, what an unhappy life does Jupiter lead with his, whom he had first enjoyed as a mistress? 'Tis, as the proverb runs, to befoul a basket and then put it upon one's head. I have in my time, in a good family, seen love shamefully and dishonestly cured by marriage; the considerations are widely different. We love at once, without any tie, two things contrary in themselves.

Socrates was wont to say, that the city of Athens pleased as ladies do whom men court for love; every one loved to come thither to take a turn, and pass away his time; but no one liked it so well as to espouse it, that is, to inhabit there, and to make it his constant residence. I have been vexed to see husbands hate their wives only

because they themselves do them wrong; we should not, at all events, methinks, love them the less for our own faults; they should at least upon the account of repentance and compassion, be dearer to us.

They are different ends, he says, and yet in some sort compatible; marriage has utility, justice, honor, and constancy for its share; a flat, but more universal pleasure; love founds itself wholly upon pleasure, and, indeed, has it more full, lively and sharp; a pleasure inflamed by difficulty; there must be in it sting and smart; 'tis no longer love, if without darts and fire. The bounty of ladies is too profuse in marriage, and dulls the point of affection and desire; to evade which inconvenience, do but observe what pains Lycurgus and Plato take in their laws.

Women are not to blame at all, when they refuse the rules of life that are introduced into the world, forasmuch as the men made them without their consent. There is naturally contention and brawling between them and us; and the strictest friendship we have with them, is yet mixed with tumult and tempest. In the opinion of our author, we deal inconsiderately with them in this; after we have discovered, that they are, without comparison, more able and ardent in the practice of love than we, and that the old priest testified as much, who had been one while a man, and then a woman,

"Venus huic erat utraque nota:"

and moreover, that we have learned from their own mouths the proof that, in several ages, was made by an emperor and empress of Rome, both famous for ability in that affair! for he in one night deflowered ten Sarmatian virgins who were his captives: but she had five-and-twenty bouts in one night, changing her man according to her need and liking,

"Adhuc ardens rigidæ tentigine vulvæ:
Et lassata viris, nondum satiata, recessit;"

and that upon the dispute which happened in Catalonia, wherein a wife complaining of her husband's too frequent addresses to her, not so much, as I conceive, that she was incommodated by it (for I believe no miracles out of religion) as under this pretense, to

curtail and curb in this, which is the fundamental act of marriage, the authority of husbands over their wives, and to show that their frowardness and malignity go beyond the nuptial bed, and spurn under foot even the graces and sweets of Venus; the husband, a man truly brutish and unnatural, replied that even on fasting days he could not subsist with less than ten courses: whereupon came out that notable sentence of the queen of Arragon, by which, after mature deliberation of her council, this good queen, to give a rule and example to all succeeding ages of the moderation required in a just marriage, set down six times a day as a legitimate and necessary stint; surrendering and quitting a great deal of the needs and desires of her sex, that she might, she said, establish an easy, and consequently, a permanent and immutable rule. Hereupon the doctors cry out; what must the female appetite and concupiscence be, when their reason, their reformation and virtue, are taxed at such a rate? considering the divers judgments of our appetites; for Solon, master of the law school, taxes us at but three a month, that men may not foil in point of conjugal frequentation: after having, I say, believed and preached all this, we go and enjoin them continency for their particular share, and upon the extremest penalties.

There is no passion so hard to contend with as this, which we would have them only resist, not simply as an ordinary vice, but as an execrable abomination, worse than irreligion and parricide; while we, at the same time, go to't without offense or reproach. Even those among us, who have tried the experiment, have sufficiently confessed what difficulty, or rather impossibility, they have found by material remedies to subdue, weaken, and cool the body. We, on the contrary, would have them at once sound, vigorous, plump, high-fed, and chaste; that is to say, both hot and cold, for the marriage, which we tell them is to keep them from burning, is but small refreshment to them as we order the matter. If they take one whose vigorous age is yet boiling, he will be proud to make it known elsewhere;

"Sit tandem pudor; aut eamus in jus;
Multis mentula millibus redempta,
Non est hæ tua, Basse; vendidis ti;"

Polemon the philosopher was justly by his wife brought before the judge for sowing in a barren field the seed that was due to one that was fruitful: if, on the other hand, they take a decayed fellow, they are in a worse condition in marriage than either maids or widows. We think them well provided for, because they have a man to lie with, as the Romans concluded Clodia Læta, a vestal nun, violated, because Caligula had approached her, though it was declared he did no more but approach her: but, on the contrary, we by that increase their necessity, forasmuch as the touch and company of any man whatever rouses their desires, that in solitude would be more quiet. And to the end 'tis likely, that they might render their chastity more meritorious by this circumstance and consideration, Boleslaus and Kinge, his wife, king and queen of Poland, vowed it by mutual consent, being in bed together, on their very wedding day, and kept their vow in spite of all matrimonial conveniences.

We train them up from their infancy to the traffic of love; their grace, dressing, knowledge, language, and whole instruction tend that way: their governesses imprint nothing in them but the idea of love, if for nothing else but by continually representing it to them, to give them a distaste for it. My daughter, the only child I have, is now of an age that forward young women are allowed to be married at; she is of a slow, thin, and tender complexion, and has accordingly been brought up by her mother after a retired and particular manner, so that she but now begins to be weaned from her childish simplicity. She was one day reading before me in a French book, where she happened to meet the word *fouteau,* the name of a tree very well known; the woman to whose conduct she is committed stopped her short a little roughly, and made her skip over that dangerous step. I let her alone, not to trouble their rules, for I never concern myself in that sort of government; feminine polity has a mysterious procedure; we must leave it to them; but if I am not mistaken, the commerce of twenty lackeys could not, in six months' time, have so imprinted in her fancy the meaning, usage, and all the consequences of the sound of these wicked

syllables, as this good old woman did by reprimand and interdiction.

"Motus doceri gaudet Ionicos
  Matura virgo, et frangitur artubus
Jam nunc, et incestos amores
  De tenero meditatur ungui."

Let them but give themselves the rein a little, let them but enter
into liberty of discourse, we are but children to them in this science.
Hear them but describe our pursuits and conversation, they will
very well make you understand that we bring them nothing they
have not known before, and digested without our help. Is it perhaps, as Plato says, that they have formerly been debauched young
fellows? I happened one day to be in a place where I could hear
some of their talk without suspicion; I am sorry I cannot repeat
it. By'r lady, said I, we had need go study the phrases of Amadis,
and the tales of Boccaccio and Aretin, to be able to discourse with
them: we employ our time to much purpose indeed. There is neither
word, example, nor step they are not more perfect in than our
books; 'tis a discipline that springs with their blood,

"Et mentem ipsa Venus dedit,"

which these good instructors, nature, youth, and health are continually inspiring them with; they need not learn, they breed it:

"Nec tantum niveo gavisa est ulla columbo,
  Compar, vel si quid dicitur improbius,
Oscula mordenti semper decerpere rostro,
  Quantum præcipue multivola est mulier."

So that if the natural violence of their desire were not a little
restrained by fear and honor, which were wisely contrived for
them, we should be all shamed. All the motions in the world resolve
into and tend to this conjunction; 'tis a matter infused throughout:
'tis a center to which all things are directed. We yet see the edicts of
the old and wise Rome, made for the service of love; and the precepts of Socrates for the instruction of courtesans:

"Necnon libelli Stoici, inter sericos
  Jacere pulvillos amant:"

[229]

Zeno, among his laws, also regulated the motions to be observed in getting a maidenhood. What was the philosopher Strato's book of "Carnal Conjunction?" And what did Theophrastus treat of in those he intituled, the one "The Lover," and the other "Of Love?" Of what Aristippus in his "Of Former Delights?" What do the so long and lively description in Plato of the loves of his time pretend to? and the book called "The Lover," of Demetrius Phalereus? and Clinias, or the Ravished Lover, of Heralides, and that of Antisthenes, "Of Getting Children," or, "Of Weddings," and the other, "Of the Master or the Lover?" And that of Aristo: "Of Amorous Exercises?" What those of Cleanthes: one, "Of Love," the other, "Of the Art of Loving?" The amorous dialogues of Sphæreus? and the fable of Jupiter and Juno, of Chrysippus, impudent beyond all toleration? And his fifty so lascivious epistles? I will let alone the writings of the philosophers of the Epicurean sect, protectress of voluptuousness. Fifty deities were, in time past, assigned to this office; and there have been nations where, to assuage the lust of those who came to their devotion, they kept men and women in their temples for the worshippers to lie with; and it was an act of ceremony to do this before they went to prayers: *"Nimirum propter continentiam incontineniia necessatia est; incendium ignibus extinguiter."*

In the greatest part of the world, that member of our body was deified; in the same province, some flayed off the skin to offer and consecrate a piece; others offered and consecrated their seed. In another, the young men publicly cut through betwixt the skin and the flesh of that part in several places, and thrust pieces of wood into the openings as long and thick as they would receive; and of these pieces of wood afterward made a fire as an offering to their gods; and were reputed neither vigorous nor chaste, if by the force of that cruel pain, they seemed to be at all dismayed. Elsewhere the most sacred magistrate was reverenced and acknowledged by that member: and in several ceremonies the effigy of it was carried in pomp to the honor of various divinities. The Egyptian ladies, in their Bacchanalia, each carried one finely-carved of wood about their necks, as large and heavy as she could so carry it; besides

which, the statue of their god presented one, which in greatness surpassed all the rest of his body. The married women, near the place where I live, make of their kerchiefs the figure of one upon their foreheads, to glorify themselves in the enjoyment they have of it; and coming to be widows, they throw it behind, and cover it with their headcloths. The most modest matrons of Rome thought it an honor to offer flowers and garlands to the god Priapus; and they made the virgins, at the time of their espousals, sit upon his shameful parts. And I know not whether I have not in my time seen some air of like devotion. What was the meaning of that ridiculous thing our forefathers wore on the forepart of their breeches, and that is still worn by the Swiss? To what end do we make a show of our implements in figure under our gaskins, and often, which is worse, above their natural size, by falsehood and imposture? I have half a mind to believe that this sort of vestment was invented in the better and more conscientious ages, that the world might not be deceived, and that every one should give a public account of his proportions; the simple nations wear them yet, and near about the real size. In those days, the tailor took measure of it, as the shoemaker does now of a man's foot. That good man, who, when I was young, gelded so many noble and ancient statues in his great city, that they might not corrupt the sight of the ladies, according to the advice of this other ancient worthy, *"Flagitii principium est, nudare inter cives corpora,"* should have called to mind, that, as in the mysteries of the Bona Dea all masculine appearance was excluded, he did nothing, if he did not geld horses and asses, in short, all nature:

> "Omne adeo genus in terris, hominumque, ferarumque,
> Et genus æquoreum, pecudes, pictæque volucres,
> In furias ignemque ruunt."

The gods, says Plato, have given us one disobedient and unruly member that, like a furious animal, attempts, by the violence of its appetite, to subject all things to it; and so they have given to women one like a greedy and ravenous animal, which, if it be refused food in season, grows wild, impatient of delay, and infusing

its rage into their bodies, stops the passages, and hinders respiration, causing a thousand ills, till, having imbibed the fruit of the common thirst, it has plentifully bedewed the bottom of their matrix. Now my legislator should also have considered, that, peradventure, it were a chaster and more fruitful usage to let them know the fact as it is betimes, than permit them to guess according to the liberty and heat of their own fancy; instead of the real parts they substitute, through hope and desire, others that are three times more extravagant; and a certain friend of mine lost himself by producing his in place and time when the opportunity was not present to put them to their more serious use. What mischief do not those pictures of prodigious dimension do that the boys make upon the staircases and galleries of the royal houses? they give the ladies a cruel contempt of our natural furniture. And what do we know but that Plato, after other well-instituted republics, ordered that the men and women, old and young, should expose themselves naked to the view of one another, in his gymnastic exercises, upon that very account? The Indian women who see the men stark naked, have at least cooled the sense of seeing. And let the women of the kingdom of Pegu say what they will, who below the waist have nothing to cover them but a cloth slit before, and so straight, that what decency and modesty soever they pretend by it, at every step all is to be seen, that it is an invention to allure the men to them, and to divert them from boys, to whom that nation is generally inclined; yet peradventure, they lose more by it than they get, and one may venture to say, that an entire appetite is more sharp than one already half-glutted by the eyes. Livia was wont to say, that to a virtuous woman a naked man was but a statue. The Lacedæmonian woman, more virgins when wives than our daughters are, saw every day the young men of their city stripped naked in their exercises, themselves little heeding to cover their thighs in walking, believing themselves, says Plato, sufficiently covered by their virtue without any other robe. But those of whom St. Augustine speaks, have given nudity a wonderful power of temptation, who have made it a doubt, whether women at the day of judgment shall rise again in their own sex, and not rather in ours, for fear of tempting us again in that

holy state. In brief, we allure and flesh them by all sorts of ways; wo incessantly heat and stir up their imagination, and then we find fault. Let us confess the truth; there is scarce one of us who does not more apprehend the shame that accrues to him by the vices of his wife than by his own, and that is not more solicitous (a wonderful charity) of the conscience of his virtuous wife than of his own; who had not rather commit theft and sacrilege, and that his wife was a murderess and a heretic, than that she should not be more chaste than her husband; an unjust estimate of vices. Both we and they are capable of a thousand corruptions more prejudicial and unnatural than lust; but we weigh vices, not according to nature, but according to our interest; by which means they take so many unequal forms.

The austerity of our decrees renders the application of women to this vice more violent and vicious than its own condition needs, and engages it in consequences worse than their cause; they will readily offer to go to the law courts to seek for gain, and to the wars to get reputation, rather than, in the midst of ease and delights, to have to keep so difficult a guard. Do not they very well see that there is neither merchant nor soldier who will not leave his business to run after this sport, or the porter or cobbler, toiled and tired out as they are with labor and hunger?

> "Num tu, quæ tenuit dives Achæmenes,
> Aut pinguis Phrygiæ Mygdonias opes,
> Permutare velis crine Licymniæ,
> Plenas aut Arabum domos,
> Dum fragrantia detorquet ad oscula
> Cervicem, aut facili sævitia negat,
> Quæ poscente magis gaudeat eripi,
> Interdum rapere occupet?"

I do not know whether the exploits of Alexander and Cæsar really surpass the resolution of a beautiful young woman, bred up after our fashion in the light and commerce of the world, assailed by so many contrary examples, and yet keeping herself entire in the midst of a thousand continual and powerful solicitations. There is no doing more difficult than that not doing, nor more active: I hold

it more easy to carry a suit of armor all the days of one's life than
a maidenhood; and the vow of virginity of all others is the most
noble, as being the hardest to keep: *"Diaboli virtus in lumbis est,"*
says St. Jerome. We have doubtless, resigned to the ladies the most
difficult and most vigorous of all human endeavors, and let us
resign to them the glory too. This ought to encourage them to be
obstinate in it; 'tis a brave thing for them to defy us, and to spurn
under foot that vain pre-eminence of valor and virtue that we pretend to have over them; they will find, if they do but observe it,
that they will not only be much more esteemed for it but also much
more beloved. A gallant man does not give over his pursuit for
being refused, provided it be a refusal of chastity, and not of
choice; we may swear, threaten, and complain to much purpose;
we therein do but lie, for we love them all the better: there is no
allurement like modesty, if it be not rude and crabbed. 'Tis stupidity and meanness to be obstinate against hatred and disdain;
but against a virtuous and constant resolution, mixed with good
will, 'tis the exercise of a noble and generous soul. They may
acknowledge our service to a certain degree, and give us civilly
to understand that they disdain us not; for the law that enjoins
them to abominate us because we adore them, and to hate us
because we love them, is certainly very cruel, if but for the difficulty of it. Why should they not give ear to our offers and requests,
so long as they are kept within the bounds of modesty? wherefore
should we fancy them to have other thoughts within, and to be
worse than they seem? A queen of our time ingeniously said, "that
to refuse these courtesies is a testimony of weakness in women and
a self-accusation of facility, and that a lady could not boast of her
chastity who was never tempted." The limits of honor are not cut
so short; they may give themselves a little rein, and relax a little
without being faulty: there lies on the frontier some space free,
indifferent and neuter. He that has beaten and pursued her into her
fort is a strange fellow if he be not satisfied with his fortune: the
price of the conquest is considered by the difficulty. Would you
know what impression your service and merit have made in her
heart? Judge of it by her behavior. Some may grant more, who do

not grant so much. The obligation of a benefit wholly relates to the good will of those who confer it: the other coincident circumstances are dumb, dead, and casual; it costs her dearer to grant you that little, than it would do her companion to grant all. If in anything rarity give estimation, it ought especially in this: do not consider how little it is that is given, but how few have it to give; the value of money alters according to the coinage and stamp of the place. Whatever the spite and indiscretion of some may make them say in the excess of their discontent, virtue and truth will in time recover all the advantage. I have known some whose reputation has for a great while suffered under slander, who have afterward been restored to the world's universal approbation by their mere constancy without care or artifice; every one repents, and gives himself the lie for what he has believed and said; and from girls a little suspected they have been afterward advanced to the first rank among the ladies of honor. Somebody told Plato that all the world spoke ill of him. "Let them talk," said he, "I will live so as to make them change their note." Besides the fear of God, and the value of so rare a glory, which ought to make them look to themselves, the corruption of the age we live in compels them to it; and if I were they, there is nothing I would not rather do than intrust my reputation in so dangerous hands. In my time the pleasure of telling (a pleasure little inferior to that of doing) was not permitted but to those who had some faithful and only friend; but now the ordinary discourse and common table-talk is nothing but boasts of favors received and the secret liberality of ladies. In earnest, 'tis too abject, too much meanness of spirit, in men to suffer such ungrateful, indiscreet, and giddy-headed people so to persecute, forage, and rifle those tender and charming favors.

This our immoderate and illegitimate exasperation against this vice springs from the most vain and turbulent disease that afflicts human minds, which is jealousy;

"Quis vetat apposito lumen de lumine sumi?
Dent licet assidue, nil tamen inde perit;"

she, and envy, her sister, seem to me to be the most foolish of the whole troop. As to the last, I can say little about it; 'tis a passion that, though said to be so mighty and powerful, had never to do with me. As to the other, I know it by sight, and that's all. Beasts feel it; the shepherd Cratis, having fallen in love with a she-goat, the he-goat, out of jealousy, came to butt him as he lay asleep, and beat out his brains. We have raised this fever to a greater excess by the examples of some barbarous nations; the best disciplined have been touched with it, and 'tis reason, but not transported:

> "Ense maritali nemo confossus adulter
> Purpureo Stygias sanguine tinxit aquas:"

Lucullus, Cæsar, Pompey, Antony, Cato, and other brave men were cuckolds, and knew it, without making any bustle about it; there was in those days but one coxcomb, Lepidus, that died for grief that his wife had used him so.

> "Ah! tum te miserum malique fati,
> Quem attractis pedibus, patente porta,
> Percurrent raphanique mugilesque."

and the god of our poet, when he surprised one of his companions with his wife, satisfied himself by putting them to shame only,

> "Atque aliquis de dis non tristibus optat
> Sic fieri turpis:"

and nevertheless took anger at the lukewarm embraces she gave him, complaining that upon that account she was grown jealous of his affection:

> "Quid causas petis ex alto? fiducia cessit
> Quo tibi, diva, mei?"

nay, she entreats arms for a bastard of hers,

> "Arma rogo genitrix nato,"

which are freely granted; and Vulcan speaks honorably of Æneas,

> "Arma acri facienda viro,"

with in truth, a more than human humanity. And I am willing to leave this excess of kindness to the gods:

> "Nec divis homines componier æquum est."

As to the confusion of children, besides that the gravest legislators ordain and affect it in their republics, it touches not the women, where this passion is, I know not how, much better seated:

> "Sæpe etiam Juno, maxima cœlicoluam,
> Conjugis in culpa flagravit quotidiana."

When jealousy seizes these poor souls, weak and incapable of resistance, 'tis pity to see how miserably it torments and tyrannizes over them; it insinuates itself into them under the title of friendship, but after it has once possessed them, the same causes that served for a foundation of good will serve them for a foundation of mortal hatred. 'Tis, of all the diseases of the mind, that which the most things serve for aliment, and the fewest for remedy: the virtue, health, merit, reputation of the husband are incendiaries of their fury and ill will:

> "Nullæ sunt inimicitiæ, nisi amoris, acerbæ."

This fever defaces and corrupts all they have of beautiful and good besides; and there is no action of a jealous woman, let her be how chaste and how good a housewife soever, that does not relish of anger and wrangling: 'tis a furious agitation, that rebounds them to an extremity quite contrary to its cause. This was very manifest in one Octavius at Rome, who, having lain with Pontia Posthumia, found his love so much augmented by fruition, that he solicited with all importunity to marry her, which seeing he could not persuade her to, this excessive affection precipitated him to the effects of the most cruel and mortal hatred, for he killed her. In like manner, the ordinary symptoms of this other amorous disease are intestine hatreds, private conspiracies, and cabals,

> "Notumque furens quid famina possit,"

and a rage which so much the more frets itself, as it is compelled to excuse itself by a pretense of good will.

Now, the duty of chastity is of a vast extent; is it their will that we would have them restrain? That is a very supple and active thing; a thing very nimble, to be stayed. How? if dreams sometimes engage them so far that they cannot deny them: it is not in them, nor, peradventure, in chastity itself, seeing that is a female, to defend itself from lust and desire. If we are only to trust to their will, what a case are we in, then? Do but imagine what crowding there would be among men in pursuance of the privilege to run full speed, without tongue or eyes, into every woman's arms who would accept them. The Scythian women put out the eyes of all their slaves and prisoners of war, that they might have their pleasure of them, and they never the wiser. Oh, the furious advantage of opportunity! Should any one ask me, what was the first thing to be considered in love matters, I should answer, that it was how to take a fitting time; and so the second; and so the third—'tis a point that can do everything. I have sometimes wanted fortune, but I have also sometimes been wanting to myself in matters of attempt. There is greater temerity required in this age of ours, which our young men excuse, under the name of heat; but should women examine it more strictly, they would find that it rather proceeds from contempt. I was always superstitiously afraid of giving offense, and have ever had a great respect for her I loved: besides, he who in this traffic takes away the reverence, defaces at the same time the luster. I would in this affair have a man a little play the child, the timorous, and the servant. If not altogether in this, I have in other things some air of the foolish bashfulness whereof Plutarch makes mention; and the course of my life has been divers ways hurt and blemished with it; a quality very ill suiting my universal form: and, indeed, what are we but sedition and discrepancy? I am as much out of countenance to be denied as I am to deny; and it so much troubles me to be troublesome to others, that on occasions where duty compels me to try the good will of any one in a thing that is doubtful and that will be chargeable to him, I do it very faintly, and very

much against my will: but if it be for my own particular (whatever
Homer truly says, that modesty is a foolish virtue in an indigent
person), I commonly commit it to a third person to blush for me,
and deny those who employ me with the same difficulty: so that
it has sometimes befallen me to have had a mind to deny when I
had not the power to do it.

'Tis folly, then to attempt to bridle in women a desire that is so
powerful in them, and so natural to them. And when I hear them
brag of having so maidenly and so temperate a will, I laugh at
them: they retire too far back. If it be an old toothless trot, or a
young dry consumptive thing, though it be not altogether to be
believed, at least they may say it with more similitude of truth.
But they who still move and breathe, talk at that ridiculous rate to
their own prejudice, by reason that inconsiderate excuses are a
kind of self-accusation; like a gentleman, a neighbor of mine,
suspected to be insufficient,

> "Languidior tenera cui pendens sicula beta,
>   Nunquam se mediam sustulit ad tunicam,"

who three or four days after he was married, to justify himself,
went about boldly swearing that he had ridden twenty stages the
night before: an oath that was afterward made use of to convict
him of his ignorance in that affair, and to divorce him from his
wife. Besides, it signifies nothing, for there is neither continency
nor virtue where there are no opposing desires. It is true they may
say, but we will not yield; saints themselves speak after that
manner. I mean those who boast in good gravity of their coldness
and insensibility, and who expect to be believed with a serious
countenance; for when 'tis spoken with an affected look, when
their eyes give the lie to their tongue, and when they talk in the
cant of their profession which always goes against the hair, 'tis
good sport. I am a great servant of liberty and plainness; but there
is no remedy; if it be not wholly simple or childish, 'tis silly, and
unbecoming ladies in this commerce, and presently runs into impudence. Their disguises and figures only serve to cozen fools; lying
is there in its seat of honor; 'tis a by-way, that by a back door

leads us to truth. If we cannot curb their imagination, what would we have from them. Effects? There are enough of them that evade all foreign communication, by which chastity may be corrupted;

"Illud sœpe facit, quod sine teste facit;"

and those which we fear the least, are, peradventure, most to be feared; their sins that make the least noise are the worst:

"Offendor mæcha simpliciore minus."

There are ways by which they may lose their virginity without prostitution, and, which is more, without their knowledge: *"Ob-sterix, virginis cujusdam integritatem manu velut explorans, sive malevolentia, sive inscitia, sive casu, dum inspicit, perdidit."* Such a one, by seeking her maidenhood, has lost it; another by playing with it, has destroyed it. We cannot precisely circumscribe the actions, we interdict them; they must guess at our meaning under general and doubtful terms, the very idea we invent for their chastity is ridiculous: for, among the greatest examples arrived at my knowledge, Fatua, the wife of Faunus, is one: who never, after her marriage, suffered herself to be seen by any man whatever: and the wife of Hiero, who never perceived her husband's stinking breath, imagining that it was common to all men. They must become insensible and invisible to satisfy us.

Now let us confess that the knot of this judgment of duty principally lies in the will; there have been husbands who have suffered cuckoldom, not only without reproach or taking offense at their wives, but with singular obligation to them and great commendation of their virtue. Such a woman has been, who prized her honor above her life, and yet has prostituted it to the furious lust of a mortal enemy, to save her husband's life, and who, in so doing did that for him she would not have done for herself! This is not the place wherein we are to multiply these examples; they are too high and rich to be set off with so poor a foil as I can give them here; let us reserve them for a nobler place; but for examples of ordinary luster, do we not every day see women among us who surrender themselves for their husbands' sole benefit, and by their express order and mediation? and, of old, Phaulius the Argian

who offered his to King Philip out of amibition: as Galba did it out of civility, who having entertained Mæcenas at supper, and observing that his wife and he began to cast sheep's eyes at one another and to complot love by signs, let himself sink down upon his cushion, like one in a profound sleep, to give opportunity to their desires: which he handsomely confessed, for, at the same time, a servant making bold to lay hands on the plate that stood upon the table, he frankly cried, "What, you rogue? do you not see that I only sleep for Mæcenas?" Such a woman there may be, whose manners may be lewd enough, and yet whose will may be more reformed than another, who outwardly carries herself after a more regular manner. As we see some, who complain of having vowed chastity before they knew what they did; and I have also known others really complain of having been given up to debauchery before they were of the years of discretion. The vice of the parents, or the impulse of nature, which is a rough counselor, may be the cause.

In the east Indies, though chastity is of singular reputation, yet custom permitted a married woman to prostitute herself to any one who presented her with an elephant, and that with glory to have been valued at so high a rate. Phædo the philosopher, a man of birth, after the taking of his country Elis, made it his trade to prostitute the beauty of his youth, so long as it lasted, to any one that would, for money, thereby to gain his living; and Solon was the first in Greece, 'tis said, who by his laws gave liberty to women, at the expense of their chastity, to provide for the necessities of life; a custom that Herodotus says had been received in many governments before his time. And besides, what fruit is there of this painful solicitude? For what justice soever there is in this passion, we are yet to consider whether it turns to account or no: does any one think to curb them, with all his industry?

> "Pone seram; cohibe: sed quis custodiet ipsos
> Custodes? cauta est, et ab illis incipit uxor."

What commodity will not serve their turn, in so knowing an age? Curiosity is vicious throughout; but 'tis pernicious here. 'Tis

folly to examine into a disease for which there is no physic that does not inflame and make it worse; of which the shame grows still greater, and more public by jealousy, and of which the revenge more wounds our children than it heals us. You wither and die in the search of so obscure a proof. How miserably have they of my time arrived at that knowledge, who have been so unhappy as to have found it out? If the informer, does not at the same time apply a remedy and bring relief, 'tis an injurious information, and that better deserves a stab than the lie. We no less laugh at him who takes pains to prevent it, than at him who is a cuckold, and knows it not. The character of cuckold is indelible: who once has it carries it to his grave; the punishment proclaims it more than the fault. It is to much purpose to drag out of obscurity and doubt our private misfortunes, thence to expose them on tragic scaffolds; and misfortunes that only hurt us by being known; for we say a good wife, or a happy marriage, not that they are really so, but because no one says to the contrary. Men should be so discreet as to evade this tormenting and unprofitable knowledge: and the Romans had a custom, when returning from any expedition, to send home before to acquaint their wives with their coming, that they might not surprise them; and to this purpose it is, that a certain nation has introduced a custom, that the priest shall on the wedding-day unlock the bride's cabinet, to free the husband from the doubt and curiosity of examining in the first assault, whether she comes a virgin to his bed, or that she has been at the trade before.

But the world will be talking. I know a hundred honest men cuckolds, that are handsomely, and not discreditably met; a worthy man is pitied, but not disesteemed for it. Order it so that your virtue may conquer your misfortune; that good men may curse the occasion, and that he who wrongs you may tremble but to think on't. And, moreover, who escapes being talked of at the same rate, from the least even to the greatest?

"Tot qui legionibus imperitavit,
Et melior quam tu multis fuit, improbe, rebus."

[242]

You hear how many honest men are reproached with this in your presence; you may believe that you are no more spared behind your back. Nay, the very ladies will be laughing too; and what are they so apt to laugh at in this virtuous age of ours, as at a peaceable and well-composed marriage? There is not one among you but has made somebody cuckold: and nature runs much in parallel, in compensation, and turn for turn. The frequency of this accident ought long since to have made it more easy; 'tis now passed into custom.

Miserable passion! which has this also, that it is incommunicable.

"Fors etiam nostris invidit questibus aures:"

for to what friend dare you intrust your griefs, who, if he does not laugh at them, will not make use of the occasion to get a share of the quarry? The sharps, as well as the sweets of marriage, are kept secret by the wise; and among its other troublesome conditions this to a prating fellow, as I am, is one of the chief, that custom has rendered it indecent and prejudicial to communicate to any one all that a man knows and all that a man feels.

To give women the same counsel against jealousy, would be so much time lost; their very being is so made up of suspicion, vanity, and curiosity, that to cure them by any legitimate way is not to be hoped. They often recover of this infirmity by a form of health much more to be feared than the disease itself; for as there are enchantments that cannot take away the evil, but by throwing it upon another, they also willingly transfer this fever to their husbands, when they shake it off themselves. And yet I know not, to speak truth, whether a man can suffer worse from them than their jealousy; 'tis the most dangerous of all their conditions, as the head is of all their members. Pittacus used to say, that every one had his trouble, and that his was the jealous head of his wife; but for which he should think himself perfectly happy. A mighty inconvenience, sure, which could poison the whole life of so just, so wise, and so valiant a man; what must we other little fellows do? The senate of Marseilles had reason to grant him his request who begged leave to kill himself that he might be delivered from the

ESSAYS OF MICHEL DE MONTAIGNE

clamor of his wife; for 'tis a mischief that is never removed but by removing the whole piece; and that has no remedy but flight or patience, though both of them very hard. He was, methinks, an understanding fellow who said, 'twas a happy marriage between a blind wife and a deaf husband.

Let us also consider whether the great and violent severity of obligation we enjoin them, does not produce two effects contrary to our design: namely, whether it does not render the pursuants more eager to attack, and the women more easy to yield. For as to the first, by raising the value of the place we raise the value and the desire of the conquest. Might it not be Venus herself, who so cunningly enhanced the price of her merchandise, by making the laws her bawds; knowing how insipid a delight it would be that was not heightened by fancy and hardness to achieve? In short, 'tis all swine's flesh, varied by sauces, as Flaminius' host said. Cupid is a roguish god, who makes it his sport to contend with devotion and justice: 'tis his glory that his power mates all powers, and that all other rules give place to his;

"Materiam culpæ prosequiturque suæ."

As to the second point; should we not be less cuckolds, if we less feared to be so? according to the humor of women whom interdiction incites, and who are more eager, being forbidden.

"Ubi velis, nolunt; ubi nolis, volunt ultro;
Concessa pudet ire via."

What better interpretation can we make of Messalina's behavior? She, at first, made her husband a cuckold in private, as in the common use: but, bringing her business about with too much ease, by reason of her husband's stupidity, she soon scorned that way, and presently fell to making open love, to own her lovers, and to favor and entertain them in the sight of all: she would make him know and see how she used him. This animal, not to be roused with all this, and rendering her pleasures dull and flat by his too stupid facility, by which he seemed to authorize and make them lawful; what does she? Being the wife of a living and healthful

[244]

emperor, and at Rome, the theater of the world, in the face of the sun, and with solemn ceremony, and to Silius, who had long before enjoyed her, she publicly married herself one day that her husband was gone out of the city. Does it not seem as if she was going to become chaste by her husband's negligence? or that she sought another husband who might sharpen her appetite by his jealousy, and who by watching should incite her? But the first difficulty she met with was also the last: this beast suddenly roused: these sleepy, sluggish sort of men are often the most dangerous; I have found by experience, that this extreme toleration, when it comes to dissolve, produces the most severe revenge; for taking fire on a sudden, anger and fury being combined in one, discharge their utmost force at the first onset,

> "Irarumque omnes effundit habenas:"

he put her to death, and with her a great number of those with whom she had intelligence, and even one of them who could not help it, and whom she had caused to be forced to her bed with scourges.

What Virgil says of Venus and Vulcan, Lucretius had better expressed of a stolen enjoyment between her and Mars:

> "Belli fera mœnera Mavors
> Armipotens regit, in gremium qui sæpe tuum se
> Rejicit, æterno devinctas vulnere amoris
>
> . . . .
>
> Pascit amore avidos inhians in te, Dea, visus,
> Eque tuo pendet resupini spiritus ore:
> Hunc tu, Diva, tuo recubantem corpore sancto
> Circumfusa super, suaveis ex ore loquelas
> Funde."

When I consider this *rejicit, pascit, inhians, molli, fovet, medullas, labefacta, pendet, percurrit,* and that noble *circumfusa,* mother of the gentle *infusus;* I contemn those little quibbles and verbal allusions that have been since in use. Those worthy people stood in need of no subtilty to disguise their meaning; their language is downright, and full of natural and continued vigor; they are all

epigram; not only the tail, but the head, body, and feet. There is nothing forced, nothing languishing, but everything keeps the same pace: *"Contextus totus virilis est; non sunt circa flosculos occupati."* 'Tis not a soft eloquence, and without offense only; 'tis nervous and solid, that does not so much please, as it fills and ravishes the greatest minds. When I see these brave forms of expression, so lively, so profound, I do not say that 'tis Well said, but Well thought. 'Tis the sprightliness of the imagination that swells and elevates the words: *"Pectus est quod disertum facit."* Our people call language, judgment, and fine words, full conceptions. This painting is not so much carried on by dexterity of hand, as by having the object more vividly imprinted in the soul. Gallus speaks simply, because he conceives simply: Horace does not content himself with a superficial expression; that would betray him; he sees farther and more clearly into things; his mind breaks into and rummages all the magazine of words and figures wherewith to express himself, and he must have them more than ordinary because his conception is so. Plutarch says, that he sees the Latin tongue by the things: 'tis here the same; the sense illuminates and produces the words, no more words of air, but of flesh and bone; they signify more than they say. Moreover, those who are not well skilled in a language, present some image of this; for in Italy, I said whatever I had a mind to in common discourse, but in more serious talk, I durst not have trusted myself with an idiom that I could not wind and turn out of its ordinary pace; I would have a power of introducing something of my own.

The handling and utterance of fine wits is that which sets off language; not so much by innovating it, as by putting it to more vigorous and various services, and by straining, bending, and adapting it to them. They do not create words, but they enrich their own, and give them weight and signification by the uses they put them to, and teach them unwonted notions, but withal, ingeniously and discreetly. And how little this talent is given to all, is manifest by the many French scribblers of this age; they are bold and proud enough not to follow the common road, but want of invention and discretion ruins them; there is nothing seen in their writings but

a wretched affectation of a strange new style, with cold and absurd disguises, which instead of elevating, depress the matter; provided they can but trick themselves out with new words, they care not what they signify; and to bring in a new word by the head and shoulders, they leave the old one, very often more sinewy and significant than the other.

There is stuff enough in our language, but there is a defect in cutting out; for there is nothing that might not be made out of our terms of hunting and war, which is a fruitful soil to borrow from; and forms of speaking, like herbs, improve and grow stronger by being transplanted. I find it sufficiently abundant, but not sufficiently pliable and vigorous; it commonly quails under a powerful conception; if you would maintain the dignity of your style, you will often perceive it to flag and languish under you, and there Latin steps in to its relief, as Greek does to others. Of some of these words I have just picked out we do not so easily discern the energy, by reason that the frequent use of them has in some sort abased their beauty, and rendered it common; as in our ordinary language there are many excellent phrases and metaphors to be met with, of which the beauty is withered by age, and the color is sullied by too common handling; but that nothing lessens the relish to an understanding man, nor does it derogate from the glory of those ancient authors who, 'tis likely, first brought those words into that luster.

The sciences treat of things too refinedly, after an artificial, very different from the common and natural way. My page makes love, and understands it; but read to him Leo Hebræus and Ficinus, where they speak of love, its thoughts and actions, he understands it not. I do not find in Aristotle most of my ordinary motions; they are there covered and disguised in another robe for the use of the schools. Well may they speed; but were I of the trade, I would as much naturalize art as they artify nature. Let us let Bembo and Equicola alone.

When I write, I can very well spare both the company and the remembrance of books, lest they should interrupt my progress; and also, in truth, the best authors too much humble and discourage

me; I am very much of the painter's mind, who, having represented cocks most wretchedly ill, charged all his boys not to suffer any natural cock to come into his shop; and had rather need to give myself a little luster, of the invention of Antigenides the musician, who, when he was to sing or play, took care beforehand that the auditory should, either before or after, be glutted with some other ill musicians. But I can hardly be without Plutarch; he is so universal, and so full, that upon all occasions, and what extravagant subject soever you take in hand, he will still be at your elbow and hold out to you a liberal and not to be exhausted hand of riches and embellishments. It vexes me that he is so exposed to be the spoil of those who are conversant with him: I can scarce cast an eye upon him but I purloin either a leg or a wing.

And also for this design of mine 'tis convenient for me to write at home, in a wild country, where I have nobody to assist or relieve me; where I hardly see a man who understands the Latin of his Pater noster, and of French as little, if not less. I might have it better elsewhere, but then the work would have been less my own; and its principal end and perfection is to be exactly mine. I readily correct an accidental error, of which I am full, as I run carelessly on; but for my ordinary and constant imperfections, it were a kind of treason to put them out. When another tells me, or that I say to myself, "Thou art too thick of figures: this is a word of Gascon growth: that is a dangerous phrase (I do not reject any of those that are used in the common streets of France; they who would fight custom with grammar are fools); this is an ignorant discourse: this is a paradoxical discourse; that is going too far: thou makest thyself too merry at times: men will think thou sayest a thing in good earnest which thou only speakest in jest." "Yes," say I, "but I correct the faults of inadvertence, not those of custom. Do I not talk at the same rate throughout? Do I not represent myself to the life? 'Tis enough that I have done what I designed; all the world knows me in my book, and my book in me."

Now I have an apish, imitating quality; when I used to write verses (and I never made any but Latin) they evidently discovered

the poet I had last read, and some of my first essays have a little exotic taste: I speak something another kind of language at Paris than I do at Montaigne. Whoever I steadfastly look upon easily leaves some impression of his upon me; whatever I consider I usurp, whether a foolish countenance, a disagreeable look, or a ridiculous way of speaking; and vices most of all, because they seize and stick to me, and will not leave hold without shaking. I swear more by imitation than by complexion: a murderous imitation, like that of the apes so terrible both in stature and strength, that Alexander met with in a certain country of the Indies, and which he would have had much ado any other way to have subdued; but they afforded him the means by that inclination of theirs to imitate whatever they saw done; for by that, the hunters were taught to put on shoes in their sight, and to tie them fast with many knots, and to muffle up their heads in caps all composed of running nooses, and to seem to anoint their eyes with glue; so did those poor beasts employ their imitation to their own ruin: they glued up their own eyes, haltered and bound themselves. The other faculty of playing the mimic, and ingeniously acting the words and gestures of another, purposely to make people merry and to raise their admiration, is no more in me than in a stock. When I swear my own oath 'tis only, by God! of all oaths the most direct. They say that Socrates swore by the dog; Zeno had for his oath the same interjection at this time in use among the Italians, Cappari; Pythagoras swore by water and air. I am so apt, without thinking of it, to receive these superficial impressions, that if I have Majesty or Highness in my mouth three days together, they come out instead of Excellency and Lordship eight days after; and what I say to-day in sport and fooling I shall say the same to-morrow seriously. Wherefore, in writing, I more unwillingly undertake beaten arguments, lest I should handle them at another's expense. Every subject is equally fertile to me: a fly will serve the purpose, and 'tis well if this I have in hand has not been undertaken at the recommendation of as flighty a will. I may begin with that which pleases me best, for the subjects are all linked to one another.

But my soul displeases me in that it ordinarily produces its

deepest and most airy conceits and which please me best, when I least expect or study for them, and which suddenly vanish, having, at the instant, nothing to apply them to; on horseback, at table, and in bed: but most on horseback, where I am most given to think. My speaking is a little nicely jealous of silence and attention: if I am talking my best, who ever interrupts me, stops me. In traveling, the necessity of the way will often put a stop to discourse; besides which I, for the most part, travel without company fit for regular discourses, by which means I have all the leisure I would to entertain myself. It falls out as it does in my dreams; while dreaming I recommend them to my memory (for I am apt to dream that I dream), but, the next morning, I may represent to myself of what complexion they were, whether gay, or sad, or strange, but what they were, as to the rest, the more I endeavor to retrieve them, the deeper I plunge them in oblivion. So of thoughts that come accidentally into my head, I have no more but a vain image remaining in my memory; only enough to make me torment myself in their quest to no purpose.

Well, then, laying books aside, and more simply and materially speaking, I find, after all, that LOVE is nothing else but the thirst of enjoying the object desired; or Venus any other thing than the pleasure of discharging one's vessels, just as the pleasure nature gives in discharging other parts, that either by immoderation or indiscretion become vicious. According to Socrates, love is the appetite of generation, by the mediation of beauty. And when I consider the ridiculous titillation of this pleasure, the absurd, crack-brained, wild motions with which it inspires Zeno and Cratippus, the indiscreet rage, the countenance inflamed with fury and cruelty in the sweetest effects of love, and then that austere air, so grave, severe, ecstatic, in so wanton an action; that our delights and our excrements are promiscuously shuffled together; and that the supreme pleasure brings along with it, as in pain, fainting and complaining; I then believe it to be true as Plato says, that the gods made man for their sport,

"Quænam ista jocandi
Sævitia!"

[250]

and that it was in mockery that nature has ordered the most agitative of actions and the most common, to make us equal and to put fools and wise men, beasts and us, on a level. Even the most contemplative and prudent man, when I imagine him in this posture, I hold him an impudent fellow to pretend to be prudent and contemplative; they are the peacocks' feet, that abate his pride.

> "Ridentem dicere verum
> Quid vetat?"

They who banish serious imaginations from their sports, do, says one, like him who dares not adore the statue of a saint, if not covered with a veil. We eat and drink, indeed, as beasts do; but these are not actions that obstruct the functions of the soul, in these we maintain our advantage over them; this other action subjects all other thought, and by its imperious authority makes an ass of all Plato's divinity and philosophy; and yet there is no complaint of it. In everything else a man may keep some decorum, all other operations submit to the rules of decency; this cannot so much as in imagination appear other than vicious or ridiculous: find out, if you can, therein any serious and discreet procedure. Alexander said, that he chiefly knew himself to be mortal by this act, and sleeping; sleep suffocates and suppresses the faculties of the soul; the familiarity with women likewise dissipates and exhausts them: doubtless 'tis a mark, not only of our original corruption, but also of our vanity and deformity.

On the one side, nature pushes us on to it, having fixed the most noble, useful, and pleasant of all her functions to this desire; and, on the other side, leaves us to accuse and avoid it, as insolent and indecent, to blush at it, and to recommend abstinence. Are we not brutes, to call that work brutish which begets us? People of so many differing religions have concurred in several proprieties, as sacrifices, lamps, burning incense, fasts, and offerings; and among others, in the condemning this act; all opinions tend that way, besides the widespread custom of circumcision, which may be regarded as a punishment. We have, peradventure, reason to blame ourselves for being guilty of so foolish a production as man,

and to call the act, and the parts that are employed in the act, shameful (mine, truly, are now shameful and pitiful). The Essenians, of whom Pliny speaks, kept up their country for several ages without either nurse or baby-clouts, by the arrival of strangers who, following this pretty humor, came continually to them: a whole nation being resolute, rather to hazard a total extermination, than to engage themselves in female embraces, and rather to lose the succession of men, than to beget one. 'Tis said, that Zeno never had to do with a woman but once in his life, and then out of civility, that he might not seem too obstinately to disdain the sex. Every one avoids seeing a man born, every one runs to see him die; to destroy him, a spacious field is sought out, in the face of the sun; but, to make him, we creep into as dark and private a corner as we can; 'tis a man's duty to withdraw himself bashfully from the light to create; but 'tis glory and the fountain of many virtues to know how to destroy what we have made; the one is injury, the other favor; for Aristotle says that to do any one a kindness, in a certain phrase of his country, is to kill him. The Athenians, to couple the disgrace of these two actions, having to purge the isle of Delos, and to justify themselves to Apollo, interdicted at once all birth and burials in the precincts thereof. *"Nostri nosmet pœnitet."*

There are some nations that will not be seen to eat. I know a lady, and of the best quality, who has the same opinion, that chewing disfigures the face, and takes away much from the ladies' grace and beauty; and therefore unwillingly appears at a public table with an appetite; and I know a man also, who cannot endure to see another eat, nor himself to be seen eating; and who is more shy of company when putting in than when putting out. In the Turkish empire, there are a great number of men, who to excel others, never suffer themselves to be seen when they make their repast; who never have any more than one a week; who cut and mangle their faces and limbs; who never speak to any one; fanatic people who think to honor their nature by disnaturing themselves; who value themselves upon their contempt of themselves, and purport to grow better by being worse. What monstrous animal

is this, that is a horror to himself, to whom his delights are grievous, and who weds himself to misfortune? There are people who conceal their life,

"Exsilioque domos et dulcia limina mutant,"

and withdraw them from the sight of other men; who avoid health and cheerfulness, as dangerous and prejudicial qualities. Not only many sects, but many peoples, curse their birth, and bless their death; and there is a place where the sun is abominated, and darkness adored. We are only ingenious in using ourselves ill; 'tis the real quarry our intellects fly at; and intellect, when misapplied, is a dangerous tool!

"O miseri! quorum gaudia crimen habent!"

Alas, poor man! thou hast enough inconveniences that are inevitable, without increasing them by thine own invention; and art miserable enough by nature, without being so by art; thou hast real and essential deformities enough, without forging those that are imaginary. Dost thou think thou art too much at ease, unless half thy ease is uneasy? dost thou find that thou hast not performed all the necessary offices that nature has enjoined thee, and that she is idle in thee, if thou dost not oblige thyself to other and new offices? Thou dost not stick to infringe her universal and undoubted laws; but stickest to thy own special and fantastic rules, and by how much more particular, uncertain, and contradictory they are, by so much thou employest thy whole endeavor in them; the laws of thy parish occupy and bind thee; those of God and the world concern thee not. Run but a little over the examples of this kind; thy life is full of them.

While the verses of these two poets treat so reservedly and discreetly of wantonness as they do, methinks they discover it much more openly. Ladies cover their necks with network, priests cover several sacred things, and painters shadow their pictures to give them greater luster: and 'tis said that the sun and wind strike more violently by reflection than in a direct line. The Egyptian

wisely answered him who asked him what he had under his cloak; "it is hid under my cloak," said he, "that thou mayest not know what it is:" but there are certain other things that people hide only to show them. Hear this fellow who speaks plainer,

"Et nudum pressi corpus ad usque meum:"

methinks, I am eunuched with the expression. Let Martial turn up Venus' coats as high as he may, he cannot show her so naked; he, who says all that is to be said, gluts and disgusts us. He who is afraid to express himself, draws us on to guess at more than is meant; there is treachery in this sort of modesty, and specially when they half open, as these do, so fair a path to imagination. Both the action and description should relish of theft.

The more respectful, more timorous, more coy, and secret love of the Spaniards and Italians pleases me. I know not who of old wished his throat as long as that of a crane, that he might the longer taste what he swallowed: it had been better wished as to this quick and precipitous pleasure, especially in such natures as mine that have the fault of being too prompt. To stay its flight and delay it with preambles; all things—a glance, a bow, a word, a sign, stand for favor and recompense between them. Were it not an excellent piece of thrift in him who could dine on the steam of the roast? 'Tis a passion that mixes with very little solid essence, far more vanity and feverish raving; and we should serve and pay it accordingly. Let us teach the ladies to set a better value and esteem upon themselves, to amuse and fool us: we give the last charge at the first onset; the French impetuosity will still show itself; by spinning out their favors, and exposing them in small parcels, even miserable old age itself will find some little share of reward, according to its worth and merit. He who has no fruition but in fruition, who wins nothing unless he sweeps the stakes, who takes no pleasure in the chase but in the quarry, ought not to introduce himself in our school: the more steps and degrees there are, so much higher and more honorable is the uppermost seat; we should take a pleasure in being conducted to it, as in magnificent palaces, by various porticoes and passages, long and pleasant

galleries, and many windings. This disposition of things would turn to our advantage; we should there longer stay and longer love; without hope and without desire we proceed not worth a pin. Our conquest and entire possession is what they ought infinitely to dread: when they wholly surrender themselves up to the mercy of our fidelity and constancy they run a mighty hazard; they are virtues very rare and hard to be found; the ladies are no sooner ours, than we are no more theirs:

> "Posquam cupidæ mentis satiata libido est,
> Verba nihil metuere, nihil perjuria curant;"

And Thrasonides, a young man of Greece, was so in love with his passion that, having gained a mistress' consent, he refused to enjoy her, that he might not by fruition quench and stupefy the unquiet ardor of which he was so proud, and with which he so fed himself. Dearness is a good sauce to meat: do but observe how much the manner of salutation, particular to our nation, has, by its faculties, made kisses, which Socrates says are so powerful and dangerous for the stealing of hearts, of no esteem. It is a nauseous custom and injurious for the ladies, that they must be obliged to lend their lips to every fellow who has three footmen at his heels, however disgusting he may be in himself,

> "Cujus livida naribus caninis
> Dependet glacies, rigetque barba . . .
> Centum occurrere malo culilingis:"

and we ourselves do not get much by it; for as the world is divided, for three beautiful women we must kiss three-score ugly ones; and to a tender stomach, like those of my age, an ill kiss overpays a good one.

In Italy they passionately court even their common women who sell themselves for money, and justify the doing so by saying, "that there are degrees of fruition, and that by such service they would procure for themselves that which is most entire; the women sell nothing but their bodies; the will is too free and too much its own to be exposed to sale." So that these say, 'tis the will they

undertake; and they have reason. 'Tis indeed the will that we are to serve and gain by wooing. I abhor to imagine mine, a body without affection: and this madness is, methinks, cousin-german to that of the boy, who would needs pollute the beautiful statue of Venus, made by Praxiteles; or that of the furious Egyptian, who violated the dead carcass of a woman he was embalming: which was the occasion of the law then made in Egypt, that the corpses of beautiful young women, of those of good quality, should be kept three days before they should be delivered to those whose office it was to take care for the interment. Periander did more wonderfully, who extended his conjugal affection (more regular and legitimate) to the enjoyment of his wife Melissa after she was dead. Does it not seem a lunatic humor in the Moon, seeing she could no otherwise enjoy her darling Endymion, to lay him for several months asleep, and to please herself with the fruition of a boy, who stirred not but in his sleep? I likewise say that we love a body without a soul or sentiment when we love a body without its consent and concurring desire. All enjoyments are not alike: there are some that are etic and languishing: a thousand other causes besides good will may procure us this favor from the ladies; this is not a sufficient testimony of affection: treachery may lurk there, as well as elsewhere: they sometimes go to't by halves,

> "Tanquam thura merumque parent . . .
> Absentem, marmoreamve putes:"

I know some who had rather lend that than their coach, and who only impart themselves that way. You are to examine whether your company pleases them upon any other account, or, as some strong-chined groom, for that only; in what degree of favor and esteem you are with them,

> "Tibi si datur uni;
> Quo lapide illa diem candidiore notet."

What if they eat your bread with the sauce of a more pleasing imagination?

> "Te tenet, absentes alios suspirat amores."

What? have we not seen one in these days of ours who made use of this act for the purpose of a most horrid revenge, by that means to kill and poison, as he did, a worthy lady?

Such as know Italy will not think it strange if, for this subject, I seek not elsewhere for examples; for that nation may be called the regent of the world in this. They have more generally handsome and fewer ugly women than we: but for rare and excellent beauties we have as many as they. I think the same of their intellects: of those of the common sort, they have evidently far more: brutishness is immeasurably rarer there; but in individual characters, of the highest form, we are nothing indebted to them. If I should carry on the comparison, I might say, as touching valor, that, on the contrary, it is, to what it is with them, common and natural with us; but sometimes we see them possessed of it to such a degree as surpasses the greatest examples we can produce. The marriages of that country are defective in this; their custom commonly imposes so rude and so slavish a law upon the women, that the most distant acquaintance with a stranger is as capital an offense as the most intimate; so that all approaches being rendered necessarily substantial, and seeing that all comes to one account, they have no hard choice to make; and when they have broken down the fence, we may safely presume they get on fire. *"Luxuria ipsis vinculis, sicut fera bestia, irritata, deinde emissa."* They must give them a little more rein;

> "Vidi ego nuper equum, contra sua frena tenacem,
>   Ore reluctanti fulminis ire modo:"

the desire of company is allayed by giving it a little liberty. We are pretty much in the same case: they are extreme in constraint, we in license. 'Tis a good custom we have in France, that our sons are received into the best families, there to be entertained and bred up pages, as in a school of nobility; and 'tis looked upon as a discourtesy and an affront to refuse this to a gentleman. I have taken notice (for so many families, so many differing forms) that the ladies, who have been strictest with their maids, have had no better luck than those who allowed them a greater liberty. There

should be moderation in these things; one must leave a great deal of their conduct to their own discretion; for, when all comes to all, no discipline can curb them throughout. But it is true withal that she who comes off with flying colors from a school of liberty, brings with her whereon to repose more confidence than she who comes away sound from a severe and strict school.

Our fathers dressed up their daughters' looks in bashfulness and fear (their courage and desires being the same); we ours in confidence and assurance; we understand nothing of the matter; we must leave it to the Sarmatian women, who may not live with a man till with their own hands they have first killed another in battle. For me, who have no other title left me to these things but by the ears, 'tis sufficient if, according to the privilege of my age, they retain me for one of their counsel. I advise them then, and us men too, to abstinence; but if the age we live in will not endure it, at least modesty and discretion. For, as in the story of Aristippus who, speaking to some young men who blushed to see him go into a scandalous house, said: "The vice is in not coming out, not in going in," let her who has no care of her conscience, have yet some regard to her reputation; and though she be rotten within, let her carry a fair outside at least.

I commend a gradation and delay in bestowing their favors: Plato declares that, in all sorts of love, facility and promptness are forbidden to the defendant. 'Tis a sign of eagerness, which they ought to disguise with all the art they have, so rashly, wholly, and hand-over-head to surrender themselves. In carrying themselves orderly and measuredly in the granting their last favors, they much more allure our desires and hide their own. Let them still fly before us, even those who have most mind to be overtaken: they better conquer us by flying, as the Scythians did. To say the truth, according to the law that nature has imposed upon them, it is not properly for them either to will or desire; their part is to suffer, obey, and consent: and for this it is that nature has given them a perpetual capacity, which in us is but at times and uncertain; they are always fit for the encounter, that they may be always ready when we are so, *"Pati natæ."* And whereas she has

ordered that our appetites shall be manifest by a prominent demonstration, she would have theirs to be hidden and concealed within, and has furnished them with parts improper for ostentation, and simply defensive. Such proceedings as this that follows must be left to the Amazonian license: Alexander marching his army through Hyrcania, Thalestris, queen of the Amazons, came with three hundred light horse of her own sex, well mounted and armed, having left the remainder of a very great army that followed her, behind the neighboring mountains, to give him a visit; where she publicly and in plain terms told him that the fame of his valor and victories had brought her thither to see him, and to make him an offer of her forces to assist him in the pursuit of his enterprises: and that finding him so handsome, young, and vigorous, she, who was also perfect in all those qualities, advised that they might lie together, to the end that from the most valiant woman of the world, and the bravest man then living, there might spring some great and wonderful issue for the time to come. Alexander returned her thanks for all the rest, but to give leisure for the accomplishment of her last demand, he detained her thirteen days in that place, which were spent in royal feasting and jollity, for the welcome of so courageous a princess.

We are, almost throughout, unjust judges of their actions, as they are of ours; I confess the truth when it makes against me, as well as when 'tis on my side. 'Tis an abominable intemperance that pushes them on so often to change, and that will not let them limit their affection to any one person whatever; as is evident in that goddess, to whom are attributed so many changes and so many lovers. But 'tis true withal, that 'tis contrary to the nature of love, if it be not violent; and contrary to the nature of violence, if it be constant. And they who wonder, exclaim, and keep such a clutter to find out the causes of this frailty of theirs, as unnatural and not to be believed, how comes it to pass they do not discern how often they are themselves guilty of the same, without any astonishment or miracle at all? It would, peradventure, be more strange to see the passion fixed; 'tis not a simply corporeal passion; if there be no end to avarice and ambition, there is doubtless no more

in desire; it still lives after satiety; and 'tis impossible to prescribe either constant satisfaction, or end; it ever goes beyond its possession. And by that means inconstancy, peradventure, is in some sort more pardonable in them than in us: they may plead, as well as we, the inclination to variety and novelty common to us both; and secondly, without us, that they buy a pig in a poke: Joan, queen of Naples, caused her first husband Andreasso to be hanged at the bars of her window in a halter of gold and silk, woven with her own hand, because in matrimonial performances she neither found his parts nor abilities answer the expectation she had conceived from his stature, beauty, youth, and activity, by which she had been caught and deceived. They may say, there is more pains required in doing than in suffering; and so they are on their part always at least provided for necessity, whereas on our part it may fall out otherwise. For this reason it was that Plato wisely made a law, that before marriage, to determine of the fitness of persons, the judges should see the young men who pretended to it stripped stark naked, and the women but to the girdle only. When they come to try us, they do not; perhaps, find us worthy of their choice:

> "Experta latus, madidoque simillima loro
> Inguina, nec lassa stare coacta manu,
> Deserit imbelles thalamos."

'Tis not enough that a man's will be good; weakness and insufficiency lawfully break a marriage,

> "Et quærendum aliunde foret nervosius illud,
> Quod posset zonam solvere virgineam:"

why not? and according to her own standard, an amorous intelligence, more licentious and active,

> "Si blando nequeat superesse labori."

But it is not great impudence to offer our imperfections and imbecilities, where we desire to please and leave a good opinion and esteem of ourselves? For the little that I am able to do now,

> "Ad unum
Mollis opus."

I would not trouble a woman, that I am to reverence and fear.

> "Fuge suspicari,
> Cujus undenum trepidavit ætas
> Claudare lustrum."

Nature should satisfy herself in having rendered this age miserable, without rendering it ridiculous too. I hate to see it, for one poor inch of pitiful vigor which comes upon it but thrice a week, to strut and set out itself with as much eagerness as if it could do mighty feats; a true flame of flax; and laugh to see it so boil and bubble and then in a moment so congealed and extinguished. This appetite ought to appertain only to the flower of beautiful youth: trust not to its seconding that indefatigable, full, constant, magnanimous ardor you think in you, for it will certainly leave you in the lurch at your greatest need; but rather transfer it to some tender, bashful, and ignorant boy, who yet trembles at the rod and blushes;

> "Indum sanguineo veluti violaverit ostro
> Si quis ebur, vel mista rubent ubi lilia multa
> Alba rosa."

Who can stay till the morning without dying for shame to behold the disdain of the fair eyes of her who knows so well his fumbling impertinence,

> "Et taciti fecere tamen convicia vultus,"

has never had the satisfaction and the glory of having cudgeled them till they were weary, with the vigorous performance of one heroic night. When I have observed any one to be vexed with me, I have not presently accused her levity, but have been in doubt, if I had not reason rather to complain of nature; she has doubtless used me very uncivilly and unkindly,

> "Si non longa satis, si non bene mentula crassa:
> Nimirum sapiunt, videntque parvam
> Matronæ quoque mentulam illibenter:"

and done me a most enormous injury. Every member I have, as much one as another, is equally my own, and no other more properly makes me a man than this.

[261]

I universally owe my entire picture to the public. The wisdom of my instruction consists in liberty, in truth, in essence: disdaining to introduce those little, feigned, common, and provincial rules into the catalogue of its real duties; all natural, general, and constant, of which civility and ceremony are daughters indeed, but illegitimate. We are sure to have the vices of appearance, when we shall have had those of essence: when we have done with these, we run full drive upon the others, if we find it must be so; for there is danger that we shall fancy new offices, to excuse our negligence toward the natural ones and to confound them; and to manifest this, is it not seen that in places where faults are crimes, crimes are but faults; that in nations where the laws of decency are most rare and most remiss, the primitive laws of common reason are better observed: the innumerable multitude of so many duties stifling and dissipating our care. The application of ourselves to light and trivial things diverts us from those that are necessary and just. Oh, how these superficial men take an easy and plausible way in comparison of ours! These are shadows wherewith we palliate and pay one another; but we do not pay, but inflame the reckoning toward that great Judge who tucks up our rags and tatters above our shameful parts, and stickles not to view us all over, even to our inmost and most secret ordures: it were a useful decency of our maidenly modesty, could it keep him from this discovery. In fine, whoever could reclaim man from so scrupulous a verbal superstition, would do the world no great disservice. Our life is divided between folly and prudence: whoever will write of it but what is reverend and canonical, will leave above the one-half behind. I do not excuse myself to myself; and if I did, it should rather be for my excuses that I would excuse myself, than for any other fault: I excuse myself of certain humors, which I think more strong in number than those that are on my side. In consideration of which, I will further say this (for I desire to please every one, though it will be hard to do, *"esse unum hominen accommodatum ad tantam morum ac sermonum et voluntatum varietatem,"*) that they ought not to condemn me for what I make authorities, received and approved by so many ages, to utter: and that there is no reason that for want

of rhyme, they should refuse me the liberty they allow even to churchmen of our nation and time, and these among the most notable, of which here are two of their brisk verses,

"Rimula, dispeream, ni monogramma tua est."

"Un vit d'amy la contente et bien traicte:"

besides how many others. I love modesty, and 'tis not out of judgment that I have chosen this scandalous way of speaking; 'tis nature that has chosen it for me. I commend it not, no more than other forms that are contrary to common use: but I excuse it, and by circumstances both general and particular, alleviate its accusation.

But to proceed. Whence, too, can proceed that usurpation of sovereign authority you take upon you over the women, who favor you at their own expense,

"Si furtiva dedit nigra munuscula nocte,"

so that you presently assume the interest, coldness, and authority of a husband? 'Tis a free contract: why do you not then keep to it, as you would have them do? there is no prescription upon voluntary things. 'Tis against the form, but it is true withal, that I in my time have conducted this bargain as much as the nature of it would permit, as conscientiously and with as much color of justice, as any other contract; and that I never pretended other affection than what I really had, and have truly acquainted them with its birth, vigor, and declination, its fits and intermissions: a man does not always hold on at the same rate. I have been so sparing of my promises, that I think I have been better than my word. They have found me faithful even to service of their inconstancy, a confessed and sometimes multiplied inconstancy. I never broke with them while I had any hold at all, and what occasion soever they have given me, never broke with them to hatred or contempt; for such privacies, though obtained upon never so scandalous terms, do yet oblige to some good will. I have sometimes, upon their tricks and evasions, discovered a little indiscreet anger and impatience; for I am naturally subject to rash emotions, which though light and short, often spoil my market. At any time they have consulted my judgment, I never stuck to give them sharp and paternal counsels, and to pinch them

to the quick. If I have left them any cause to complain of me, 'tis rather to have found in me, in comparison of the modern use, a love foolishly conscientious, than anything else. I have kept my word in things wherein I might easily have been dispensed; they sometimes surrendered themselves with reputation, and upon articles that they were willing enough should be broken by the conqueror. I have, more than once, made pleasure in its greatest effort strike to the interest of their honor; and where reason importuned me, have armed them against myself; so that they ordered themselves more decorously and securely by my rules, when they frankly referred themselves to them, than they would have done by their own. I have ever, as much as I could, wholly taken upon myself alone the hazard of our assignations, to acquit them; and have always contrived our meetings after the hardest and most unusual manner, as less suspected, and, moreover, in my opinion, more accessible. They are chiefly more open, where they think they are most securely shut; things least feared are least interdicted and observed; one may more boldly dare what nobody thinks you dare, which by its difficulty becomes easy. Never had any man his approaches more impertinently generative; this way of loving is more according to discipline: but how ridiculous it is to our people, and how ineffectual, who better knows than I? yet I shall not repent me of it; I have nothing there more to lose;

> "Me tabula sacer
> Votiva paries, indicat uvida
> Suspendisse potenti
> Vestimenta maris deo:"

'tis now time to speak out. But as I might, peradventure, say to another, "Thou talkest idly, my friend; the love of thy time has little commerce with faith and integrity;"

> "Hæc si tu postules
> Ratione certa facere, nihilo plus agas,
> Quam si des operam, ut cum ratione insanias:"

on the contrary, also, if it were for me to begin again, certainly it should be by the same method and the same progress, how fruitless soever it might be to me; folly and insufficiency are commendable

in an incommendable action; the farther I go from their humor in this, I approach so much nearer to my own. As to the rest, in this traffic, I did not suffer myself to be totally carried away; I pleased myself in it, but did not forget myself; I retained the little sense and discretion that nature has given me, entire for their service and my own; a little emotion, but no dotage. My conscience, also, was engaged in it, even to debauch and licentiousness; but, as to ingratitude, treachery, malice, and cruelty, never. I would not purchase the pleasure of this vice at any price, but content myself with its proper and simple cost: *"Nullum intra se vitium est."* I almost equally hate a stupid and slothful laziness, as I do a toilsome and painful employment; this pinches, the other lays me asleep. I like wounds as well as bruises, and cuts as well as dry blows. I found in this commerce, when I was the most able for it, a just moderation between these extremes. Love is a sprightly, lively, and gay agitation; I was neither troubled nor afflicted with it, but heated, and, moreover, disordered; a man must stop there; it hurts nobody but fools. A young man asked the philosopher Panetius, if it was becoming a wise man to be in love? "Let the wise man look to that," answered he, "but let not thou and I, who are not so, engage ourselves in so stirring and violent an affair, that enslaves us to others, and renders us contemptible to ourselves." He said true, that we are not to intrust a thing so precipitous in itself, to a soul that has not wherewithal to withstand its assaults and disprove practically the saying of Agesilaus, that prudence and love cannot live together. 'Tis a vain employment, 'tis true, unbecoming, shameful, and illegitimate; but carried on after this manner, I look upon it as wholesome, and proper to enliven a drowsy soul, and to rouse up a heavy body; and, as an experienced physician, I would prescribe it to a man of my form and condition, as soon as any other recipe whatever, to rouse and keep him in vigor till well advanced in years, and to defer the approaches of age. While we are but in the suburbs, and that the pulse yet beats,

"Dum nova canities, dum prima et recta senectus,
Dum superest Lachesi quod torqueat, et pedibus me
Porto meis, nullo dextram subeunte bacillo,"

we have need to be solicited and tickled by some such nipping incitation as this. Do but observe what youth, vigor, and gayety it inspired Anacreon withal: and Socrates, who was then older than I, speaking of an amorous object: "Leaning," said he, "my shoulder to her shoulder, and my head to hers, as we were reading together in a book, I felt, without dissembling, a sudden sting in my shoulder like the biting of a flea, which I still felt above five days after, and a continual itching crept into my heart." So that merely the accidental touch, and of a shoulder, heated and altered a soul cooled and enervated by age, and the strictest liver of all mankind. And, pray, why not? Socrates was a man, and would neither be, nor seem, any other thing. Philosophy does not contend against natural pleasures, provided they be moderate: and only preaches moderation, not a total abstinence; the power of its resistance is employed against those that are adulterate and strange. Philosophy says that the appetites of the body ought not to be augmented by the mind, and ingeniously warns us not to stir up hunger by saturity; not to stuff, instead of merely filling, the belly; to avoid all enjoyments that may bring us to want; and all meats and drinks that bring thirst and hunger: as, in the service of love, she prescribes us to take such an object as may simply satisfy the body's need, and does not stir the soul, which ought only barely to follow and assist the body, without mixing in the affair. But have I not reason to hold, that these precepts, which, indeed, in my opinion, are somewhat over strict, only concern a body in its best plight; and that in a body broken with age, as in a weak stomach, 'tis excusable to warm and support it by art, and by the mediation of the fancy, to restore the appetite and cheerfulness it has lost of itself.

May we not say that there is nothing in us, during this earthly prison, that is purely either corporeal or spiritual; and that we injuriously break up a man alive; and that it seems but reasonable that we should carry ourselves as favorably, at least, toward the use of pleasure as we do toward that of pain? Pain was (for example) vehement even to perfection in the souls of the saints by penitence: the body had there naturally a share by the right of union, and yet might have but little part in the cause; and yet are

they not contented that it should barely follow and assist the afflicted soul; they have afflicted itself with grievous and special torments, to the end that by emulation of one another the soul and body might plunge man into misery by so much more salutiferous as it is more severe. In like manner, is it not injustice, in bodily pleasures, to subdue and keep under the soul, and say that it must therein be dragged along as to some enforced and servile obligation and necessity? 'Tis rather her part to hatch and cherish them, there to present herself, and to invite them, the authority of ruling belonging to her; as it is also her part, in my opinion, in pleasures that are proper to her, to inspire and infuse into the body all the sentiment it is capable of, and to study how to make them sweet and useful to it. For it is good reason, as they say, that the body should not pursue its appetites to the prejudice of the mind; but why is it not also reason that the mind should not pursue hers to the prejudice of the body?

I have no other passion to keep me in breath. What avarice, ambition, quarrels, lawsuits do for others who, like me, have no particular vocation, love would much more commodiously do; it would restore to me vigilance, sobriety, grace, and the care of my person; it would reassure my countenance, so that the grimaces of old age, those deformed and dismal looks, might not come to disgrace it; would again put me upon sound and wise studies, by which I might render myself more loved and esteemed, clearing my mind of the despair of itself and of its use, and redintegrating it to itself; would divert me from a thousand troublesome thoughts, a thousand melancholic humors that idleness and the ill posture of our health loads us withal at such an age; would warm again, in dreams at least, the blood that nature is abandoning; would hold up the chin, and a little stretch out the nerves, the vigor and gayety of life of that poor man who is going full drive toward his ruin. But I very well understand that it is a commodity hard to recover: by weakness and long experience our taste is become more delicate and nice; we ask most when we bring least, and are harder to choose when we least deserve to be accepted; and knowing ourselves for what we are, we are less confident and more distrustful; nothing

can assure us of being beloved, considering our condition and theirs. I am out of countenance to see myself in company with those young wanton creatures,

> "Cujus in indomito constantior inguine nervus,
> Quam nova collibus arbor inhæret."

To what end should we go insinuate our misery amid their gay and sprightly humor?

> "Possint ut juvenes visere fervidi,
> Multo non sine risu,
> Dilapsam in cinere facem."

They have strength and reason on their side; let us give way; we have nothing to do there: and these blossoms of springing beauty suffer not themselves to be handled by such benumbed hands nor dealt with by mere material means, for, as the old philosopher answered one who jeered him because he could not gain the favor of a young girl he made love to, "Friend, the hook will not stick in such soft cheese." It is a commerce that requires relation and correspondence; the other pleasures we receive may be acknowledged by recompenses of another nature, but this is not to be paid but with the same kind of coin. In earnest, in this sport, the pleasure I give more tickles my imagination than that they give me; now, he has nothing of generosity in him who can receive pleasure where he confers none—it must needs be a mean soul that will owe all, and can be content to maintain relations with persons to whom he is a continual charge; there is no beauty, grace, nor privacy so exquisite that a gentleman ought to desire at this rate. If they can only be kind to us out of pity, I had much rather die than live upon charity. I would have right to ask, in the style wherein I heard them beg in Italy: *"Fate ben per voi,"* or after the manner that Cyrus exhorted his soldiers, "Who loves himself let him follow me." "Consort yourself," some one will say to me, "with women of your own condition, whom like fortune will render more easy to your desire." Oh ridiculous and insipid composition!

> "Nolo
> Barbam vellere mortuo leoni."

Xenophon lays it for an objection and an accusation against Menon, that he never made love to any but old women. For my part, I take more pleasure in but seeing the just and sweet mixture of two young beauties, or only in meditating on it in my fancy, than myself in acting second in a piteous and imperfect conjunction; I leave that fantastic appetite to the Emperor Galba, who was only for old curried flesh; and to this poor wretch,

> "O, ego Di faciant talem te cernere possim,
> Caraque mutatis oscula ferre comis,
> Amplectique meis corpus non pingue lacertis!"

Among chief deformities I reckon forced and artificial beauties; Hemon, a young fellow of Chios, thinking by fine dressing to acquire the beauty that nature had denied him, came to the philosopher Arcesilaus and asked him if it was possible for a wise man to be in love—"Yes," replied he, "provided it be not with a farded and adulterated beauty like thine." Ugliness of a confessed antiquity is to me less old and less ugly than another that is polished and plastered up. Shall I speak it, without the danger of having my throat cut? love, in my opinion, is not properly and naturally in its season, but in the age next to childhood;

> "Quem si puellarum insereres choro,
> Mille sagaces falleret hospites,
> Discrimen obscurum, solutis
> Crinibus ambiguoque vultu;"

nor beauty neither; for whereas Homer extends it so far as to the budding of the beard, but to himself has remarked this as rare; and the reason why the Sophist Bion so pleasantly called the first appearing hairs of adolescence *Aristogitons* and *Harmodiuses* is sufficiently known. I find it in virility already in some sort a little out of date, though not so much as in old age;

> "Importunus enim transvolat aridas
> Quercus:"

and Marguerite, queen of Navarre, like a woman, very far extends the advantage of women, ordaining that it is time at thirty years old,

to convert the title of fair into that of good. The shorter authority we give to love over our lives 'tis so much the better for us. Do but observe his port; 'tis a beardless boy. Who knows not how, in his school they proceed contrary to all order; study, exercise, and usage are there ways for insufficiency; there novices rule; "*Amor ordinem nescit.*" Doubtless his conduct is much more graceful when mixed with inadvertency and trouble; miscarriages and ill successes give him point and grace; provided it be sharp and eager, 'tis no great matter whether it be prudent or no; do but observe how he goes reeling, tripping, and playing: you put him in the stocks when you guide him by art and wisdom; and he is restrained of his divine liberty when put into those hairy and callous clutches.

As to the rest, I often hear the women set out this intelligence as entirely spiritual, and disdain to put the interest the senses there have into consideration; everything there serves; but I can say that I have often seen that we have excused the weakness of their understandings in favor of their outward beauty, but have never yet seen that in favor of mind, how mature and full soever, any of them would hold out a hand to a body that was never so little in decadence. Why does not some one of them take it into her head to make that noble practical bargain between body and soul, purchasing a philosophical and spiritual intelligence and generation at the price of her thighs, which is the highest price she can get for them? Plato ordains in his laws that he who has performed any signal and advantageous exploit in war may not be refused during the whole expedition, his age or ugliness notwithstanding, a kiss or any other amorous favor from any woman whatever. What he thinks to be so just in recommendation of military valor, why may it not be the same in recommendation of any other good quality? and why does not some woman take a fancy to possess over her companions the glory of this chaste love? I may well say chaste,

"Nam si quando ad prælia ventum est
Ut quondam in stipulis magnus sine viribus ignis
Incassum furit:"

the vices that are stifled in the thought are not the worst.

To conclude this notable commentary, which has escaped from me in a torrent of babble, a torrent sometimes impetuous and hurtful.

> "Ut missum sponsi furtivo munere malum
> Procurrit casto virginis e gremio,
> Quod miseræ oblitæ molli sub veste locatum,
> Dum aventu matris prosilit, excutitur,
> Atque illud prono præceps agitur decursu
> Huic manat tristi conscius ore rubor."

I say that males and females are cast in the same mold, and that, education and usage excepted, the difference is not great. Plato indifferently invites both the one and the other to the society of all studies, exercises, and vocations, both military and civil, in his commonwealth; and the philosopher Antisthenes rejected all distinction between their virtue and ours. It is much more easy to accuse one sex than to excuse the other; 'tis according to the saying "The Pot and the Kettle."

XVI

OF COACHES

I T IS very easy to verify, that great authors, when they write of causes, not only make use of those they think to be the true causes, but also of those they believe not to be so, provided they have in them some beauty and invention: they speak true and usefully enough, if it be ingeniously. We cannot make ourselves sure of the supreme cause, and therefore clutter a great many together, to see if it may not accidentally be among them,

> "Namque unam dicere causam
> Non satis est, verum plures, unde una tamen sit."

Will you ask me, whence comes the custom of blessing those who sneeze? we break wind three several ways; that which sallies from below is too filthy; that which breaks out from the mouth carries with it some reproach of having eaten too much; the third eruption is sneezing, which because it proceeds from the head, and is without offense, we give it this civil reception: do not laugh at this distinction; for they say 'tis Aristotle's.

I think I have read in Plutarch (who of all the authors I ever conversed with is he who has best mixed art with nature, and judgment with knowledge), his giving as a reason for the rising of the stomach in those who are at sea, that it is occasioned by fear; having first found out some reason by which he proves that fear may produce such an effect. I, who am very subject to it, know well that this cause concerns not me; and know it, not by argument, but by necessary

experience. Without instancing what has been told me, that the same thing often happens in beasts, especially hogs who are out of all apprehension of danger; and what an acquaintance of mine told me of himself that, though very subject to it, the disposition to vomit has three of four times gone off him, being very afraid in a violent storm, as it happened to that ancient, *"Pejus vexabar, quam ut periculum mihi succurreret;"* I was never afraid upon the water, nor, indeed, in any other peril (and I have had enough before my eyes that would have sufficed, if death be one), so as to be astounded and to lose my judgment. Fear springs sometimes as much from want of judgment as from want of courage. All the dangers I have been in I have looked upon without winking, with an open, sound, and entire sight; and, indeed, a man must have courage to fear. It formerly served me better than other help, so to order and regulate my retreat, that it was, if not without fear, nevertheless without affright and astonishment; it was agitated, indeed, but not amazed or stupefied. Great souls go yet much farther, and present to us flights, not only steady and temperate, but moreover lofty. Let us make a relation of that which Alcibiades reports of Socrates, his fellow in arms: "I found him," says he, "after the rout of our army, him and Lachez, last among those who fled, and considered him at my leisure and in security, for I was mounted upon a good horse, and he on foot, as he had fought. I took notice, in the first place, how much judgment and resolution he showed, in comparison of Lachez, and then the bravery of his march, nothing different from his ordinary gait; his sight firm and regular, considering and judging what passed about him, looking one while upon those, and then upon others, friends and enemies, after such a manner as encouraged those, and signified to the others that he would sell his life dear to any one who should attempt to take it from him, and so they came off; for people are not willing to attack such kind of men, but pursue those they see are in a fright." This is the testimony of this great captain, which teaches us, what we every day see, that nothing so much throws us into dangers as an inconsiderate eagerness of getting ourselves clear of them: *"Quo timoris minus est, eo minus ferme periculi est."* Our people are to blame who say that such a

one is afraid of death, when they would express that he thinks of it and foresees it: foresight is equally convenient in what concerns us, whether good or ill. To consider and judge of danger, is, in some sort, the reverse to being astounded. I do not find myself strong enough to sustain the force and impetuosity of this passion of fear, nor of any other vehement passion whatever: if I was once conquered and beaten down by it, I should never rise again very sound. Whoever should once make my soul lose her footing, would never set her upright again: she retastes and researches herself too profoundly, and too much to the quick, and therefore would never let the wound she had received heal and cicatrize. It has been well for me that no sickness has yet discomposed her: at every charge made upon me, I preserve my utmost opposition and defense; by which means the first that should rout me would keep me from rallying again. I have no after-game to play: on which side soever the inundation breaks my banks, I lie open, and am drowned without remedy. Epicurus says, that a wise man can never become a fool; I have an opinion reverse to this sentence, which is that he who has once been a very fool, will never after be very wise. God grants me cold according to my cloth, and passions proportionable to the means I have to withstand them: nature having laid me open on the one side, has covered me on the other; having disarmed me of strength, she has armed me with insensibility and an apprehension that is regular, or, if you will, dull.

I cannot now long endure (and when I was young could much less) either coach, litter, or boat, and hate all other riding but on horseback, both in town and country. But I can bear a litter worse than a coach; and, by the same reason, a rough agitation upon the water, whence fear is produced, better than the motions of a calm. At the little jerks of oars, stealing the vessel from under us, I find, I know not how, both my head and my stomach disordered: neither can I endure to sit upon a tottering chair. When the sail or the current carries us equally, or that we are towed, the equal agitation does not disturb me at all: 'tis an interrupted motion that offends me, and, most of all when most slow: I cannot otherwise express it. The physicians have ordered me to squeeze and gird myself about

the bottom of the belly with a napkin to remedy this evil; which however I have not tried, being accustomed to wrestle with my own defects, and overcome them myself.

Would my memory serve me, I should not think my time ill spent in setting down here the infinite variety that history presents us of the use of coaches in the service of war: various, according to the nations, and according to the age; in my opinion, of great necessity and effect; so that it is a wonder that we have lost all knowledge of them. I will only say this, that very lately, in our fathers' time, the Hungarians made very advantageous use of them against the Turks; having in every one of them a targetter and a musketeer, and a number of harquebuses piled ready and loaded, and all covered with a pavesade like a galliot. They formed the front of their battle with three thousand such coaches, and after the cannon had played, made them all pour in their shot upon the enemy, who had to swallow that volley before they tasted of the rest, which was no little advance; and that done, these chariots charged into their squadrons to break them and open a way for the rest: besides the use they might make of them to flank the soldiers in a place of danger when marching to the field, or to cover a post, and fortify it in haste. In my time, a gentleman on one of our frontiers, unwieldly of body, and finding no horse able to carry his weight, having a quarrel, rode through the country in a chariot of this fashion, and found great convenience in it. But let us leave these chariots of war.

As if their effeminacy had not been sufficiently known by better proofs, the last kings of our first race traveled in a chariot drawn by four oxen. Marc Antony was the first at Rome who caused himself to be drawn in a coach by lions, and a singing wench with him.

Heliogabalus did since as much, calling himself Cybele, the mother of the gods; and also drawn by tigers, taking upon him the person of the god Bacchus; he also sometimes harnessed two stags to his coach, another time four dogs, and another, four naked wenches, causing himself to be drawn by them in pomp, stark naked too. The Emperor Firmus caused his chariot to be drawn by ostriches of a prodigious size, so that it seemed rather to fly than roll.

The strangeness of these inventions puts this other fancy in my

[275]

head: that it is a kind of pusillanimity in monarchs, and a testimony that they do not sufficiently understand themselves what they are, when they study to make themselves honored and to appear great by excessive expense: it were indeed excusable in a foreign country, but among their own subjects, where they are in sovereign command, and may do what they please, it derogates from their dignity the most supreme degree of honor to which they can arrive: just as, methinks, it is superfluous in a private gentleman to go finely dressed at home; his house, his attendants, and his kitchen, sufficiently answer for him. The advice that Isocrates gives his king, seems to be grounded upon reason; that he should be splendid in plate and furniture; forasmuch as it is an expense of duration that devolves on his successors; and that he should avoid all magnificences that will in a short time be forgotten. I loved to go fine when I was a younger brother, for want of other ornament; and it became me well: there are some upon whom their rich clothes weep. We have strange stories of the frugality of our kings about their own persons and in their gifts: kings who were great in reputation, valor, and fortune. Demosthenes vehemently opposes the law of his city that assigned the public money for the pomp of their public plays and festivals: he would that their greatness should be seen in numbers of ships well equipped, and good armies well provided for; and there is good reason to condemn Theophrastus who, in his Book on Riches, establishes a contrary opinion, and maintains that sort of expense to be the true fruit of abundance. They are delights, says Aristotle, that only please the baser sort of the people, and that vanish from the memory so soon as the people are sated with them, and for which no serious and judicious man can have any esteem. This money would, in my opinion, be much more royally, as more profitably, justly, and durably, laid out in ports, havens, walls, and fortifications; in sumptuous buildings, churches, hospitals, colleges, the reforming of streets and highways; wherein Pope Gregory XIII. will leave a laudable memory to future times: and wherein our Queen Catherine would to long posterity manifest her natural liberality and munificence, did her means supply her affection. Fortune has done me a great despite, in interrupting the noble

structure of the Pont-Neuf of our great city, and depriving me of the hope of seeing it finished before I die.

Moreover, it seems to the subjects, who are spectators of these triumphs, that their own riches are exposed before them, and that they are entertained at their own expense: for the people are apt to presume of kings, as we do of our servants, that they are to take care to provide us all things necessary in abundance, but not touch it themselves: and therefore the Emperor Galba, being pleased with a musician who played to him at supper, called for his money box, and gave him a handful of crowns that he took out of it, with these words: "This is not the public money, but my own." Yet it so falls out that the people, for the most part, have reason on their side, and that the princes feed their eyes with what they have need of to fill their bellies.

Liberality itself is not in its true luster in a sovereign hand: private men have therein the most right: for, to take it exactly, a king has nothing properly his own; he owes himself to others: authority is not given in favor of the magistrate, but of the people; a superior is never made so for his own profit, but for the profit of the inferior, and a physician for the sick person, and not for himself: all magistracy, as well as all art, has its end out of itself: *"Nulla ars in se versatur:"* wherefore the tutors of young princes, who make it their business to imprint in them this virtue of liberality, and preach to them to deny nothing and to think nothing so well spent as what they give (a doctrine that I have known in great credit in my time), either have more particular regard to their own profit than to that of their master, or ill understand to whom they speak. It is too easy a thing to inculcate liberality on him who has as much as he will to practice it with at the expense of others; and, the estimate not being proportioned to the measure of the gift but to the measure of the means of him who gave it, it comes to nothing in so mighty hands; they find themselves prodigal, before they can be reputed liberal. And it is but a little recommendation, in comparison with other royal virtues: and the only one, as the tyrant Dionysius said, that suits well with tyranny itself. I should rather teach him this verse of the ancient laborer,

"Τῇ χειρὶ δεῖ σπείρειν, ἀλλὰ μὴ ὅλῳ τῷ ξυλακῷ;"

[278]

he must scatter it abroad, and not lay it on a heap, in one place: and that, seeing he is to give, or, to say better, to pay and restore to so many people according as they have deserved, he ought to be a loyal and discreet disposer. If the liberality of a prince be without measure or discretion, I had rather he were covetous.

Royal virtue seems most to consist in justice; and of all the parts of justice that best denotes a king which accompanies liberality, for this they have particularly reserved to be performed by themselves, whereas all other sorts of justice they remit to the administration of others. An immoderate bounty is a very weak means to acquire for them good will; it checks more people than it allures: *"Quo in plures usus sis, minus in multos uti possis. . . . Quid autem est stultius, quam, quod libenter facias, curare ut id diutius facere non possis;"* and if it be conferred without due respect of merit, it puts him out of countenance who receives it, and is received ungraciously. Tyrants have been sacrificed to the hatred of the people by the hands of those very men they have unjustly advanced; such kind of men thinking to assure to themselves the possession of benefits unduly received, if they manifest to have him in hatred and disdain of whom they hold them, and in this associate themselves to the common judgment and opinion.

The subjects of a prince excessive in gifts grow excessive in asking, and regulate their demands, not by reason, but by example. We have, seriously, very often reason to blush at our own impudence: we are overpaid, according to justice, when the recompense equals our service, for do we owe nothing of natural obligation to our princes? If he bear our charges, he does too much; 'tis enough that he contribute to them: the overplus is called benefit, which cannot be exacted: for the very name Liberality sounds of Liberty.

There is no end on't, as we use it; we never reckon what we have received; we are only for the future liberality: wherefore, the more a prince exhausts himself in giving, the poorer he grows in friends. How shall he satisfy immoderate desires, that still increase as they are fulfilled? He who has his thoughts upon taking, never thinks of what he has taken; covetousness has nothing so properly and so much its own as ingratitude.

[279]

The example of Cyrus will not do amiss in this place, to serve the kings of these times for a touchstone to know whether their gifts are well or ill bestowed, and to see how much better that emperor conferred them than they do, by which means they are reduced to borrow of unknown subjects, and rather of them whom they have wronged, than of them on whom they have conferred their benefits, and so receive aids, wherein there is nothing of gratuitous but the name. Crœsus reproached him with his bounty, and cast up to how much his treasure would amount if he had been a little closer-handed. He had a mind to justify his liberality, and therefore sent dispatches into all parts to the grandees of his dominions whom he had particularly advanced, entreating every one of them to supply him with as much money as they could, for a pressing occasion, and to send him particulars of what each could advance. When all these answers were brought to him, every one of his friends, not thinking it enough barely to offer him so much as he had received from his bounty, and adding to it a great deal of his own, it appeared that the sum amounted to a great deal more than Crœsus' reckoning. Whereupon Cyrus: "I am not," said he, "less in love with riches than other princes, but rather a better husband; you see with how small a venture I have acquired the inestimable treasure of so many friends, and how much more faithful treasurers they are to me than mercenary men without obligation or affection would be: and my money better laid up than in chests, bringing upon me the hatred, envy, and contempt of other princes."

The emperors excused the superfluity of their plays and public spectacles by reason that their authority in some sort (at least in outward appearance) depended upon the will of the people of Rome, who time out of mind, had been accustomed to be entertained and caressed with such shows and excesses. But they were private citizens, who had nourished this custom to gratify their fellow-citizens and companions (and chiefly out of their own purses) by such profusion and magnificence; it had quite another taste when the masters came to imitate it: *"Pecuniarum translatio a justis dominis ad a lienosnon debet liberalis videri."* Philip, seeing that his son went about by presents to gain the affection of the Mace-

donians, reprimanded him in a letter after this manner; "What! hast thou a mind that thy subjects shall look upon thee as their cash-keeper and not as their king? Wilt thou tamper with them to win their affections? Do it, then, by the benefits of thy virtue, and not by those of thy chest."

And yet it was, doubtless, a fine thing to bring and plant within the amphitheater a great number of vast trees, with all their branches in their full verdure, representing a great shady forest, disposed in excellent order; and, the first day, to throw into it a thousand ostriches and a thousand stags, a thousand boars and a thousand fallow-deer, to be killed and disposed of by the people: the next day to cause a hundred great lions, a hundred leopards, and three hundred bears to be killed in his presence; and for the third day, to make three hundred pair of gladiators fight it out to the last, as the Emperor Probus did. It was also very fine to see those vast amphitheaters, all faced with marble without, curiously wrought with figures and statues, and the inside sparkling with rare decorations and enrichments,

"Baltheus en gemmis, en illita porticus auro:"

all the sides of this vast space filled and environed, from the bottom to the top, with three or four score rows of seats, all of marble also, and covered with cushions,

"Exeat, inquit,
Si pudor est, et de pulvino surgat equestri,
Cujus res legi non sufficit."

where a hundred thousand men might sit at their ease: and the place below, where the games were played, to make it, by art, first open and cleave in chasms, representing caves that vomited out the beasts designed for the spectacle; and then, secondly, to be overflowed by a deep sea, full of sea monsters, and laden with ships of war, to represent a naval battle: and, thirdly, to make it dry and even again for the combat of the gladiators; and, for the fourth scene, to have it strown with vermilion grain and storax, instead of sand, there to

make a solemn feast for all that infinite number of people; the last act of one only day.

> "Quoties los descendentis arenæ
> Vidimus in partes, ruptaque voragine terræ
> Emersisse feras, et eisdem sæpe latebris
> Aurea cum croceo creverunt arbuta libro! . . .
> Nec solum nobis silvestria cernere monstra
> Contigit; æquoreos ego cum certantibus ursis
> Spectavi vitulos, et equorum nomine dignum,
> Sed deforme pecus."

Sometimes they made a high mountain advance itself, covered with fruit trees and other leafy trees, sending down rivulets of water from the top, as from the mouth of a fountain; otherwhiles, a great ship was seen to come rolling in, which opened and divided of itself, and after having disgorged from the hold four or five hundred beasts for fight, closed again, and vanished without help. At other times, from the floor of this place, they made spouts of perfumed water dart their streams upward, and so high as to sprinkle all that infinite multitude. To defend themselves from the injuries of the weather, they had that vast place one while covered over with purple curtains of needlework, and by and by with silk of one or another color, which they drew off or on in a moment, as they had a mind.

> "Quamvis non modico caleant spectacula sole,
> Vela reducunter, cum venit Hermogenes."

The network also that was set before the people to defend them from the violence of these turned out beasts, was woven of gold:

> "Auro quoque torta refulgent
> Retia."

If there be anything excusable in such excesses as these, it is where the novelty and invention create more wonder than the expense; even in these vanities, we discover how fertile those ages were in other kind of wits than these of ours. It is with this sort of fertility, as with all other products of nature; not that she there and then employed her utmost force: we do not go; we rather run up and down,

and whirl this way and that; we turn back the way we came. I am afraid our knowledge is weak in all senses; we neither see far forward nor far backward: our understanding comprehends little, and lives but a little while; 'tis short both in extent of time and extent of matter.

> "Vixere fortes ante Agamemnona
> Multi, sed omnes illacrymabilas
> Urgentur, ignotique longa
> Nocte."

> "Et supera bellum Thebanum, et funera Trojæ,
> Multi alias alii quoque res cecinere poetæ:"

And the narrative of Solon, of what he had got out of the Egyptian priests, touching the long life of their state, and their manner of learning and preserving foreign histories, is not, methinks, a testimony to be slighted upon this consideration. *"Si interminatam in omnes partes magnitudinem regionum videremus, et temporum, in quam se injiciens animus et intendens, ita late longeque peregrinatur, ut nullam oram ultimi videat, in qua possit insistere: in hæc immensitate . . . infinita vis innumerabili umappareret formarum."* Though all that has arrived, by report, of our knowledge of times past should be true, and known by some one person, it would be less than nothing in comparison of what is unknown. And of this same image of the world, which glides away while we live upon it, how wretched and limited is the knowledge of the most curious; not only of particular events, which fortune often renders exemplary and of great concern, but of the state of great governments and nations, a hundred more escape us than ever come to our knowledge. We make a mighty business of the invention of artillery and printing, which other men at the other end of the world, in China, had a thousand years ago. Did we but see as much of the world as we do not see, we should perceive, we may well believe, a perpetual multiplication and vicissitude of forms. There is nothing single and rare in respect of nature, but in respect of our knowledge, which is a wretched foundation whereon to ground our rules, and that represents to us a very false image of things. As we nowadays vainly con-

clude the declension and decrepitude of the world, by the arguments
we extract from our own weakness and decay;

"Jamque adeo est affecta ætas effoet aque tellus;"

so did he vainly conclude as to its birth and youth, by the vigor he
observed in the wits of his time, abounding in novelties and the invention of divers arts:

"Verum, ut opinor, habet novitatem summa, recensque
Natura est mundi, neque pridem exordia cœpit:
Quare etiam quædam nunc artes expoliuntur,
Nunc etiam augescunt; nunc addita navigiis sunt
Multa."

Our world has lately discovered another (and who can assure us
that it is the last of its brothers, since the Dæmons, the Sybils, and
we ourselves have been ignorant of this till now?) as large, well
peopled, and fruitful, as this whereon we live; and yet so raw and
childish, that we are still teaching it its A B C; 'tis not above fifty
years since it knew neither letters, weights, measures, vestments,
corn nor vines; it was then quite naked in the mother's lap, and only
lived upon what she gave it. If we rightly conclude of our ends, and
this poet of the youthfulness of that age of his, that other world will
only enter into the light when this of ours shall make its exit; the
universe will fall into paralysis; one member will be useless, the
other in vigor. I am very much afraid that we have greatly precipitated its declension and ruin by our contagion; and that we have
sold it our opinions and our arts at a very dear rate. It was an infant
world, and yet we have not whipped and subjected it to our discipline, by the advantage of our natural worth and force, neither have
we won it by our justice and goodness, nor subdued it by our
magnanimity. Most of their answers, and the negotiations we have
had with them, witness that they were nothing behind us in pertinency and clearness of natural understanding. The astonishing
magnificence of the cities of Cusco and Mexico, and among many
other things, the garden of the king, where all the trees, fruits, and
plants, according to the order and stature they have in a garden,

were excellently formed in gold; as, in his cabinet, were all the animals bred upon his territory and in its seas; and the beauty of their manufactures, in jewels, feathers, cotton, and painting, gave ample proof that they were as little inferior to us in industry. But as to what concerns devotion, observance of the laws, goodness, liberality, loyalty, and plain dealing, it was of use to us that we had not so much as they; for they have lost, sold, and betrayed themselves by this advantage over us.

As to boldness and courage, stability, constancy against pain, hunger, and death, I should not fear to oppose the examples I find among them, to the most famous examples of elder times, that we find in our records on this side of the world. For, as to those who subdued them, take but away the tricks and artifices they practiced to gull them, and the just astonishment it was to those nations, to see so sudden and unexpected an arrival of men with beards, differing in language, religion, shape, and countenance, from so remote a part of the world, and where they had never heard there was any habitation, mounted upon great unknown monsters, against those who had not only never seen a horse, but had never seen any other beast trained up to carry a man or any other loading; shelled in a hard and shining skin, with a cutting and glittering weapon in his hand, against them, who, out of wonder at the brightness of a looking-glass or a knife, would truck great treasures of gold and pearl; and who had neither knowledge, nor matter with which, at leisure, they could penetrate our steel: to which may be added the lightning and thunder of our cannon and harquebuses, enough to frighten Cæsar himself, if surprised, with so little experience, against people naked, except where the invention of a little quilted cotton was in use, without other arms, at the most, than bows, stones, staves, and bucklers of wood; people surprised under color of friendship and good faith, by the curiosity of seeing strange and unknown things; take but away, I say, this disparity from the conquerors, and you take away all the occasion of so many victories. When I look upon that invincible ardor wherewith so many thousands of men, women, and children, so often presented and threw themselves into inevitable dangers for the defense of their gods and

liberties; that generous obstinacy to suffer all extremities and difficulties, and death itself, rather than submit to the dominion of those
by whom they had been so shamefully abused; and some of them
choosing to die of hunger and fasting, being prisoners, rather than
to accept of nourishment from the hands of their so basely victorious enemies: I see, that whoever would have attacked them upon
equal terms of arms, experience, and number, would have had a
hard, and, peradventure, a harder game to play, than in any other
war we have seen.

Why did not so noble a conquest fall under Alexander, or the
ancient Greeks and Romans; and so great a revolution and mutation of so many empires and nations, fall into hands that would
have gently leveled, rooted up, and made plain and smooth whatever was rough and savage among them, and that would have
cherished and propagated the good seeds that nature had there
produced; mixing not only with the culture of land and the ornament of cities, the arts of this part of the world, in what was necessary, but also the Greek and Roman virtues, with those that were
original of the country? What a reparation had it been to them, and
what a general good to the whole world, had our first examples
and deportments in those parts allured those people to the admiration and imitation of virtue, and had begotten between them and
us a fraternal society and intelligence? How easy had it been to
have made advantage of souls so innocent, and so eager to learn,
having, for the most part, naturally so good inclinations before?
Whereas on the contrary, we have taken advantage of their ignorance and inexperience, with greater ease to incline them to treachery, luxury, avarice, and toward all sorts of inhumanity and
cruelty, by the pattern and example of our manners. Who ever
enhanced the price of merchandise at such a rate? So many cities
leveled with the ground, so many nations exterminated, so many
millions of people fallen by the edge of the sword, and the richest
and most beautiful part of the world turned upside down, for the
traffic of pearl and pepper? Mechanic victories! Never did ambition, never did public animosities engage men against one another
in such miserable hostilities, in such miserable calamities.

Certain Spaniards, coasting the sea in quest of their mines, landed in a fruitful and pleasant and very well peopled country, and there made to the inhabitants their accustomed professions: "that they were peaceable men, who were come from a very remote country, and sent on the behalf of the king of Castile, the greatest prince of the habitable world, to whom the pope, God's vicegerent upon earth, had given the principality of all the Indies; that if they would become tributaries to him, they should be very gently and courteously used;" at the same time requiring of them victuals for their nourishment, and gold whereof to make some pretended medicine; setting forth, moreover, the belief in one only God, and the truth of our religion, which they advised them to embrace, whereunto they also added some threats. To which they received this answer: "That as to their being peaceable, they did not seem to be such, if they were so. As to their king, since he was fain to beg, he must be necessitous and poor; and he who had made him this gift, must be a man who loved dissension, to give that to another which was none of his own, to bring it into dispute against the ancient possessors. As to victuals, they would supply them; that of gold they had little; it being a thing they had in very small esteem as of no use to the service of life, whereas their only care was to pass it over happily and pleasantly: but that what they could find excepting what was employed in the service of their gods, they might freely take. As to one only God, the proposition had pleased them well; but that they would not change their religion, both because they had so long and happily lived in it, and that they were not wont to take advice of any but their friends, and those they knew: as to their menaces, it was a sign of want of judgment, to threaten those whose nature and power were to them unknown; that, therefore, they were to make haste to quit their coast, for they were not used to take the civilities and professions of armed men and strangers in good part; otherwise they should do by them as they had done by those others," showing them the heads of several executed men round the walls of their city. A fair example of the babble of these children. But so it is that the Spaniards did not, either in this or in several other places, where they did not find the

merchandise they sought, make any stay or attempt, whatever other conveniences were there to be had; witness my Cannibals.

Of the two most puissant monarchs of that world, and, peradventure, of this, kings of so many kings, and the last they turned out, he of Peru, having been taken in a battle, and put to so excessive a ransom as exceeds all belief, and it being faithfully paid, and he having, by his conversation, given manifest signs of a frank, liberal, and constant spirit, and of a clear and settled understanding, the conquerors had a mind, after having exacted one million three hundred and twenty-five thousand and five hundred weight of gold, besides silver, and other things which amounted to no less (so that their horses were shod with massy gold), still to see, at the price of what disloyalty and injustice whatever, what the remainder of the treasures of this king might be, and to possess themselves of that also. To this end a false accusation was preferred against him, and false witnesses brought to prove that he went about to raise an insurrection in his provinces, to procure his own liberty; whereupon, by the virtuous sentence of those very men who had by this treachery conspired his ruin, he was condemned to be publicly hanged, after having made him buy off the torment of being burned alive, by the baptism they gave immediately before execution; a horrid and unheard-of barbarity which, nevertheless, he underwent without giving way either in word or look, with a truly grave and royal behavior. After which, to calm and appease the people, aroused and astounded at so strange a thing, they counterfeited great sorrow for his death, and appointed most sumptuous funerals.

The other king of Mexico, having for a long time defended his beleaguered city, and having in this siege manifested the utmost of what suffering and perseverance can do, if ever prince and people did, and his misfortune having delivered him alive into his enemies' hands, upon articles of being treated like a king, neither did he in his captivity discover anything unworthy of that title. His enemies, after their victory, not finding so much gold as they expected, when they had searched and rifled with their utmost diligence, they went about to procure discoveries by the most cruel torments they could invent upon the prisoners they had taken: but

having profited nothing by these, their courage being greater than
their torments, they arrived at last to such a degree of fury, as,
contrary to their faith and the law of nations, to condemn the king
himself, and one of the principal noblemen of his court to the rack,
in the presence of one another. This lord, finding himself overcome
with pain, being environed with burning coals, pitifully turned his
dying eyes toward his master, as it were to ask him pardon that he
was able to endure no more; whereupon the king darting at him a
fierce and severe look, as reproaching his cowardice and pusillanimity, with a harsh and constant voice said to him thus only:
"And what dost thou think I suffer? am I in a bath? am I more
at ease than thou?" Whereupon the other immediately quailed under the torment and died upon the spot. The king, half roasted, was
carried thence; not so much out of pity (for what compassion ever
touched so barbarous souls, who, upon the doubtful information
of some vessel of gold to be made a prey of, caused not only a man,
but a king, so great in fortune and desert, to be broiled before their
eyes), but because his constancy rendered their cruelty still more
shameful. They afterward hanged him, for having nobly attempted
to deliver himself by arms from so long a captivity and subjection,
and he died with a courage becoming so magnanimous a prince.

Another time, they burned in the same fire, four hundred and
sixty men alive at once, the four hundred of the common people,
the sixty, the principal lords of a province, mere prisoners of war.
We have these narratives from themselves: for they not only own
it, but boast of it and publish it. Could it be for a testimony of their
justice, or their zeal to religion? Doubtless these are ways too
differing and contrary to so holy an end. Had they proposed to
themselves to extend our faith, they would have considered that it
does not amplify in the possession of territories, but in the gaining
of men; and would have more than satisfied themselves with the
slaughters occasioned by the necessity of war, without indifferently
mixing a massacre, as upon wild beasts, as universal as fire and
sword could make it: having only, by intention, saved so many as
they meant to make miserable slaves of, for the work and service
of their mines; so that many of the captains were put to death upon

the place of conquest, by order of the kings of Castile, justly offended with the horror of their deportment, and almost all of them hated and disesteemed. God meritoriously permitted that all this great plunder should be swallowed up by the sea in transportation, or in the civil wars wherewith they devoured one another: and most of the men themselves were buried in a foreign land, without any fruit of their victory.

That the revenue from these countries, though in the hands of so parsimonious and so prudent a prince, so little answers the expectation given of it to his predecessors, and to that original abundance of riches which was found at the first landing in those new discovered countries (for though a great deal be fetched thence, yet we see 'tis nothing in comparison of that which might be expected) is, that the use of coin was there utterly unknown, and that consequently their gold was found all hoarded together, being of no other use but for ornament and show, as a furniture reserved from father to son by many puissant kings, who were ever draining their mines to make this vast heap of vessels and statues for the decoration of their palaces and temples; whereas our gold is always in motion and traffic; we cut it into a thousand small pieces, and cast it into a thousand forms, and scatter and disperse it in a thousand ways. But suppose our kings should thus hoard up all the gold they could get in several ages, and let it lie idle by them.

Those of the kingdom of Mexico were in some sort more civilized, and more advanced in arts, than the other nations about them. Therefore did they judge, as we do, that the world was near its period, and looked upon the desolation we brought among them as a certain sign of it. They believed that the existence of the world was divided into five ages, and in the life of five successive suns, of which four had already ended their time, and that this which gave them light was the fifth. The first perished, with all other creatures, by an universal inundation of water; the second by the heavens falling upon us and suffocating every living thing; to which age they assigned the giants, and showed bones to the Spaniards according to the proportion of which the stature of men amounted to twenty feet; the third by fire, which burned and consumed all; the

fourth by an emotion of the air and wind, which came with such violence as to beat down even many mountains, wherein the men died not, but were turned into baboons (what impressions will not the weakness of human belief admit?). After the death of this fourth sun, the world was twenty-five years in perpetual darkness: in the fifteenth of which a man and a woman were created, who restored the human race: ten years after, upon a certain day, the sun appeared newly created, and since the account of their years takes beginning from that day: the third day after its creation the ancient gods died, and the new ones were since born daily. After what manner they think this last sun shall perish my author knows not; but their number of this fourth change agrees with the great conjunction of stars which eight hundred and odd years ago, as astrologers suppose, produced great alterations and novelties in the world.

As to pomp and magnificence, upon the account of which I engaged in this discourse, neither Greece, Rome, nor Egypt, whether for utility, difficulty, or state, can compare any of their works with the highway to be seen in Peru, made by the kings of the country, from the city of Quito to that of Cusco (three hundred leagues), straight, even, five-and-twenty paces wide, paved and provided on both sides with high and beautiful walls; and close by them, and all along on the inside, two perennial streams, bordered with a beautiful sort of a tree which they call Molly. In this work, where they met with rocks and mountains, they cut them through, and made them even, and filled up pits and valleys with lime and stone to make them level. At the end of every day's journey are beautiful palaces, furnished with provisions, vestments, and arms, as well for travelers as for the armies that are to pass that way. In the estimate of this work I have reckoned the difficulty which is especially considerable in that place; they did not build with any stones less than ten feet square, and had no other conveniency of carriage but by drawing their load themselves by force of arm, and knew not so much as the art of scaffolding, nor any other way of standing to their work, but by throwing up earth against the building as it rose higher, taking it away again when they had done.

Let us here return to our coaches. Instead of these, and of all other sorts of carriages, they caused themselves to be carried upon men's shoulders. This last king of Peru, the day that he was taken, was thus carried between two upon staves of gold, and set in a chair of gold in the middle of his army. As many of these sedan-men as were killed to make him fall (for they would take him alive), so many others (and they contended for it) took the place of those who were slain, so that they could never beat him down, what slaughter soever they made of these people, till a light-horseman, seizing upon him, brought him down.

XVII

THAT TO STUDY PHILOSOPHY
IS TO LEARN TO DIE

CICERO says "that to study philosophy is nothing but to prepare one's self to die." The reason of which is, because study and contemplation do in some sort withdraw from us our soul, and employ it separately from the body, which is a kind of apprenticeship and a resemblance of death; or else, because all the wisdom and reasoning in the world do in the end conclude in this point, to teach us not to fear to die. And to say the truth, either our reason mocks us, or it ought to have no other aim but our contentment only, nor to endeavor anything but, in sum, to make us live well, and, as the Holy Scripture says, at our ease. All the opinions of the world agree in this, that pleasure is our end, though we make use of divers means to attain it: they would, otherwise, be rejected at the first motion; for who would give ear to him that should propose affliction and misery for his end? The controversies and disputes of the philosophical sects upon this point are merely verbal—*"Transcurramus solertissimas nugas"*—there is more in them of opposition and obstinacy than is consistent with so sacred a profession; but whatsoever personage a man takes upon himself to perform, he ever mixes his own part with it.

Let the philosophers say what they will, the main thing at which we all aim, even in virtue itself, is pleasure. It amuses me to rattle in their ears this word, which they so nauseate to hear; and if it signify some supreme pleasure and excessive contentment, it is more due to the assistance of virtue than to any other assistance

whatever. This pleasure, for being more gay, more sinewy, more robust, and more manly, is only the more seriously voluptuous, and we ought to give it the name of pleasure, as that which is more favorable, gentle, and natural, and not that of vigor, from which we have denominated it. The other, and meaner pleasure, if it could deserve this fair name, it ought to be by way of competition, and not of privilege. I find it less exempt from traverses and inconveniences than virtue itself; and, besides that the enjoyment is more momentary, fluid, and frail, it has its watchings, fasts, and labors, its sweat and its blood; and, moreover, has particular to itself so many several sorts of sharp and wounding passions, and so dull a satiety attending it, as equal it to the severest penance. And we mistake if we think that these incommodities serve it for a spur and a seasoning to its sweetness (as in nature one contrary is quickened by another), or say, when we come to virtue, that like consequences and difficulties overwhelm and render it austere and inaccessible; whereas, much more aptly than in voluptuousness, they ennoble, sharpen, and heighten the perfect and divine pleasure they procure us. He renders himself unworthy of it who will counterpoise its cost with its fruit, and neither understands the blessing nor how to use it. Those who preach to us that the quest of it is craggy, difficult, and painful, but its fruition pleasant, what do they mean by that but to tell us that is always unpleasing? For what human means will ever attain its enjoyment? The most perfect have been fain to content themselves to aspire unto it, and to approach it only, without ever possessing it. But they are deceived, seeing that of all the pleasures we know, the very pursuit is pleasant. The attempt ever relishes of the quality of the thing to which it is directed, for it is a good part of, and consubstantial with, the effect. The felicity and beatitude that glitters in Virtue, shines throughout all her appurtenances and avenues, even to the first entry and utmost limits.

Now, of all the benefits that virtue confers upon us, the contempt of death is one of the greatest, as the means that accommodates human life with a soft and easy tranquillity, and gives us a pure and pleasant taste of living, without which all other pleasure would be extinct. Which is the reason why all the rules center and concur

in this one article. And although they all in like manner, with common accord, teach us also to despise pain, poverty, and the other
accidents to which human life is subject, it is not, nevertheless, with
the same solicitude, as well by reason these accidents are not of so
great necessity, the greater part of mankind passing over their
whole lives without ever knowing what poverty is, and some without sorrow or sickness, as Xenophilus the musician, who lived a
hundred and six years in perfect and continual health; as also because, at the worst, death can, whenever we please, cut short and
put an end to all other inconveniences. But as to death, it is inevitable:

> "Omnes eodem cogimur; omnium
> Versatur urna serius ocius
> Sors exitura, et nos in æternum
> Exilium impositura cymbæ,"

and, consequently, if it frights us, 'tis a perpetual torment, for
which there is no sort of consolation. There is no way by which it
may not reach us. We may continually turn our heads this way and
that, as in a suspected country, *"quæ, quasi saxum Tantalo, semper
impendet."* Our courts of justice often send back condemned criminals to be executed upon the place where the crime was committed;
but, carry them to fine houses by the way, prepare for them the
best entertainment you can—

> "Non Siculæ dapes
> Dulcem elaborabunt saporem:
> Non avium citharæque cantus
> Somnum reducent."

Do you think they can relish it? and that the fatal end of their
journey being continually before their eyes, would not alter and
deprave their palate from tasting these regalios?

> "Audit iter, numeratque dies, spatioque viarum
> Metitur vitam; torquetur peste futura."

The end of our race is death; 'tis the necessary object of our aim,
which, if it fright us, how is it possible to advance a step without a
fit of ague? The remedy the vulgar use is not to think on't; but from

[295]

what brutish stupidity can they derive so gross a blindness? They must bridle the ass by the tail.

"Qui capite ipse suo instituit vestigia retro,"

'tis no wonder if he be often trapped in the pitfall. They affright people with the very mention of death, and many cross themselves, as it were the name of the devil. And because the making a man's will is in reference to dying, not a man will be persuaded to take a pen in hand to that purpose till the physician has passed sentence upon him, and totally given him over, and then between grief and terror, God knows in how fit a condition of understanding he is to do it.

The Romans, by reason that this poor syllable *death* sounded so harshly to their ears, and seemed so ominous, found out a way to soften and spin it out by a periphrasis, and instead of pronouncing such a one is dead, said, "Such a one has lived," or "Such a one has ceased to live;" for, provided there was any mention of life in the case, though past, it carried yet some sound of consolation. And from them it is that we have borrowed our expression, "The late monsieur such and such a one." Peradventure, as the saying is, the term we have lived is worth our money. I was born between eleven and twelve o'clock in the forenoon the last day of February, 1533, according to our computation, beginning the year the 1st of January, and it is now just fifteen days since I was complete nine-and-thirty years old; I make account to live, at least, as many more. In the meantime, to trouble a man's self with the thought of a thing so far off, were folly. But what? Young and old die upon the same terms; no one departs out of life otherwise than if he had but just before entered into it; neither is any man so old and decrepit, who, having heard of Methuselah, does not think he has yet twenty years good to come. Fool that thou art, who has assured unto thee the term of life? Thou dependest upon physicians' tales: rather consult effects and experience. According to the common course of things, 'tis long since that thou hast lived by extraordinary favor: thou hast already outlived the ordinary term of life. And that is so, reckon up thy acquaintance, how many more have died before they

arrived at thy age than have attained unto it; and of those who have ennobled their lives by their renown, take but an account, and I dare lay a wager thou wilt find more who have died before than after five-and-thirty years of age. It is full both of reason and piety too, to take example by the humanity of Jesus Christ Himself; now, He ended His life at three-and-thirty years. The greatest man, that was no more than a man, Alexander, died also at the same age. How many several ways has death to surprise us?

> "Quid quisque, vitet, nunquam homini satis
> Cautum est in horas."

To omit fevers and pleurisies, who would ever have imagined that a duke of Brittany should be pressed to death in a crowd as that duke was, at the entry of Pope Clement, my neighbor, into Lyons? Hast thou not seen one of our kings killed at a tilting, and did not one of his ancestors die by the jostle of a hog? Æschylus, threatened with the fall of a house, was to much purpose circumspect to avoid that danger, seeing that he was knocked on the head by a tortoise falling out of an eagle's talons in the air. Another was choked with a grapestone; an emperor killed with the scratch of a comb in combing his head. Æmilius Lepidus with a stumble at his own threshold, and Aufidius with a jostle against the door as he entered the council-chamber. And between the very thighs of woman, Cornelius Gallus the prætor; Tigillinus, captain of the watch at Rome; Ludovico, son of Guido di Gonzaga, Marquis of Mantua; and (of worse example) Speusippus, a Platonic philosopher, and one of our popes. The poor judge Bebius gave adjournment in a case for eight days, but he himself meanwhile, was condemned by death, and his own stay of life expired. While Caius Julius, the physician, was anointing the eyes of a patient, death closed his own; and, if I may bring in an example of my own blood, a brother of mine, Captain St. Martin, a young man, three-and-twenty years old, who had already given sufficient testimony of his valor, playing a match at tennis, received a blow of a ball a little above his right ear, which, as it gave no manner of sign of wound or contusion, he took no notice of it, nor so much as sat down to re-

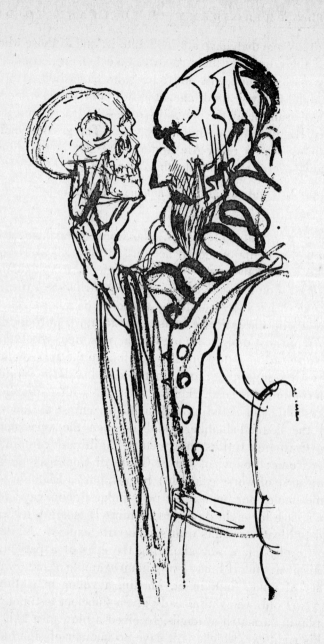

pose himself, but, nevertheless, died within five or six hours after, of an apoplexy occasioned by that blow.

These so frequent and common examples passing every day bo fore our eyes, how is it possible a man should disengage himself from the thought of death, or avoid fancying that it has us, every moment, by the throat? What matter is it, you will say, which way it comes to pass, provided a man does not terrify himself with the expectation? For my part, I am of this mind, and if a man could by any means avoid it, though by creeping under a calf's skin, I am one that should not be ashamed of the shift; all I aim at is, to pass my time at my ease, and the recreations that will most contribute to it, I take hold of, as little glorious and exemplary as you will.

> "Prætulerim . . . delirus inersque videri,
> Dum mea delectent mala me, vel denique fallant,
> Quam sapere, et ringi."

But 'tis folly to think of doing anything that way. They go, they come, they gallop and dance, and not a word of death. All this is very fine: but withal, when it comes either to themselves, their wives, their children, or friends, surprising them at unawares and unprepared, then what torment, what outcries, what madness and despair! Did you ever see anything so subdued, so changed, and so confounded? A man must, therefore, make more early provision for it; and this brutish negligence, could it possibly lodge in the brain of any man of sense (which I think utterly impossible), sells us its merchandise too dear. Were it an enemy that could be avoided, I would then advise to borrow arms even of cowardice itself; but seeing it is not, and that it will catch you as well flying and playing the poltroon, as standing to't like an honest man—

> "Nempe et fugacem persequitur virum,
> Nec parcit imbellis juventæ
> Poplitibus timidoque tergo."

And seeing that no temper of arms is of proof to secure us—

> "Ille licet ferro cautus se condat, et ære,
> Mors tamen inclusum protrahet inde caput"

[299]

—let us learn bravely to stand our ground, and fight him. And to begin to deprive him of the greatest advantage he has over us, let us take a way quite contrary to the common course. Let us disarm him of his novelty and strangeness, let us converse and be familiar with him, and have nothing so frequent in our thoughts as death. Upon all occasions represent him to our imagination in his every shape; at the stumbling of a horse, at the falling of a tile, at the least prick with a pin, let us presently consider, and say to ourselves, "Well, and what if it had been death itself?" and, thereupon, let us encourage and fortify ourselves. Let us evermore, amidst our jollity and feasting, set the remembrance of our frail condition before our eyes, never suffering ourselves to be so far transported with our delights, but that we have some intervals of reflecting upon, and considering how many several ways this jollity of ours tends to death, and with how many dangers it threatens it. The Egyptians were wont to do after this manner, who in the height of their feasting and mirth, caused a dried skeleton of a man to be brought into the room to serve for a memento to their guests.

> "Omnem crede diem tibi diluxisse supremum:
> Grata superveniet, quæ non sperabitur, hora."

Where death waits for us is uncertain; let us look for him everywhere. The premeditation of death is the premeditation of liberty; he who has learned to die, has unlearned to serve. There is nothing of evil in life, for him who rightly comprehends that the privation of life is no evil: to know how to die, delivers us from all subjection and constraint. Paulus Æmilius answered him whom the miserable king of Macedon, his prisoner, sent to entreat him that he would not lead him in his triumph, "Let him make that request to himself."

In truth, in all things, if nature do not help a little, it is very hard for art and industry to perform anything to purpose. I am in my own nature not melancholic, but meditative; and there is nothing I have more continually entertained myself withal than imaginations of death, even in the most wanton time of my age:

> "Jucundum quum ætas florida ver ageret."

In the company of ladies, and at games, some have perhaps thought me possessed with some jealousy, or the uncertainty of some hope, while I was entertaining myself with the remembrance of some one, surprised, a few days before, with a burning fever of which he died, returning from an entertainment like this, with his head full of idle fancies of love and jollity, as mine was then, and that, for aught I knew, the same destiny was attending me.

"Jam fuerit, nec post unquam revocare licebit."

Yet did not this thought wrinkle my forehead any more than any other. It is impossible but we must feel a sting in such imaginations as these, at first; but with often turning and re-turning them in one's mind, they, at last, become so familiar as to be no trouble at all; otherwise, I, for my part, should be in a perpetual fright and frenzy; for never man was so distrustful of his life, never man so uncertain as to its duration. Neither health, which I have hitherto ever enjoyed very strong and vigorous, and very seldom interrupted, does prolong, nor sickness contract my hopes. Every minute, methinks, I am escaping, and it eternally runs in my mind, that what may be done to-morrow, may be done to-day. Hazards and dangers do, in truth, little or nothing hasten our end; and if we consider how many thousands more remain and hang over our heads, besides the accident that immediately threatens us, we shall find that the sound and the sick, those that are abroad at sea, and those that sit by the fire, those who are engaged in battle, and those who sit idle at home, are the one as near it as the other. *"Nemo altero fragilior est: nemo in crastinum sui certior."* For anything I have to do before I die, the longest leisure would appear too short, were it but an hour's business I had to do.

A friend of mine the other day turning over my tablets, found therein a memorandum of something I would have done after my decease, whereupon I told him, as it was really true, that though I was no more than a league's distance only from my own house, and merry and well, yet when that thing came into my head, I made haste to write it down there, because I was not certain to live till I came home. As a man that am eternally brooding over my own

thoughts, and confine them to my own particular concerns, I am at all hours as well prepared as I am ever like to be, and death, whenever he shall come, can bring nothing along with him I did not expect long before. We should always, as near as we can, be booted and spurred, and ready to go, and, above all things, take care, at that time, to have no business with any one but one's self:

> "Quid brevi fortes jaculamur ævo
> Multa?"

for we shall there find work enough to do, without any need of addition. One man complains, more than of death, that he is thereby prevented of a glorious victory; another, that he must die before he has married his daughter, or educated his children; a third seems only troubled that he must lose the society of his wife; a fourth, the conversation of his son, as the principal comfort and concern of his being. For my part, I am, thanks be to God, at this instant in such a condition, that I am ready to dislodge, whenever it shall please Him, without regret for anything whatsoever. I disengage myself throughout from all worldly relations; my leave is soon taken of all but myself. Never did any one prepare to bid adieu to the world more absolutely and unreservedly, and to shake hands with all manner of interest in it, than I expect to do. The deadest deaths are the best.

> "'Miser, O miser,' aiunt, 'omnia ademit
> Una dies infesta mihi tot præmia vitæ.'"

And the builder,

> "'Manent,' says he, 'opera interrupta, minæque
> Murorum ingentes.'"

A man must design nothing that will require so much time to the finishing, or, at least, with no such passionate desire to see it brought to perfection. We are born to action.

> "Quum moriar medium solvar et inter opus."

I would always have a man to be doing, and, as much as in him lies, to extend and spin out the offices of life; and then let death take

me planting my cabbages, indifferent to him, and still less of my garden's not being finished. I saw one die, who, at his last gasp, complained of nothing so much as that destiny was about to cut the thread of a chronicle history he was then compiling, when he was gone no farther than the fifteenth or sixteenth of our kings.

"Illud in his rebus non addunt, nec tibi earum
Jam desiderium rerum super insidit una."

We are to discharge ourselves from these vulgar and hurtful humors. To this purpose it was that men first appointed the places of sepulture adjoining the churches, and in the most frequented places of the city, to accustom, says Lycurgus, the common people, women, and children, that they should not be startled at the sight of a corpse, and to the end, that the continual spectacle of bones, graves, and funeral obsequies should put us in mind of our frail condition.

"Quin etiam exhilarare viris convivia cæde
Mos olim, et miscere epulis spectacula dira
Certantum ferro, sæpe et super ipsa cadentum
Pocula, respersis non parco sanguine mensis."

And as the Egyptians after their feasts were wont to present the company with a great image of death, by one that cried out to them, "Drink and be merry, for such shalt thou be when thou art dead;" so it is my custom to have death not only in my imagination, but continually in my mouth. Neither is there anything of which I am so inquisitive, and delight to inform myself, as the manner of men's deaths, their words, looks, and bearing; nor any places in history I am so intent upon; and it is manifest enough, by my crowding in examples of this kind, that I have a particular fancy for that subject. If I were a writer of books, I would compile a register, with a comment, of the various deaths of men: he who should teach men to die, would at the same time teach them to live. Dicearchus made one, to which he gave that title; but it was designed for another and less profitable end.

Peradventure, some one may object, that the pain and terror of dying so infinitely exceed all manner of imagination, that the best fencer will be quite out of his play when it comes to the push. Let

them say what they will: to premeditate is doubtless a very great advantage; and besides, is it nothing to go so far, at least, without disturbance or alteration? Moreover, nature herself assists and encourages us: if the death be sudden and violent, we have not leisure to fear; if otherwise, I perceive that as I engage further in my disease, I naturally enter into a certain loathing and disdain of life. I find I have much more ado to digest this resolution of dying, when I am well in health, than when languishing of a fever; and by how much I have less to do with the commodities of life, by reason that I begin to lose the use and pleasure of them, by so much I look upon death with less terror. Which makes me hope, that the farther I remove from the first, and the nearer I approach to the latter, I shall the more easily exchange the one for the other. And, as I have experienced in other occurrences, that, as Cæsar says, things often appear greater to us at a distance than near at hand, I have found, that being well, I have had maladies in much greater horror than when really afflicted with them. The vigor wherein I now am, the cheerfulness and delight wherein I now live, make the contrary estate appear in so great a disproportion to my present condition, that, by imagination, I magnify those inconveniences by one-half, and apprehend them to be much more troublesome, than I find them really to be, when they lie the most heavy upon me; I hope to find death the same.

Let us but observe in the ordinary changes and declinations we daily suffer, how nature deprives us of the light and sense of our bodily decay. What remains to an old man of the vigor of his youth and better days?

"Heu! senibus vitæ portio quanta manet."

Cæsar, to an old weather-beaten soldier of his guards, who came to ask him leave that he might kill himself, taking notice of his withered body and decrepit motion, pleasantly answered, "Thou fanciest, then, that thou art yet alive." Should a man fall into this condition on the sudden, I do not think humanity capable of enduring such a change: but nature, leading us by the hand, an easy and, as it were, an insensible pace step by step conducts us to that

miserable state, and by that means makes it familiar to us, so that we are insensible of the stroke when our youth dies in us, though it be really a harder death than the final dissolution of a languishing body, than the death of old age; forasmuch as the fall is not so great from an uneasy being to none at all, as it is from a sprightly and flourishing being to one that is troublesome and painful. The body, bent and bowed, has less force to support a burden; and it is the same with the soul, and therefore it is, that we are to raise her up firm and erect against the power of this adversary. For, as it is impossible she should ever be at rest, while she stands in fear of it; so, if she once can assure herself, she may boast (which is a thing as it were surpassing human condition) that it is impossible that disquiet, anxiety, or fear, or any other disturbance, should inhabit or have any place in her.

> "Non vultus instantis tyranni
>   Mente quati solida, neque Auster
>   Dux inquieti turbidus Adriæ,
>   Nec fulminantis magna Jovis manus."

She is then become sovereign of all her lusts and passions, mistress of necessity, shame, poverty, and all the other injuries of fortune. Let us, therefore, as many of us as can, get this advantage; 'tis the true and sovereign liberty here on earth, that fortifies us wherewithal to defy violence and injustice, and to contemn prisons and chains.

> "In manicis et
> Compedibus sævo te sub custode tenebo.

> "Ipse Deus, simul atque volam, me solvet.   Opinor,
>   Hoc sentit; moriar; mors ultima linea rerum est."

Our very religion itself has no surer human foundation than the contempt of death. Not only the argument of reason invites us to it—for why should we fear to lose a thing, which being lost cannot be lamented?—but, also, seeing we are threatened by so many sorts of death, is it not infinitely worse eternally to fear them all, than once to undergo one of them? And what matters it, when it shall happen, since it is inevitable? To him that told Socrates, "The thirty tyrants have sentenced thee to death;" "And nature them,"

[305]

said he. What a ridiculous thing it is to trouble ourselves about taking the only step that is to deliver us from all trouble! As our birth brought us the birth of all things, so in our death is the death of all things included. And therefore to lament that we shall not be alive a hundred years hence, is the same folly as to be sorry we were not alive a hundred years ago. Death is the beginning of another life. So did we weep, and so much it cost us to enter into this, and so did we put off our former veil in entering into it. Nothing can be a grievance that is but once. Is it reasonable so long to fear a thing that will so soon be despatched? Long life, and short, are by death made all one; for there is no long, nor short, to things that are no more. Aristotle tells us that there are certain little beasts upon the banks of the river Hypanis, that never live above a day: they which die at eight of the clock in the morning, die in their youth, and those that die at five in the evening, in their decrepitude: which of us would not laugh to see this moment of continuance put into the consideration of weal or woe? The most and the least, of ours, in comparison with eternity, or yet with the duration of mountains, rivers, stars, trees, and even of some animals, is no less ridiculous.

But nature compels us to it. "Go out of this world," says she, "as you entered into it; the same pass you made from death to life, without passion or fear, the same, after the same manner, repeat from life to death. Your death is a part of the order of the universe, 'tis a part of the life of the world.

" 'Inter se mortales mutua vivunt

. . . .

Et, quasi cursores, vitai lampada tradunt.'

"Shall I exchange for you this beautiful contexture of things? 'Tis the condition of your creation; death is a part of you, and while you endeavor to evade it, you evade yourselves. This very being of yours that you now enjoy is equally divided between life and death. The day of your birth is one day's advance toward the grave.

" 'Prima, quæ vitam dedit, hora carpsit.'
" 'Nascentes morimus, finisque ab origne pendet.'

[306]

"All the whole time you live, you purloin from life, and live at the expense of life itself. The perpetual work of your life is but to lay the foundation of death. You are in death, while you are in life, because you still are after death, when you are no more alive; or, if you had rather have it so, you are dead after life, but dying all the while you live; and death handles the dying much more rudely than the dead, and more sensibly and essentially. If you have made your profit of life, you have had enough of it; go your way satisfied.

" 'Cur non ut plenus vitæ conviva recedis?'

"If you have not known how to make the best use of it, if it was unprofitable to you, what need you to care to lose it, to what end would you desire longer to keep it?

" 'Cur amplius addere quæris,
Rursum quod pereat malé, èt ingratum occidat omne?'

"Life in itself is neither good nor evil; it is the scene of good or evil, as you make it. And, if you have lived a day, you have seen all: one day is equal and like to all other days. There is no other light, no other shade; this very sun, this moon, these very stars, this very order and disposition of things, is the same your ancestors enjoyed, and that shall also entertain your posterity.

" 'Non alium videre patres, aliumve nepotes
Aspicient.'

"And, come the worst that can come, the distribution and variety of all the acts of my comedy are performed in a year. If you have observed the revolution of my four seasons, they comprehend the infancy, the youth, the virility, and the old age of the world: the year has played his part, and knows no other art but to begin again; it will always be the same thing.

" 'Versamur ibidem, atque insumus usque.'
" 'Atque in se sua per vestigia volvitur annus.'

"I am not prepared to create for you any new recreations.

" 'Nam tibi præterea quod machiner, inveniamque
Quod placeat, nihil est; eadem sunt omnia semper.'

[307]

"Give place to others, as others have given place to you. Equality is the soul of equity. Who can complain of being comprehended in the same destiny, wherein all are involved. Besides, live as long as you can, you shall by that nothing shorten the space you are to be dead; 'tis all to no purpose; you shall be every whit as long in the condition you so much fear, as if you had died at nurse.

> " 'Licet quot vis viven do vincere secla,
>   Mors æterna tamen nihilominus illa manebit.'

"And yet I will place you in such a condition as you shall have no reason to be displeased.

> " 'In vera nescis nullum fore morte alium te,
>   Qui possit vivus tibi te lugere peremptum,
>   Stansque jacentem.'

"Nor shall you so much as wish for the life you are so concerned about.

> " 'Nec sibi enim quisquam tum se vitamque requirit.
>   .   .   .   .
>   Nec desiderium nostri nos afficit ullum.'

"Death is less to be feared than nothing, if there could be anything less than nothing.

> " 'Multo . . . mortem minus ad nos esse putandum,
>   Si minus esse potest, quam quod nihil esse videmus.'

"Neither can it any way concern you, whether you are living or dead: living, by reason that you are still in being; dead because you are no more. Moreover, no one dies before his hour: the time you leave behind was no more yours, than that was lapsed and gone before you came into the world; nor does it any more concern you.

> " 'Respice enim, quam nil ad nos anteacta vetustas
>   Temporis æterni fuerit.'

"Wherever your life ends, it is all there. The utility of living consists not in the length of days, but in the use of time; a man may have lived long, and yet lived but a little. Make use of time while it is present with you. It depends upon your will, and not

upon the number of days, to have a sufficient length of life. Is it possible you can imagine never to arrive at the place toward which you are continually going? and yet there is no journey but hath its end. And, if company will make it more pleasant or more easy to you, does not all the world go the self-same way?

" 'Omnia te, vitâ perfuncta, sequentur.'

"Does not all the world dance the same brawl that you do? Is there anything that does not grow old, as well as you? A thousand men, a thousand animals, a thousand other creatures, die at the same moment that you die:

" 'Nam nox nulla diem, neque noctem aurora sequuta est,
    Quæ non audierit mistos vagitibus ægris
    Ploratus, mortis comites et funerisiatri.'

"To what end should you endeavor to draw back, if there be no possibility to evade it? you have seen examples enough of those who have been well pleased to die, as thereby delivered from heavy miseries; but have you ever found any who have been dissatisfied with dying? It must, therefore, needs be very foolish to condemn a thing you have neither experimented in your own person, nor by that of any other. Why dost thou complain of me and of destiny? Do we do thee any wrong? Is it for thee to govern us, or for us to govern thee? Though, peradventure thy age may not be accomplished, yet thy life is: a man of low stature is as much a man as a giant: neither men nor their lives are measured by the ell. Chiron refused to be immortal, when he was acquainted with the conditions under which he was to enjoy it, by the god of time itself and its duration, his father Saturn. Do but seriously consider how much more insupportable and painful an immortal life would be to man than what I have already given him. If you had not death, you would externally curse me for having deprived you of it; I have mixed a little bitterness with it, to the end, that seeing of what convenience it is, you might not too greedily and indiscreetly seek and embrace it: and that you might be so established in this moderation, as neither to nauseate life, nor have an antipathy for dying, which I have decreed you shall once do, I have tempered the one and the

other between pleasure and pain. It was I that taught Thales, the most eminent of your sages, that to live and to die were indifferent; which made him, very wisely, answer him, 'Why then he did not die?' 'Because,' said he, 'it is indifferent.' Water, earth, air, and fire, and the other parts of this creation of mine, are no more instruments of thy life than they are of thy death. Why dost thou fear thy last day? it contributes no more to thy dissolution, than every

one of the rest: the last step is not the cause of lassitude; it does but confess it. Every day travels toward death: the last only arrives at it." These are the good lessons our mother Nature teaches.

I have often considered with myself whence it should proceed, that in war the image of death, whether we look upon it in ourselves or in others, should, without comparison, appear less dreadful than at home in our own houses (for if it were not so, it would be an army of doctors and whining milksops), and that being still in all places the same, there should be, notwithstanding, much more assurance in peasants and the meaner sort of people, than in others of better quality. I believe, in truth, that it is those terrible ceremonies and preparations wherewith we set it out, that more terrify

us than the thing itself; a new, quite contrary way of living; the cries of mothers, wives, and children: the visits of astounded and afflicted friends; the attendance of pale and blubbering servants; a dark room, set round with burning tapers; our beds environed with physicians and divines; in sum, nothing but ghostliness and horror round about us: we seem dead and buried already. Children are afraid even of those they are best acquainted with, when disguised in a visor; and so 'tis with us; the visor must be removed as well from things as from persons; that being taken away, we shall find nothing underneath but the very same death that a mean servant, or a poor chambermaid, died a day or two ago, without any manner of apprehension. Happy is the death that leaves us no leisure to prepare things for all this foppery.

XVIII

OF VANITY

THERE is, peradventure, no more manifest vanity than to write
of it so vainly. That which divinity has so divinely expressed
to us ought to be carefully and continually meditated by understanding men. Who does not see that I have taken a road, in which,
incessantly and without labor, I shall proceed so long as there shall
be ink and paper in the world? I can give no account of my life by
my actions; fortune has placed them too low; I must do it by my
fancies. And yet I have seen a gentleman who only communicated
his life by the workings of his belly; you might see in his house a
show of a row of basins of seven or eight days' excrements; that
was all his study, all his discourse; all other talk stunk in his
nostrils. Here, but not so nauseous, are the excrements of an old
mind, sometimes thick, sometimes thin, and always indigested. And
when shall I have done representing the continual agitation and
mutation of my thoughts, as they come into my head, seeing that
Diomedes wrote six thousand books upon the sole subject of grammar? What, then, ought prating to produce, since prattling and the
first beginning to speak, stuffed the world with such a horrible
number of volumes? So many words about words only. Oh Pythagoras, why didst not thou allay this tempest? They accused one
Galba of old for living idly; he made answer, "That every one
ought to give account of his actions but not of his leisure." He was
mistaken, for justice has also cognizance and correction over
holiday-makers.

But there should be some restraint of law against foolish and impertinent scribblers, as well as against vagabonds and idle persons; which if there were, both I and a hundred others would be banished the kingdom. I do not speak this in jest: scribbling seems to be a sign of a disordered and licentious age: When did we write so much as since our civil wars? when the Romans so much, as when their commonwealth was upon the point of ruin? Besides that, the refining of wits does not make people wiser in a government: this idle employment springs from this, that every one applies himself negligently to the duty of his vocation, and is easily debauched from it. The corruption of the age is made up by the particular contribution of every individual man; some contribute treachery, others injustice, irreligion, tyranny, avarice, cruelty, according to their power; the weaker sort contribute folly, vanity, and idleness; of these I am one. It seems as if it were the season for vain things, when the hurtful oppress us; in a time when doing ill is common, to do but what signifies nothing is a kind of commendation. 'Tis my comfort, that I shall be one of the last who shall be called in question; and while the greater offenders are being brought to account, I shall have leisure to amend: for it would, methinks, be against reason to punish little inconveniences, while we are infested with the greater. As the physician Philotimus said to one who presented him his finger to dress, and who he perceived, both by his complexion and his breath, had an ulcer in his lungs: "Friend, it is not now time to concern yourself about your fingers' ends."

And yet I saw, some years ago, a person, whose name and memory I have in very great esteem, in the very height of our great disorders, when there was neither law nor justice, nor magistrate who performed his office, no more than there is now, publish I know not what pitiful reformations about cloths, cookery, and law chicanery. Those are amusements wherewith to feed a people that are ill-used, to show that they are not totally forgotten. Those others do the same, who insist upon prohibiting particular ways of speaking, dances, and games, to a people totally abandoned to all sorts of execrable vices. 'Tis no time to bathe and cleanse one's self when

one is seized by a violent fever; 'tis for the Spartans alone to fall to combing and curling themselves, when they are just upon the point of running headlong into some extreme danger of their life.

For my part, I have yet a worse custom, that if my shoe go awry, I let my shirt and my cloak do so too; I scorn to mend myself by halves. When I am in a bad plight, I fasten upon the mischief; I abandon myself through despair; I let myself go toward the precipice, and, as the saying is, "throw the helve after the hatchet;" I am obstinate in growing worse, and think myself no longer worth my own care; I am either well or ill throughout. 'Tis a favor to me, that the desolation of this kingdom falls out in the desolation of my age: I better suffer that my ill be multiplied, than if my well had been disturbed. The words I utter in mishap are words of anger: my courage sets up its bristles, instead of letting them down; and, contrary to others, I am more devout in good than in evil fortune, according to the precept of Xenophon, if not according to his reason; and am more ready to turn up my eyes to heaven to return thanks, than to crave. I am more solicitous to improve my health, when I am well, than to restore it when I am sick; prosperities are the same discipline and instruction to me that adversities and rods are to others. As if good fortune were a thing inconsistent with good conscience, men never grow good but in evil fortune. Good fortune is to me a singular spur to modesty and moderation: an entreaty wins, a threat checks me; favor makes me bend, fear stiffens me.

Among human conditions this is common enough: to be better pleased with foreign things than with our own, and to love innovation and change:

> "Ipsa dies ideo nos grato perluit haustu,
> Quod permutatis hora recurrit equis:"

I have my share. Those who follow the other extreme, of being quite satisfied and pleased with and in themselves, of valuing what they have above all the rest, and of concluding no beauty can be greater than what they see, if they are not wiser than we, are really more happy; I do not envy their wisdom, but their good fortune.

This greedy humor of new and unknown things helps to nourish

in me the desire of travel; but a great many more circumstances contribute to it; I am very willing to quit the government of my house. There is, I confess, a kind of convenience in commanding, though it were but in a barn, and in being obeyed by one's people; but 'tis too uniform and languid a pleasure, and is, moreover, of necessity mixed with a thousand vexatious thoughts: one while the poverty and the oppression of your tenants: another, quarrels among neighbors: another, the trespasses they make upon you, afflict you;

> "Aut verberatæ grandine vinæ,
> Fundusque mundax, arbore nunc aquas
> Culpante, nunc torrentia agros
> Sidera, nunc hyemes iniquas:"

and that God scarce in six months sends a season wherein your bailiff can do his business as he should; but that if it serves the vines, it spoils the meadows;

> "Aut nimiis torret fervoribus ætherius sol,
> Aut subiti perimunt imbres, gelidæque pruinæ,
> Flabraque ventorum violento turbine vexant;"

to which may be added, the new and neat-made shoe of the man of old, that hurts your foot; and that a stranger does not understand how much it costs you, and what you contribute, to maintain that show of order that is seen in your family, and that, peradventure, you buy too dear.

I came late to the government of a house: they whom nature sent into the world before me long eased me of that trouble; so that I had already taken another bent more suitable to my humor. Yet, for so much as I have seen, 'tis an employment more troublesome than hard; whoever is capable of anything else, will easily do this. Had I a mind to be rich, that way would seem too long; I had served my kings, a more profitable traffic than any other. Since I pretend to nothing but the reputation of having got nothing or dissipated nothing, conformably to the rest of my life, improper either to do good or ill of any moment, and that I only desire to pass on, I can do it, thanks be to God, without any great endeavor. At the worst,

evermore prevent poverty by lessening your expense; 'tis that which I made my great concern, and doubt not but to do it before I shall be compelled. As to the rest, I have sufficiently settled my thoughts to live upon less than I have, and live contentedly: *"Non æstimatione census, verum victu atque cultu, terminantur pecuniæ modus."* My real need does not so wholly take up all I have, that Fortune has not whereon to fasten her teeth without biting to the quick. My presence, heedless and ignorant as it is, does me great service in my domestic affairs; I employ myself in them, but it goes against the hair, finding that I have this in my house, that though I burn my candle at one end by myself, the other is not spared.

Journeys do me no harm but only by their expense, which is great, and more than I am well able to bear, being always wont to travel with not only a necessary, but a handsome equipage; I must make them so much shorter and fewer; I spend therein but the froth, and what I have reserved for such uses, delaying and deferring my motion till that be ready. I will not that the pleasure of going abroad spoil the pleasure of being retired at home; on the contrary, I intend they shall nourish and favor one another. Fortune has assisted me in this, that since my principal profession in this life was to live at ease, and rather idly than busily, she has deprived me of the necessity of growing rich to provide for the multitude of my heirs. If there be not enough for one, of that whereof I had so plentifully enough, at his peril be it; his prudence will not deserve that I should wish him any more. And every one, according to the example of Phocion, provides sufficiently for his children who so provides for them as to leave them as much as was left him. I should by no means like Crates' way. He left his money in the hands of a banker with this condition—"That if his children were fools, he should then give it to them; if wise, he should then distribute it to the most foolish of the people;" as if fools, for being less capable of living without riches, were more capable of using them.

At all events, the damage occasioned by my absence seems not to deserve, so long as I am able to support it, that I should waive the occasions of diverting myself by that troublesome assistance.

There is always something that goes amiss. The affairs, one while

of one house, and then of another, tear you to pieces; you pry into everything too near; your perspicacity hurts you here, as well as in other things. I steal away from occasions of vexing myself, and turn from the knowledge of things that go amiss; and yet I cannot so order it, but that every hour I jostle against something or other that displeases me; and the tricks that they most conceal from me, are those that I the soonest come to know; some there are that, not to make matters worse, a man must himself help to conceal. Vain vexations; vain sometimes, but always vexations. The smallest and slightest impediments are the most piercing: and as little letters most tire the eyes, so do little affairs most disturb us. The rout of little ills more offend than one, how great soever. By how much domestic thorns are numerous and slight, by so much they prick deeper and without warning, easily surprising us when least we suspect them. I am no philosopher; evils oppress me according to their weight, and they weigh as much according to the form as matter, and very often more. If I have therein more perspicacity than the vulgar, I have also more patience; in short, they weigh with me, if they do not hurt me. Life is a tender thing, and easily molested. Since my age has made me grow more pensive and morose, *"Nemo enim resistit sibi, cum cœperit impelli,"* for the most trivial cause imaginable, I irritate that humor, which after-ward nourishes and exasperates itself of its own motion; attracting and heaping up matter upon matter whereon to feed:

"Stillicidi casus lapidem cavat:"

these continual tricklings consume and ulcerate me. Ordinary inconveniences are never light, they are continual and inseparable, especially when they spring from the members of a family, continual and inseparable. When I consider my affairs at distance and in gross, I find, because perhaps my memory is none of the best, that they have gone on hitherto improving beyond my reason or expectation; my revenue seems greater than it is; its prosperity betrays me: but when I pry more narrowly into the business, and see how all things go,

"Tum vero in curas animum diducimus omnes;"

[317]

I have a thousand things to desire and to fear. To give them quite over, is very easy for me to do; but to look after them without trouble, is very hard. 'Tis a miserable thing to be in a place where everything you see employs and concerns you; and I fancy that I more cheerfully enjoy the pleasures of another man's house, and with greater and a purer relish, than those of my own. Diogenes answered according to my humor him who asked him what sort of wine he liked the best: "That of another," said he.

My father took a delight in building at Montaigne, where he was born; and in all the government of domestic affairs I love to follow his example and rules, and I shall engage those who are to succeed me, as much as in me lies, to do the same. Could I do better for him, I would; and am proud that his will is still performing and acting by me. God forbid, that in my hands I should ever suffer any image of life, that I am able to render to so good a father, to fail. And wherever I have taken in hand to strengthen some old foundations of walls, and to repair some ruinous buildings, in earnest I have done it more out of respect to his design, than my own satisfaction; and am angry at myself, that I have not proceeded further to finish the beginnings he left in his house, and so much the more, because I am very likely to be the last possessor of my race, and to give the last hand to it. For, as to my own particular application, neither the pleasure of building, which they say is so bewitching, nor hunting, nor gardens, nor the other pleasures of a retired life, can much amuse me. And 'tis what I am angry at myself for, as I am for all other opinions that are incommodious to me; which I would not so much care to have vigorous and learned, as I would have them easy and convenient for life; they are true and sound enough, if they are useful and pleasing. Such as hear me declare my ignorance in husbandry, whisper in my ear that it is disdain, and that I neglect to know its instruments, its seasons, its order, how they dress my vines, how they graft, and to know the names and forms of herbs and fruits, and the preparing the meat on which I live, the names and prices of the stuffs I wear, because, say they, I have set my heart upon some higher knowledge; they kill me in saying so. This were

folly, and rather stupidity than glory; I had rather be a good horse-man than a good logician:

"Quin tu aliquid saltem potius, quorum indiget usus,
Viminibus mollique paras detexere junco."

We occupy our thoughts about the general, and about universal causes and conducts, which will very well carry on themselves with-out our care; and leave our own business at random, and Michael much more our concern than man. Now I am, indeed, for the most part at home; but I would be there better pleased than anywhere else:

"Sit meæ sedes utinam senectæ,
Sit modus lasso maris, et viarum,
Militiæque."

I know not whether or no I shall bring it about. I could wish that, instead of some other member of his succession, my father had re-signed to me the passionate affection he had in his old age to his household affairs; he was happy in that he could accommodate his desires to his fortune, and satisfy himself with what he had; politi-cal philosophy may to much purpose condemn the meanness and sterility of my employment, if I can once come to relish it, as he did. I am of opinion that the most honorable calling is to serve the public, and to be useful to many; *"Fructus enim ingenii et virtutis, omnisque præstantiæ, tum maximus capitur, quum in proximum quemque confertur:"* for myself, I disclaim it; partly out of con-science (for where I see the weight that lies upon such employments, I perceive also the little means I have to supply it; and Plato, a master in all political government himself, nevertheless, took care to abstain from it), and partly out of cowardice. I content myself with enjoying the world without bustle; only to live an excusable life, and such as may neither be a burden to myself nor to any other.

Never did any man more fully and feebly suffer himself to be governed by a third person than I should do, had I any one to whom to intrust myself. One of my wishes at this time should be, to have a son-in-law that knew handsomely how to cherish my old age, and to rock it asleep; into whose hands I might deposit, in full sovereignty, the management and use of all my goods, that he might dispose of them as I do, and get by them what I get, provided that he on his

[319]

part were truly acknowledging, and a friend. But we live in a world where loyalty of one's own children is unknown.

He who has the charge of my purse in my travels, has it purely and without control; he could cheat me thoroughly if he came to reckoning; and, if he is not a devil, I oblige him to deal faithfully with me by so entire a trust. *"Multi fallere docuerunt, dum timent falli; et aliis jus peccandi, suspicando, fecerunt."* The most common security I take of my people is ignorance; I never presume any to be vicious till I have first found them so; and repose the most confidence in the younger sort, that I think are least spoiled by ill example. I had rather be told at two months' end that I have spent four hundred crowns, than to have my ears battered every night with three, five, seven: and I have been, in this way, as little robbed as another. It is true, I am willing enough not to see it; I, in some sort, purposely, harbor a kind of perplexed, uncertain knowledge of my money: up to a certain point, I am content to doubt. One must leave a little room for the infidelity or indiscretion of a servant; if you have left enough, in gross, to do your business, let the overplus of Fortune's liberality run a little more freely at her mercy; 'tis the gleaner's portion. After all, I do not so much value the fidelity of my people, as I contemn their injury. What a mean and ridiculous thing it is for a man to study his money, to delight in handling and telling it over and over again! 'Tis by this avarice makes its approaches.

In eighteen years that I have had my estate in my own hands, I could never prevail with myself either to read over my deeds, or examine my principal affairs, which ought, of necessity, to pass under my knowledge and inspection. 'Tis not a philosophical disdain of wordly and transitory things; my taste is not purified to that degree, and I value them at as great a rate, at least, as they are worth; but 'tis, in truth, an inexcusable and childish laziness and negligence. What would I not rather do than read a contract? or than, as a slave to my own business, tumble over a company of old musty writings? or, which is worse, those of another man, as so many do nowadays, to get money? I grudge nothing but care and trouble, and endeavor nothing so much as to be careless and at ease.

I had been much fitter, I believe, could it have been without obligation and servitude, to have lived upon another man's fortune than
my own: and, indeed, I do not know, when I examine it nearer,
whether, according to my humor, what I have to suffer from my
affairs and servants, has not in it something more abject, troublesome, and tormenting than there would be in serving a man better
born than myself, who would govern me with a gentle rein, and
a little at my own ease: *"Servitus obedientia est fracti animi et
abjecti, arbitrio carentis suo."* Crates did worse, who threw himself
into the liberty of poverty, only to rid himself of the inconveniences
and cares of his house. This is what I would not do; I hate poverty
equally with pain; but I could be content to change the kind of life
I live for another that was humbler and had fewer affairs.

When absent from home, I strip myself of all these thoughts, and
should be less concerned for the ruin of a tower, than I am, when
present, at the fall of a tile. My mind is easily composed at distance,
but suffers as much as that of the meanest peasant when I am at
home; the reins of my bridle being wrongly put on, or a strap
flapping against my leg, will keep me out of humor a day together.
I raise my courage well enough against inconveniences; lift up my
eyes I cannot.

"Sensus, o superi, sensus."

I am at home responsible for whatever goes amiss. Few masters
(I speak of those of medium condition, such as mine), and if there
be any such, they are more happy, can rely so much upon another,
but that the greatest part of the burden will lie upon their own
shoulders. This takes much from my grace in entertaining visitors,
so that I have, peradventure, detained some rather out of expectation of a good dinner, than by my own behavior; and lose much of
the pleasure I ought to reap at my own house from the visitation and
assembling of my friends. The most ridiculous carriage of a gentleman in his own house, is to see him bustling about the business of
the place, whispering one servant, and looking an angry look at
another; it ought insensibly to slide along, and to represent an
ordinary current; and I think it unhandsome to talk much to our

guests of their entertainment, whether by way of bragging or excuse. I love order and cleanliness.

"Et cantharus et lanx
Ostendunt mihi me"

more than abundance: and at home have an exact regard to necessity, little to outward show. If a footman falls to cuffs at another man's house, or stumble and throw a dish before him as he is carrying it up, you only laugh and make a jest on't; you sleep while the master of the house is arranging a bill of fare with his steward for your morrow's entertainment. I speak according as I do myself: quite appreciating, nevertheless, good husbandry in general, and how pleasant, quiet and prosperous household management, carried regularly on, is to some natures; and not wishing to fasten my own errors and inconveniences to the thing, nor to give Plato the lie, who looks upon it as the most pleasant employment to every one to do his particular affairs without wrong to another.

When I travel I have nothing to care for but myself, and the laying out my money; which is disposed of by one single precept; too many things are required to the raking it together; in that I understand nothing; in spending, I understand a little, and how to give some show to my expense, which is indeed its principal use; but I rely too ambitiously upon it, which renders it unequal and difform, and, moreover, immoderate, in both the one and the other aspect; if it make a show, if it serve the turn, I indiscreetly let it run; and as indiscreetly tie up my purse-strings, if it does not shine and does not please me. Whatever it be, whether art or nature, that imprints in us the condition of living by reference to others, it does us much more harm than good; we deprive ourselves of our own utilities, to accommodate appearances to the common opinion; we care not so much what our being is, as to us and in reality, as what it is to the public observation. Even the goods of the mind, and wisdom itself, seems fruitless to us, if only enjoyed by ourselves, and if it produce not itself to the view and approbation of others. There is a sort of men whose gold runs in streams underground imperceptibly; others expose it all in plates and branches, so that to

the one a liard is worth a crown, and to the others the inverse: the world esteeming its use and value, according to the show. All over-nice solicitude about riches smells of avarice: even the very dispos-ing of it, with a too systematic and artificial liberality is not worth a painful superintendence and solicitude: he that will order his expense to just so much, makes it too pinched and narrow. The keeping or spending are, of themselves, indifferent things, and re-ceive no color of good or ill, but according to the application of the will.

The other cause that tempts me out to these journeys is, inaptitude for the present manners in our state. I could easily console myself for this corruption in regard to the public interest;

> "Perjoraque sæcula ferri
> Temporibus, quorum sceleri non invenit ipsa
> Nomen, et a nullo posuit natura metallo;"

but not to my own. I am, in particular, too much oppressed by them: for, in my neighborhood, we are, of late, by the long license of our civil wars, grown old in so riotous a form of state,

> "Quippe ubi fas versum atque nefas,"

that in earnest, 'tis a wonder how it can subsist.

> "Armati terram exercent, semperque recentes
> Convectare juvat prædas, et vivere rapto."

In fine, I see by our example, that the society of men is maintained and held together, at what price soever; in what condition soever they are placed, they still close and stick together, both moving and in heaps; as ill united bodies, that shuffled together without order, find of themselves a means to unite and settle, often better than they could have been disposed by art. King Philip mustered up a rabble of the most wicked and incorrigible rascals he could pick out, and put them all together into a city he had caused to be built for that purpose, which bore their name: I believe that they, even from vices themselves, erected a government among them, and a com-modious and just society. I see, not one action, or three, or a hun-dred, but manners, in common and received use, so ferocious, es-pecially in inhumanity and treachery, which are to me the worst of

all vices, that I have not the heart to think of them without horror; and almost as much admire as I detest them: the exercise of these signal villainies carries with it as great signs of vigor and force of soul, as of error and disorder. Necessity reconciles and brings men together; and this accidental connection afterward forms itself into laws: for there have been such, as savage as any human opinion could conceive, who, nevertheless, have maintained their body with as much health and length of life as any Plato or Aristotle could invent. And certainly, all these descriptions of polities, feigned by art, are found to be ridiculous and unfit to be put in practice.

These great and tedious debates about the best form of society, and the most commodious rules to bind us, are debates only proper for the exercise of our wits; as in the arts there are several subjects, which have their being in agitation and controversy, and have no life but there. Such an idea of government might be of some value in a new world; but we take a world already made, and formed to certain customs; we do not beget it, as Pyrrha or Cadmus did. By what means soever we may have the privilege to redress and reform it anew, we can hardly writhe it from its wonted bent, but we shall break all. Solon being asked, whether he had established the best laws he could for the Athenians; "Yes," said he, "of those they would have received." Varro excuses himself after the same manner: "that if he were to begin to write of religion, he would say what he believed; but seeing it was already received, he would write rather to use than nature."

Not according to opinion, but in truth and reality, the best and most excellent government for every nation is that under which it is maintained: its form and essential convenience depend upon custom. We are apt to be displeased at the present condition; but I, nevertheless, maintain that to desire command in a few in a republic, or another sort of government in monarchy than that already established, is both vice and folly.

"Ayme l'estat, tel que tu le veois estre:
S'il est royal ayme la royauté,
S'il est de peu, ou bien communauté,
Ayme l'aussi; car Dieu t'y a faict naistre."

So wrote the good Monsieur de Pibrac, whom we have lately lost, a man of so excellent a wit, such sound opinions and such gentle manners. This loss, and that at the same time we have had of Monsieur de Foix, are of so great importance to the crown, that I do not know whether there is another couple in France worthy to supply the places of these two Gascons, in sincerity and wisdom in the king's council. They were both variously great men, and certainly according to the age, rare and great, each of them in his kind: but what destiny was it that placed them in these times, men so remote from and so disproportioned to our corruption and intestine tumults?

Nothing presses so hard upon a state as innovation: change only gives form to injustice and tyranny. When any piece is loosened, it may be proper to stay it; one may take care that the alteration and corruption natural to all things do not carry us too far from our beginnings and principles; but to undertake to found so great a mass anew, and to change the foundations of so vast a building, is for them to do, who to make clean, efface; who reform particular defects by an universal confusion, and cure diseases by death: *"Non tam commutandarum quam evertendarum rerum cupidi."* The world is unapt to be cured; and so impatient of anything that presses it, that it thinks of nothing but disengaging itself at what price soever. We see by a thousand examples, that it ordinarily cures itself to its cost. The discharge of a present evil is no cure, if there be not a general amendment of condition. The surgeon's end is not only to cut away the dead flesh; that is but the progress of his cure; he has a care, over and above, to fill up the wound with better and more natural flesh, and to restore the member to its due state. Whoever only proposes to himself to remove that which offends him, falls short: for good does not necessarily succeed evil; another evil may succeed, and a worse, as it happened to Cæsar's murderers, who brought the republic to such a pass, that they had reason to repent the meddling with the matter. The same has since happened to several others, even down to our own times; the French, my contemporaries, know it well enough. All great mutations shake and disorder a state.

Whoever would look direct at a cure, and well consider of it

[325]

before he began, would be very willing to withdraw his hands from meddling in it. Pacuvius Calavius corrected the vice of this proceeding by a notable example. His fellow-citizens were in mutiny against their magistrates; he being a man of great authority in the city of Capua, found means one day to shut up the senators in the palace; and calling the people together in the market place, there told them that the day was now come wherein at full liberty they might revenge themselves on the tyrants by whom they had been so long oppressed, and whom he had now, all alone and unarmed, at his mercy. He then advised that they should call these out, one by one, by lot, and should individually determine as to each, causing whatever should be decreed to be immediately executed; with this proviso, that they should, at the same time, depute some honest man in the place of him who was condemned, to the end there might be no vacancy in the senate. They had no sooner heard the name of one senator but a great cry of universal dislike was raised up against him. "I see," says Pacuvius, "that he must out; he is a wicked fellow; let us look out a good one in his room." Immediately there was a profound silence, every one being at a stand whom to choose. But one, more impudent than the rest, having named his man, there arose yet a greater consent of voices against him, an hundred imperfections being laid to his charge, and as many just reasons why he should not stand. These contradictory humors growing hot, it fared worse with the second senator and the third, there being as much disagreement in the election of the new, as consent in the putting out of the old. In the end growing weary of this bustle to no purpose, they began, some one way and some another, to steal out of the assembly: every one carrying back this resolution in his mind, that the oldest and best known evil was ever more supportable than one that was new and untried.

Seeing how miserably we are agitated (for what have we not done)!

> "Eheu! cicatricum et sceleris pudet,
> Fratrumque: quid nos dura refugimus
> Ætas? quid intactum nefasti
> Liquimus? Unde manus inventus

> Metu Deorum continuit? quibus
> Pepercit aris."

I do not presently concludo.

> "Ipsa si velit Salus,
> Servare prorsus non potest hanc familiam;"

we are not, peradventure, at the last gasp. The conservation of states is a thing that, in all likelihood, surpasses our understanding; a civil government is, as Plato says, a mighty and puissant thing, and hard to be dissolved; it often continues against mortal and intestine diseases, against the injury of unjust laws, against tyranny, the corruption and ignorance of magistrates, the license and sedition of the people. In all our fortunes, we compare ourselves to what is above us, and still look toward those who are better; but let us measure ourselves with what is below us: there is no condition so miserable wherein a man may not find a thousand examples that will administer consolation. 'Tis our vice that we more unwillingly look upon what is above, than willingly upon what is below; and Solon was used to say, that "whoever would make a heap of all the ills together, there is no one who would not rather choose to bear away the ills he has than to come to an equal division with all other men from that heap, and take his share." Our government is, indeed, very sick, but there have been others more sick, without dying. The gods play at tennis with us and bandy us every way:

> "Enimvero Dii nos homines quasi pilas habent."

The stars have fatally destined the state of Rome for an example of what they could do in this kind; in it are comprised all the forms and adventures that concern a state: all that order or disorder, good or evil fortune, can do. Who, then, can despair of his condition, seeing the shocks and commotions wherewith Rome was tumbled and tossed, and yet withstood them all? If the extent of dominion be the health of a state (which I by no means think it is, and Isocrates pleases me when he instructs Nicocles not to envy princes who have large dominions, but those who know how to preserve those which have fallen into their hands), that of Rome was never so sound as

[327]

when it was most sick. The worst of her forms was the most fortunate; one can hardly discern any image of government under the first emperors; it was the most horrible and tumultuous confusion that can be imagined: it endured it, notwithstanding, and therein continued, preserving not a monarchy limited within its own bounds, but so many nations so differing, so remote, so ill-affected, so confusedly commanded, and so unjustly conquered:

> "Nec gentibus ullis
> Commodat in populum, terræ pelagique potentem,
> Invidiam fortuna suam."

Everything that totters does not fall. The contexture of so great a body holds by more nails than one; it holds even by its antiquity, like old buildings, from which the foundations are worn away by time, without rough-cast or mortar, which yet live and support themselves by their own weight:

> "Nec jam validis radicibus hærens,
> Pondere tuta suo est."

Moreover, it is not rightly to go to work, to examine only the flank and the foss, to judge of the security of a place; we must observe which way approaches can be made to it, and in what condition the assailant is: few vessels sink with their own weight, and without some exterior violence. Now, let us every way cast our eyes; everything about us totters; in all the great states, both of Christendom and elsewhere, that are known to us, if you will but look, you will there see evident menace of alteration and ruin:

> "Et sua sunt illis incommoda; parque per omnes
> Tempestas."

Astrologers may very well, as they do, warn us of great revolutions and imminent mutations: their prophecies are present and palpable, they need not go to heaven to foretell this. There is not only consolation to be extracted from this universal combination of ills and menaces, but, moreover, some hopes of the continuation of our state, forasmuch as, naturally nothing falls where all falls:

universal sickness is particular health: conformity is antagonistic to dissolution. For my part, I despair not, and fancy that I discover ways to save us:

> "Deus hæc fortasse benigna
> Reducet in sedem vice."

Who knows but that God will have it happen, as in human bodies that purge and restore themselves to a better state by long and grievous maladies, which render them more entire and perfect health than that they took from them? That which weighs the most with me is, that in reckoning the symptoms of our ill, I see as many natural ones, and that heaven sends us, and properly its own, as of those that our disorder and human imprudence contribute to it. The very stars seem to declare that we have already continued long enough, and beyond the ordinary term. This also afflicts me, that the mischief which nearest threatens us, is not an alteration in the entire and solid mass, but its dissipation and divulsion, which is the most extreme of our fears.

I, moreover, fear, in these fantasies of mine, the treachery of my memory, lest, by inadvertence, it should make me write the same thing twice. I hate to examine myself, and never review, but very unwillingly, what has once escaped my pen. I here set down nothing new. These are common thoughts, and having, peradventure, conceived them an hundred times, I am afraid I have set them down somewhere else already. Repetition is everywhere troublesome, though it were in Homer; but 'tis ruinous in things that have only a superficial and transitory show. I do not love over insisting, even in the most profitable things, as in Seneca; and the usage of his stoical school displeases me, to repeat, upon every subject, at full length and width the principles and presuppositions that serve in general, and always to reallege anew common and universal reasons.

My memory grows cruelly worse every day;

> "Pocula Lethæos ut si ducentia somnos,
> Arente fauce traxerim,"

I must be fain for the time to come (for hitherto, thanks be to God, nothing has happened much amiss), whereas others seek time and

opportunity to think of what they have to say, to avoid all preparation, for fear of tying myself to some obligation upon which I must
insist. To be tied and bound to a thing puts me quite out, and to
depend upon so weak an instrument as my memory. I never read
this following story that I am not offended at it with a personal and
natural resentment: Lyncestes, accused of conspiracy against Alexander, the day that he was brought out before the army, according
to the custom, to be heard as to what he could say for himself, had
learned a studied speech, of which, haggling and stammering, he
pronounced some words. While growing more and more perplexed,
while struggling with his memory, and trying to recollect what he
had to say, the soldiers nearest to him charged their pikes against
him and killed him, looking upon him as convict; his confusion and
silence served them for a confession; for having had so much
leisure to prepare himself in prison, they concluded that it was
not his memory that failed him, but that his conscience tied up his
tongue and stopped his mouth. And, truly, well said; the place,
the assembly, the expectation, astound a man, even when he has but
the ambition to speak well; what can a man do when it is an
harangue upon which his life depends?

For my part, the very being tied to what I am to say is enough
to loose me from it. When I wholly commit and refer myself to my
memory, I lay so much stress upon it that it sinks under me; it
grows dismayed with the burden. So much as I trust to it, so much
do I put myself out of my own power, even to the finding it difficult
to keep my own countenance; and have been sometimes very much
put to it to conceal the slavery wherein I was engaged; whereas my
design is to manifest, in speaking, a perfect calmness both of face
and accent, and casual and unpremeditated motions, as rising from
present occasions, choosing rather to say nothing to purpose than
to show that I came prepared to speak well, a thing especially unbecoming a man of my profession, and of too great obligation on
him who cannot retain much. The preparation begets a great deal
more expectation than it will satisfy. A man often strips himself
to his doublet, to leap no further than he would have done in his
gown: *"Nihil est his, qui placere volunt, tam adversarium, quam*

expectatio." It is recorded of the orator Curio, that when he proposed the division of his oration into three or four parts, or three or four arguments or reasons, it often happened either that he forgot some one, or added one or two more. I have always avoided falling into this inconvenience, having ever hated these promises and prescriptions, not only out of distrust of my memory, but also because this method relishes too much of the artist: "*Simpliciora militares decent.*" 'Tis enough that I have promised to myself never again to take upon me to speak in a place of respect, for as to speak-

[331]

ing, when a man reads his speech, besides that it is very absurd, it is a mighty disadvantage to those who naturally could give it a grace by action; and to rely upon the mercy of my present invention, I would much less do it; 'tis heavy and perplexed, and such as would never furnish me in sudden and important necessities.

Permit, reader, this essay its course also, and this further sitting to finish the rest of my picture: I add, but I correct not. First, because I conceive that a man having once parted with his labors to the world, he has no further right to them; let him do better if he can, in some new undertaking, but not adulterate what he has already sold. Of such dealers nothing should be bought till after they are dead. Let them well consider what they do before they produce it to the light: who hastens them? My book is always the same, saving that upon every new edition (that the buyer may not go away quite empty) I take the liberty to add (as 'tis but an ill-jointed mosaic) some few bits over and above; they are but over-weight, that do not disfigure the primitive form of the essays, but, by a little ambitious subtlety, give a kind of particular value to every one of those that follow. Thence, however, will easily happen some transposition of chronology, my stories taking place according to their patness, and not always according to their age.

Secondly, because as to what concerns myself, I fear to lose by change: my understanding does not always go forward, it goes backward too. I do not much less suspect my fancies for being the second or the third, than for being the first, or present, or past; we often correct ourselves as foolishly as we do others. I am grown older by a great many years since my first publications, which were in the year 1580; but I very much doubt whether I am grown an inch the wiser. I now, and I anon, are two several persons; but whether better, I cannot determine. It were a fine thing to be old, if we only traveled toward improvement; but 'tis a drunken, stumbling, reeling, infirm motion: like that of reeds, which the air casually waves to and fro at pleasure. Antiochus had in his youth strongly written in favor of the academy; in his old age, he wrote as much against it; would not, which of these two soever I should follow, be still Antiochus? After having established the uncer-

tainty, to go about to establish the certainty of human opinions, was it not to establish doubt, and not certainty, and to promise, that had he had yet another age to live, he would be always upon terms of altering his judgment, not so much for the better, as for something else?

The public favor has given me a little more confidence than I expected; but what I most fear is, lest I should glut the world with my writings; I had rather, of the two, nettle my reader, than tire him, as a learned man of my time has done. Praise is always pleasing, let it come from whom, or upon what account it will; yet ought a man to understand why he is commended, that he may know how to keep up the same reputation still; imperfections themselves may get commendation. The vulgar and common estimation is seldom happy in hitting; and I am much mistaken, if, among the writings of my time, the worst are not those which have most gained the popular applause. For my part, I return my thanks to those good-natured men, who are pleased to take my weak endeavors in good part; the faults of the workmanship are nowhere so apparent, as in a matter which of itself has no recommendation. Blame not me, reader, for those that slip in here, by the fancy or inadvertency of others; every hand, every artisan, contribute their own materials; I neither concern myself with orthography (and only care to have it after the old way) nor pointing, being very inexpert both in the one and the other. Where they wholly break the sense, I am very little concerned, for they at least discharge me; but where they substitute a false one, as they so often do, and wrest me to their conception, they ruin me. When the sentence, nevertheless, is not strong enough for my proportion, a civil person ought to reject it as spurious, and none of mine. Whoever shall know how lazy I am, and how indulgent to my own humor, will easily believe that I had rather write as many more essays, than be tied to revise these over again for so childish a correction.

I said elsewhere, that being planted in the very center of this new religion, I am not only deprived of any great familiarity with men of other kind of manners than my own, and of other opinions, by which they hold together, as by a tie that supersedes all other

obligations; but, moreover, I do not live without danger, among men to whom all things are equally lawful, and of whom the most part cannot offend the laws more than they have already done; from which the extremest degree of license proceeds. All the particular circumstances respecting me being summed up together, I do not find one man of my country, who pays so dear for the defense of our laws both in loss and damages (as the lawyers say) as myself; and some there are who vapor and brag of their zeal and constancy, that if things were justly weighed, do much less than I. My house, as one that has ever been open and free to all comers, and civil to all (for I could never persuade myself to make it a garrison of war, war being a thing that I prefer to see as remote as may be), has sufficiently merited popular kindness, and so that it would be a hard matter justly to insult over me upon my own dunghill; and I look upon it as a wonderful and exemplary thing, that it yet continues a virgin from blood and plunder during so long a storm, and so many neighboring revolutions and tumults. For to confess the truth, it had been possible enough for a man of my complexion to have shaken hands with any one constant and continued form whatever; but the contrary invasions and incursions, alternations and vicissitudes of fortune round about me, have hitherto more exasperated than calmed and mollified the temper of the country, and involved me, over and over again, with invincible difficulties and dangers.

I escape, 'tis true, but am troubled that it is more by chance, and something of my own prudence, than by justice; and am not satisfied to be out of the protection of the laws, and under any other safeguard than theirs. As matters stand, I live, above one half, by the favors of others; which is an untoward obligation. I do not like to owe my safety either to the generosity or affection of great persons, who allow me my legality and my liberty, nor to the obliging manners of my predecessors, or my own; for what if I were another kind of man? If my deportment, and the frankness of my conversation, or relationship, oblige my neighbors, 'tis cruel that they should acquit themselves of that obligation in only permitting me to live, and that they may say "We allow him the free liberty of

having divine service read in his own private chapel when it is interdicted in all churches round about, and allow him the use of his goods and his life, as one who protects our wives and cattle in time of need." For my house has for many descents shared in the reputation of Lycurgus the Athenian, who was the general depositary and guardian of the purses of his fellow-citizens. Now I am clearly of opinion that a man should live by right and by authority, and not either by recompense or favor. How many gallant men have rather chosen to lose their lives than to be debtors for them? I hate to subject myself to any sort of obligation, but above all, to that which binds me by the duty of honor. I think nothing so dear as what has been given me, and this because my will lies at pawn under the title of gratitude, and more willingly accept of services that are to be sold; I feel that for the last I give nothing but money, but for the other I give myself.

The knot that binds me by the laws of courtesy binds me more than that of civil constraint; I am much more at ease when bound by a scrivener, than by myself. Is it not reason that my conscience should be much more engaged when men simply rely upon it? In a bond, my faith owes nothing, because it has nothing lent it; let them trust to the security they have taken without me. I had much rather break the wall of a prison, and the laws themselves than my own word. I am nice, even to superstition, in keeping my promises, and, therefore, upon all occasions, have a care to make them uncertain and conditional. To those of no great moment, I add the jealousy of my own rule, to make them weight; it wracks and oppresses me with its own interest. Even in actions wholly my own and free, if I once say a thing, I conceive that I have bound myself, and that delivering it to the knowledge of another, I have positively enjoined it my own performance. Methinks I promise it, if I but say it: and therefore am not apt to say much of that kind. The sentence that I pass upon myself is more severe than that of a judge, who only considers the common obligation; but my conscience looks upon it with a more severe and penetrating eye. I lag in those duties to which I should be compelled if I did not go: *"Hoc ipsum*

ita justum est, quod recte fit, si est voluntarium." If the action has not some splendor of liberty, it has neither grace nor honor:

"Quod me jus cogit, vix voluntate impetrent:"

where necessity draws me, I love to let my will take its own course: "*Quia quicquid imperio cogitur exigenti magis, quam præstanti, acceptum refertur.*" I know some who follow this rule, even to injustice; who will sooner give than restore, sooner lend than pay, and will do them the least good to whom they are most obliged. I don't go so far as that, but I'm not far off.

I so much love to disengage and disobligate myself, that I have sometimes looked upon ingratitude, affronts, and indignities which I have received from those to whom either by nature or accident I was bound in some duty of friendship, as an advantage to me; taking this occasion of their ill usage, for an acquittance and discharge of so much of my debt. And though I still continue to pay them all the external offices of public reason, I notwithstanding, find a great saving in doing that upon the account of justice which I did upon the score of affection, and am a little eased of the attention and solicitude of my inward will: "*Est prudentis sustinere, ut currum, sic impetum benevolentia;*" 'tis in me, too urging and pressing where I take; at least, for a man who loves not to be strained at all. And this husbanding my friendship serves me for a sort of consolation in the imperfections of those in whom I am concerned. I am very sorry they are not such as I could wish they were, but then I also am spared somewhat of my application and engagement toward them. I approve of a man who is the less fond of his child for having a scald head, or for being crooked; and not only when he is ill-conditioned, but, also, when he is of unhappy disposition, and imperfect in his limbs (God himself has abated so much from his value and natural estimation), provided he carry himself in this coldness of affection with moderation and exact justice: proximity, with me, lessens not defects, but rather aggravates them.

After all, according to what I understand in the science of benefit and acknowledgment, which is a subtle science, and of great use,

I know no person whatever more free and less indebted than I am at this hour. What I do owe, is simply to common and natural obligations; as to anything else, no man is more absolutely clear:

> "Nec sunt mihi nota potentum
> Munera."

Princes give me a great deal, if they take nothing from me; and do me good enough, if they do me no harm; that's all I ask from them. Oh, how am I obliged to Almighty God, that he was pleased I should immediately receive from his bounty all I have, and especially reserved all my obligation to himself! How earnestly do I beg of his holy compassion, that I may never owe essential thanks to any one! Oh happy liberty wherein I have thus far lived! May it continue with me to the last. I endeavor to have no express need of any one: *"In me omnis spes est mihi."* 'Tis what every one may do in himself, but more easily they whom God has placed in a condition exempt from natural and urgent necessities. It is a wretched and dangerous thing to depend upon others; we ourselves, in whom is ever the most just and safest dependence, are not sufficiently sure. I have nothing mine but myself, and yet the possession is, in part, defective and borrowed. I fortify myself both in courage, which is the strongest assistant, and also in fortune, therein wherewith to satisfy myself, though everything else should forsake me. Eleus Hippias not only furnished himself with knowledge, that he might, at need, cheerfully retire from all other company to enjoy the Muses; nor only with the knowledge of philosophy, to teach his soul to be contented with itself, and bravely to subsist without outward conveniences, when fate would have it so; he was, moreover, so careful as to learn to cook, to shave himself, to make his own clothes, his own shoes and drawers, to provide for all his necessities in himself and to wean himself from the assistance of others. A man more freely and cheerfully enjoys borrowed conveniences, when it is not an enjoyment forced and constrained by need; and when he has, in his own will and fortune, the means to live without them. I know myself very well; but 'tis hard for me to imagine any so pure liberality of any one toward me, any

so frank and free hospitality, that would not appear to me discreditable, tyrannical, and tainted with reproach, if necessity had reduced me to it. As giving is an ambitious and authoritative quality, so is accepting a quality of submission; witness the insulting and quarrelsome refusal that Bajazet made of the presents that Tamerlane sent him; and those that were offered on the part of the Emperor Solyman to the emperor of Calicut, so angered him, that he not only rudely rejected them, saying, that neither he nor any of his predecessors had ever been wont to take, and that it was their office to give; but, moreover, caused the ambassadors sent with the gifts to be put into a dungeon. When Thetis, says Aristotle, flatters Jupiter; when the Lacedæmonians flatter the Athenians, they do not put them in mind of the good they have done them, which is always odious, but of the benefits they have received from them. Such as I see so frequently employ every one in their affairs, and thrust themselves into so much obligation, would never do it, did they but relish as I do the sweetness of a pure liberty, and did they but weigh, as wise men should, the burden of obligation: 'tis, sometimes, peradventure, fully paid, but 'tis never dissolved. 'Tis a miserable slavery to a man who loves to be at full liberty in all respects. Such as know me, both above and below me in station, are able to say whether they have ever known a man less importuning, soliciting, entreating, and pressing upon others than I. If I am so, and a degree beyond all modern example, 'tis no great wonder, so many parts of my manners contributing to it: a little natural pride, an impatience of being refused, the moderation of my desires and designs, my incapacity for business, and my most beloved qualities, idleness and freedom; by all these together I have conceived a mortal hatred to being obliged to any other, or by any other than myself. I leave no stone unturned to do without it, rather than employ the bounty of another in any light or important occasion or necessity whatever. My friends strangely trouble me, when they ask me to ask a third person; and I think it costs me little less to disengage him who is indebted to me, by making use of him, than to engage myself to him who owes me nothing. These conditions being removed, and provided they require of me nothing of any

great trouble or care (for I have declared mortal war against all care), I am very ready to do every one the best service I can. But I have yet more avoided receiving than sought occasions of giving, and moreover, according to Aristotle, it is more easy. My fortune has allowed me but little to do others good withal, and the little it can afford, is put into a pretty close hand. Had I been born a great person, I should have been ambitious to have made myself beloved, not to make myself feared or admired: shall I more plainly express it? I should more have endeavored to please than to profit others. Cyrus very wisely, and by the mouth of a great captain, and still greater philosopher, prefers his bounty and benefits much before his valor and warlike conquests; and the elder Scipio, wherever he would raise himself in esteem, sets a higher value upon his affability and humanity, than on his prowess and victories, and has always this glorious saying in his mouth: "That he has given his enemies as much occasion to love him as his friends." I will then say, that if a man must, of necessity, owe something, it ought to be by a more legitimate title than that whereof I am speaking, to which the necessity of this miserable war compels me; and not in so great a debt as that of my total preservation both of life and fortune: it overwhelms me.

I have a thousand times gone to bed in my own house with an apprehension that I should be betrayed and murdered that very night; compounding with fortune, that it might be without terror and with quick despatch; and, after my Paternoster, have cried out,

"Impius hæc tam culta novalia miles habebit!"

What remedy? 'tis the place of my birth, and that of most of my ancestors; they have here fixed their affection and name. We inure ourselves to whatever we are accustomed to; and in so miserable a condition as ours is, custom is a great bounty of nature, which benumbs our senses to the sufferance of many evils. A civil war has this with it worse than others wars have, to make us stand sentinels in our own houses:

"Quam miserum, porta vitam muroque tueri,
Vixque suæ tutum viribis esse domus!"

[339]

'Tis a grievous extremity for a man to be jostled even in his own house and domestic repose. The country where I live is always the first in arms, and the last that lays them down, and where there is never an absolute peace:

> "Tum quoque, cum pax est, trepidant formidine belli.
>   Quoties pacem fortuna lacessit;
>   Hac iter est bellis . . . Melius, Fortuna, dedisses
>   Orbe sub Eoo sedem, gelidaque sub Arcto,
>   Errantesque domos."

I sometimes extract the means to fortify myself against these considerations, from indifference and indolence, which, in some sort, bring us on to resolution. It often befalls me to imagine and expect mortal dangers with a kind of delight: I stupidly plunge myself headlong, into death, without considering or taking a view of it, as into a deep and obscure abyss which swallows me up at one leap, and involves me in an instant in a profound sleep, without any sense of pain. And in these short and violent deaths, the consequence that I foresee administers more consolation to me than the effect does fear. They say, that as life is not better for being long, so death is better for being not long. I do not so much evade being dead, as I enter into confidence with dying. I wrap and shroud myself in the storm that is to blind and carry me away with the fury of a sudden and insensible attack. Moreover, if it should fall out, that, as some gardeners say, roses and violets spring more odoriferous near garlic and onions, by reason that the last suck and imbibe all the ill odor of the earth; so, if these depraved natures should also attract all the malignity of my air and climate, and render it so much better and purer by their vicinity, I should not lose all. That cannot be: but there may be something in this, that goodness is more beautiful and attractive when it is rare; and that contrariety and diversity fortify and consolidate well-doing within itself, and inflame it by the jealousy of opposition and by glory. Thieves and robbers, of their special favor, have no particular spite at me; no more have I to them: I should have my hands too full. Like consciences are lodged under several sorts of robes; like cruelty, disloyalty, rapine; and so much the worse, and more falsely when

the more secure and concealed under color of the laws. I less hate
an open professed injury than one that is treacherous; an enemy in
arms, than an enemy in a gown. Our fever has seized upon a body
that is not much the worse for it; there was fire before and now 'tis
broken out into a flame; the noise is greater, not the evil. I ordinarily answer such as ask me the reason of my travels, "That I know
very well what I fly from, but not what I seek." If they tell me that
there may be as little health among foreigners, and that their manners are no better than ours; I first reply, that it is hard to be
believed,

"Tam multæ scelerum facies!"

secondly, that it is always gain to change an ill condition for one
that is uncertain; and that the ills of others ought not to afflict us
so much as our own.

I will not here omit that I never mutiny so much against France,
that I am not perfectly friends with Paris; that city has ever had
my heart from my infancy, and it has fallen out, as of excellent
things, that the more beautiful cities I have seen since, the more
the beauty of this still wins upon my affection. I love her for herself, and more in her own native being, than in all the pomp of
foreign and acquired embellishments. I love her tenderly, even to
her warts and blemishes. I am French only by this great city, great
in people, great in the felicity of her situation; but, above all, great
and incomparable in variety and diversity of commodities: the
glory of France, and one of the most noble ornaments of the world.
May God keep our divisions far remote from her. Entire and united,
I think her sufficiently defended from all other violences. I give
her caution that, of all sorts of people, those will be the worst
that shall set her in discord; I have no fear for her, but of herself;
and, certainly, I have as much fear for her as for any other part of
the kingdom. While she shall continue, I shall never want a retreat,
where I may stand at bay, sufficient to make me amends for parting
with any other retreat.

Not because Socrates has said so, but because it is, in truth, my
own humor, and, peradventure, not without some excess, I look

upon all men as my compatriots, and embrace a Polander as a Frenchman, preferring the universal and common tie to all national ties whatever. I am not much taken with the sweetness of a native air: acquaintance wholly new and wholly my own, appear to me full as good as the other common and fortuitous ones with our neighbors: friendships that are purely of our own acquiring ordinarily carry it above those to which the communication of climate or of blood oblige us. Nature has placed us in the world free and unbound: we imprison ourselves in certain straits, like the kings of Persia, who obliged themselves to drink no other water but that of the river Choaspes, foolishly quitted claim to their right in all other streams, and, so far as concerned themselves, dried up all the other rivers of the world. What Socrates did toward his end, to look upon a sentence of banishment as worse than a sentence of death against him, I shall, I think, never be either so decrepit or so strictly habituated to my own country to be of that opinion. These celestial lives have images enough that I embrace more by esteem than affection; and they have some also so elevated and extraordinary that I cannot embrace them so much as by esteem, forasmuch as I cannot conceive them. That fancy was singular in a man who thought the whole world his city; it is true that he disdained travel, and had hardly ever set his foot out of the Attic territories. What say you to his complaint of the money his friends offered to save his life, and that he refused to come out of prison by the mediation of others, in order not to disobey the laws in a time when they were otherwise so corrupt? These examples are of the first kind for me: of the second, there are others that I could find out in the same person; many of these rare examples surpass the force of my action, but some of them, moreover, surpass the force of my judgment.

Besides these reasons, travel is in my opinion a very profitable exercise; the soul is there continually employed in observing new and unknown things, and I do not know, as I have often said, a better school wherein to model life than by incessantly exposing to it the diversity of so many other lives, fancies, and usances, and by making it relish so perpetual a variety of forms of human nature.

The body is, therein, neither idle nor overwrought; and that moderate agitation puts it in breath. I can keep on horseback, tormented with the stone as I am, without alighting or being weary, eight or ten hours together.

"Vires ultra sortemque senectæ:"

No season is enemy to me but the parching heat of a scorching sun; for the umbrellas made use of in Italy, ever since the time of the ancient Romans, more burden a man's arm than they relieve his head. I would fain know how it was that the Persians, so long ago, and in the infancy of luxury, made ventilators where they wanted them, and planted shades, as Xenophon reports they did. I love rain, and to dabble in the dirt, as well as ducks do. The change of air and climate never touches me; every sky is alike; I am only troubled with inward alterations which I breed within myself, and those are not so frequent in travel. I am hard to be got out, but being once upon the road, I hold out as well as the best. I take as much pains in little as in great attempts, and am as solicitous to equip myself for a short journey, if but to visit a neighbor, as for the longest voyage. I have learned to travel after the Spanish fashion, and to make but one stage of a great many miles; and in excessive heats I always travel by night, from sunset to sunrise. The other method of baiting by the way, in haste and hurry to gobble up a dinner is, especially in short days, very inconvenient. My horses perform the better; never any horse tired under me that was able to hold out the first day's journey. I water them at every brook I meet, and have only a care they have so much way to go before I come to my inn, as will digest the water in their bellies. My unwillingness to rise in a morning gives my servants leisure to dine at their ease before they set out; for my own part, I never eat too late; my appetite, comes to me in eating, and not else; I am never hungry but at table.

Some of my friends blame me for continuing this traveling humor, being married and old. But they are out in't; 'tis the best time to leave a man's house, when he has put it into a way of continuing without him, and settled such order as corresponds with its

former government. 'Tis much greater imprudence to abandon it to a less faithful housekeeper, and who will be less solicitous to look after your affairs.

The most useful and honorable knowledge and employment for the mother of a family is the science of good housewifery. I see some that are covetous indeed, but very few that are good managers. 'Tis the supreme quality of a woman, which a man ought to seek before any other, as the only dowry that must ruin or preserve our houses. Let men say what they will, according to the experience I have learned, I require in married women the economical virtue above all other virtues; I put my wife to't, as a concern of her own, leaving her, by my absence, the whole government of my affairs. I see and am vexed to see, in several families I know, monsieur about dinner time come home all jaded and ruffled about his affairs, when madam is still pouncing and tricking up herself, forsooth, in her closet; this is for queens to do, and that's a question, too; 'tis ridiculous and unjust that the laziness of our wives should be maintained with our sweat and labor. No man, so far as in me lies, shall have a clearer, a more quiet, and free fruition of his estate than I. If the husband bring matter, nature herself will that the wife find the form.

As to the duties of conjugal friendship, that some think to be impaired by these absences, I am quite of another opinion. It is, on the contrary, an intelligence that easily cools by a too frequent and assiduous companionship. Every strange woman appears charming, and we all find by experience that being continually together is not so pleasing, as to part for a time and meet again. These interruptions fill me with fresh affection toward my family, and render my house more pleasant to me. Change warms my appetite to the one and then to the other. I know that the arms of friendship are long enough to reach from the one end of the world to the other, and especially this, where there is a continual communication of offices that rouse the obligation and remembrance. The Stoics say, that there is so great connection and relation among the sages, that he who dines in France nourishes his companion in Egypt; and that whoever does but hold out his finger, in what part of the world

soever, all the sages upon the habitable earth feel themselves assisted by it. Fruition and possession principally appertain to the imagination; it more fervently and constantly embraces what it is in quest of, than what we hold in our arms. Let a man but consider and cast up his daily thoughts, and he will find, that he is most absent from his friend, when in his company; his presence relaxes your attention, and gives your thoughts liberty to absent themselves at every turn, and upon every occasion. When I am away at Rome, I keep and govern my house, and the conveniences I there left; see my wall rise, my trees shoot, and my revenue increase or decrease, very near as well as when I am there:

"Ante oculos errat domus, errat forma locorum."

If we enjoy nothing but what we touch, we may say farewell to the money in our chests, and to our sons when they are gone a hunting. We will have them nearer to us; in the garden, or half a day's journey from home, far? What is ten leagues; far or near? If near, what is eleven, twelve, or thirteen, and so by degrees. In earnest, if there be a woman who can tell her husband what step ends the near and what step begins the remote, I would advise her to stop between:

"Excludat jurgia finis. . . .
Utor permisso; caudæque pilos ut equinæ
Paulatim vello, et demo unum, demo etiam unum,
Dum cadat elusus ratione ruentis acervi:"

and let them boldly call philosophy to their assistance; in whose teeth it may be cast, that seeing it neither discerns the one nor the other end of the joint, between the too much and the little, the long and the short, the light and the heavy, the near and the remote; that seeing it discovers neither the beginning nor the end, it must needs judge very uncertainly of the middle: *"Rerum natura nullam nobis dedit cognitionem finium."* Are they not still wives and friends to the dead, who are not at the end of this, but in the other world? We embrace not only the absent, but those who have been, and those who are not yet. We do not promise in marriage to be continually

twisted and linked together, like some little animals that we see, or, like the bewitched folks of Kerenty, tied together like dogs; and a wife ought not to be so greedily enamored of her husband's foreparts, that she cannot endure to see him turn his back, if occasion be. But may not this saying of that excellent painter of women's humors be here introduced, to show the reason of their complaints?

> "Uxor, si cesses, aut te amare cogitat,
>   Aut tete amari, aut potare, aut animo obsequi;
>   Et tibi bene esse soli, cum sibi sit male;"

or may it not be, that of itself opposition and contradiction entertain and nourish them; and that they sufficiently accommodate themselves, provided they incommodate you?

In true friendship, wherein I am perfect, I more give myself to my friend, than I endeavor to attract him to me; I am not only better pleased in doing him service, than if he conferred a benefit upon me, but, moreover, had rather he should do himself good than me, and he most obliges me when he does so; and if absence be either more pleasant or convenient for him, 'tis also more acceptable to me than his presence; neither is it properly absence, when we can write to one another. I have sometimes made good use of our separation from one another: we better filled, and further extended the possession of life in being parted. He lived, enjoyed, and saw for me, and I for him, as fully as if he had himself been there: one part of us remained idle, and we were too much blended in one another when we were together; the distance of place rendered the conjunction of our wills more rich. This insatiable desire of personal presence, a little implies weakness in the fruition of souls.

As to what concerns age, which is alleged against me, 'tis quite contrary; 'tis for youth to subject itself to common opinions, and to curb itself to please others; it has wherewithal to please both the people and itself; we have but too much ado to please ourselves alone. As natural conveniences fail, let us supply them with those that are artificial. 'Tis injustice to excuse youth for pursuing its

pleasures, and to forbid old men to seek them. When young, I concealed my wanton passions with prudence; now I am old, I chase away melancholy by debauch. And thus do the Platonic laws forbid men to travel till forty or fifty years old, so that travel might be more useful and instructive in so mature an age. I should sooner subscribe to the second article of the same Laws, which forbids it after threescore.

"But, at your age, you will never return from so long a journey." What care I for that? I neither undertake it to return, nor to finish it: my business is only to keep myself in motion, while motion pleases me; I only walk for the walk's sake. They, who run after a benefice or a hare, run not; they only run who run at base, and to exercise their running. My design is divisible throughout: it is not grounded upon any great hopes; every day concludes my expectation: and the journey of my life is carried on after the same manner. And yet I have seen places enough a great way off, where I could have wished to have stayed. And why not, if Chrysippus, Cleanthes, Diogenes, Zeno, Antipater, so many sages of the sourest sect, readily abandoned their country, without occasion of complaint, and only for the enjoyment of another air. In earnest, that which most displeases me in all my travels is, that I cannot resolve to settle my abode where I should best like, but that I must always propose to myself to return, to accommodate myself to the common humor.

If I feared to die in any other place than that of my birth; if I thought I should die more uneasily, remote from my own family, I should hardly go out of France; I should not, without fear, step out of my parish; I feel death always twitching me by the throat, or by the back. But I am of another temper; 'tis in all places alike to me. Yet, might I have my choice, I think I should rather choose to die on horseback than in a bed; out of my own house, and far from my own people. There is more heartbreaking than consolation in taking leave of one's friends; I am willing to omit that civility, for that, of all the offices of friendship, is the only one that is unpleasant; and I could, with all my heart, dispense with that great and eternal farewell. If there be any convenience in so

many standers by, it brings an hundred inconveniences along with it. I have seen many dying miserably, surrounded with all this train: 'tis a crowd that chokes them. 'Tis against duty, and is a testimony of little kindness and little care, to permit you to die in repose; one torments your eyes, another your ears, another your tongue; you have neither sense nor member that is not worried by them. Your heart is wounded with compassion to hear the mourning of friends; and perhaps, with anger, to hear the counterfeit condolings of pretenders. Whoever has been delicate and sensitive, when well, is much more so when ill. In such a necessity, a gentle hand is required, accommodated to his sentiment, to scratch him just in the place where he itches, otherwise scratch him not at all. If we stand in need of a wise woman to bring us into the world, we have much more need of a still wiser man to help us out of it. Such a one, and a friend to boot, a man ought to purchase at any cost for such an occasion. I am not yet arrived to that pitch of disdainful vigor, that is fortified in itself, that nothing can assist, or disturb; I am of a lower form; I endeavor to hide myself; and to escape from this passage, not by fear, but by art. I do not intend in this act of dying to make proof and show of my constancy. For whom should I do it? all the right and interest I have in reputation will then cease. I content myself with a death involved within itself, quiet, solitary, and all my own, suitable to my retired and private life; quite contrary to the Roman superstition, where a man was looked upon as unhappy who died without speaking, and who had not his nearest relations to close his eyes. I have enough to do to comfort myself, without having to console others; thoughts enough in my head, not to need that circumstances should possess me with new; and matter enough to occupy me without borrowing. This affair is out of the part of society; 'tis the act of one single person. Let us live and be merry among our friends; let us go rapine and die among strangers; a man may find those, for his money, who will shift his pillow and rub his feet, and will trouble him no more than he would have them; who will present to him an indifferent countenance, and suffer him to govern himself, and to complain according to his own method.

I wean myself daily by my reason from this childish and inhuman humor, of desiring by our suffering to move the compassion and mourning of our friends: we stretch our own incommodities beyond their just extent when we extract tears from others; and the constancy which we commend in every one in supporting his adverse fortune, we accuse and reproach in our friends when the evil is our own; we are not satisfied that they should be sensible of our condition only, unless they be, moreover, afflicted. A man should diffuse joy, but, as much as he can, smother grief. He who makes himself lamented without reason, is a man not to be lamented when there shall be real cause: to be always complaining, is the way never to be lamented; by making himself always in so pitiful a taking, he is never commiserated by any. He who makes himself out dead when he is alive, is subject to be thought living, when he is dying. I have seen some who have taken it ill when they have been told that they looked well, and that their pulse was good; restrain their smiles, because they betrayed a recovery, and be angry at their health because it was not to be lamented: and, which is a great deal more, these were not women. I describe my infirmities, such as they really are, at most, and avoid all expressions of evil prognostic and composed exclamations. If not mirth, at least a temperate countenance in the standers by, is proper in the presence of a wise sick man: he does not quarrel with health, for seeing himself in a contrary condition; he is pleased to contemplate it sound and entire in others, and at least to enjoy it for company: he does not, for feeling himself melt away, abandon all living thoughts, nor avoid ordinary discourse. I would study sickness while I am well; when it has seized me, it will make its impression real enough, without the help of my imagination. We prepare ourselves beforehand for the journeys we undertake, and resolve upon them; we leave the appointment of the hour when to take horse to the company, and in their favor defer it.

I find this unexpected advantage in the publication of my manners, that it in some sort serves me for a rule. I have, at times, some consideration of not betraying the history of my life: this public declaration obliges me to keep my way, and not to give the lie to

the image I have drawn of my qualities, commonly less deformed and contradictory than consists with the malignity and infirmity of the judgments of this age. The uniformity and simplicity of my manners produce a face of easy interpretation; but because the fashion is a little new and not in use, it gives too great opportunity to slander. Yet so it is, that whoever would fairly assail me, I think I so sufficiently assist his purpose in my known and avowed imperfections, that he may that way satisfy his ill-nature, without fighting with the wind. If I myself, to anticipate accusation and discovery, confess enough to frustrate his malice, as he conceives, 'tis but reason that he make use of his right of amplification, and to wiredraw my vices as far as he can; attack has its rights beyond justice; and let him make the roots of those errors I have laid open to him, shoot up into trees: let him make his use, not only of those I am really affected with, but also of those that only threaten me; injurious vices, both in quality and number; let him cudgel me that way. I should willingly follow the example of the philosopher Bion: Antigonus being about to reproach him with the meanness of his birth, he presently cut him short with this declaration: "I am," said he, "the son of a slave, a butcher, and branded, and of a strumpet my father married in the lowest of his fortune; both of them were whipped for offenses they had committed. An orator bought me, when a child, and finding me a pretty and hopeful boy, bred me up, and when he died left me all his estate, which I have transported into this city of Athens, and here settled myself to the study of philosophy. Let the historians never trouble themselves with inquiring about me: I will tell them about it." A free and generous confession enervates reproach, and disarms slander. So it is, that, one thing with another, I fancy men as often commend as undervalue me beyond reason; as methinks also, from my childhood, in rank and degree of honor, they have given me a place rather above than below my right. I should find myself more at ease in a country where these degrees were either regulated or not regarded. Among men, when an altercation about the precedence either of walking or sitting exceeds three replies, 'tis reputed uncivil. I never stick at giving or taking place out of rule, to avoid the trouble of such

[350]

ceremony; and never any man had a mind to go before me but I permitted him to do it.

Besides this profit I make of writing of myself, I have also hoped for this other advantage, that if it should fall out that my humor should please or jump with those of some honest man before I die, he would then desire and seek to be acquainted with me. I have given him a great deal of made-way; for all that he could have, in many years, acquired by close familiarity, he has seen in three days in this memorial, and more surely and exactly. A pleasant fancy: many things that I would not confess to any one in particular, I deliver to the public, and send my best friends to a bookseller's shop, there to inform themselves concerning my most secret thoughts;

"Excutienda damus præcordia."

Did I, by good direction, know where to seek any one proper for my conversation, I should certainly go a great way to find him out: for the sweetness of suitable and agreeable company cannot in my opinion, be bought too dear. Oh! what a thing is a true friend! how true is that old saying, that the use of a friend is more pleasing and necessary than the elements of water and fire!

To return to my subject: there is, then, no great harm in dying privately, and far from home; we conceive ourselves obliged to retire from natural actions less unseemly, and less terrible than this. But, moreover, such as are reduced to spin out a long languishing life, ought not, perhaps, to wish to trouble a great family with their continual miseries; therefore the Indians, in a certain province, thought it just to knock a man on the head when reduced to such a necessity; and in another of their provinces, they all forsook him to shift for himself as well as he could. To whom do they not, at last, become tedious and insupportable? the ordinary offices of life do not go that length. You teach your best friends to be cruel perforce; hardening wife and children by long use neither to regard nor to lament your sufferings. The groans of the stone are grown so familiar to my people, that nobody takes any notice of them. And though we should extract some pleasure from their

conversation (which does not always happen by reason of the disparity of conditions, which easily begets contempt or envy toward any one whatever), is it not too much to make abuse of this half a lifetime? The more I should see them constrain themselves out of affection to be serviceable to me, the more I should be sorry for their pains. We have liberty to lean, but not to lay our whole weight upon others, so as to prop ourselves by their ruin; like him who caused little children's throats to be cut to make use of their blood for the care of a disease he had, or that other, who was continually supplied with tender young girls to keep his old limbs warm in the night, and to mix the sweetness of their breath with his, sour and stinking. Decrepitude is a solitary quality. I am sociable even to excess, yet I think it reasonable that I should now withdraw my troubles from the sight of the world, and keep them to myself. Let me shrink and draw up myself in my own shell, like a tortoise, and learn to see men without hanging upon them. I should endanger them in so slippery a passage: 'tis time to turn my back to company.

"But, in these travels, you will be taken ill in some wretched place, where nothing can be had to relieve you." I always carry most things necessary about me: and besides, we cannot evade fortune if she once resolves to attack us. I need nothing extraordinary when I am sick, I will not be beholden to my bolus to do that for me which nature cannot. At the very beginning of my fevers and sicknesses that cast me down, while still entire, and but little disordered in health, I reconcile myself to Almighty God by the last Christian offices, and find myself by so doing less oppressed and more easy, and have got, methinks, so much the better of my disease. And I have yet less need of a notary or counselor than of a physician. What I have not settled of my affairs when I was in health, let no one expect I should do it when I am sick. What I will do for the service of death is always done; I dare not so much as one day defer it, and if nothing be done, 'tis as much as to say either that doubt hindered my choice (and sometimes 'tis well chosen not to choose), or that I was positively resolved not to do anything at all.

I write my book for few men and for few years. Had it been

matter of duration, I should have put it into firmer language. According to the continual variation that ours has been subject to, up to this day, who can expect that its present form should be in use fifty years hence? It slips every day through our fingers, and since I was born, it is altered above one-half. We say that it is now perfect; and every age says the same of its own. I shall hardly trust to that, so long as it varies and changes as it does. 'Tis for good and useful writings to rivet it to them, and its reputation will go according to the fortune of our state. For which reason I am not afraid to insert in it several private articles, which will spend their use among the men that are now living, and that concern the particular knowledge of some who will see further into them than every common reader. I will not, after all, as I often hear dead men spoken of, that men should say of me: "He judged he lived so and so; he would have done this or that; could he have spoken when he was dying, he would have said so or so, and have given this thing or t'other; I knew him better than any." Now, as much as decency permits, I here discover my inclinations and affections; but I do it more willingly and freely by word of mouth to any one who desires to be informed. So it is that in these memoirs, if any one observe, he will find that I have either told or designed to tell all; what I cannot express, I point out with my finger:

"Verum animo satis hæc vestigia parva sagaci
Sunt, per quæ possis cognoscere cœtera tute."

I leave nothing to be desired, or to be guessed at, concerning me. If people must be talking of me, I would have it to be justly and truly: I would come again, with all my heart, from the other world to give any one the lie who should report me other than I was, though he did it to honor me. I perceive that people represent, even living men, quite another thing than what they really are; and had I not stoutly defended a friend, whom I have lost, they would have torn him into a thousand contrary pieces.

To conclude the account of my poor humors, I confess that in my travels I seldom reach my inn but that it comes into my mind to consider whether I could there be sick, and dying, at my ease. I

desire to be lodged in some private part of the house, remote from all noise, ill scents, and smoke. I endeavor to flatter death by these frivolous circumstances; or, to say better, to discharge myself from all other incumbrances, that I may have nothing to do, nor be troubled with anything but that, which will lie heavy enough upon me without any other load. I would have my death share in the ease and conveniences of my life; 'tis a great part of it, and of great importance, and I hope it will not in the future contradict the past. Death has some forms that are more easy than others, and receives divers qualities, according to every one's fancy. Among the natural deaths, that which proceeds from weakness and stupor I think the most favorable; among those that are violent, I can worse endure to think of a precipice than of the fall of a house that will crush me in a moment, and of a wound with a sword than of a harquebus shot; I should rather have chosen to poison myself with Socrates, than stab myself with Cato. And, though it be all one, yet my imagination makes as great a difference as between death and life, between throwing myself into a burning furnace and plunging into the channel of a river: so idly does our fear more concern itself in the means than the effect. It is but an instant, 'tis true, but withal an instant of such weight, that I would willingly give a great many days of my life to pass it over after my own fashion. Since every one's imagination renders it more or less terrible, and since every one has some choice among the several forms of dying, let us try a little further to find some one that is wholly clear from all offense. Might not one render it even voluptuous, as they did who died with Antony and Cleopatra? I set aside the brave and exemplary efforts produced by philosophy and religion: but, among men of little mark, there have been found some such as Petronius and Tigellinus at Rome, condemned to despatch themselves, who have, as it were, rocked death asleep with the delicacy of their preparations; they have made it slip and steal away in the height of their accustomed diversions, among girls and good fellows; not a word of consolation, no mention of making a will, no ambitious affectation of constancy, no talk of their future condition; among sports, feastings, wit, and mirth, common and indifferent dis-

courses, music, and amorous verses. Were it not possible for us to imitate this resolution, after a more decent manner? Since there are deaths that are good for fools, deaths good for tho wise, let us find out such as are fit for those who are between both. My imagination suggests to me one that is easy, and, since we must die, to be desired. The Roman tyrants thought they did, in a manner, give a criminal life, when they gave him the choice of his death. But was not Theophrastus, that so delicate, so modest, and so wise a philosopher, compelled by reason when he dared say this verse, translated by Cicero,

"Vitam regit fortuna, non sapientia?"

Fortune assists the facility of the bargain of my life, having placed it in such a condition that for the future it can be neither advantage nor hindrance to those who are concerned in me; 'tis a condition that I would have accepted at any time of my life; but in this occasion of trussing up my baggage, I am particularly pleased that in dying I shall neither do them good nor harm. She has so ordered it, by a cunning compensation, that they who may pretend to any considerable advantage by my death will, at the same time, sustain a material inconvenience. Death sometimes is more grievous to us, in that it is grievous to others, and interests us in their interest as much as in our own, and sometimes more.

In this conveniency of lodging that I desire, I mix nothing of pomp and amplitude—I hate it rather; but a certain plain neatness, which is oftenest found in places where there is less of art, and that Nature has adorned with some grace that is all her own. *"Non ampliter, sed munditer convivium." "Plus salis quam sumptus."* And besides, 'tis for those whose affairs compel them to travel in the depth of winter through the Grisons country, to be surprised upon the way with great inconveniences. I, who for the most part travel for my pleasure, do not order my affairs so ill. If the way be foul on my right hand, I turn on my left; if I find myself unfit to ride, I stay where I am; and, so doing, in earnest I see nothing that is not as pleasant and commodious as my own house. 'Tis true, that I always find superfluity superfluous, and observe a kind of trouble

even in abundance itself. Have I left anything behind me unseen, I go back to see it; 'tis still on my way; I trace no certain line, either straight or crooked. Do I not find in the place to which I go what was reported to me—as it often falls out that the judgments of others do not jump with mine, and that I have found their reports for the most part false—I never complain of losing my labor: I have, at least, informed myself that what was told me was not true.

I have a constitution of body as free, and a palate as indifferent, as any man living: the diversity of manners of several nations only affects me in the pleasure of variety: every usage has its reason. Let the plate and dishes be pewter, wood, or earth; my meat be broiled or roasted; let them give me butter or oil, of nuts or olives, hot or cold, 'tis all one to me; and so indifferent, that growing old, I accuse this generous faculty, and would wish that delicacy and choice should correct the indiscretion of my appetite, and sometimes help my stomach. When I have been abroad out of France, and that people, out of courtesy, have asked me if I would be served after the French manner, I laughed at the question, and always frequented tables the most filled with foreigners. I am ashamed to see my countrymen besotted with this foolish humor of quarreling with forms contrary to their own; they seem to be out of their element when out of their own village: wherever they go, they keep to their own fashion, and abominate those of strangers. Do they meet with a compatriot in Hungary? Oh the happy chance! They are thencefoward inseparable; they cling together, and their whole discourse is to condemn the barbarous manners they see about them. And why barbarous, but because they are not French? And those have made the best use of their travels, who have observed most to speak against. Most of them go, for no other end but to come back again; they proceed in their travel with vast gravity and circumspection, with a silent and incommunicable prudence, preserving themselves from the contagion of an unknown air. What I am saying of them puts me in mind of something like it I have at times observed in some of our young courtiers; they will not mix with any but men of their own sort, and look upon us as men of another world, with disdain or pity. Put them upon any discourse

but the intrigues of the court, and they are utterly at a loss; as very owls and novices to us as we are to them. 'Tis truly said, that a well-bred man is a compound man. I, on the contrary, travel very much sated with our own fashions; I do not look for Gascons in Sicily; I have left enough of them at home; I rather seek for Greeks and Persians; they are the men I endeavor to be acquainted with, and the men I study; 'tis there that I bestow and employ myself. And which is more, I fancy that I have met with but few customs that are not as good as our own; I have not, I confess, traveled very far; scarce out of the sight of the vanes of my own house.

As to the rest, most of the accidental company a man falls into upon the road, beget him more trouble than pleasure; I waive them as much as I civilly can, especially now that age seems in some sort to privilege and sequester me from the common forms. You suffer for others, or others suffer for you; both of them inconveniences of importance enough, but the latter appears to me the greater. 'Tis a rare fortune, but of inestimable solace, to have a worthy man, one of a sound judgment, and of manners conformable to your own, who takes a delight to bear you company. I have been at an infinite loss for such upon my travels. But such a companion should be chosen and acquired from your first setting out. There can be no pleasure to me without communication: there is not so much as a sprightly thought comes into my mind, that it does not grieve me to have produced alone, and that I have no one to communicate it to. *"Si cum hac exceptione detur sapientia, ut illam inclusam teneam, nec enuntiem, rejiciam."* This other has strained it one note higher: *"Si contigerit ea vita sapienti ut omnium rerum affluentibus copiis, quamvis omnia, quæ cognitione digna sunt, summo otio secum ipse consideret et contempletur, tamen, si solitudo tanta sit, ut hominem videre non possit, excedat e vita."* Architas pleases me when he says, "that it would be unpleasant even in heaven itself, to wander in those great and divine celestial bodies without a companion." But yet 'tis much better to be alone, than in foolish and troublesome company. Aristippus loved to live as a stranger in all places:

"Me si fata meis paterentur ducere vitam
Auspiciis,"

I should choose to pass the greatest part of my life on horseback.

> "Visere gestiens,
> Qua parte debacchentur ignes,
> Qua nebulæ, pluviique rores."

"Have you not more easy diversions at home? What do you there want? Is not your house situated in a sweet and healthful air, sufficiently furnished, and more than sufficiently large? Has not the royal majesty been more than once there entertained with all its train? Are there not more below your family in good ease than there are above it in eminence? Is there any local, extraordinary, indigestible thought that afflicts you?"

> "Quæ te nunc coquat, et vexet sub pectore fixa."

"Where do you think to live without disturbance?" *"Nunquam simpliciter Fortuna indulget."* You see, then, it is only you that trouble yourself; you will everywhere follow yourself, and everywhere complain; for there is no satisfaction here below, but either for brutish or for divine souls. He who, on so just an occasion, has no contentment, where will he think to find it? How many thousands of men terminate their wishes in such a condition as yours? Do but reform yourself; for that is wholly in your own power, whereas, you have no other right but patience toward fortune: *"Nulla placidi quies est nisi quam ratio composuit."*

I see the reason of this advice, and see it perfectly well; but he might sooner have done, and more pertinently, in bidding me in one word, be wise; that resolution is beyond wisdom; 'tis her precise work and product. Thus the physician keeps preaching to a poor languishing patient to "be cheerful;" but he would advise him a little more discreetly in bidding him "be well." For my part, I am but a man of the common sort. 'Tis a wholesome precept, certain, and easy to be understood, "Be content with what you have," that is to say, with reason; and yet to follow this advice is no more in the power of the wise men of the world than in me. 'Tis a common saying, but of a terrible extent: what does it not comprehend? All things fall under discretion and qualification. I know very well that, to take it by the letter, this pleasure of traveling is a testimony of

uneasiness and irresolution, and, in sooth, these two are our governing and predominating qualities. Yes, I confess, I see nothing, not so much as in a dream, in a wish, whereon I could set up my rest; variety only, and the possession of diversity, can satisfy me; that is, if anything can. In traveling, it pleases me that I may stay where I like, without inconvenience, and that I have a place wherein commodiously to divert myself. I love a private life, because 'tis my own choice that I love it, not by any dissenting from or dislike of public life, which, peradventure, is as much according to my complexion. I serve my prince more cheerfully, because it is by the free election of my own judgment and reason, without any particular obligation; and that I am not reduced and constrained so to do for being rejected or disliked by the other party; and so of all the rest; I hate the morsels that necessity carves me; any commodity upon which I had only to depend would have me by the throat:

"Alter remus aquas, alter mihi radat arenas;"

one cord will never hold me fast enough. You will say there is vanity in this way of living. But where is there not? All these fine precepts are vanity, and all wisdom is vanity *"Dominus novit cognationes sapientum, quoniam vanœ sunt."* These exquisite subtleties are only fit for sermons; they are discourses that will send us all saddled into the other world. Life is a material and corporal motion, an action imperfect and irregular of its own proper essence; I make it my business to serve it according to itself.

"Quisque suos patimur manes."

"Sic est faciendum, ut contra naturam universam nihil contendamus; ea tamen conservata, propriam sequamur." To what end are these elevated points of philosophy, upon which no human being can rely? and those rules that exceed both our use and force?

I see often that we have theories of life set before us which neither the proposer, nor those who hear him, have any hope nor, which is more, any inclination to follow. Of the same sheet of paper whereon the judge has but just written a sentence against an adulterer, he steals a piece whereon to write a love-letter to his com-

ESSAYS OF MICHEL DE MONTAIGNE

panion's wife. She whom you have but just now illicitly embraced
will presently, even in your own hearing, more loudly inveigh
against the same fault in her companion than a Portia would do;
and men there are who will condemn others to death for crimes that
they themselves do not repute so much as faults. I have, in my
youth, seen a man of good rank with one hand present to the people
verses that excelled both in wit and debauchery, and with the other,
at the same time, the most ripe and pugnacious theological reformation that the world has been treated withal these many years.
And so men proceed; we let the laws and precepts follow their way;
ourselves keep another course, not only from debauchery of manners, but ofttimes by judgment and contrary opinion. Do you hear
a philosophical lecture; the invention, eloquence, pertinency immediately strike upon your mind, and move you; there is nothing
that touches or stings your conscience; 'tis not to this they address
themselves. Is not this true? It made Aristo say, that neither a bath
nor a lecture did aught, unless it scoured and made men clean?
One may stop at the outward skin; but it is after the marrow is
picked out: as, after we have quaffed off the wine out of a fine cup,
we examine the design and workmanship. In all the courts of ancient philosophy, this is to be found, that the same teacher publishes
rules of temperance, and at the same time lessons in love and
wantonness: Xenophon, in the very bosom of Clinias, wrote against
the Aristippic virtue. 'Tis not there is any miraculous conversion
in it that makes them thus wavering; 'tis that Solon represents himself, sometimes in his own person, and sometimes in that of a legislator; one while he speaks for the crowd, and another for himself;
taking the free and natural rules for his own share, feeling assured
of a firm and entire health:

"Curentur dubii medicis majoribus ægri."

Antisthenes allows a sage to love, and to do whatever he thinks
convenient, without regard to the laws: forasmuch as he is better
advised than they, and has a greater knowledge of virtue. His
disciple Diogenes said, that "men to pertubations were to oppose
reason; to fortune, courage; to the laws, nature." For tender

stomachs, constrained and artificial recipes must be prescribed: good and strong stomachs serve themselves simply with the prescriptions of their own natural appetite; after this manner do our physicians proceed, who eat melons and drink iced wines, while they confine their patients to syrups and sops. "I know not," said the courtesan Lais, "what they may talk of books, wisdom, and philosophy; but these men knock as often at my door as any others." At the same rate that our license carries us beyond what is lawful and allowed, men have, often beyond universal reason, stretched the precepts and rules of our life:

> "Nemo satis credit tantum delinquere, quantum
>   Permittas."

It were to be wished that there was more proportion between the command and the obedience; and the mark seems to be unjust to which one cannot attain. There is no so good man, who so squares all his thoughts and actions to the laws, that he is not faulty enough to deserve hanging ten times in his life; and he may well be such a one, as it were great injustice and great harm to punish and ruin:

> "Ole, quid ad te
> De cute quid faciat ille, vel illa sua?"

and such a one there may be, who has no way offended the laws, who nevertheless, would not deserve the character of a virtuous man, and whom philosophy would justly condemn to be whipped; so unequal and perplexed is this relation. We are so far from being good men, according to the laws of God, that we cannot be so according to our own: human wisdom never yet arrived at the duties it had itself prescribed; and could it arrive there, it would still prescribe to itself others beyond, to which it would ever aspire and pretend; so great an enemy to consistency is our human condition. Man enjoins himself to be necessarily in fault: he is not very discreet to cut out his own duty, by the measure of another being than his own. To whom does he prescribe that which he does not expect any one should perform? Is he unjust in not doing what it is impossible for him to do? The laws which condemn us not to be able, condemn us for not being able.

At the worst, this difform liberty of presenting ourselves two several ways, the actions after one manner, and the reasoning after another, may be allowed to those who only speak of things; but it cannot be allowed to those who speak of themselves, as I do; I must march my pen as I do my feet. The common life ought to have relation to the other lives; the virtue of Cato was vigorous beyond the reason of the age he lived in; and for a man who made it his business to govern others, a man dedicated to the public service, it might be called a justice, if not unjust, at least vain, and out of season. Even my own manners, which differ not above an inch from those current among us, render me, nevertheless, a little rough and unsociable at my age. I know not whether it be without reason that I am disgusted with the world I frequent; but I know very well that it would be without reason, should I complain of its being disgusted with me, seeing I am so with it. The virtue that is assigned to the affairs of the world, is a virtue of many wavings, corners, and elbows, to join and adapt itself to human frailty, mixed and artificial, not straight, clear, constant, nor purely innocent. Our annals to this very day reproach one of our kings for suffering himself too simply to be carried away by the conscientious persuasions of his confessor; affairs of state have bolder precepts:

> "Exeat aula
> Qui vult esse pius."

I formerly tried to employ in the service of public affairs, opinions and rules of living, as rough, new, unpolished or unpolluted, as they were either born with me, or brought away from my education, and wherewith I serve my own turn, if not so commodiously, at least securely, in my own particular concerns; a scholastic and novice virtue; but I have found them unapt and dangerous. He who goes into a crowd, must now go one way, and then another, keep his elbows close, retire, or advance, and quit the straight way, according to what he encounters; and must live not so much according to his own method, as to that of others; not according to what he proposes to himself, but according to what is proposed to him, according to the time, according to the men, according to the occasions.

Plato says, that whoever escapes from the world's handling with clean breeches, escapes by miracle: and says withal, that when he appoints his philosopher the head of a government, he does not mean a corrupt one like that of Athens, and much less such a one as this of ours, wherein wisdom itself would be to seek. A good herb, transplanted into a soil contrary to its own nature, much sooner conforms itself to the soil, than it reforms the soil to it. I find, that if I had wholly to apply myself to such employments, it would require a great deal of change and new modeling in me, before I could be any way fit for it. And though I could so far prevail upon myself (and why might I not with time and diligence work such a feat), I would not do it. The little trial I have had of public employment has been so much disgust to me; I feel at times temptations toward ambition, rising in my soul; but I obstinately oppose them:

"At tu, Catulle, obstinatus obdura."

I am seldom called to it and as seldom offer myself uncalled; liberty and laziness, the qualities most predominant in me, are qualities diametrically contrary to that trade. We cannot well distinguish the faculties of men; they have divisions and limits hard and delicate to choose; to conclude from the discreet conduct of a private life, a capacity for the management of public affairs, is to conclude ill; a man may govern himself well, who cannot govern others so; and compose Essays, who could not work effects: men there may be who can order a siege well, who would ill marshal a battle; who can speak well in private, who would ill harangue a people or a prince; nay, 'tis peradventure rather a testimony in him who can do the one, that he cannot do the other, than otherwise. I find that elevated souls are not much more proper for mean things, than mean souls are for high ones. Could it be imagined that Socrates should have administered occasion of laughter, at the expense of his own reputation, to the Athenians, for having never been able to sum up the votes of his tribe to deliver it to the council? Truly, the veneration I have for the perfections of this great man deserves that his fortune should furnish, for the excuse of my principal imperfections, so magnificent an example. Our sufficiency

is cut out into small parcels; mine has no latitude, and is also very contemptible in number. Saturninus, to those who had conferred upon him the command in chief, "Companions," said he, "you have lost a good captain, to make of him a bad general."

Whoever boasts, in so sick a time as this, to employ a true and sincere virtue in the world's service, either knows not what it is, opinions growing corrupt with manners (and in truth, to hear them describe it, to hear the most of them glorify themselves in their deportments, and lay down their rules; instead of painting virtue, they paint pure vice and injustice, and so represent it false in the education of princes); or if he does know it, boasts unjustly and let him say what he will, does a thousand things of which his own conscience must necessarily accuse him. I should willingly take Seneca's word of the experience he made upon the like occasion, provided he would deal sincerely with me. The most honorable mark of goodness in such a necessity, is freely to confess both one's own faults and those of others; with the power of its virtue to stay one's inclination toward evil; unwillingly to follow this propension; to hope better, to desire better. I perceive that in these divisions wherein we are involved in France, every one labors to defend his cause; but, even the very best of them with dissimulation and disguise: he, who would write roundly of the true state of the quarrel, would write rashly and wrongly. The most just party is at best but a member of a decayed and worm-eaten body; but of such a body, the member that is least affected, calls itself sound, and with good reason, forasmuch as our qualities have no title but in comparison; civil innocence is measured according to times and places. Imagine this in Xenophon, related as a fine commendation of Agesilaus: that, being entreated by a neighboring prince with whom he had formerly had war, to permit him to pass through his country, he granted his request, giving him free passage through Peloponnesus; and not only did not imprison or poison him, being at his mercy, but courteously received him according to the obligation of his promise, without doing him the least injury or offense. To such ideas as theirs this were an act of no especial note; elsewhere, and in another age, the frankness and magnanimity of such an action would be thought

wonderful; our crack-rope capets would have laughed at it, so little does the Spartan innocence resemble that of France. We are not without virtuous men, but 'tis according to our notions of virtue. Whoever has his manners established in regularity above the standard of the age he lives in, let him either wrest or blunt his rules, or, which I would rather advise him to, let him retire, and not meddle with us at all, what will he get by it?

> "Egregium sanctumque virum si cerno, bimembri
> Hoc monstrum puero, et miranti jam sub aratro
> Piscibus inventis, et fœtæ comparo mulæ."

One may regret better times, but cannot fly from the present; we may wish for other magistrates, but we must, notwithstanding, obey those we have; and, peradventure, 'tis more laudable to obey the bad than the good. So long as the image of the ancient and received laws of this monarchy shall shine in any corner of the kingdom, there will I be. If they unfortunately happen to thwart and contradict one another, so as to produce two parts, of doubtful and difficult choice, I will willingly choose to withdraw and escape the tempest; in the meantime nature or the hazards of war may lend me a helping hand. Between Cæsar and Pompey, I should frankly have declared myself; but, as among the three robbers who came after, a man must have been necessitated either to hide himself, or have gone along with the current of the time; which I think one may fairly do when reason no longer guides.

> "Quo diversus abis?"

This medley is a little from my subject; I go out of my way; but 'tis rather by license than oversight; my fancies follow one another, but sometimes at a great distance, and look toward one another, but 'tis with an oblique glance. I have read a dialogue of Plato, of the like motley and fantastic composition, the beginning about love, and all the rest to the end about rhetoric; they stick not at these variations, and have a marvelous grace in letting themselves be carried away at the pleasure of the wind, or at least to seem as if they were. The titles of my chapters do not always comprehend the

whole matter; they often denote it by some mark only, as these others, Andria, the Eunuchus; or these, Sylla, Cicero, Torquatus. I love a poetic progress, by leaps and skips; 'tis an art, as Plato says, light, nimble, demoniac. There are pieces in Plutarch where he forgets his theme; where the proposition of his argument is only found by incidence, stuffed and half stifled in foreign matter. Do but observe his footings in the Dæmon of Socrates. Lord! how beautiful are these frolicsome sallies, those variations and digressions, and then, most of all, when they seem most fortuitous, and introduced for want of heed. 'Tis the indiligent reader who loses my subject, and not I; there will always be found some words or other in a corner, that is to the purpose, though it lie very close. I ramble indiscreetly and tumultuously; my style and my wit wander at the same rate. He must fool it a little who would not be deemed wholly a fool, say both the precepts, and, still more, the examples of our masters. A thousand poets flag and languish after a prosaic manner; but the best old prose (and I strew it here up and down indifferently for verse) shines throughout with the luster, vigor and boldness of poetry, and not without some air of its fury. And certainly prose ought to have the pre-eminence in speaking. The poet, says Plato, seated upon the muses' tripod, pours out with fury whatever comes into his mouth, like the pipe of a fountain, without considering and weighing it; and things escape him of various colors, of contrary substance, and with an irregular torrent. Plato himself is throughout poetical; and the old theology, as the learned tell us, is all poetry; and the first philosophy is the original language of the gods. I would have my matter distinguish itself; it sufficiently shows where it changes, where it concludes, where it begins, and where it rejoins, without interlacing it with words of connection introduced for the relief of weak or negligent ears, and without explaining myself. Who is he that had not rather not be read at all, than after a drowsy or cursory manner? *"Nihil est tam utile, quod in transitu prosit."* If to take a book in hand were to take it in head; to look upon it were to consider it; and to run it slightly over were to make it a man's own, I were then to blame to make myself out so ignorant as I say I am. Seeing I cannot fix the atten-

tion of my reader by the weight of what I write, *manco male*, I am much mistaken if I should chance to do it by my intricacies. "Nay, but he will afterward repent that he ever perplexed himself about it." 'Tis very true, but he will yet be there perplexed. And, besides, there are some humors in which intelligence produces disdain; who will think better of me for not understanding what I say, and will conclude the depth of my sense by its obscurity; which, to speak in good sooth, I mortally hate; and would avoid it if I could. Aristotle boasts somewhere in his writings that he affected it: a vicious affectation. The frequent breaks into chapters that I made my method in the beginning of my book, having since seemed to me to dissolve the attention before it was raised, as making it disdain to settle itself to so little, I, upon that account, have made them longer, such as require proposition and assigned leisure. In such an employment, to whom you will not give an hour you give nothing; and you do nothing for him for whom you only do it while you are doing something else. To which may be added that I have, peradventure, some particular obligation to speak only by halves, to speak confusedly and discordantly. I am therefore angry at this trouble-feast reason, and its extravagant projects that worry one's life, and its opinions, so fine and subtle, though they be all true; I think too dear bought and too inconvenient. On the contrary, I make it my business to bring vanity itself in repute, and folly too, if it produce me any pleasure; and let myself follow my own natural inclinations, without carrying too strict a hand upon them.

I have seen elsewhere palaces in ruins, and statues both of gods and men: these are men still. 'Tis all true; and yet, for all that, I cannot so often revisit the tomb of that so great and so puissant city, that I do not admire and reverence it. The care of the dead is recommended to us; now, I have been bred up from my infancy with these dead; I had knowledge of the affairs of Rome, long before I had any of those of my own house; I knew the capitol and its plan, before I knew the Louvre; and the Tiber, before I knew the Seine. The qualities and fortunes of Lucullus, Metellus, and Scipio, have ever run more in my head than those of any of my own country; they are all dead; so is my father as absolutely dead as they, and

is removed as far from me and life in eighteen years, as they are in sixteen hundred; whose memory, nevertheless, friendship and society, I do not cease to hug and embrace with a perfect and lively union. Nay, of my own inclination, I pay more service to the dead; they can no longer help themselves, and therefore, methinks, the more require my assistance; 'tis there that gratitude appears in its

full luster. Benefits are not so generously placed, where there is retrogradation and reflection. Arcesilaus, going to visit Ctesibius who was sick, and finding him in a very poor condition, privately conveyed some money under his pillow; and by concealing it from him, acquitted him, moreover, from the acknowledgment due to such a benefit. Such as have merited from me friendship and gratitude, have never lost these by being no more; I have better and more carefully paid them when gone and ignorant of what I did; I speak most affectionately of my friends, when they can no longer know it. I have had a hundred quarrels in defending Pompey, and for the cause of Brutus: this acquaintance yet continues between us; we

have no other hold even on present things but by fancy. Finding myself of no use to this age I throw myself back upon that other; and am so enamored of it, that the free, just, and flourishing state of that ancient Rome (for I neither love it in its birth nor its old age) interests me to a degree of passion; and therefore I cannot so often revisit the places of their streets and houses and those ruins profound as the Antipodes, that it does not always put me into the dumps. Is it by nature, or through error of fancy, that the sight of places which we know have been frequented and inhabited by persons whose memories are recommended in story, in some sort works more upon us than to hear a recital of their acts or to read their writings? *"Tanta vis admonitionis inest in locis. . . . . Et id quidem in hac urbe infinitum; quacumque, enim ingredimur, in aliquam historiam vestigium ponimus."* It pleases me to consider their face, port, and vestments; I ruminate those great names between my teeth, and make them ring in my ears: *"Ego illos veneror, et tantis nominibus semper assurgo."* Of things that are in some part great and admirable, I admire even the common parts; I could wish to see them talk, walk and sup. It were ingratitude to contemn the relics and images of so many worthy and valiant men as I have seen live and die, and who, by their example, give us so many good instructions, knew we how to follow them.

And, moreover, this very Rome that we now see, deserves to be beloved; so long, and by so many titles, confederate to our crown; the only common and universal city; the sovereign magistrate that commands there, is equally acknowledged elsewhere; 'tis the metropolitan city of all the Christian nations; the Spaniard and Frenchman is there at home; to be a prince of that state, there needs no more but to be of Christendom wheresoever. There is no place upon earth, that heaven has embraced with such an influence and constancy of favor; her very ruins are grand and glorious,

"Laudandis pretiosior ruinis;"

she yet in her very tomb retains the marks and images of empire: *"Ut palam sit, uno in loco guadentis opus esse naturæ."* Some would blame and be angry at themselves to perceive themselves tickled

with so vain a pleasure: our humors are never too vain that are pleasant: let them be what they may, if they constantly content a man of common understanding, I could not have the heart to blame him.

I am very much obliged to fortune, in that, to this very hour, she has offered me no outrage beyond what I was well able to bear. Is it not her custom to let those live in quiet by whom she is not importuned?

> "Quanto quisque sibi plura negaverit,
> A diis plura feret: nil cupientium
> Nudus castra peto. . . .
> Multa petentibus
> Desunt multa."

If she continue her favor, she will dismiss me very well satisfied:

> "Nihil supra
> Deos lacesso."

But beware a shock: there are a thousand who perish in the port. I easily comfort myself for what shall here happen when I shall be gone; present things trouble me enough:

> "Fortunæ cætera mando."

Besides, I have not that strong obligation that they say ties men to the future, by the issue that succeeds to their name and honor; and peradventure, ought less to covet them, if they are to be so much desired. I am but too much tied to the world, and to this life, of myself: I am content to be in fortune's power by circumstances properly necessary to my being, without otherwise enlarging her jurisdiction over me; and have never thought, that to be without children was a defect that ought to render life less complete or less contented: a sterile vocation has its conveniences too. Children are of the number of things that are not so much to be desired, especially now, that it would be so hard to make them good: *"Bona jam nec nasci licet, ita corrupta sunt semina;"* and yet they are justly to be lamented by such as lose them when they have them.

He who left me my house in charge, foretold that I was like to

ruin it, considering my humor so little inclined to look after household affairs. But he was mistaken; for I am in the same condition
now as when I first entered into it, or rather somewhat better; and
yet without office, or any place of profit.

As to the rest, if fortune has never done me any violent or extraordinary injury, neither has she done me any particular favor;
whatever we derive from her bounty, was there above a hundred
years before my time: I have, as to my own particular, no essential
and solid good that I stand indebted for to her liberality. She has,
indeed, done me some airy favors, honorary and titular favors,
without substance, and those, in truth, she has not granted, but
offered me, who God knows, am all material, and who take nothing
but what is real and indeed massive too, for current pay: and who,
if I dare confess so much, should not think avarice much less excusable than ambition; nor pain less to be avoided than shame; nor
health less to be coveted than learning, or riches than nobility.

Among those empty favors of hers, there is none that so much
pleases vain humor natural to my country, as an authentic bull of
a Roman burgess-ship, that was granted me when I was last there,
glorious in seals and gilded letters; and granted with all gracious
liberality. And because 'tis couched in a mixed style, more or less
favorable, and that I could have been glad to have seen a copy of it
before it had passed the seal, I will, to satisfy such as are sick of the
same curiosity I am, transcribe it here in its exact form.

"Quod Horatius Maximus, Martius Cecius, Alexander Mutus,
almæ urbis Conservatores, de Illustrissimo viro Michaele
Montano, equite Sancti Michaelis, et a cubiculo regis Christianissimi, Romana civitate donando, ad Senatum retulerunt;
S. P. Q. R. de ea re ita fieri censuit.

"Quum, veteri more et instituto, cupide illisem per studioseque
suscepti sint, qui virtute ac nobilitate præstantes, magno Reipublicæ
nostræ usui atque ornamento fuissent, vel esse aliquando possent:
Nos, majorum nostrorum exemplo atque auctoritate permoti, præ-
claram hanc consuetudinem nobis imitandam ac servandam fore
censemus. Quamobrem quum Illustrissimus Michael Montanus,

[371]

eques Sancti Michaelis, et a cubiculo regis Christianissimi, Romani nominis studiosissimus, et familiæ laude atque splendore, et propriis virtutum meritis dignissimus sit, qui summo, Senatus Populique Romani judicio ac studio in Romanam civitatem adsciscatur; placere Senatui P. Q. R. Illustrissimum Michaelem Montanum, rebus omnibus orantissimum, atque huic inclyto Populo carissimum, ipsum posterosque in Romanam civitatem adscribi, ornarique omnibus et præmiis et honoribus, quibus illi fruuntur, qui cives patriciique Romani nati, aut jure optimo facti sunt. In quo censere Senatum P. Q. R. se non tam illi jus civitatis largiri, quam debitum tribuere, neque magis beneficium dare, quam ab ipso accipere, qui, hoc civitatis munere accipiendo, singulari civitatem ipsam ornamento atque honore affecerit. Quam quidem S. C. auctoritatem iidem Conservatores per senatus P. Q. R. scribas in acta referri, atque in Capitolii curia servari, privilegiumque hujusmodi fieri, solitoque urbis sigillo communiri curarunt. Anno ab urbe condita CXC.CCC.XXXI.; post Christum natum M.D.LXXXI. 3 idus Martii.

Horatius Fuscus,
Sacri S. P. Q. R. scriba.
Vincent. Martholus,
Sacri S. P. Q. R. scriba."

Being, before, burgess of no city at all, I am glad to be created one of the most noble that ever was or ever shall be. If other men would consider themselves at the rate I do, they would, as I do, discover themselves to be full of inanity and foppery; to rid myself of it, I cannot, without making myself away. We are all steeped in it, as well one as another; but they who are not aware on't have somewhat the better bargain; and yet, I know not, whether they have or no.

This opinion and common usage to observe others more than ourselves, has very much relieved us that way; 'tis a very displeasing object: we can there see nothing but misery and vanity: nature, that we may not be dejected with the sight of our own deformities, has wisely thrust the action of seeing outward. We go forward with the

current: but to turn back toward ourselves is a painful motion; so is the sea moved and troubled when the waves rush against one another. Observe, says every one, the motions of the heavens, of public affairs; observe the quarrel of such a person, take notice of such a one's pulse, of such another's last will and testament; in sum, be always looking high or low, on one side, before, or behind you. It was a paradoxical command anciently given us by the god of Delphos: "Look into yourself; discover yourself; keep close to yourself; call back your mind and will, that elsewhere consume themselves into yourself; you run out, you spill yourself; carry a more steady hand: men betray you, men spill you, men steal you from yourself. Dost thou not see that this world we live in keeps all its sight confined within, and its eyes open to contemplate itself? 'Tis always vanity for thee, both within and without; but 'tis less vanity when less extended. Excepting thee, oh man, said that god, everything studies itself first, and has bounds to its labors and desires, according to its need. There is nothing so empty and necessitous as thou, who embracest the universe; thou are the explorator without knowledge; the magistrate without jurisdiction: and, after all, the fool of the farce."

XIX

OF PHYSIOGNOMY

ALMOST all the opinions we have are taken on authority and trust; and 'tis not amiss; we could not choose worse than by ourselves, in so weak an age. That image of Socrates' discourses, which his friends have transmitted to us, we approve upon no other account than a reverence to public sanction; 'tis not according to our own knowledge; they are not after our way; if anything of the kind should spring up now, few men would value them. We discern no graces that are not pointed and puffed out and inflated by art; such as glide on in their own purity and simplicity easily escape so gross a sight as ours; they have a delicate and concealed beauty, such as requires a clear and purified sight to discover its secret light. Is not simplicity, as we take it, cousin-german to folly, and a quality of reproach? Socrates makes his soul move a natural and common motion; a peasant said this; a woman said that; he has never anybody in his mouth but carters, joiners, cobblers, and masons; his are inductions and similitudes drawn from the most common and known actions of men; every one understands him. We should never have recognized the nobility and splendor of his admirable conceptions under so mean a form; we, who think all things low and flat, that are not elevated by learned doctrine, and who discern no riches but in pomp and show. This world of ours is only formed for ostentation; men are only puffed up with wind, and are bandied to and fro like tennis-balls. He proposed to himself

no vain and idle fancies; his design was to furnish us with precepts
and things that more really and fitly serve the use of life;

> "Servare modu, finemque tenere,
> Naturamque sequi."

He was also always one and the same, and raised himself, not by
starts but by complexion, to the highest pitch of vigor; or, to say
better, mounted not at all, but rather brought down, reduced and
subjected all asperities and difficulties to his original and natural
condition; for, in Cato 'tis most manifest, that 'tis a procedure extended far beyond the common ways of men: in the brave exploits
of his life, and in his death, we find him always mounted upon the
great horse; whereas the other ever creeps upon the ground, and
with a gentle and ordinary pace, treats of the most useful matters,
and bears himself, both at his death and in the rudest difficulties
that could present themselves, in the ordinary way of human life.

It has fallen out well, that the man most worthy to be known and
to be presented to the world for example, should be he of whom we
have the most certain knowledge; he has been pried into by the most
clear-sighted men that ever were; the testimonies we have of him
are admirable both in fidelity and fullness. 'Tis a great thing that
he was able so to order the pure imaginations of a child, that, without altering or wresting them, he thereby produced the most beautiful effects of our soul: he presents it neither elevated nor rich; he
only represents it sound, but assuredly with a brisk and full health.
By these common and natural springs, by these ordinary and popular fancies, without being moved or put out, he set up not only the
most regular, but the most high and vigorous beliefs, actions, and
manners that ever were. 'Tis he who brought again from heaven,
where she lost her time, human wisdom, to restore her to man, with
whom her most just and greatest business lies. See him plead before
his judges; observe by what reasons he rouses his courage to the hazards of war; with what arguments he fortifies his patience against
calumny, tyranny, death, and the perverseness of his wife; you will
find nothing in all this borrowed from arts and sciences: the simplest
may there discover their own means and strength; 'tis not possible

more to retire or to creep more low. He has done human nature a great kindness, in showing it how much it can do of itself.

We are all of us richer than we think we are; but we are taught to borrow and to beg, and brought up more to make use of what is another's than of our own. Man can in nothing fix himself to his actual necessity: of pleasure, wealth, and power, he grasps at more than he can hold; his greediness is incapable of moderation. And I find that in curiosity of knowing he is the same; he cuts himself out more work than he can do, and more than he needs to do: extending the utility of knowledge, to the full of its matter: *"Ut omnium rerum, sic litterarum quoque, intemperantia laboramus."* And Tacitus had reason to commend the mother of Agricola, for having restrained her son in his too violent appetite of learning.

'Tis a good, if duly considered, which has in it, as the other goods of men have, a great deal of vanity and weakness, proper and natural to itself, and that costs very dear. Its acquisition is far more hazardous than that of all other meat or drink; for, as to other things, what we have bought we carry home in some vessel, and there have full leisure to examine our purchase, how much we shall eat or drink of it, and when: but sciences we can, at the very first, stow into no other vessel than the soul; we swallow them in buying, and return from the market, either already infected or amended: there are some that only burden and overcharge the stomach, instead of nourishing; and, moreover, some, that under color of curing, poison us. I have been pleased, in places where I have been, to see men in devotion vow ignorance as well as chastity, poverty, and penitence: 'tis also a gelding of our unruly appetites, to blunt this cupidity that spurs us on to the study of books, and to deprive the soul of this voluptuous complacency that tickles us with the opinion of knowledge: and 'tis plenarily to accomplish the vow of poverty, to add unto it that of the mind. We need little doctrine to live at our ease; and Socrates teaches us, that this is in us, and the way how to find it, and the manner how to use it. All our sufficiency which exceeds the natural is well-nigh superfluous and vain: 'tis much if it does not rather burden and cumber us than do us good: *"Paucis opus est literis ad mentem bonam:"* 'tis a feverish excess

of the mind; a tempestuous and unquiet instrument. Do but recollect yourself, and you will find in yourself natural arguments against death, true, and the fittest to serve you in time of necessity; 'tis they that make a peasant, and whole nations, die with as much firmness as a philosopher. Should I have died less cheerfully before I had read Cicero's Tusculans? I believe not; and when I find myself at the best, I perceive that my tongue is enriched indeed, but my courage little or nothing elevated by them; that is just as nature framed it at first, and defends itself against the conflict, only after a natural and ordinary way. Books have not so much served me for instruction as exercise. What if knowledge, trying to arm us with new defenses against natural inconveniences, has more imprinted in our fancies their weight and greatness, than her reasons and subtleties to secure us from them? They are subtleties, indeed, with which she often alarms us to little purpose. Do but observe, how many slight and frivolous, and, if nearly examined, incorporeal arguments, the closest and wisest authors scatter about one good one: they are but verbal quirks and fallacies to amuse and gull us: but forasmuch as it may be with some profit, I will sift them no further; many of that sort are here and there dispersed up and down this book, either borrowed or by imitation. Therefore one ought to take a little heed not to call that force which is only a pretty knack of writing, and that solid which is only sharp, or that good which is only fine: *"Quæ magis gustata, quam potata delectant:"* everything that pleases, does not nourish: *"Ubi non ingenii, sed animi negotium agitur."*

To see the trouble that Seneca gives himself to fortify himself against death; to see him so sweat and pant to harden and encourage himself, and bustle so long upon this perch, would have lessened his reputation with me, had he not very bravely held himself at the last. His so ardent and frequent agitations discover that he was in himself impetuous and passionate (*"Magnus animus remissius loquitur, et securius . . . non est alius ingenio, alius animo color"*); he must be convinced at his own expense; and he in some sort discovers that he was hard pressed by his enemy. Plutarch's way, by how much it is more disdainful and farther stretched, is, in my opinion, so much more manly and persuasive;

[377]

and I am apt to believe that his soul had more assured and more regular motions. The one more sharp, pricks and makes us start, and more touches the soul; the other more constantly solid, forms, establishes, and supports us, and more touches the understanding. That ravishes the judgment, this wins it. I have likewise seen other writings, yet more reverenced than these, that in the representation of the conflict they maintain against the temptations of the flesh, paint them so sharp, so powerful and invincible, that we ourselves, who are of the common herd, are as much to wonder at the strangeness and unknown force of their temptation, as at the resisting it.

To what end do we so arm ourselves with this harness of science? Let us look down upon the poor people that we see scattered upon the face of the earth, prone and intent upon their business, that neither know Aristotle nor Cato, example nor precept; from these nature every day extracts effects of constancy and patience, more pure and manly than those we so inquisitively study in the schools; how many do I ordinarily see who slight poverty, how many who desire to die, or who die without alarm or regret? He who is now digging in my garden, has this morning buried his father or his son. The very names by which they call diseases, sweeten and mollify the sharpness of them; the phthisic is with them no more than a cough, dysentery but a looseness, the pleurisy but a stitch; and, as they gently name them, so they patiently endure them; they are very great and grievous indeed, when they hinder their ordinary labor; they never keep their beds but to die. *"Simplex illa et aperta virtus in obscuram et solertem scientiam versa est."*

I was writing this about a time when a great load of our intestine troubles for several months lay with all its weight upon me; I had the enemy at my door on one side, and the free-booters, worse enemies than they, on the other, *"Non armis, sed vitiis, certatur;"* and underwent all sorts of military injuries at once:

> "Hostis adest dextra lævaque a parte timendus.
> Vicinoque malo terret utrumque latus."

A monstrous war! Other wars are bent against strangers, this against itself, destroying itself with its own poison. It is of so malignant

and ruinous a nature, that it ruins itself with the rest: and with its own rage mangles and tears itself to pieces. We more often see it dissolve of itself, than through scarcity of any necessary thing, or by force of the enemy. All discipline evades it: it comes to compose sedition, and is itself full of it; would chastise disobedience, and itself is the example; and, employed for the defense of the laws, rebels against its own. What a condition are we in! Our physic makes us sick!

> "Nostre mal s' empoisonne
> Du secours qu'on luy donne"

> "Exuperat magis, ægrescitque medendo."

> "Omnia fanda, nefanda, malo permista furore,
> Justificam nobis mentem avertere deorum."

In the beginning of these popular maladies, one may distinguish the sound from the sick: but when they come to continue, as ours have done, the whole body is then infected from head to foot; no part is free from corruption, for there is no air that men so greedily draw in, that diffuses itself so soon and that penetrates so deep, as that of license. Our armies only subsist and are kept together by the cement of foreigners; for of Frenchmen there is now no constant and regular army to be made. What a shame it is! there is no longer any discipline but what we see in the borrowed soldiers. As to ourselves, our conduct is at discretion, and that not of the chief, but every one at his own. The general has a harder game to play within, than he has without; he it is who has to follow, to court the soldiers, to give way to them; he alone has to obey: all the rest is dissolution and free license. It pleases me to observe how much pusillanimity and cowardice there is in ambition; by how abject and servile ways it must arrive at its end; but it displeases me to see good and generous natures, and that are capable of justice, every day corrupted in the management and command of this confusion. Long toleration begets habit; habit, consent and imitation. We had ill-formed souls enough, without spoiling those that were generous and good; so that if we hold on, there will scarcely remain any with

whom to intrust the health of this state of ours, in case fortune chance to restore it:

"Hunc saltem everso juvenem succurrere seclo,
Ne prohibete."

What is become of the old precept, "That soldiers ought more to fear their chief than the enemy?" and of that wonderful example, that an orchard being enclosed within the precincts of a camp of the Roman army, was seen at their dislodgment the next day in the same condition, not an apple, though ripe and delicious, being pulled off, but all left to the possessor? I could wish that our youth, instead of the time they spend in less fruitful travels, and less honorable employments would bestow one half of that time in being an eyewitness of naval exploits, under some good captain of Rhodes, and the other half in observing the discipline of the Turkish armies; for they have many differences and advantages over ours; one of these is, that our soldiers become more licentious in expeditions, theirs more temperate and circumspect; for the thefts and insolencies committed upon the common people, which are only punished with a cudgel in peace, are capital in war; for an egg taken by a Turkish soldier without paying for it, fifty blows with a stick is the fixed rate; for anything else, of what sort or how trivial soever, not necessary to nourishment, they are presently impaled or beheaded without mercy. I am astonished in the history of Selim, the most cruel conqueror that ever was, to see that when he subdued Egypt, the beautiful gardens about Damascus being all open, and in a conquered land, and his army encamped upon the very place, should be left untouched by the hands of the soldiers, by reason they had not received the signal of pillage.

But is there any disease in a government, that it is worth while to physic with such a mortal drug? No, said Favonius, not even the tyrannical usurpation of a commonwealth. Plato, likewise, will not consent that a man should violate the peace of his country in order to cure it, and by no means approves of a reformation that disturbs and hazards all, and that is to be purchased at the price of the citizen's blood and ruin; determining it to be the duty of a good

patriot in such a case to let it alone, and only to pray to God for his extraordinary assistance: and he seems to be angry with his great friend Dion, for having proceeded somewhat after another manner. I was a Platonist in this point, before I knew there had ever been such a man as Plato in the world. And if this person ought absolutely to be rejected from our society (he who by the sincerity of his conscience, merited from the divine favor to penetrate so far into the Christian light, through the universal darkness wherein the world was involved in his time), I do not think it becomes us to suffer ourselves to be instructed by a heathen how great an impiety it is not to expect from God any relief simply his own and without our co-operation. I often doubt, whether among so many men as meddle in such affairs, there is not to be found some one of so weak understanding as to have been really persuaded that he went toward reformation by the worst of deformations; and advanced toward salvation by the most express causes that we have of most assured damnation; that by overthrowing government, the magistracy, and the laws, in whose protection God has placed him, by dismembering his good mother, and giving her limbs to be mangled by her old enemies, filling fraternal hearts with parricidal hatreds, calling devils and furies to his aid, he can assist the most holy sweetness and justice of the divine law. Ambition, avarice, cruelty, and revenge, have not sufficient natural impetuosity of their own; let us bait them with the glorious titles of justice and devotion. There cannot a worse state of things be imagined, than where wickedness comes to be legitimate, and assumes with the magistrates' permission, the cloak of virtue: *"Nihil in speciem fallacius, quam prava religio, ubi deorum numen prætenditur sceleribus."* The extremest sort of injustice, according to Plato, is where that which is unjust, should be reputed for just.

The common people then suffered very much, and not present damage only,

> "Undique totis
> Usque adeo turbatur agris,"

but future too; the living were to suffer, and so were they who were yet unborn; they stripped them, and consequently myself, even of

hope, taking from them all they had laid up in store to live on for many years:

"Quæ nequeunt secum ferre aut abducere, perdunt;
Et cremat insontes turba scelesta casas . . .
Muris nulla fides, squalent populatibus agri."

Besides this shock, I suffered others: I underwent the inconveniences that moderation brings along with it in such a disease: I was robbed on all hands; to the Ghibelin I was a Guelph, and to the Guelph a Ghibelin: one of my poets expresses this very well, but I know not where it is. The situation of my house, and my friendliness with my neighbors, presented me with one face; my life and my actions with another. They did not lay formal accusations to my charge, for they had no foundation for so doing; I never hide my head from the laws, and whoever would have questioned me, would have done himself a greater prejudice than me; they were only mute suspicions that were whispered about, which never want appearance in so confused a mixture, no more than envious or idle heads. I commonly myself lend a hand to injurious presumptions that fortune scatters abroad against me, by a way I have ever had of evading to justify, excuse, or explain myself; conceiving, that it were to compromise my conscience to plead in its behalf; *"Perspicuitas enim argumentatione elevatur;"* and, as if every one saw as clearly into me as I do myself, instead of retiring from an accusation, I step up to meet it, and rather give it some kind of color by an ironical and scoffing confession, if I do not sit totally mute, as of a thing not worth my answer. But such as look upon this kind of behavior of mine as too haughty a confidence, have as little kindness for me as they who interpret it the weakness of an indefensible cause; namely, the great folks, toward whom want of submission is the great fault, harsh toward all justice that knows and feels itself, and is not submissive, humble, and suppliant; I have often knocked my head against this pillar. So it is, that at what then befell me, an ambitious man would have hanged himself, and a covetous man would have done the same. I have no manner of care of getting:

"Si mihi, quod nunc est, etiam minus; et mihi vivam
Quod superest ævi, si quid superesse volent dii:

but the losses that befall me by the injury of others, whether by theft or violence, go almost as near my heart, as they would do that of the most avaricious man. The offense troubles me, without comparison, more than the loss. A thousand several sorts of mischiefs fell upon me in the neck of one another; I could more cheerfully have borne them all at once.

I was already considering to whom, among my friends, I might commit a helpless and decrepit age; and having turned my eyes quite round, I found myself bare. To let one's self fall plumb down, and from so great a height, it ought to be in the arms of a solid, vigorous, and fortunate friendship: these are very rare, if there be any. At last, I saw that it was safest for me to trust to myself in my necessity: and if it should so fall out, that I should be but upon cold terms in fortune's favor, I should so much the more pressingly recommend me to my own, and attach myself and look to myself all the more closely. Men on all occasions throw themselves upon foreign assistance to spare their own, which is alone certain and sufficient to him who knows how therewith to arm himself. Every one runs elsewhere, and to the future, forasmuch as no one is arrived at himself. And I was satisfied that they were profitable inconveniences; forasmuch as, first, ill scholars are to be admonished with the rod, when reason will not do, as a crooked piece of wood is by fire and straining reduced to straightness. I have a great while preached to myself to stick close to my own concerns, and separate myself from the affairs of others: yet I am still turning my eyes aside. A bow, a kind word or look from a great person tempts me; of which God knows how little scarcity there is in these days, and how little they signify. I, moreover, without wrinkling my forehead, hearken to the persuasions offered me, to draw me into the open market place, and so gently refuse, as if I were half willing to be overcome. Now for so indocile a spirit blows are required; this vessel which thus chops and cleaves, and is ready to fall one piece from another, must have the hoops forced down with good sound strokes of a mallet. Secondly, that this accident served me for exercise to prepare me for worse, if I, who both by the benefit of fortune, and by the condition of my manners, hoped to be among the last,

should happen to be one of the first assailed by this storm; instructing myself betimes to constrain my life, and fit it for a new state. The true liberty is to be able to do what a man will with himself: *"Potentissimus est, qui se habet in potestate."* In an ordinary and quiet time, a man prepares himself for moderate and common accidents; but in the confusion wherein we have been for these thirty years, every Frenchman, whether in particular or in general, sees himself every hour upon the point of the total ruin and overthrow of his fortune: by so much the more ought he to have his courage supplied with the strongest and most vigorous provisions. Let us thank fortune, that has not made us live in an effeminate, idle, and languishing age; some who could never have been so by other means, will be made famous by their misfortunes. As I seldom read in histories the confusions of other states without regret that I was not present, the better to consider them, so does my curiosity make me in some sort please myself in seeing with my own eyes this notable spectacle of our public death, its form and symptoms; and since I cannot hinder it, I am content to have been destined to be present therein, and thereby to instruct myself. So do we eagerly covet to see, though but in shadow and the fables of theaters, the pomp of tragic representations of human fortune; 'tis not without compassion at what we hear, but we please ourselves in rousing our displeasure, by the rarity of these pitiable events. Nothing tickles that does not pinch. And good historians skip over, as stagnant water and dead sea, calm narrations, to occupy themselves with wars and seditions, which they know are most acceptable to the readers.

I question whether I can decently confess with how small a sacrifice of its repose and tranquillity, I have passed over above the one-half of my life amid the ruin of my country. I make my patience somewhat too cheap, in accidents that do not absolutely assail myself; and do not so much regard what they take from me, as what remains safe, both within and without. There is comfort in evading, one while this, another while that, of the evils that are leveled, at ourselves too, at last, but at present hurt others only about us; as also, that in matters of public interest, the more universally my affection is dispersed, the weaker it is: to which may be added, that

it is half true: *"Tantum ex publicis malis sentimus, quantum ad privatas res pertinet;"* and that the health from which we fell was so ill, that itself relieves the regret we should have for it. It was health, but only in comparison with the sickness that has succeeded it: we are not fallen from any great height; the corruption and brigandage which are in dignity and office, seem to me the most insupportable: we are less injuriously rifled in a wood, than in a place of security. It was an universal juncture of particular members, each rotten in emulation of the others: and most of them with inveterate ulcers, that neither admitted nor required any cure. This convulsion, therefore, really more animated than pressed me, by the assistance of my conscience, which was not only at peace within itself, but elevated, and I did not find any reason to complain of myself. Also, as God never sends evils, any more than goods, absolutely pure to men, my health continued at that time more than usually good; and, as I can do nothing without it, there are few things that I cannot do with it. It afforded me means to rouse up all my faculties, and to lay my hand before the wound that would else, peradventure, have gone farther; and I experienced, in my patience, that I had some stand against fortune; and that it must be a great shock could throw me out of the saddle. I do not say this to provoke her to give me a more vigorous charge: I am her humble servant, and submit to her pleasure; let her be content in God's name. Do you ask if I am sensible of her assaults? Yes, certainly. But, as those who are possessed and oppressed with sorrow, sometimes suffer themselves, nevertheless, by intervals to taste a little pleasure, and are sometimes surprised with a smile, so have I so much power over myself, as to make my ordinary condition quiet and free from disturbing thoughts; yet I suffer myself, withal, by fits to be surprised with the stings of those unpleasing imaginations that assault me, while I am arming myself to drive them away, or at least to wrestle with them.

But behold another aggravation of the evil which befell me in the tail of the rest! both without doors and within I was assailed with a most violent plague, violent in comparison of all others; for as sound bodies are subject to more grievous maladies, forasmuch as they are not to be forced but by such, so my very healthful

air, where no contagion, however near, in the memory of man, ever took footing, coming to be corrupted, produced most strange effects:

"Mista senum et juvenum densantur funera; nullum
Sæva caput Proserpina fugit;"

I had to suffer this pleasant condition, that the sight of my house was frightful to me; whatever I had there was without guard, and left to the mercy of any one who wished to take it. I myself, who am so hospitable, was in very great distress for a retreat for my family; a distracted family, frightful both to its friends and itself, and filling every place with horror where it attempted to settle, having to shift its abode so soon as any one's finger began but to ache; all diseases are then concluded to be the plague, and people do not stay to examine whether they are so or no. And the mischief on't is, that, according to the rules of art, in every danger that a man comes near, he must undergo a quarantine, in fear of the evil, your imagination all the while tormenting you at pleasure, and turning even your health itself into a fever. Yet all this would have much less affected me, had I not withal been compelled to be sensible of the sufferings of others, and miserably to serve six months together for a guide to this caravan; for I carry my own antidotes within myself, which are resolution and patience. Apprehension, which is particularly feared in this disease, does not much trouble me; and, if being alone, I should have been taken, it had been a less cheerless and more remote departure; 'tis a kind of death that I do not think of the worst sort; 'tis commonly short, stupid, without pain, and consoled by the public condition; without ceremony, without mourning, without a crowd. But as to the people about us, the hundredth part of them could not be saved:

"Videas desertaque regna
Pastorum, et longe saltus lateque vacantes."

In this place my largest revenue is pure manual labor; what an hundred man plowed for me, lay a long time fallow.

But then, what example of resolution did we not see in the simplicity of all this people? Generally, every one renounced all care of life; the grapes, the principal wealth of the country, remained untouched upon the vines; every man indifferently prepared for

and expected death, either to-night or to-morrow, with a countenance and voice so far from fear, as if they had come to terms with this necessity, and that it was an universal and inevitable sentence. 'Tis always such; but how slender hold has the resolution of dying? The distance and difference of a few hours, the sole consideration of company, renders its apprehension various to us. Observe these people; by reason that they die in the same month, children, young people, and old, they are no longer astonished at it: they no longer lament. I saw some who were afraid of staying behind, as in a dreadful solitude: and I did not commonly observe any other solicitude among them, than that of sepulture; they were troubled to see the dead bodies scattered about the fields, at the mercy of the wild beasts, that presently flocked thither. How differing are the fancies of men! the Neorites, a nation subjected by Alexander, threw the bodies of their dead into the deepest and less frequented part of their woods, on purpose to have them there eaten; the only sepulture reputed happy among them. Some, who were yet in health, dug their own graves; others laid themselves down in them while alive; and a laborer of mine, in dying, with his hands and feet pulled the earth upon him. Was not this to nestle and settle himself to sleep at greater ease? A bravery in some sort like that of the Roman soldiers, who, after the battle of Cannæ, were found with their heads thrust into holes in the earth, which they had made, and in suffocating themselves, with their own hands pulled the earth about their ears. In short, a whole province was, by the common usage, at once brought to a course, nothing inferior in undauntedness to the most studied and premeditated resolution.

Most of the instructions of science to encourage us herein have in them more of show than of force, and more of ornament than of effect. We have abandoned Nature, and will teach her what to do; teach her who so happily and so securely conducted us; and in the meantime, from the footsteps of her instruction, and that little which, by the benefit of ignorance, remains of her image imprinted in the life of this rustic rout of unpolished men, science is constrained every day to borrow patterns for her disciples of constancy, tranquillity and innocence. It is pretty to see that these per-

sons full of so much fine knowledge, have to imitate this foolish simplicity, and this in the primary actions of virtue; and that our wisdom must learn even from beasts, the most profitable instructions in the greatest and most necessary concerns of our life; as, how we are to live and die, manage our property, love and bring up our children, maintain justice: a singular testimony of human infirmity; and that this reason we so handle at our pleasure, finding evermore some diversity and novelty, leaves in us no apparent trace of nature. Men have done with nature as perfumers with oils: they have sophisticated her with so many argumentations and far-fetched discourses, that she is become variable and particular to each, and has lost her proper, constant, and universal face; so that we must seek testimony from beasts, not subject to favor, corruption, or diversity of opinions. It is, indeed, true that even these themselves do not always go exactly in the path of nature, but wherein they swerve, it is so little that you may always see the track; as horses that are led, make many bounds and curvets, but 'tis always at the length of the halter, and they still follow him that leads them; and as a young hawk takes its flight, but still under the restraint of its tether. *"Exsilia, tormenta, bella, morbos, naufragia meditare, . . . ut nullo sis malo tiro."* What good will this curiosity do us, to anticipate all the inconveniences of human nature, and to prepare ourselves with so much trouble against things which, peradventure, will never befall us? *"Parem passis tristitiam facit, pati posse;"* not only the blow, but the wind of the blow strikes us; or, like phrenetic people—for certainly it is a frenzy—to go immediately and whip yourself, because it may so fall out that Fortune may one day make you undergo it; and to put on your furred gown at mid-summer, because you will stand in need of it at Christmas! Throw yourselves, say they, into the experience of all the evils, the most extreme evils that can possibly befall you, and so be assured of them. On the contrary, the most easy and most natural way, would be to banish even the thoughts of them; they will not come soon enough; their true being will not continue with us long enough: our mind must lengthen and extend them; we must incorporate them in us beforehand, and there entertain them, as if they would not otherwise sufficiently press upon our senses. "We

shall find them heavy enough when they come," says one of our masters, of none of the tender sects, but of the most severe; "in the meantime, favor thyself; believe what pleases thee best: what good will it do thee to anticipate thy ill fortune, to lose the present for fear of the future; and to make thyself miserable now, because thou art to be so in time?" These are his words. Science, indeed, does us one good office, in instructing us exactly as to the dimensions of evils,

"Curis acuens mortalia corda!"

'Twere pity that any part of their greatness should escape our sense and knowledge.

'Tis certain that, for the most part, the preparation for death has administered more torment than the thing itself. It was of old truly said, and by a very judicious author, *"Minus afficit sensus fatigatio, quam cogitatio."* The sentiment of present death sometimes, of itself, animates us with a prompt resolution not to avoid a thing that is utterly inevitable: many gladiators have been seen in the olden time, who, after having fought timorously and ill, have courageously entertained death, offering their throats to the enemies' sword and bidding them despatch. The sight of future death requires a courage that is slow, and consequently hard to be got. If you know not how to die, never trouble yourself; nature will, at the time, fully and sufficiently instruct you: she will exactly do that business for you; take you no care—

"Incertam frustra, mortales, funeris horam
Quæritis, et qua sit mors aditura via." . . .

"Pœna minor, certam subito perferre ruinam;
Quod timeas, gravius sustinuisse diu."

We trouble life by the care of death, and death by the care of life: the one torments, the other frights us. It is not against death that we prepare, that is too momentary a thing; a quarter of an hour's suffering, without consequence, and without damage, does not deserve especial precepts: to say the truth, we prepare ourselves against the preparations of death. Philosophy ordains that we should always have death before our eyes, to see and consider it

before the time, and then gives us rules and precautions to provide that this foresight and thought do us no harm: just so do physicians, who throw us into diseases, to the end they may have whereon to employ their drugs and their art. If we have not known how to live, 'tis injustice to teach us how to die, and make the end difform from all the rest: if we have known how to live firmly and quietly, we shall know how to die so too. They may boast as much as they please, *"Tota philosophorum vita, commentatio mortis est;"* but I fancy that, though it be the end, it is not the aim of life; 'tis its end, its extremity, but not nevertheless its object; it ought itself to be its own aim and design; its true study is to order, govern, and suffer itself. In the number of several other offices, that the general and principal chapter of Knowing how to live comprehends, is this article of Knowing how to die; and, did not our fears give it weight, one of the lightest too.

To judge of them by utility and by the naked truth, the lessons of simplicity are not much inferior to those which learning teaches us: nay, quite the contrary. Men differ in sentiment and force; we must lead them to their own good according to their capacities and by various ways:

"Quo me cumque rapit tempestas, deferor hospes."

I never saw any peasant among my neighbors cogitate with what countenance and assurance he should pass over his last hour; nature teaches him not to think of death till he is dying; and then he does it with a better grace than Aristotle, upon whom death presses with a double weight, both of itself and of so long a premeditation; and, therefore, it was the opinion of Cæsar, that the least premeditated death was the easiest and the most happy. *"Plus dolet quam necesse est, qui anti dolet, quam necesse est."* The sharpness of this imagination springs from our curiosity: 'tis thus we ever impede ourselves, desiring to anticipate and regulate natural prescripts. It is only for the doctors to dine worse for it, when in the best health, and to frown at the image of death; the common sort stand in need of no remedy or consolation, but just in the shock, and when the blow comes; and consider on't no more than just what they endure. Is it

[390]

not, then, as we say, that the stolidity and want of apprehension in the vulgar give them that patience in present evils, and that profound carelessness of future sinister accidents? That their souls, in being more gross and dull, are less penetrable and not so easily moved? If it be so, let us henceforth, in God's name, teach nothing but ignorance: 'tis the utmost fruit the sciences promise us, to which this stolidity so gently leads its disciples.

We have no want of good masters, interpreters of natural simplicity. Socrates shall be one; for, as I remember, he speaks something to this purpose to the judges who sat upon his life and death. "I am afraid, my masters, that if I entreat you not to put me to death, I shall confirm the charge of my accusers, which is, that I pretend to be wiser than others, as having some more secret knowledge of things that are above and below us. I have neither frequented nor known death, nor have ever seen any person that has tried its qualities, from whom to inform myself. Such as fear it, presuppose they know it; as for my part, I neither know what it is, nor what they do in the other world. Death is, peradventure, an indifferent thing; peradventure, a thing to be desired. 'Tis nevertheless to be believed, if it be a transmigration from one place to another, that it is a bettering of one's condition to go and live with so many great persons deceased, and to be exempt from having any more to do with unjust and corrupt judges; if it be an annihilation of our being, 'tis yet a bettering of one's condition to enter into a long and peaceable night; we find nothing more sweet in life than quiet repose and a profound sleep, without dreams. The things that I know to be evil, as to injure's one's neighbor, and to disobey one's superior, whether it be God or man, I carefully avoid; such as I do not know whether they be good or evil, I cannot fear them. If I am to die and leave you alive, the gods alone only know whether it will go better with you or with me. Wherefore, as to what concerns me, you may do as you shall think fit. But according to my method of advising just and profitable things, I say that you will do your consciences more right, to set me at liberty, unless you see further into my cause than I do; and, judging according to my past actions, both public and private, according to my intentions, and

according to the profit that so many of our citizens, both young and old, daily extract from my conversation, and the fruit that you all reap from me, you cannot more duly acquit yourself toward my merit, than in ordering that, my poverty considered, I should be maintained at the Prytaneum, at the public expense, a thing that I have often known you, with less reason, grant to others. Do not impute it to obstinacy or disdain, that I do not, according to the custom, supplicate and go about to move you to commiseration. I have both friends and kindred, not being, as Homer says, begotten of wood or of a stone, no more than others, who might well present themselves before you with tears and mourning, and I have three desolate children with whom to move you to compassion; but I should do a shame to our city at the age I am, and in the reputation of wisdom which is now charged against me, to appear in such an abject form. What would men say of the other Athenians? I have always admonished those who have frequented my lectures, not to redeem their lives by an unbecoming action; and in the wars of my country, at Amphipolis, Potidea, Delia, and other expeditions where I have been, I have effectually manifested how far I was from securing my safety by my shame. I should, moreover, compromise your duty, and should invite you to unbecoming things; for 'tis not for my prayers to persuade you, but for the pure and solid reasons of justice. You have sworn to the gods to keep yourselves upright; and it would seem as if I suspected you, or would recriminate upon you that I do not believe that you are so; and I should testify against myself, not to believe them as I ought, mistrusting their conduct, and not purely committing my affair into their hands. I wholly rely upon them; and hold myself assured they will do in this what shall be most fit both for you and for me; good men, whether living or dead, have no reason to fear the gods."

Is not this an innocent child's pleading of an unimaginable loftiness, true, frank, and just, unexampled? and in what a necessity employed! Truly, he had very good reason to prefer it before that which the great orator Lysias had penned for him: admirably couched, indeed, in the judiciary style, but unworthy of so noble a criminal. Had a suppliant voice been heard out of the mouth of

Socrates, that lofty virtue had struck sail in the height of its glory; and ought his rich and powerful nature to have committed her defense to art, and, in her highest proof, have renounced truth and simplicity, the ornaments of his speaking, to adorn and deck herself with the embellishments of figures, and the flourishes of a premeditated speech? He did very wisely, and like himself, not to corrupt the tenor of an incorrupt life, and so sacred an image of the human form, to spin out his decrepitude another year, and to betray the immortal memory of that glorious end. He owed his life not to himself, but to the example of the world; had it not been a public damage, that he should have concluded it after a lazy and obscure manner? Assuredly, that careless and indifferent consideration of his death deserved that posterity should consider it so much the more, as indeed they did; and there is nothing so just in justice than that which fortune ordained for his recommendation; for the Athenians abominated all those who had been causers of his death to such a degree, that they avoided them as excommunicated persons, and looked upon everything as polluted that had been touched by them; no one would wash with them in the public baths, none would salute or own acquaintance with them: so that, at last, unable longer to support this public hatred, they hanged themselves.

If any one shall think that, among so many other examples that I had to choose out of in the sayings of Socrates for my present purpose, I have made an ill choice of this, and shall judge this discourse of his elevated above common conceptions, I must tell them that I have purposely selected it; for I am of another opinion, and hold it to be a discourse, in rank and simplicity, much below and behind common conceptions. He represents, in an inartificial boldness and infantine security, the pure and first impression and ignorance of nature; for it is to be believed that we have naturally a fear of pain, but not of death, by reason of itself; 'tis a part of our being, and no less essential than living. To what end should nature have begotten in us a hatred to it and a horror of it, considering that it is of so great utility to her in maintaining the succession and vicissitude of her works? and that in this universal repub-

[393]

lic, it conduces more to birth and augmentation, than to loss or ruin?

"Sic rerum summa novatur."

"Mille animas una necata dedit."

"The failing of one life is the passage to a thousand other lives." Nature has imprinted in beasts the care of themselves and of their conservation; they proceed so far as to be timorous of being worse, of hitting or hurting themselves, of our haltering and beating them, accidents subject to their sense and experience; but that we should kill them, they cannot fear, nor have they the faculty to imagine and conclude such a thing as death; it is said, indeed, that we see them not only cheerfully undergo it, horses for the most part neighing and swans singing when they die, but, moreover, seek it at need, of which elephants have given many examples.

But besides, is not the way of arguing which Socrates here makes use of, equally admirable both in simplicity and vehemence? Truly, it is much more easy to speak like Aristotle, and to live like Cæsar, than to speak and live as Socrates did; there lies the extreme degree of perfection and difficulty; art cannot reach it. Now, our faculties are not so trained up: we do not try, we do not know them; we invest ourselves with those of others, and let our own lie idle; as some one may say of me, that I have here only made a nosegay of culled flowers, and have brought nothing of my own but the thread that ties them.

In earnest, I have so far yielded to the public opinion, that those borrowed ornaments accompany me, but I would not have them totally cover and hide me; that is quite contrary to my design, who desire to make a show of nothing but what is my own, and what is my own by nature; and had I taken my own advice, I had at all hazards spoken purely alone. I more and more load myself every day, beyond my purpose and first method, upon the account of idleness and the humor of the age. If it misbecome me, as I believe it does, 'tis no matter; it may be of use to some others. Such there are who quote Plato and Homer, who never saw either of them; and as I also have taken things out of places far enough distant from their source. Without pains and without learning,

having a thousand volumes about me in the place where I write, I can presently borrow, if I please, from a dozen such scrap-gatherers, people about whom I do not much trouble myself, wherewith to trick up this treatise of Physiognomy; there needs no more but a preliminary epistle of the German cut to stuff me with illustrations. And so 'tis we go a begging for a ticklish glory, cheating the sottish world. These lumber pies of commonplaces, wherewith so many furnish their studies, are of little use but to common subjects, and serve but to show us, and not to direct us: a ridiculous fruit of learning that Socrates so pleasantly discusses against Euthydemus. I have seen books made of things that were never either studied or understood; the author committing to several of his learned friends the examination of this and t'other matter to compile it, contenting himself, for his share, with having projected the design, and by his industry to have tied together this faggot of unknown provisions; the ink and paper, at least, are his. This is to buy or borrow a book, and not to make one; 'tis to show men not that he can make a book, but that, whereof they may be in doubt, he cannot make one. A president, in my hearing, boasted that he had cluttered together two hundred and odd commonplaces in one of his judgments; in telling which, he deprived himself of the glory he had got by it: in my opinion, a pusillanimous and absurd vanity for such a subject and such a person. I do quite contrary; and among so many borrowed things, am glad if I can steal one, disguising and altering it for some new service; at the hazard of having it said that 'tis for want of understanding its natural use; I give it some particular address of my own hand, to the end it may not be so absolutely foreign. These set their thefts in show, and value themselves upon them, and so have more credit with the laws than I; we naturalists think that there is a great and incomparable preference in the honor of invention over that of quotation.

If I would have spoken by learning, I had spoken sooner; I had written in a time nearer to my studies, when I had more wit and better memory; and should sooner have trusted to the vigor of that age than of this, would I have professed writing. And what if this gracious favor which fortune has lately offered me upon the

[395]

account of this work, had befallen me in that time of my life, instead of this, wherein 'tis equally desirable to possess, soon to be lost! Two of my acquaintance, great men in this faculty, have, in my opinion, lost half, in refusing to publish at forty years old, that they might stay till threescore. Maturity has its defects as well as green years, and worse; and old age is as unfit for this kind of business as for any other. He who commits his decrepitude to the press, plays the fool if he thinks to squeeze anything out thence, that does not relish of dreaming, dotage and driveling; the mind grows costive and thick in growing old. I deliver my ignorance in pomp and state, and my learning meagerly and poorly: this accidentally and accessorily, that principally and expressly; and write specifically of nothing, but nothing, nor of any science but of that inscience. I have chosen a time when my life, which I am to give an account of, lies wholly before me: what remains has more to do with death; and of my death itself, should I find it a prating death, as others do, I would willingly give an account at my departure.

Socrates was a perfect exemplar in all great qualities, and I am vexed that he had so deformed a face and body as is said, and so unsuitable to the beauty of his soul, himself being so amorous and such an admirer of beauty: Nature did him wrong. There is nothing more probable than the conformity and relation of the body to the soul: *"Ipsi animi magni refert, quali in corpore locati sint: multa enim e corpore existunt, quæ acuant mentem: multa, quæ obtundant;"* this refers to an unnatural ugliness and deformity of limbs; but we call ugliness also an unseemliness at first sight, which is principally lodged in the face, and disgusts us on very slight grounds, by the complexion, a spot, a rugged countenance, for some reasons often wholly inexplicable, in members nevertheless of good symmetry and perfect. The deformity, that clothed a very beautiful soul in La Boetie, was of this predicament; that superficial ugliness, which nevertheless is always the most imperious, is of least prejudice to the state of the mind, and of little certainty in the opinion of men. The other, which by a more proper name, is called deformity, more substantial, strikes deeper in. Not every shoe of smooth shining leather, but every shoe well made, shows the shape

of the foot within. As Socrates said of his, it betrayed equal ugliness in his soul, had he not corrected it by education; but in saying so, I believe he did but scoff, as his custom was; never so excellent a soul made itself.

I cannot often enough repeat how great an esteem I have for beauty, that potent and advantageous quality; he called it "a short tyranny," and Plato, "the privilege of nature." We have nothing that excels it in reputation; it has the first place in the commerce of men; it presents itself in the front; seduces and prepossesses our judgments with great authority and wonderful impression. Phryne had lost her cause in the hands of an excellent advocate, if, opening her robe, she had not corrupted her judges by the luster of her beauty. And I find that Cyrus, Alexander, and Cæsar, the three masters of the world, never neglected beauty in their greatest affairs; no more did the first Scipio. The same word in Greek signifies both fair and good; and the Holy Word often says good, when it means fair; I should willingly maintain the priority in good things, according to the song that Plato calls an idle thing, taken out of some ancient poet; "health, beauty, riches." Aristotle says that the right of command appertains to the beautiful; and that, when there is a person whose beauty comes near the images of the gods, veneration is equally due to him. To him who asked why people oftener and longer frequent the company of handsome persons: "That question," said he, "is only to be asked by the blind." Most of the philosophers, and the greatest, paid for their schooling, and acquired wisdom by the favor and mediation of their beauty. Not only in the men that serve me, but also in the beasts, I consider it within two fingers' breadth of goodness.

And yet I fancy that those features and molds of face, and those lineaments, by which men guess at our internal complexions and our fortunes to come, is a thing that does not very directly and simply lie under the chapter of beauty and deformity, no more than every good odor and serenity of air promises health, nor all fog and stink, infection in a time of pestilence. Such as accuse ladies of contradicting their beauty by their manners, do not always hit right; for, in a face which is none of the best, there may dwell some

air of probity and trust; as on the contrary I have read, between two beautiful eyes, menaces of a dangerous and malignant nature. There are favorable physiognomies, so that in a crowd of victorious enemies, you shall presently choose, among men you never saw before, one rather than another, to whom to surrender, and with whom to intrust your life; and yet not properly upon the consideration of beauty.

A person's look is but a feeble warranty; and yet it is something considerable too; and if I had to lash them, I would most severely scourge the wicked ones who belie and betray the promises that nature has planted in their foreheads; I should with greater severity punish malice under a mild and gentle aspect. It seems as if there were some lucky and some unlucky faces; and I believe there is some art in distinguishing affable from merely simple faces, severe from rugged, malicious from pensive, scornful from melancholic, and such other bordering qualities. There are beauties which are not only haughty, but sour, and others that are not only gentle but more than that, insipid; to prognosticate from them future events, is a matter that I shall leave undecided.

I have, as I have said elsewhere, as to my own concern, simply and implicitly embraced this ancient rule, "That we cannot fail in following Nature," and that the sovereign precept is to "conform ourselves to her." I have not, as Socrates did, corrected my natural composition by the force of reason, and have not in the least disturbed my inclination by art; I have let myself go as I came; I contend not; my two principal parts live, of their own accord, in peace and good intelligence, but my nurse's milk, thank God, was tolerably wholesome and good. Shall I say this by the way? that I see, in greater esteem than 'tis worth, and in use solely among ourselves, a certain image of scholastic probity, a slave to precepts, and fettered with hope and fear. I would have it such as that laws and religions should not make, but perfect and authorize it; that finds it has wherewithal to support itself without help, born and rooted in us from the seed of universal reason, imprinted in every man by nature. That reason which straightens Socrates from his vicious bend, renders him obedient to the gods and men of authority

in his city; courageous in death, not because his soul is immortal, but because he is mortal. 'Tis a doctrine ruinous to all government, and much more hurtful than ingenious and subtle, which persuades the people that a religious belief is alone sufficient, and without conduct, to satisfy the divine justice. Use demonstrates to us a vast distinction between devotion and conscience.

I have a favorable aspect, both in form and interpretation.

"Quid dixi, habere me? imo habui, Chreme."

"Heu! tantum attriti corporis ossa vides;"

and that makes quite a contrary show to that of Socrates. It has often befallen me, that upon the mere credit of my presence and air, persons who had no manner of knowledge of me, have put a very great confidence in me, whether in their own affairs or mine; and I have in foreign parts thence obtained singular and rare favors. But the two following examples are, peradventure, worth particular relation: a certain person planned to surprise my house and me in it; his scheme was to come to my gates alone, and to be importunate to be let in. I knew him by name, and had fair reason to repose confidence in him, as being my neighbor and something related to me. I caused the gates to be opened to him, as I do to every one. There I found him, with every appearance of alarm, his horse panting, and all in a foam. He presently popped in my ears this flim-flam: "That, about half a league off, he had met with a certain enemy of his, whom I also knew, and had heard of their quarrel; that his enemy had given him a very brisk chase, and that having been surprised in disorder, and his party being too weak, he had fled to my gates for refuge; and that he was in great trouble for his followers, whom (he said) he concluded to be all either dead or taken." I innocently did my best to comfort, assure, and refresh him. Shortly after came four or five of his soldiers, who presented themselves in the same countenance and affright, to get in too; and after them more, and still more, very well mounted and armed, to the number of five and twenty or thirty, pretending that they had the enemy at their heels. This mystery began a little to awaken my suspicion; I was not ignorant what an age I lived in, how much my house might be envied, and I had several examples of others of

my acquaintance to whom a mishap of this sort had happened. But, thinking there was nothing to be got by having begun to do a courtesy, unless I went through with it, and that I could not disengage myself from them without spoiling all, I let myself go the most natural and simple way, as I always do, and invited them all to come in. And in truth I am naturally very little inclined to suspicion and distrust; I willingly incline toward excuse and the gentlest interpretation; I take men according to the common order, and do not more believe in those perverse and unnatural inclinations, unless convinced by manifest evidence, than I do in monsters and miracles; and I am, moreover, a man who willingly commit myself to Fortune, and throw myself headlong into her arms; and I have hitherto found more reason to applaud than to blame myself for so doing, having ever found her more discreet about, and a greater friend to my affairs, than I am myself. There are some actions in my life whereof the conduct may justly be called difficult, or, if you please, prudent; of these, supposing the third part to have been my own, doubtless the other two-thirds were absolutely hers. We make, methinks, a mistake, in that we do not enough trust heaven with our affairs, and pretend to more from our own conduct than appertains to us: and therefore it is that our designs so often miscarry. Heaven is jealous of the extent that we attribute to the right of human prudence above its own, and cuts it all the shorter by how much the more we amplify it. The last comers remained on horseback in my courtyard, while their leader, who was with me in the parlor, would not have his horse put up in the stable, saying he should immediately retire, so soon as he had news of his men. He saw himself master of his enterprise, and nothing now remained but its execution. He has since several times said (for he was not ashamed to tell the story himself) that my countenance and frankness had snatched the treachery out of his hands. He again mounted his horse; his followers, who had their eyes intent upon him, to see when he would give the signal, being very much astonished to find him come away and leave his prey behind him.

Another time, relying upon some truce, just published in the army, I took a journey through a very ticklish country. I had not

ridden far but I was discovered, and two or three parties of horse, from various places, were sent out to seize me; one of them overtook me on the third day, and I was attacked by fifteen or twenty gentlemen in visors, followed at a distance by a band of foot soldiers. I was taken, withdrawn into the thick of a neighboring forest, dismounted, robbed, my trunks rifled, my money-box taken, and my horses and equipage divided among new masters. We had, in this copse, a very long contest about my ransom, which they set so high, that it was manifest I was not known to them. They were, moreover, in a very great debate about my life; and, in truth, there were various circumstances that clearly showed the danger I was in.

"Tunc animis opus, Ænea, tunc pectore firmo."

I still insisted upon the truce, too willing they should have the gain of what they had already taken from me, which was not to be despised, without promise of any other ransom. After two or three hours that we had been in this place, and that they had mounted me upon a pitiful jade that was not likely to run from them, and committed me to the guard of fifteen or twenty harquebuseers, and dispersed my servants to others, having given order that they should carry us away prisoners several ways, and I being already got some two or three musket-shots from the place,

"Jam prece Pollucis, jam Castoris, implorata,"

behold a sudden and unexpected alteration; I saw the chief return to me with gentler language, making search among the troopers for my scattered property, and causing as much as could be recovered, to be restored to me, even to my money-box; but the best present they made me, was my liberty, for the rest did not much concern me at that time. The true cause of so sudden a change, and of this reconsideration, without any apparent impulse, and of so miraculous a repentance, in such a time, in a planned and deliberate enterprise, and become just by usage (for, at the first dash, I plainly confessed to them of what party I was, and whither I was going), truly, I do not yet rightly understand. The most prominent among them, who pulled off his visor and told me his name, repeatedly told me at the time over and over again, that I owed my deliverance to my countenance, and the liberty and boldness of

my speech, that rendered me unworthy of such a misadventure, and should secure me from its repetition. 'Tis possible that the Divine goodness willed to make use of this vain instrument for my preservation; and it, moreover, defended me the next day from other and worse ambushes, of which these my assailants had given me warning. The last of these two gentlemen is yet living, himself to tell the story; the first was killed not long ago.

If my face did not answer for me, if men did not read in my eyes and in my voice the innocence of my intention, I had not lived so long without quarrels and without giving offense, seeing the indiscreet liberty I take to say, right or wrong, whatever comes into my head, and to judge so rashly of things. This way may, with reason, appear uncivil, and ill adapted to our way of conversation; but I have never met with any who judged it outrageous or malicious, or that took offense at my liberty, if he had it from my own mouth; words repeated have another kind of sound and sense. Nor do I hate any person; and I am so slow to offend, that I cannot do it, even upon the account of reason itself; and when occasion has required me to sentence criminals, I have rather chosen to fail in point of justice than to do it: *"Ut magis peccari nolim, quam satis animi ad vindicanda peccata habeam."*

Aristotle, 'tis said, was reproached for having been too merciful to a wicked man: "I was, indeed," said he, "merciful to the man, but not to his wickedness." Ordinary judgments exasperate themselves to punishment by the horror of the fact: but it cools mine; the horror of the first murder makes me fear a second; and the deformity of the first cruelty makes me abhor all imitation of it. That may be applied to me, who am but a Knave of Clubs, which was said of Charillus, king of Sparta: "He cannot be good, seeing he is not evil to the wicked." Or thus—for Plutarch delivers it both these ways, as he does a thousand other things, variously and contradictorily—"He must needs be good, because he is so even to the wicked." Even as in lawful actions, I dislike to employ myself, when for such as are displeased at it; so, to say the truth, in unlawful things, I do not make conscious enough of employing myself, when for such as are willing.

XX

OF THE FORCE OF IMAGINATION

"Fortis *imaginatio generat casum*," say the schoolmen.

I am one of those who are most sensible of the power of imagination: every one is jostled by it, but some are overthrown by it. It has a very piercing impression upon me; and I make it my business to avoid, wanting force to resist it. I could live by the sole help of healthful and jolly company: the very sight of another's pain materially pains me, and I often usurp the sensations of another person. A perpetual cough in another tickles my lungs and throat. I more unwillingly visit the sick in whom by love and duty I am interested, than those I care not for, to whom I less look. I take possession of the disease I am concerned at, and take it to myself. I do not at all wonder that fancy should give fevers and sometimes kill such as to allow it too much scope, and are too willing to entertain it. Simon Thomas was a great physician of his time: I remember, that happening one day at Toulouse to meet him at a rich old fellow's house, who was troubled with weak lungs, and discoursing with his patient about the method of his cure, he told him, that one thing which would be very conducive to it, was to give me such occasion to be pleased with his company, that I might come often to see him, by which means, and by fixing his eye upon the freshness of my complexion, and his imagination upon the sprightliness and vigor that glowed in my youth, and possessing all his senses with the flourishing age wherein I then was, his habit to body might, peradventure, be amended; but he forgot to say that

mine, at the same time, might be made worse. Gallus Vibius so long cudgeled his brains to find out the essence and motions of madness, that, in the end, he himself went out of his wits, and to such a degree, that he could never after recover his judgment; and might brag that he was become a fool by too much wisdom. Some there are who through fear anticipate the hangman; and there was the man, whose eyes being unbound to have his pardon read to him, was found stark dead upon the scaffold, by the stroke of imagination. We start, tremble, turn pale, and blush, as we are variously moved by imagination; and, being a-bed, feel our bodies agitated with its power to that degree, as even sometimes to expiring. And boiling youth, when fast asleep, grows so warm with fancy, as in a dream to satisfy amorous desires:

> "Ut, quasi transactis sæpe omnibu' rebu' profundant
> Fluminis ingentes fluctus, vestemque cruentent."

Although it be no new thing to see horns grown in a night on the forehead of one that had none when he went to bed, notwithstanding, what befell Cippus, king of Italy, is memorable; who having one day been a very delighted spectator of a bull-fight, and having all the night dreamed that he had horns on his head, did, by the force of imagination, really cause them to grow there. Passion gave to the son of Crœsus the voice which nature had denied him. And Antiochus fell into a fever, inflamed with the beauty of Stratonice, too deeply imprinted in his soul. Pliny pretends to have seen Lucius Cossitius, who from a woman was turned into a man upon her very wedding-day. Pontanus and others report the like metamorphosis to have happened in these latter days in Italy. And, through the vehement desire of him and his mother,

> "Vota puer solvit, quæ fœmina voverat, Iphis."

Myself passing by Vitry le François, saw a man the bishop of Soissons had, in confirmation, called Germain, whom all the inhabitants of the place had known to be a girl till two-and-twenty years of age, called Mary. He was, at the time of my being there, very full of beard, old, and not married. He told us, that by straining himself in a leap his male instruments came out; and the girls of that place have, to this day, a song, wherein they advise one an-

other not to take too great strides, for fear of being turned into men, as Mary Germain was. It is no wonder if this sort of accident frequently happen; for if imagination have any power in such things, it is so continually and vigorously bent upon this subject, that to the end it may not so often relapse into the same thought and violence of desire, it were better, once for all, to give these young wenches the things they long for.

Some attribute the scars of King Dagobert and of St. Francis to the force of imagination. It is said, that by it bodies will sometimes be removed from their places; and Celsus tells us of a priest whose soul would be ravished into such an ecstasy that the body would, for a long time, remain without sense or respiration. St. Augustine makes mention of another, who, upon the hearing of any lamentable or doleful cries, would presently fall into a swoon, and be so far out of himself, that it was in vain to call, bawl in his ears, pinch or burn him, till he voluntarily came to himself; and then he would say, that he had heard voices as it were afar off, and did feel when they pinched and burned him; and to prove that this was no obstinate dissimulation in defiance of his sense of feeling, it was manifest, that all the while he had neither pulse nor breathing.

'Tis very probable, that visions, enchantments, and all extraordinary effects of that nature, derive their credit principally from the power of imagination, working and making its chiefest impression upon vulgar and more easy souls, whose belief is so strangely imposed upon, as to think they see what they do not see.

I am not satisfied whether those pleasant ligatures with which this age of ours is so occupied, that there is almost no other talk, are not mere voluntary impressions of apprehension and fear; for I know, by experience, in the case of a particular friend of mine, one for whom I can be as responsible as for myself, and a man that cannot possibly fall under any manner of suspicion of insufficiency, and as little of being enchanted, who having heard a companion of his make a relation of an unusual frigidity that surprised him at a very unseasonable time; being afterward himself engaged upon the same account, the horror of the former story on a sudden so strangely possessed his imagination, that he ran the same fortune

the other had done; and from that time forward, the scurvy remembrance of his disaster running in his mind and tyrannizing over him, he was subject to relapse into the same misfortune. He found some remedy, however, for this fancy in another fancy, by himself frankly confessing and declaring beforehand to the party with whom he was to have to do, this subjection of his, by which means, the agitation of his soul was, in some sort, appeased; and knowing that, now, some such misbehavior was expected from him, the restraint upon his faculties grew less. And afterward, at such times as he was in no such apprehension, when setting about the act (his thoughts being then disengaged and free, and his body in its true and natural estate) he was at leisure to cause the part to be handled and communicated to the knowledge of the other party, he was totally freed from that vexatious infirmity. After a man has once done a woman right, he is never after in danger of misbehaving himself with that person, unless upon the account of some excusable weakness. Neither is this disaster to be feared, but in adventures where the soul is over-extended with desire or respect, and especially, where the opportunity is of an unforeseen and pressing nature; in those cases, there is no means for a man to defend himself from such a surprise, as shall put him altogether out of sorts. I have known some, who have secured themselves from this mischance, by coming half sated elsewhere, purposely to abate the ardor of the fury, and others, who, being grown old, find themselves less impotent by being less able; and one, who found an advantage in being assured by a friend of his, that he had a counter-charm of enchantments that would secure him from this disgrace. The story itself is not much amiss, and therefore you shall have it.

A count of a very great family, and with whom I was very intimate, being married to a fair lady, who had formerly been courted by one who was at the wedding, all his friends were in very great fear; but especially an old lady his kinswoman, who had the ordering of the solemnity, and in whose house it was kept, suspecting his rival would offer foul play by these sorceries. Which fear she communicated to me. I bade her rely upon me: I had, by chance, about me a certain flat plate of gold, whereon were graven some

celestial figures, supposed good against sunstroke or pains in the head, being applied to the suture; where, that it might the better remain firm, it was sewed to a ribbon to be tied under the chin; a foppery cousin-german to this of which I am speaking. Jaques Pelletier, who lived in my house, had presented this to me for a singular rarity. I had a fancy to make some use of this knack, and therefore privately told the count, that he might possibly run the same fortune other bridegrooms had sometimes done, especially some one being in the house, who, no doubt, would be glad to do him such a courtesy: but let him boldly go to bed. For I would do him the office of a friend, and, if need were, would not spare a miracle it was in my power to do, provided he would engage to me, upon his honor, to keep it to himself; and only, when they came to bring him his caudle, if matters had not gone well with him, to give me such a sign, and leave the rest to me. Now he had had his ears so battered, and his mind so prepossessed with the eternal tattle of this business, that when he came to't, he did really find himself tied with the trouble of his imagination, and, accordingly, at the time appointed, gave me the sign. Whereupon, I whispered him in the ear, that he should rise, under pretense of putting us out of the room, and after a jesting manner pull my nightgown from my shoulders—we were of much about the same height—throw it over his own, and there keep it till he had performed what I had appointed him to do, which was, that when we were all gone out of the chamber he should withdraw to make water, should three times repeat such and such words, and as often do such and such actions; that at every of the three times, he should tie the ribbon I put into his hand about his middle, and be sure to place the medal that was fastened to it, the figures in such a posture, exactly upon his reins, which being done, and having the last of the three times so well girt and fast tied the ribbon that it could neither untie nor slip from its place, let him confidently return to his business, and withal not forget to spread my gown upon the bed, so that it might be sure to cover them both. These ape's tricks are the main of the effect, our fancy being so far seduced as to believe that such strange means must, of necessity, proceed from some abstruse science: their very inanity gives them weight and reverence. And, certain it is, that

my figures approved themselves more venerian than solar, more active than prohibitive. 'Twas a sudden whimsey, mixed with a little curiosity, that made me do a thing so contrary to my nature; for I am an enemy to all subtle and counterfeit actions, and abominate all manner of trickery, though it be for sport, and to an advantage; for though the action may not be vicious in itself, its mode is vicious.

Amasis, king of Egypt, having married Laodice, a very beautiful Greek virgin, though noted for his abilities elsewhere, found himself quite another man with his wife, and could by no means enjoy her; at which he was so enraged, that he threatened to kill her, suspecting her to be a witch. As 'tis usual in things that consist in fancy, she put him upon devotion, and having, accordingly, made his vows to Venus, he found himself divinely restored the very first night after his oblations and sacrifices. Now women are to blame to entertain us with that disdainful coy, and angry countenance, which extinguishes our vigor, as it kindles our desire; which made the daughter-in-law of Pythagoras say, "That the woman who goes to bed to a man, must put off her modesty with her petticoat, and put it on again with the same." The soul of the assailant being disturbed with many several alarms, readily loses the power of performance; and whoever the imagination has once put this trick upon, and confounded with the shame of it (and she never does it but at the first acquaintance, by reason men are then more ardent and eager, and also, at this first account a man gives of himself, he is much more timorous of miscarrying), having made an ill beginning, he enters into such fever and despite at the accident, as are apt to remain and continue with him upon following occasions.

Married people, having all their time before them, ought never to compel or so much as to offer at the feat, if they do not find themselves quite ready; and it is less unseemly to fail of handselling the nuptial sheets, when a man perceives himself full of agitation and trembling, and to await another opportunity at more private and more composed leisure, than to make himself perpetually miserable, for having misbehaved himself and been baffled at the first assault. Till possession be taken, a man that knows himself subject to this infirmity, should leisurely and by degrees make several

[408]

FORTIS IMAGINATIO GENERAT CASVM

OF THE FORCE OF IMAGINATION

little trials and light offers, without obstinately attempting, at once, to force an absolute conquest over his own mutinous and indisposed faculties. Such as know their members to be naturally obedient, need take no other care but only to counterplot their fantasies.

The indocile liberty of this member is very remarkable, so importunately unruly in its timidity and impatience, when we do not require it, and so unseasonably disobedient when we stand most in need of it: so imperiously contesting in authority with the will, and with so much haughty obstinacy denying all solicitation, both of hand and mind. And yet, though his rebellion is so universally complained of, and that proof is thence deduced to condemn him, if he had, nevertheless, feed me to plead his cause, I should, peradventure, bring the rest of his fellow-members into suspicion of complotting this mischief against him, out of pure envy at the importance and pleasure especial to his employment; and to have, by confederacy, armed the whole world against him, by malevolently charging him alone, with their common offense. For let any one consider, whether there is any one part of our bodies that does not often refuse to perform its office at the precept of the will, and that does not often exercise its function in defiance of her command. They have every one of them passions of their own, that rouse and awaken, stupefy and benumb them, without our leave or consent. How often do the involuntary motions of the countenance discover our inward thoughts, and betray our most private secrets to the bystanders. The same cause that animates this member does also, without our knowledge, animate the lungs, pulse, and heart, the sight of a pleasing object imperceptibly diffusing a flame through all our parts, with a feverish motion. Is there nothing but these veins and muscles that swell and flag without the consent, not only of the will, but even of our knowledge also? We do not command our hairs to stand on end, nor our skin to shiver either with fear or desire; the hands often convey themselves to parts to which we do not direct them; the tongue will be interdict, and the voice congealed, when we know not how to help it. When we have nothing to eat, and would willingly forbid it, the appetite does not, for all that, forbear to stir up the parts that are subject to it, no more nor

[409]

less than the other appetite we were speaking of, and in like manner, as unseasonably leaves us, when it thinks fit. The vessels that serve to discharge the belly have their own proper dilatations and compressions, without and beyond our concurrence, as well as those which are destined to purge the reins; and that which, to justify the prerogative of the will, St. Augustine urges, of having seen a man who could command his rear to discharge as often together as he pleased, Vives, his commentator, yet further fortifies with another example in his time, of one that could break wind in tune; but these cases do not suppose any more pure obedience in that part; for is anything commonly more tumultuary or indiscreet? To which let me add, that I myself knew one so rude and ungoverned, as for forty years together made his master vent with one continued and unintermitted outbursting, and 'tis like will do so till he die of it. And I could heartily wish that I only knew by reading how often a man's belly, by the denial of one single puff, brings him to the very door of an exceeding painful death; and that the emperor, who gave liberty to let fly in all places, had at the same time given us power to do it. But for our will, in whose behalf we prefer this accusation, with how much greater probability may we reproach herself with mutiny and sedition, for her irregularity and disobedience? Does she always will what we would have her to do? Does she not often will what we forbid her to will, and that to our manifest prejudice? Does she suffer herself, more than any of the rest, to be governed and directed by the results of our reason? To conclude, I should move, in the behalf of the gentleman, my client, it might be considered, that in this fact, his cause being inseparably and indistinctly conjoined with an accessory, yet he only is called in question, and that by arguments and accusations which cannot be charged upon the other; whose business, indeed, it is sometimes inopportunely to invite, but never to refuse, and invite, moreover, after a tacit and quiet manner; and therefore is the malice and injustice of his accusers most manifestly apparent. But be it how it will, protesting against the proceedings of the advocates and judges, Nature will, in the meantime, proceed after her own way, who had done but well had she endowed this member with some particular

privilege; the author of the sole immortal work of mortals; a divine work, according to Socrates; and love, the desire of immortality, and himself an immortal demon.

Some one, perhaps, by such an effect of imagination may have had the good luck to leave behind him here, the scrofula, which his companion who has come after, has carried with him into Spain. And 'tis for this reason you may see why men in such cases require a mind prepared for the thing that is to be done. Why do the physicians possess, beforehand, their patients' credulity with so many false promises of cure, if not to the end, that the effect of imagination may supply the imposture of their decoctions? They know very well that a great master of their trade has given it under his hand, that he has known some with whom the very sight of physic would work. All which conceits come now into my head by the remembrance of a story that was told me by a domestic apothecary of my father's, a blunt Swiss, a nation not much addicted to vanity and lying, of a merchant he had long known at Toulouse, who being a valetudinary, and much afflicted with the stone had often occasion to take clysters, of which he caused several sorts to be prescribed him by the physicians, according to the accidents of his disease: which, being brought him, and none of the usual forms, as feeling if it were not too hot, and the like, being omitted, he lay down, the syringe advanced, and all ceremonies performed, injection alone excepted; after which, the apothecary being gone, and the patient accommodated as if he had really received a clyster, he found the same operation and effect that those do who have taken one, indeed; and if at any time the physician did not find the operation sufficient, he would usually give him two or three more doses, after the same manner. And the fellow swore, that to save charges (for he paid as if he had really taken them) this sick man's wife, having sometimes made trial of warm water only, the effect discovered the cheat, and finding these would do no good, was fain to return to the old way.

A woman fancying she had swallowed a pin in a piece of bread, cried and lamented as though she had an intolerable pain in her throat, where she thought she felt it stick; but an ingenious fellow

that was brought to her, seeing no outward tumor nor alteration, supposing it to be only a conceit taken at some crust of bread that had hurt her as it went down, caused her to vomit, and, unseen, threw a crooked pin into the basin, which the woman no sooner saw, but believing she had cast it up, she presently found herself eased of her pain. I myself knew a gentleman, who having treated a large company at his house, three or four days after bragged in jest (for there was no such thing), that he had made them eat of a baked cat; at which a young gentlewoman, who had been at the feast, took such a horror, that falling into a violent vomiting and fever, there was no possible means to save her. Even brute beasts are subject to the force of imagination as well as we, witness dogs, who die of grief for the loss of their masters and bark and tremble and start in their sleep; so horses will kick and whinny in their sleep.

Now all this may be attributed to the close affinity and relation between the soul and the body intercommunicating their fortunes; but 'tis quite another thing when the imagination works not only upon one's own particular body, but upon that of others also. And as an infected body communicates its malady to those that, approach or live near it, as we see in the plague, the smallpox, and sore eyes, that run through whole families and cities—

"Dum spectant oculi læsos, læduntur et ipsi;
Multaque corporibus transitione nocent"

—so the imagination, being vehemently agitated, darts out infection capable of offending the foreign object. The ancients had an opinion of certain women of Scythia, that being animated and enraged against any one, they killed him only with their looks. Tortoises and ostriches hatch their eggs with only looking on them, which infers, that their eyes have in them some ejaculative virtue. And the eyes of witches are said to be assailant and hurtful:

"Nescio quis teneros oculus mihi fascinat agnos."

Magicians are no very good authority with me. But we experimentally see that women impart the marks of their fancy to the children they carry in the womb; witness her that was brought to bed of a Moor; and there was presented to Charles the emperor

and king of Bohemia, a girl from about Pisa, all over rough and covered with hair, whom her mother said to be so conceived by reason of a picture of St. John the Baptist that hung within the curtains of her bed.

It is the same with beasts; witness Jacob's sheep, and the hares and partridges that the snow turns white upon the mountains. There was at my house, a little while ago, a cat seen watching a bird upon the top of a tree: these, for some time, mutually fixing their eyes one upon another, the bird at last let herself fall dead into the cat's claws, either dazzled by the force of its own imagination, or drawn by some attractive power of the cat. Such as are addicted to the pleasures of the field have, I make no question, heard the story of the falconer, who having earnestly fixed his eyes upon a kite in the air, laid a wager that he would bring her down with the sole power of his sight, and did so, as it was said, for the tales I borrow I charge upon the consciences of those from whom I have them. The discourses are my own, and found themselves upon the proofs of reason, not of experience; to which every one has liberty to add his own examples; and who has none, let him not forbear, the number and varieties of accidents considered, to believe that there are plenty of them: if I do not apply them well, let some other do it for me. And, also, in the subject of which I treat, our manners and notions, testimonies and instances, how fabulous soever, provided they are possible, serve as well as the true; whether they have really happened or no, at Rome or Paris, to John or Peter 'tis still within the verge of human capacity, which serves me to good use. I see, and make my advantage of it, as well in shadow as in substance; and among the various readings thereof in history, I cull out the most rare and memorable to fit my own turn. There are authors whose only end and design it is, to give an account of things that have happened; mine, if I could arrive unto it, should be to deliver of what may happen. There is a just liberty allowed in the schools, of supposing similitudes, when they have none at hand. I do not, however, make any use of that privilege, and as to that matter, in superstitious religion, surpass all historical authority. In the examples which I here bring in, of what I have heard, read, done, or said, I have forbidden myself to dare to alter even the most light

and indifferent circumstances: my conscience does not falsify one tittle; what my ignorance may do, I cannot say.

And this it is that makes me sometimes doubt in my own mind, whether a divine, or a philosopher, and such men of exact and tender prudence and conscience, are fit to write history: for how can they stake their reputation upon a popular faith? how be responsible for the opinions of men they do not know? and with what assurance deliver their conjectures for current pay? Of actions performed before their own eyes, wherein several persons were actors, they would be unwilling to give evidence upon oath before a judge; and there is no man, so familiarly known to them, for whose intentions they would become absolute caution. For my part, I think it less hazardous to write of things past, than present, by how much the writer is only to give an account of things every one knows he must of necessity borrow upon trust.

I am solicited to write the affairs of my own time, by some who fancy I look upon them with an eye less blinded with passion than another, and have a clearer insight into them by reason of the free access fortune has given me to the heads of various factions; but they do not consider, that to purchase the glory of Sallust, I would not give myself the trouble, sworn enemy as I am to obligation, assiduity, or perseverance; that there is nothing so contrary to my style as a continued narrative, I so often interrupt, and cut myself short in my writing for want of breath; I have neither composition nor explanation worth anything, and am ignorant, beyond a child, of the phrases and even the very words proper to express the most common things; and for that reason it is, that I have undertaken to say only what I can say, and have accommodated my subject to my strength: should I take one to be my guide, peradventure I should not be able to keep pace with him; and in the freedom of my liberty, might deliver judgments, which upon better thoughts, and according to reason, would be illegitimate and punishable. Plutarch would tell us, of what he has delivered to us, that it is the work of others: that his examples are all and everywhere exactly true: that they are useful to posterity, and are presented with a luster that will light us the way to virtue, is his own work. It is not of so dangerous consequence, as in a medicinal drug, whether an old story be so or no.

XXI

OF EXPERIENCE

Tʜᴇʀᴇ is no desire more natural than that of knowledge. We try all ways that can lead us to it; where reason is wanting, we therein employ experience.

> "Per varios usus artem experientia fecit,
> Exemplo monstrante viam,"

which is a means much more weak and cheap; but truth is no great thing, that we ought not to disdain any mediation that will guide us to it. Reason has so many forms, that we know not to which to take; experience has no fewer; the consequence we would draw from the comparison of events is unsure, by reason they are always unlike. There is no quality so universal in this image of things, as diversity and variety. Both the Greeks and the Latins, and we, for the most express example of similitude, employ that of eggs: and yet there have been men, particularly one at Delphos, who could distinguish marks of difference among eggs so well, that he never mistook one for another; and, having many hens, could tell which had laid it. Dissimilitude intrudes itself of itself in our works; no art can arrive at perfect similitude: neither Perrozet, nor any other cardmarker, can so carefully polish and blanch the backs of his cards, that some gamesters will not distinguish them by seeing them only shuffled by another. Resemblance does not so much make one, as difference makes another. Nature has obliged herself to make nothing other, that was not unlike.

And yet I am not much pleased with his opinion, who thought by the multitude of laws to curb the authority of judges, in cutting out for them their several parcels; he was not aware that there is as much liberty and latitude in the interpretation of laws, as in their form; and they but fool themselves, who think to lessen and stop our disputes by recalling us to the express words of the Bible: forasmuch as our mind does not find the field less spacious wherein to controvert the sense of another, than to deliver his own; and as if there were less animosity and tartness in commentary than in invention. We see how much he was mistaken; for we have more laws in France than all the rest of the world put together, and more than would be necessary for the government of all the worlds of Epicurus: *"Ut olim flagitiis, sic nunc legibus laboramus:"* and yet we have left so much to the opinions and decisions of our judges, that there never was so full a liberty or so full a license. What have our legislators gained by culling out a hundred thousand particular cases, and by applying to these a hundred thousand laws? This number holds no manner of proportion with the infinite diversity of human actions; the multiplication of our inventions will never arrive at the variety of examples; add to these a hundred times as many more, it will still not happen, that of events to come, there shall one be found that, in this vast number of millions of events so chosen and recorded, shall so tally with any other one, and be so exactly coupled and matched with it, that there will not remain some circumstance and diversity which will require a diverse judgment. There is little relation between our actions, which are in perpetual mutation, and fixed and immutable laws; the most to be desired, are those that are the most rare, the most simple and general: and I am even of opinion, that we had better have none at all, than to have them in so prodigious a number as we have.

Nature always gives them better and happier than those we make ourselves. Witness the picture of the Golden Age of the poets, and the state wherein we see nations live, who have no other: some there are, who for their only judge, take the first passer-by that travels along their mountains, to determine their cause: and others who, on their market day, choose out some one among them upon

the spot to decide their controversies. What danger would there be, that the wisest among us should so determine ours, according to occurrences, and at sight, without obligation of example and consequence? For every foot, its own shoe. King Ferdinand, sending colonies to the Indies, wisely provided that they should not carry along with them any students of the long-robe, for fear lest suits should get footing in that new world, as being a science in its own nature, the mother of altercation and division: judging with Plato, "that lawyers and physicians are the pests of a country."

Whence does it come to pass that our common language, so easy for all other uses, becomes obscure, and unintelligible in wills and contracts? and that he who so clearly expresses himself, in whatever else he speaks or writes, cannot find in these, any way of declaring himself that does not fall into doubt and contradiction? if it be not that the princes of that art, applying themselves with a peculiar attention to cull out portentous words and to contrive artificial sentences, have so weighed every syllable, and so thoroughly sifted every sort of quirking connection, that they are now confounded and intangled in the infinity of figures and minute divisions, and can no more fall within any rule or prescription, nor any certain intelligence: "*Confusum est, quidquid usque in pulverem sectum est.*" As you see children trying to bring a mass of quicksilver to a certain number of parts; the more they press and work it, and endeavor to reduce it to their own will, the more they irritate the liberty of this generous metal; it evades their endeavor, and sprinkles itself into so many separate bodies as frustrate all reckoning; so is it here; for in subdividing these subtleties, we teach men to increase their doubts; they put us into a way of extending and diversifying difficulties, and lengthen and disperse them. In sowing and retailing questions, they make the world fructify and increase in uncertainties and disputes, as the earth is made fertile by being crumbled and dug deep: "*Difficultatim facit doctrina.*" We doubted of Ulpian, and are now still more perplexed with Bartolus and Baldus. We should efface the trace of this innumerable diversity of opinions; not adorn ourselves with it, and fill posterity with crotchets. I know not what to say to it; but experience

makes it manifest, that so many interpretations dissipate truth, and break it. Aristotle wrote to be understood; if he could not do this, much less will another that is not so good at it; and a third than he who expressed his own thoughts. We open the matter, and spill it in pouring out: of one subject we make a thousand, and in multiplying and subdividing them, fall again into the infinity of atoms of Epicurus. Never did two men make the same judgment of the same thing; and 'tis impossible to find two opinions exactly alike, not only in several men, but in the same man, at diverse hours. I often find matter of doubt in things of which the commentary has disdained to take notice; I am most apt to stumble in an even country, like some horses that I have known, that make most trips in the smoothest way.

Who will not say that glosses augment doubts and ignorance, since there's no one book to be found, either human or divine, which the world busies itself about, whereof the difficulties are cleared by interpretation. The hundredth commentator passes it on to the next, still more knotty and perplexed than he found it. When were we ever agreed among ourselves: "this book has enough; there is now no more to be said about it?" This is most apparent in the law; we give the authority of law to infinite doctors, infinite decrees, and as many interpretations: yet do we find any end of the need of interpreting? is there, for all that, any progress or advancement toward peace, or do we stand in need of any fewer advocates and judges, than when this great mass of law was yet in its first infancy? On the contrary, we darken and bury intelligence; we can no longer discover it, but at the mercy of so many fences and barriers. Men do not know the natural disease of the mind; it does nothing but ferret and inquire, and is eternally wheeling, juggling, and perplexing itself like silkworms, and then suffocates itself in its work; *"Mus in pice."* It thinks it discovers at a great distance, I know not what glimpse of light and imaginary truth; but while running to it, so many difficulties, hindrances and new inquisitions cross it, that it loses its way, and is made drunk with the motion: not much unlike Æsop's dogs, that seeing something like a dead body floating in the sea, and not being able to approach it, set to

work to drink the water and lay the passage dry, and so choked themselves. To which, what one Crates said of the writings of Heraclitus, falls pat enough, "that they required a reader who could swim well," so that the depth and weight of his doctrine might not overwhelm and stifle him. 'Tis nothing but particular weakness that makes us content with what others or ourselves have found out in this chase after knowledge: one of better understanding will not rest so content; there is always room for one to follow, nay, even for ourselves; and another road: there is no end of our inquisitions; our end is in the other world. 'Tis a sign either that the mind has grown short-sighted when it is satisfied, or that it has got weary. No generous mind can stop in itself; it will still tend further, and beyond its power; it has sallied beyond its effects; if it do not advance and press forward, and retire, and rush and wheel about, 'tis but half alive: its pursuits are without bound or method; its aliment is admiration, the chase, ambiguity, which Apollo sufficiently declared in always speaking to us in a double, obscure, and oblique sense; not feeding, but amusing and puzzling us. 'Tis an irregular and perpetual motion, without model and without aim; its inventions heat, pursue, and interproduce one another.

> "Ainsi veoid on, en un ruisseau coulant,
> Sans fin l'une eau, apres l'aultre roulant;
> Et tout de reng, d'une eternel conduict,
> L'une suyt l'aultre, et l'une l'aultre fuyt.
> Par cette-cy, celle-là est poulsee,
> Et cette-cy par l'aultre est devancée:
> Tousiours l'eau va dans l'eau; et tousiours est-ce
> Mesme ruisseau, et tousiours eau diverse."

There is no more ado to interpret interpretations than to interpret things; and more books upon books than upon any other subject; we do nothing but comment upon one another. Every place swarms with commentaries; of authors there is great scarcity. Is it not the principal and most reputed knowledge of our later ages to understand the learned? Is it not the common and final end of all studies? Our opinions are grafted upon one another; the first serves as a stock to the second, the second to the third, and so forth; thus step

by step we climb the ladder: whence it comes to pass that he who is mounted highest, has often more honor than merit, for he is got up but an inch upon the shoulders of the last but one.

How often, and, peradventure, how foolishly, have I extended my book, to make it speak of itself; foolishly, if for no other reason but this, that it should remind me of what I say of others who do the same; that the frequent amorous glances they cast upon their work witness that their hearts pant with self-love; and that even the disdainful severity wherewith they scourge them, are but the dandlings and caressings of maternal love; as Aristotle, whose valuing and undervaluing himself often springs from the same air of arrogance. My own excuse is, that I ought in this to have more liberty than others, forasmuch as I write specifically of myself and of my writings, as I do of my other actions; that my theme turns upon itself; but I know not whether others will accept this excuse.

I have observed in Germany, that Luther has left as many divisions and disputes about the doubt of his opinions, and more than he himself raised upon the Holy Scriptures. Our contest is verbal: I ask what nature is, what pleasure, circle and substitution are? the question is about words, and is answered accordingly. A stone is a body; but if a man should further urge: "And what is a body?" —"Substance." "And what is substance?" and so on, he would drive the respondent to the end of his Calepin. We exchange one word for another, and often for one less understood. I better know what Man is, than I know what Animal is, or Mortal, or Rational. To satisfy one doubt, they pop me in the ear with three; 'tis the Hydra's head. Socrates asked Menon, "What virtue was." "There is," says Menon, "the virtue of a man and of a woman, of a magistrate and of a private person, of an old man and of a child." "Very fine," cried Socrates, "we were in quest of one virtue, and thou hast brought us a whole swarm." We put one question, and they return us a whole hive. As no event, no face, entirely resembles another, so do they not entirely differ: an ingenious mixture of nature. If our faces were not alike, we could not distinguish man from beast; if they were not unlike, we could not distinguish one man from another; all things hold by some similitude; every example halts

and the relation which is drawn from experience is always faulty and imperfect. Comparisons are ever coupled at one end or the other; so do the laws serve, and are fitted to every one of our affairs, by some wrested, biased, and forced interpretation.

Since the ethic laws, that concern the particular duty of every one in himself, are so hard to be framed, as we see they are, 'tis no wonder if those which govern so many particulars are much more so. Do but consider the form of this justice that governs us; 'tis a true testimony of human weakness, so full is it of error and contradiction. What we find to be favor and severity in justice—and we find so much of them both, that I know not whether the medium is as often met with—are sickly and unjust members of the very body and essence of justice. The country people run to bring me news in great haste, that they have just left in a forest of mine a man with a hundred wounds upon him, who was yet breathing, and begged of them water for pity's sake, and help to carry him to some place of relief; they tell me they dared not go near him, but have run away, lest the officers of justice should catch them there; and as happens to those who are found near a murdered person, they should be called in question about this accident, to their utter ruin, having neither money nor friends to defend their innocence. What could I have said to these people? 'Tis certain that this office of humanity would have brought them into trouble.

How many innocent people have we known that have been punished, and this without the judge's fault; and how many that have not arrived at our knowledge? This happened in my time: certain men were condemned to die for a murder committed: their sentence, if not pronounced, at least determined and concluded on. The judges, just in the nick, are informed by the officers of an inferior court hard by, that they have some men in custody, who have directly confessed the murder, and made an indubitable discovery of all the particulars of the fact. Yet it was gravely deliberated whether or not they ought to suspend the execution of the sentence already passed upon the first accused: they considered the novelty of the example judicially, and the consequence of reversing judgments; that the sentence was passed, and the judges

deprived of repentance; and in the result, the poor devils were sacrificed by the forms of justice. Philip, or some other, provided against a like inconvenience, after this manner. He had condemned a man in a great fine toward another by an absolute judgment. The truth some time after being discovered, he found that he had passed an unjust sentence. On one side was the reason of the cause; on the other side, the reason of the judicial forms: he in some sort satisfied both, leaving the sentence in the state it was, and out of his own purse recompensing the condemned party. But he had to do with a reparable affair; my men were irreparably hanged. How many condemnations have I seen, more criminal than the crimes themselves?

All which makes me remember the ancient opinions "That 'tis of necessity a man must do wrong by retail, who will do right in gross; and injustice in little things, who would come to do justice in great: that human justice is formed after the model of physic, according to which, all that is useful is also just and honest; and of what is held by the Stoics, that Nature herself proceeds contrary to justice in most of her works: and of what is received by the Cyrenaics, that there is nothing just of itself, but that customs and laws make justice: and what the Theodorians held, that theft, sacrilege, and all sorts of uncleanness, are just in a sage, if he knows them to be profitable to him." There is no remedy: I am in the same case that Alcibiades was, that I will never, if I can help it, put myself into the hands of a man who may determine as to my head; where my life and honor shall more depend upon the skill and diligence of my attorney than on my own innocence. I would venture myself with such justice as would take notice of my good deeds, as well as my ill; where I had as much to hope as to fear: indemnity is not sufficient pay to a man who does better than not to do amiss. Our justice presents to us but one hand, and that the left hand, too; let him be who he may, he shall be sure to come off with loss.

In China, of which kingdom the government and arts, without commerce with, or knowledge of ours, surpass our examples in several excellent features, and of which the history teaches me how much greater and more various the world is than either the

ancients or we have been able to penetrate, the offices deputed by the prince to visit the state of his provinces, as they punish those who behave themselves ill in their charge, so do they liberally reward those who have conducted themselves better than the common sort, and beyond the necessity of their duty; these there present themselves, not only to be approved but to get; not simply to be paid, but to have a present made to them.

No judge, thank God, has ever yet spoken to me in the quality of a judge, upon any account whatever, whether my own or that of another, whether criminal or civil; nor no prison has ever received me, not even as a visitor. Imagination renders the very outside of a jail displeasing to me; I am so enamored of liberty, that should I be interdicted the remotest corner of the Indies, I should live a little less at my ease; and while I can find earth or air open in any other part of the world, I shall never lurk in any place where I must hide myself. Good God! how ill should I endure the condition wherein I see so many people, nailed to a corner of the kingdom, deprived of the right to enter the principal cities and courts, and the liberty of the public roads, for having quarreled with our laws. If those under which I live should but wag a finger at me by way of menace, I would immediately go seek out others, let them be where they would. All my little prudence in the civil wars wherein we are now engaged, is employed that they may not hinder my liberty of coming and going.

Now, the laws keep up their credit, not for being just, but because they are laws; 'tis the mystic foundation of their authority; they have no other, and it well answers their purpose. They are often made by fools, still oftener by men who, out of hatred to equality, fail in equity; but always by men, vain and irresolute authors. There is nothing so much, nor so grossly, nor so ordinarily faulty, as the laws. Whoever obeys them because they are just, does not justly obey them as he ought. Our French laws, by their irregularity and deformity, lend, in some sort, a helping hand to the disorder and corruption that all manifest in their dispensation and execution; the command is so perplexed and inconstant, that it in some sort excuses alike disobedience, and defect in the interpre-

tation, the administration and the observation of it. What fruit, then, soever we may extract from experience, that will little advantage our institution, which we draw from foreign examples, if we make so little profit of that we have of our own, which is more familiar to us, and, doubtless, sufficient to instruct us in that whereof we have need. I study myself more than any other subject; 'tis my metaphysic, my physic.

> "Qua Deus hanc mundi temperet arte domum;
> Qua venit exoriens, qua deficit, unde coactis
> Cornibus in plenum menstrua luna redit:
> Unde salo superant venti, quid flamine captet
> Eurus, et in nubes unde perennis aqua;
> Sit ventura dies, mundi quæ subruat arces,
> Quærite, quos agitat mundi labor."

In this university, I suffer myself to be ignorantly and negligently led by the general law of the world; I shall know it well enough when I feel it; my learning cannot make it alter its course; it will not change itself for me; 'tis folly to hope it, and a greater folly to concern one's self about it, seeing it is necessarily alike, public and common. The goodness and capacity of the governor ought absolutely to discharge us of all care of the government; philosophical inquisitions and contemplations serve for no other use but to increase our curiosity. The philosophers, with great reason, send us back to the rules of nature; but they have nothing to do with so sublime a knowledge; they falsify them, and present us her face painted with too high and too adulterate a complexion, whence spring so many different pictures of so uniform a subject. As she has given us feet to walk with, so has she given us prudence to guide us in life; not so ingenious, robust, and pompous a prudence, as that of their invention; but yet one that is easy, quiet, and salutary, and that very well performs what the other promises, in him who has the good luck to know how to employ it sincerely and regularly, that is to say, according to nature. The most simply to commit one's self to nature, is to do it most wisely. Oh, what a soft, easy, and wholesome pillow is ignorance and incuriosity, whereon to repose a well-contrived head!

I had rather understand myself well in myself, than in Cicero. Of the experience I have of myself, I find enough to make me wise, if I were but a good scholar; whoever will call to mind the excess of his past anger, and to what a degree that fever transported him, will see the deformity of this passion better than in Aristotle, and conceive a more just hatred against it; whoever will remember the ills he has undergone, those that have threatened him, and the light occasions that have removed him from one state to another, will by that prepare himself for future changes, and the knowledge of his condition. The life of Cæsar has no greater example for us than our own: though popular and of command, 'tis still a life subject to all human accidents. Let us but listen to it; we apply to ourselves all whereof we have principal need; whoever shall call to memory how many and many times he has been mistaken in his own judgment, is he not a great fool if he does not ever after suspect it? When I find myself convinced, by the reason of another, of a false opinion, I do not so much learn what he has said to me that is new, and the particular ignorance—that would be no great acquisition—as, in general, I learn my own debility and the treachery of my under-standing, whence I extract the reformation of the whole mass. In all my other errors, I do the same, and find from this rule great utility to life; I regard not the species and individual, as a stone that I have stumbled at; I learn to suspect my steps throughout, and am careful to place them right. To learn that a man has said or done a foolish thing is nothing; a man must learn that he is nothing but a fool, a much more ample and important instruction. The false steps that my memory has so often made, even then when it was most secure and confident of itself, are not idly thrown away; it may now swear to me and assure me as much as it will, I shake my ears, and dare not trust it; the first opposition that is made to its testimony, puts me into suspense, and I dare not rely upon it in anything of moment, nor warrant it in another person's concerns: and were it not that what I do for want of memory, others do more often for want of good faith, I should always, in matter of fact, rather choose to take the truth from another's mouth, than from my own. If every one would pry into the effects and circumstances of the passions

[425]

that sway him, as I have done into those which I am most subject to, he would see them coming, and would a little break their impetuosity and career; they do not always seize us on a sudden; there is threatening and degrees:

"Fluctus uti primo cœpit cum albescere vento,
Paulatim sese tollit mare, et altius undas
Erigit, inde imo consurgit ad æthera fundo."

Judgment holds in me a magisterial seat; at least it carefully endeavors to make it so: it leaves my appetites to take their own course, hatred and friendship, nay even that I bear to myself, without change or corruption; if it cannot reform the other parts according to its own model, at least it suffers not itself to be corrupted by them, but plays its game apart.

That advice to every one, "to know themselves," should be of important effect, since the god of wisdom and light caused it to be written on the front of his temple, as comprehending all he had to advise us. Plato says also, that prudence is no other thing than the execution of this ordinance; and Socrates minutely verifies it in Xenophon. The difficulties and obscurity are not discerned in any science but by those who are got into it; for a certain degree of intelligence is required to be able to know that a man knows not: and we must push against a door to know whether it be bolted against us or no; whence this Platonic subtlety springs, that "neither they who know are to inquire, forasmuch as they know; nor they who do not know forasmuch as to inquire they must know what they inquire of." So in this, "of knowing a man's self," that every man is seen so resolved and satisfied with himself, that every man thinks himself sufficiently intelligent, signifies that every one knows nothing about the matter; as Socrates gives Euthydemus to understand. I, who profess nothing else, therein find so infinite a depth and variety that all the fruit I have reaped from my learning serves only to make me sensible how much I have to learn. To my weakness, so often confessed, I owe the propension I have to modesty, to the obedience of belief prescribed me, to a constant coldness and moderation of opinions, and a hatred of that trouble-

some and wrangling arrogance, wholly believing and trusting in itself, the capital enemy of discipline and truth. Do but hear them domineer; the first fopperies they utter, 'tis in the style wherewith men establish religions and laws. *"Nihil est turpius, quam cognitioni et perceptioni, assertionem approbationemque præcurrere."* Aristarchus said, that anciently there were scarce seven sages to be found in the world; and in his time scarce so many fools; have not we more reason than he to say so in this age of ours? Affirmation and obstinacy are express signs of want of wit. A fellow has stumbled and knocked his nose against the ground a hundred times in a day, and yet he will be at his Ergo's as resolute and sturdy as before; so that one would conclude he had had some new soul and vigor of understanding infused into him since, and that it happened to him, as to that ancient son of the earth, who took fresh courage and vigor by his fall:

> "Cui cum tetigere parentem.
> Jam defecta vigent renovato ropore membra:"

does not this incorrigible coxcomb think that he assumes a new understanding, by undertaking a new dispute? 'Tis by my own experience that I accuse human ignorance, which is, in my opinion, the surest part of the world's school. Such as will not conclude it in themselves, by so vain an example as mine, or their own, let them believe it from Socrates, the master of masters; for the philosopher Antisthenes, said to his disciples, "Let us go and hear Socrates: I will be a pupil with you;" and, maintaining this doctrine of the Stoic sect, "that virtue was sufficient to make a life completely happy, having no need of any other thing whatever:" except of the force of Socrates, added he.

The long attention that I employ in considering myself, also fits me to judge tolerably of others; and there are few things whereof I speak better and with better excuse. I happen very often more exactly to see and distinguish the qualities of my friends than they do themselves; I have astonished some with the pertinence of my description, and have given them warning of themselves. By having from my infancy been accustomed to contemplate my own life in

[427]

those of others, I have acquired a complexion studious in that particular; and when I am once intent upon it, I let few things about me, whether countenances, humors, or discourses, that serve to that purpose, escape me. I study all, both what I am to avoid, and what I am to follow. Also in my friends, I discover by their productions their inward inclinations; not by arranging this infinite variety of so diverse and unconnected actions into certain species and chapters, and distinctly distributing my parcels and divisions under known heads and classes;

> "Sed neque quam multæ species, et nomine quæ sint,
> Est numerus."

The wise speak, and deliver their fancies more specifically, and piece by piece; I, who see no further into things than as use informs me, present mine generally without rule and experimentally: I pronounce my opinion by disjointed articles, as a thing that cannot be spoken at once and in gross: relation and conformity are not to be found in such low and common souls as ours. Wisdom is a solid and entire building, of which every piece keeps its place and bears its mark; *"Sola sapientia in se tota conversa est."* I leave it to artists, and I know not whether or no they will be able to bring it about, in so perplexed, minute, and fortuitous a thing, to marshal into distinct bodies this infinite diversity of faces, to settle our inconstancy, and set it in order. I do not only find it hard to piece our actions to one another, but I, moreover, find it hard properly to design each by itself by any principal quality, so ambiguous and variform they are, with diverse lights. That which is remarked for rare in Perseus, king of Macedon, "that his mind fixing itself to no one condition, wandered in all sorts of living, and represented manners so wild and vagabond, that it was neither known to himself or any other what kind of man he was," seems almost to fit all the world; and, especially, I have seen another of his make, to whom I think this conclusion might more properly be applied; no moderate settledness, still running headlong from one extreme to another, upon occasions not to be guessed at; no line of path without traverse and wonderful contrariety; no one quality simple and unmixed;

so that the best guess men can one day make will be, that he affected
and studied to make himself known by being not to be known. A
man had need have sound ears to hear himself frankly criticised;
and as there are few who can endure to hear it without being
nettled, those who hazard the undertaking it to us manifest a singular effect of friendship; for 'tis to love sincerely indeed, to venture
to wound and offend us, for our own good. I think it harsh to judge
a man whose ill qualities are more than his good ones: Plato requires three things in him who will examine the soul of another:
knowledge, benevolence, boldness.

I am sometimes asked, what I should have thought myself fit for,
had any one designed to make use of me in my younger years;

> "Dum melior vires sanguis dabat, æmula necdum
> Temporibus geminis canebat sparsa senectus:"

"for nothing," say I; and I am very willing to profess not knowing
how to do anything, that I may so be excused from enslaving myself
to another. But I had told the truth to that master of mine, and had
regulated his manners, if he had so pleased; not in gross, by scholastic lessons, which I understand not, and from which I see no
true reformation spring in those that do; but by observing them by
leisure, at all opportunities, and simply and naturally judging
them as an eyewitness, distinctly one by one; giving him to understand upon what terms he was in the common opinion, in opposition
to his flatterers. There is none of us who would not be worse than
kings, if so continually corrupted as they are with that sort of
vermin; and we see that Alexander, that great king and philosopher, could not defend himself from them. I should have had
fidelity, judgment, and freedom enough for that purpose. It would
be a nameless office, otherwise it would lose its grace and its effect;
and 'tis a part that is not indifferently fit for all men: for truth
itself has not the privilege to be spoken at all times and indiscrimi-
nately: its use, noble as it is, has its circumscriptions and limits. It
often falls out, as the world goes, that a man lets it slip into the
ear of a prince, not only to no purpose, but moreover injuriously
and unjustly; and no man shall make me believe that a virtuous

remonstrance may not be viciously applied, and that the interest of the substance is not often to give way to that of the form.

For such a purpose, I would have a man who is content with his own fortune,

"Quod sit, esse velit; nihilque malit,"

and of moderate station; forasmuch as, on the one hand, he would not be afraid to touch his master's heart to the quick, for fear by that means of losing his preferment; and, on the other hand, being of no high quality, he would have more easy communication with all sorts of people. I would have this office limited to only one person; for to allow the privilege of this liberty and privacy to many, would beget an inconvenient irreverence; and of that one, I would above all things require the fidelity of silence.

A king is not to be believed, when he brags of his constancy in standing the shock of the enemy for his glory, if, for his profit and amendment, he cannot stand the liberty of a friend's advice, which has no other power but to pinch his ear, the remainder of its effect being still in his own hands. Now, there is no condition of men whatever who stand in so great need of true and free advice and warning, as they do; they sustain a public life, and have to satisfy the opinion of so many spectators, that, as those about them conceal from them whatever should divert them from their own way, they insensibly find themselves involved in the hatred and detestation of their people, often upon occasions which they might have avoided without any prejudice even of their pleasures themselves, had they been advised and set right in time. Their favorites commonly have more regard to themselves than to their master; and indeed it answers with them, forasmuch as, in truth, most offices of real friendship, when applied to the sovereign, are under a rude and dangerous hazard, so that therein there is great need, not only of very great affection and freedom, but of courage too.

In fine, all this hodge-podge which I scribble here, is nothing but a register of the essays of my own life, which, for the internal soundness, is exemplary enough, to take instruction against the grain; but as to bodily health, no man can furnish out more profit-

able experience than I, who present it pure, and no way corrupted and changed by art or opinion. Experience is properly upon its own dunghill in the subject of physic, where reason wholly gives it place: Tiberius said that whoever had lived twenty years ought to be responsible to himself for all things that were hurtful or wholesome to him, and know how to order himself without physic; and he might have learned it of Socrates, who, advising his disciples to be solicitous of their health as a chief study, added that it was hard if a man of sense, having a care to his exercise and diet, did not better know than any physician what was good or ill for him. And physic itself professes always to have experience for the test of its operations; so Plato had reason to say that, to be a right physician, it would be necessary that he who would become such, should first himself have passed through all the diseases he pretends to cure, and through all the accidents and circumstances whereof he is to judge. 'Tis but reason they should get the pox, if they will know how to cure it; for my part, I should put myself into such hands; the others but guide us, like him who paints seas and rocks and ports sitting at table, and there makes the model of a ship sailing in all security; but put him to the work itself, he knows not at which end to begin. They make such a description of our maladies, as a town-crier does of a lost horse or dog—such a color, such a height, such an ear—but bring it to him, and he knows it not, for all that. If physic should one day give me some good and visible relief, then, truly, I will cry out in good earnest:

"Tandem efficaci do manus scientiæ."

The arts that promise to keep our bodies and souls in health promise a great deal; but, withal, there are none that less keep their promise. And, in our time, those who make profession of these arts among us, less manifest the effects than any other sort of men; one may say of them, at the most, that they sell medicinal drugs; but that they are physicians, a man cannot say. I have lived long enough to be able to give an account of the custom that has carried me so far; for him who has a mind to try it, as his taster, I have made the experiment. Here are some of the articles, as my

[431]

memory shall supply me with them; I have no custom that has not varied according to circumstances; but I only record those that I have been best acquainted with, and that hitherto have had the greatest possession of me.

My form of life is the same in sickness as in health; the same bed, the same hours, the same meat, and even the same drink, serve me in both conditions alike; I add nothing to them but the moderation of more or less, according to my strength and appetite. My health is, to maintain my wonted state without disturbance. I see that sickness puts me off it on one side, and if I will be ruled by the physicians, they will put me off on the other; so that by fortune and by art I am out of my way. I believe nothing more certainly than this, that I cannot be hurt by the use of things to which I have been so long accustomed. 'Tis for custom to give a form to a man's life, such as it pleases him; she is all in all in that: 'tis the beverage of Circe, that varies our nature as she best pleases. How many nations, and but three steps from us, think the fear of the night-dew, that so manifestly is hurtful to us, a ridiculous fancy; and our own watermen and peasants laugh at it. You make a German sick if you lay him upon a mattress, as you do an Italian if you lay him on a featherbed; and a Frenchman, if without curtains or fire. A Spanish stomach cannot hold out to eat as we can; nor ours to drink like the Swiss. A German made me very merry at Augsburg, by finding fault with our hearths, by the same arguments which we commonly make use of in decrying their stoves: for, to say the truth, the smothered heat, and then the smell of that heated matter of which the fire is composed, very much offend such as are not used to them; not me; and, indeed, the heat being always equal, constant and universal, without flame, without smoke, and without the wind that comes down our chimney, they may many ways sustain comparison with ours. Why do we not imitate the Roman architecture? for they say that anciently fires were not made in the houses, but on the outside, and at the foot of them, whence the heat was conveyed to the whole fabric by pipes contrived in the wall, which were drawn twining about the rooms that were to be warmed: which I have seen plainly described somewhere in Seneca.

This German hearing me commend the conveniences and beauties of this city, which truly deserves it, began to compassionate me that I had to leave it; and the first inconvenience he alleged to me was, the heaviness of head that the chimneys elsewhere would bring upon me. He had heard some one make this complaint, and fixed it upon us, being by custom deprived of the means of perceiving it at home. All heat that comes from the fire weakens and dulls me; and yet Evenus said, that fire was the best condiment of life: I rather choose any other way of making myself warm.

We are afraid to drink our wines, when toward the bottom of the cask; in Portugal those fumes are reputed delicious, and it is the beverage of princes. In short, every nation has many customs and usages that are not only unknown to other nations, but savage and miraculous in their sight. What should we do with those people who admit of no evidence that is not in print, who believe not men if they are not in a book, nor truth, if it be not of competent age? we dignify our fopperies, when we commit them to the press: 'tis of a great deal more weight to say, "I have read such a thing," than if you only say, "I have heard such a thing." But I, who no more disbelieve a man's mouth than his pen, and who know that men write as indiscreetly as they speak, and who look upon this age as one that is past, as soon quote a friend as Aulus Gellius or Macrobius; and what I have seen, as what they have written. And, as 'tis held of virtue, that it is not greater for having continued longer, so do I hold of the truth, that for being older it is none the wiser. I often say that it is mere folly that makes us run after foreign and scholastic examples; their fertility is the same now that it was in the time of Homer and Plato. But is it not that we seek more honor from the quotation, than from the truth of the matter in hand? As if it were more to the purpose, to borrow our proofs from the shops of Vascosan or Plantin, than from what is to be seen in our own village; or else, indeed, that we have not the wit to cull out and make useful what we see before us, and to judge of it clearly enough to draw it into example; for if we say that we want authority to give faith to our testimony, we speak from the purpose; forasmuch as, in my opinion, of the most ordinary, common, and known things,

could we but find out their light, the greatest miracles of nature might be formed, and the most wonderful example, especially upon the subject of human actions.

Now, upon this subject, setting aside the examples I have gathered from books, and what Aristotle says of Andron the Argian, that he traveled over the arid sands of Lybia without drinking: a gentleman, who has very well behaved himself in several employments, said, in a place where I was, that he had ridden from Madrid to Lisbon, in the heat of summer, without any drink at all. He is very healthful and vigorous for his age, and has nothing extraordinary in the use of his life, but this, to live sometimes two or three months, nay, a whole year, as he has told me, without drinking. He is sometimes thirsty, but he lets it pass over, and he holds that it is an appetite which easily goes off of itself; and he drinks more out of caprice than either for need or pleasure.

Here is another example: 'tis not long ago that I found one of the learnedest men in France, and a man of considerable fortune, studying in a corner of a hall that they had separated for him with tapestry, and about him a rabble of his servants making all sorts of noise and confusion. He told me, and Seneca almost says the same of himself, he made an advantage of this uproar; that, beaten with this rattle, he so much the more collected and retired himself into himself for contemplation, and that this tempest of voices repercussed his thoughts within himself; when a student at Padua, he had his study so long situated amid the rattle of coaches and the tumult of the square, that he not only formed himself to the contempt, but even to the use of noise, for the service of his studies. Socrates answered Alcibiades, who was astonished how he could endure the perpetual scolding of his wife, "Why," said he, "as those do who are accustomed to the ordinary noise of wheels drawing water." I am quite otherwise; I have a tender head and easily discomposed; when 'tis bent upon anything, the least buzzing of a fly tears it into pieces.

Seneca in his youth having, by the example of Sextius, put on a positive resolution of eating nothing that had had life, and for a whole year dispensed with animal food, and, as he said, with

pleasure: only left off, that he might not be suspected of taking up this rule from some new religion by which it was prescribed: he adopted, in like manner, from the precepts of Attalus a custom not to lie upon any sort of bedding that gave way under his weight, and, even to his old age, made use of such as would not yield to any pressure. What the usage of his time made him account roughness, that of ours makes us look upon as effeminacy.

Do but observe the difference between the way of living of my laborers and my own; the Scythians and Indians have nothing more remote both from my capacity and my manners. I have picked up boys from begging, to serve me: who soon after have quitted both my kitchen and livery, only that they might return to their former course of life; and I found one afterward, picking mussels out of the sewer for his dinner, whom I could neither by entreaties nor threats reclaim from the sweetness he found in indigence. Beggars have their magnificences and delights, as well as the rich, and, 'tis said, their dignities and polities. These are effects of custom; she can mold us, not only into what form she pleases (the sages say we ought to apply ourselves to the best, which she will soon make easy to us), but also to change and variation, which is the most noble and most useful instruction of all she teaches us. The best of my bodily conditions is that I am flexible and not very obstinate: I have inclinations more my own and ordinary, and more agreeable than others; but I am diverted from them with very little ado, and easily slip into a contrary course. A young man ought to cross his own rules, to awaken his vigor and to keep it from growing faint and rusty; and there is no course of life so weak and sottish, as that which is carried on by rule and discipline;

> "Ad primum lapidem vectari quum placet, hora
> Sumitur ex libro; si prurit frictus ocelli
> Angulus, inspecta genesi, collyria quærit;"

he shall often throw himself even into excesses, if he will take my advice; otherwise the least debauch will destroy him, and render him troublesome and disagreeable in company. The worst quality in a well-bred man is over fastidiousness, and an obligation to a

certain particular way; and it is particular, if not pliable and supple. It is a kind of reproach, not to be able, or not to dare, to do what we see those about us do; let such as these stop at home. It is in every man unbecoming, but in a soldier vicious and intolerable; who, as Philopœmen said, ought to accustom himself to every variety and inequality of life.

Though I have been brought up, as much as was possible, to liberty and independence, yet so it is that, growing old, and having by indifference more settled upon certain forms (my age is now past instruction, and has henceforward nothing to do but to keep itself up as well as it can), custom has already, ere I was aware, so imprinted its character in me, in certain things, that I look upon it as a kind of excess to leave them off; and, without a force upon myself, cannot sleep in the day-time, nor eat between meals, nor breakfast, nor go to bed, without a great interval between eating and sleeping, as of three hours after supper; nor get children but before I sleep, nor standing upon my feet; nor endure my own sweat; nor quench my thirst either with pure water or pure wine; nor keep my head long bare, nor cut my hair after dinner; and I should be as uneasy without my gloves as without my shirt, or without washing when I rise from table or out of my bed; and I could not lie without a canopy and curtains, as if they were essential things. I could dine without a tablecloth, but without a clean napkin, after the German fashion, very incommodiously; I foul them more than the Germans or Italians do, and make but little use either of spoon or fork. I am sorry they did not keep up the fashion, begun after the example of kings, to change our napkins at every service, as they do our plates. We are told of that laborious soldier Marius, that growing old, he became nice in his drink, and never drank but out of a particular cup of his own: I, in like manner, have suffered myself to fancy a certain form of glasses, and not willingly to drink in common glasses, nor more than from a strange common hand: all metal offends me in comparison of a clear and transparent matter: let my eyes taste too, according to their capacity. I owe several other such niceties to custom. Nature has also, on the other side, helped me to some of hers; as not to be able to endure more

than two full meals in one day, without overcharging my stomach, nor a total abstinence from one of those meals without filling myself with wind, drying up my mouth, and dulling my appetite; the finding great inconvenience from overmuch evening air; for of late years in night marches, which often happen to be all night long, after five or six hours my stomach begins to be queasy, with a violent pain in my head, so that I always vomit before the day can break. When the others go to breakfast, I go to sleep; and when I rise, I am as brisk and gay as before. I had always been told that the night dew never rises but in the beginning of the night; but for some years past, long and familiar intercourse with a lord, possessed with the opinion that the night dew is more sharp and dangerous about the declining of the sun, an hour or two before it sets, which he carefully avoids, and despises that of the night, he almost impressed upon me, not so much his reasoning as his experiences. What, shall mere doubt and inquiry strike our imagination, so as to change us? Such as absolutely and on a sudden give way to these propensions, draw total destruction upon themselves. I am sorry for several gentlemen who, through the folly of their physicians have in their youth and health wholly shut themselves up; it were better to endure a cough, than, by disuse, forever to lose the commerce of common life in things of so great utility. Malignant science to interdict us the most pleasant hours of the day! Let us keep our possession to the last; for the most part, a man hardens himself by being obstinate and corrects his constitution, as Cæsar did the falling-sickness, by dint of contempt. A man should addict himself to the best rules, but not enslave himself to them, except to such, if there be any such, where obligation and servitude are of profit.

Both kings and philosophers go to stool, and ladies too; public lives are bound to ceremony; mine, that is obscure and private, enjoys all natural dispensation; soldier and Gascon are also qualities a little subject to indiscretion; wherefore I shall say of this act of relieving nature, that it is desirable to refer it to certain prescribed and nocturnal hours, and compel one's self to this by custom, as I have done; but not to subject one's self, as I have done

in my declining years, to a particular convenience of place and seat for that purpose, and make it troublesome by long sitting: and yet, in the fouler offices, is it not in some measure excusable to require more care and cleanliness? *"Natura homo mundum et elegans animal est."* Of all the actions of nature, I am the most impatient of being interrupted in that. I have seen many soldiers troubled with the unruliness of their bellies; whereas mine and I never fail of our punctual assignation, which is at leaping out of bed, if some indispensable business or sickness does not molest us.

I think then, as I said before, that sick men cannot better place themselves anywhere in more safety, than in sitting still in that course of life wherein they have been bred and trained up; change, be it what it will, distempers and puts one out. Do you believe that chestnuts can hurt a Perigourdin or a Lucchese, or milk and cheese the mountain people? We enjoin them not only a new, but a contrary, method of life; a change that the healthful cannot endure. Prescribe water to a Breton of three score and ten; shut a seaman up in a stove; forbid a Basque footman to walk: you will deprive them of motion, and in the end of air and light.

> "An vivere tanti est?
> Cogimur a suetis animum suspendere rebus,
> Atque, ut vivamus, vivere desinimus. . . .
> Hos superesse reor, quibus et spirabilis aer
> Et lux, qua regimur, redditur ipsa gravis."

If they do no other good, they do this at least, that they prepare patients betimes for death, by little and little undermining and cutting off the use of life.

Both well and sick, I have ever willingly suffered myself to obey the appetites that pressed upon me. I give great authority to my propensions and desires; I do not love to cure one disease by another; I hate remedies that are more troublesome than the disease itself. To be subject to the stone and subject to abstain from eating oysters, are two evils instead of one: the disease torments us on the one side, and the remedy on the other. Since we are ever in danger of mistaking, let us rather run the hazard of a

mistake, after we have had the pleasure. The world proceeds quite
the other way, and thinks nothing profitable that is not painful;
it has great suspicion of facility. My appetite, in various things,
has of its own accord happily enough accommodated itself to the
health of my stomach. Relish and pungency in sauces were pleasant
to me when young but my stomach disliking them since, my taste
incontinently followed. Wine is hurtful to sick people, and 'tis the
first thing that my mouth then finds distasteful, and with an invincible dislike. Whatever I take against my liking, does me harm;
and nothing hurts me, that I eat with appetite and delight. I never
received harm by any action that was very pleasant to me; and
accordingly have made all medicinal conclusions largely give way
to my pleasure; and I have, when I was young,

> "Quem circumcursans huc atque huc sæpe Cupido
> Fulgebat crocina splendidus in tunica,"

given myself the rein as licentiously and inconsiderately to the
desire that was predominant in me, *"Et militavi non sine gloria,"*
as any other whomsoever; yet more in continuation and holding out,
than in sally:

> "Sex me vix memini sustinuisse vices."

'Tis certainly a misfortune and a miracle at once, to confess at
what a tender age I first came under the subjection of love: it was
indeed, by chance; for it was long before the years of choice or
knowledge; I do not remember myself so far back; and my fortune
may well be coupled with that of Quartilla, who could not remember when she was a maid:

> "Inde tragus, celeresque pili, mirandaque matri
> Barba meæ."

Physicians modify their rules according to the violent longings
that happen to sick persons, ordinarily with good success; this great
desire cannot be imagined so strange and vicious, but that nature
must have a hand in it. And then how easy a thing is it to satisfy
the fancy? In my opinion, this part wholly carries it, at least, above
all the rest. The most grievous and ordinary evils are those that

fancy loads us with; this Spanish saying mightily pleases in several senses; *"Defienda me Dios de my."* I am sorry when I am sick, that I have not some longing that might give me the pleasure of satisfying it; all the rules of physic would hardly be able to divert me from it. I do the same when I am well; I can see very little more to be hoped or wished for. 'Twere pity a man should be so weak and languishing, as not to have even wishing left to him.

The art of physic is not so fixed, that we need be without authority for whatever we do; it changes according to climates and moons; according to Fernel and to Scaliger. If your physician does not think it good for you to sleep, to drink wine, or to eat such and such meats, never trouble yourself; I will find you another that shall not be of his opinion; the diversity of medical arguments and opinions embraces all sorts of forms. I saw a miserable sick person panting and burning for thirst, that he might be cured, who was afterward laughed at for his pains by another physician, who condemned that advice as prejudicial to him: had he not tormented himself to good purpose? There lately died of the stone, a man of that profession, who had made use of extreme abstinence to contend with his disease: his fellow-physicians say that, on the contrary, this abstinence had dried him up, and baked the gravel in his kidneys.

I have observed, that both in wounds and sicknesses, speaking discomposes and hurts me, as much as any irregularity I can commit. My voice pains and tires me, for 'tis loud and forced; so that when I have gone to whisper some great persons about affairs of consequence, they have often desired me to moderate my voice.

This story deserves a place here. Someone in a certain Greek school speaking loud as I do, the master of the ceremonies sent to him to speak softly: "Tell him, then, he must send me," replied the other, "the tone he would have me speak in." To which the other replied, "That he should take the tone from the ears of him to whom he spake." It was well said, if to be understood: "Speak according to the affair you are speaking about to your auditor," for if it mean, " 'tis sufficient that he hear you; or, govern yourself by him," I do not find it to be reason. The tone and motion of my voice carries with it a great deal of the expression and signification

of my meaning, and 'tis I who am to govern it, to make myself understood: there is a voice to instruct, a voice to flatter, and a voice to reprehend. I will not only that my voice reach him, but, peradventure, that it strike and pierce him. When I rattle my footman with sharp and bitter language, it would be very pretty for him to say, "Pray, master, speak lower, I hear you very well." *"Est quædam vox ad auditum accommodata, non magnitudine, sed proprietate."* Speaking is half his who speaks, and half his who hears; the latter ought to prepare himself to receive it, according to its bias; as with tennis players, he who receives the ball, shifts and prepares, according as he sees him move who strikes the stroke, and according to the stroke itself.

Experience has, moreover, taught me this, that we ruin ourselves by impatience. Evils have their life and limits, their diseases and their recovery.

The constitution of maladies is formed by the pattern of the constitution of animals; they have their fortune and their days limited from their birth; he who attempts imperiously to cut them short by force in the middle of their course, lengthens and multiplies them, and incenses instead of appeasing them. I am of Brantor's opinion, that "we are neither obstinately and willfully to oppose evils, nor truckle under them for want of courage; but that we are naturally to give way to them, according to their condition and our own." We ought to grant free passage to diseases; I find they stay less with me, who let them alone; and I have lost some, reputed the most tenacious and obstinate, by their own decay, without help and without art, and contrary to its rules. Let us a little permit Nature to take her own way; she better understands her own affairs than we. "But such an one died;" and so shall you: if not of that disease, of another. And how many have not escaped dying, who have had three physicians always at their tails? Example is a vague and universal mirror, and of various reflections. If it be a delicious medicine, take it: 'tis always so much present good. I will never stick at the name nor the color, if it be pleasant and grateful to the palate: pleasure is one of the chiefest kinds of profit. I have suffered colds, gouty defluxions, relaxations, palpi-

tations of the heart, meagrims, and other accidents, to grow old
and die in time a natural death; I have so lost them when I was half
fit to keep them: they are sooner prevailed upon by courtesy than
huffing. We must patiently suffer the laws of our condition; we are
born to grow old, to grow weak, and to be sick, in despite of all
medicine. 'Tis the first lesson the Mexicans teach their children;
so soon as ever they are born they thus salute them: "Thou art
come into the world, child, to endure: endure, suffer and say
nothing." 'Tis injustice to lament that which has befallen any one,
which may befall every one: *"Indignare, si quid in te inique pro-
prie constitutum est."*

See an old man who begs of God that he will maintain his health
vigorous and entire; that is to say, that he restore him to youth:

"Stulte, quid hæc frustra votis puerilibus optas?"

is it not folly? his condition is not capable of it. The gout, the stone,
and indigestion are symptoms of long years; as heat, rains, and
winds are of long journeys. Plato does not believe that Æsculapius
troubled himself to provide, by regimen to prolong life in a weak
and wasted body, useless to his country and to his profession, or to
beget healthful and robust children; and does not think this care
suitable to the divine justice and prudence, which is to direct all
things to utility. My good friend, your business is done; nobody
can restore you; they can, at the most, but patch you up, and prop
you a little, and by that means prolong your misery an hour or two:

"Non secus instantem cupiens fulcire ruinam,
　　Diversis contra nititur obiicibus;
　Donec certa dies, omni campage soluta,
　　Ipsum cum rebus subruat auxilium."

We must learn to suffer what we cannot evade; our life, like the
harmony of the world, is composed of contrary things—of diverse
tones, sweet and harsh, sharp and flat, sprightly and solemn: the
musician who should only effect some of these, what would he be
able to do? he must know how to make use of them all, and to mix
them; and so we should mingle the goods and evils which are consubstantial with our life; our being cannot subsist without this

mixture, and the one part is no less necessary to it than the other. To attempt to kick against natural necessity, is to represent the folly of Ctesiphon who undertook to kick with his mule.

I consult little about the alterations I feel; for these doctors take advantage; when they have you at their mercy, they cudgel your ears with their prognostics; and having once surprised me, weakened with sickness, injuriously handled me with their dogmas and magisterial fopperies—one while menacing me with great pains, and another with approaching death—by which threats I was indeed moved and shaken, but not subdued nor jostled from my place; and though my judgment was neither altered nor distracted, yet it was at least disturbed; 'tis always agitation and combat.

Now, I use my imagination as gently as I can, and would discharge it, if I could, of all trouble and contest; a man must assist, flatter, and deceive it, if he can; my mind is fit for that office; it needs no appearances throughout; could it persuade as it preaches, it would successfully relieve me. Will you have an example? It tells me: "that 'tis for my good to have the stone; that the structure of my age must naturally suffer some decay, and it is now time it should begin to disjoin and to confess a breach; 'tis a common necessity, and there is nothing in it either miraculous or new; I therein pay what is due to old age, and I cannot expect a better bargain; that society ought to comfort me, being fallen into the most common infirmity of my age; I see everywhere men tormented with the same disease, and am honored by the fellowship, forasmuch as men of the best quality are most frequently afflicted with it; 'tis a noble and dignified disease; that of such as are struck with it, few have it to a less degree of pain; that these are put to the trouble of a strict diet and the daily taking of nauseous potions, whereas I owe my better state purely to my good fortune; for some ordinary broths of Eringo or burst-wort that I have twice or thrice taken to oblige the ladies who, with greater kindness than my pain was sharp, would needs present me half of theirs, seemed to me equally easy to take and fruitless in operation, the others have to pay a thousand vows to Æsculapius, and as many crowns to their physicians, for the voiding a little gravel, which I often

do by the aid of nature; even the decorum of my countenance is not disturbed in company; and I can hold my water ten hours, and as long as any man that is in perfect health. The fear of this disease," says mind, "formerly affrighted thee, when it was unknown to thee; the cries and despairing groans of those who make it worse by their impatience, begot a horror in thee. 'Tis an infirmity that punishes the members by which thou hast most offended. Thou art a conscientious fellow:"

Que venit indigne pœna, dolenda venit."

"consider this chastisement; 'tis very easy in comparison of others, and inflicted with a paternal tenderness; do but observe how late it comes; it only seizes on and incommodes that part of thy life, which is, one way and another sterile and lost; having, as it were by composition, given time for the license and pleasures of thy youth. The fear and the compassion that the people have of this disease serve thee for matter of glory; a quality, whereof if thou hast thy judgment purified, and that thy reason has somewhat cured it, thy friends, notwithstanding, discern some tincture in thy complexion. 'Tis a pleasure to hear it said of one's self: what strength of mind, what patience! Thou art seen to sweat with pain, to turn pale and red, to tremble, to vomit blood, to suffer strange contractions and convulsions, at times to let great tears drop from thine eyes, to urine thick, black, and dreadful water, or to have it suppressed by some sharp and craggy stone, that cruelly pricks and tears the neck of the bladder, while all the while thou entertainest the company with an ordinary countenance; drolling by fits with thy people; making one in a continuous discourse, now and then making excuse for thy pain, and representing thy suffering less than it is. Dost thou call to mind the men of past time, who so greedily sought diseases to keep their virtue in breath and exercise? Put the case that nature sets thee on and impels thee to this glorious school, into which thou wouldst never have entered of thy own free will. If thou tellest me that it is a dangerous and mortal disease, what others are not so? for 'tis a physical cheat to except any that they say do not go direct to death; what matters if they go

thither by accident, or if they easily slide and slip into the path that leads us to it? But thou dost not die because thou art sick; thou diest because thou art living; death kills thee without the help of sickness; and sickness has deferred death in some, who have lived longer by reason that they thought themselves always dying; to which may be added, that as in wounds, so in diseases, some are medicinal and wholesome. The stone is often no less long-lived than you; we see men with whom it has continued from their infancy even to their extreme old age; and if they had not broken company, it would have been with them longer still; you more often kill it than it kills you. And though it should present to you the image of approaching death, were it not a good office to a man of such an age, to put him in mind of his end? And, which is worse, thou hast no longer anything that should make thee desire to be cured. Whether or no, common necessity will soon call thee away. Do but consider how skillfully and gently she puts thee out of concern with life, and weans thee from the world; not forcing thee with a tyrannical subjection, like so many other infirmities which thou seest old men afflicted withal, that hold them in continual torment, and keep them in perpetual and unintermitted weakness and pains, but by warnings and instructions at intervals, intermixing long pauses of repose, as it were to give thee opportunity to meditate and ruminate upon thy lesson, at thy own ease and leisure. To give thee means to judge aright, and to assume the resolution of a man of courage, it presents to thee the state of thy entire condition, both in good and evil; and one while a very cheerful and another an insupportable life, in one and the same day. If thou embracest not death, at least thou shakest hands with it once a month; whence thou hast more cause to hope that it will one day surprise thee without menace; and that being so often conducted to the water side, but still thinking thyself to be upon the accustomed terms, thou and thy confidence will at one time or another be unexpectedly wafted over. A man cannot reasonably complain of diseases that fairly divide the time with health."

I am obliged to fortune for having so often assaulted me with the same sort of weapons; she forms and fashions me by use,

hardens and habituates me, so that I can know within a little for how much I shall be quit. For want of natural memory, I make one of paper; and as any new symptom happens in my disease, I set it down, whence it falls out that, having now almost passed through all sorts of examples, if anything astounding threatens me, turning over these little loose notes, as the Sybil's leaves, I never fail of finding matter of consolation from some favorable prognostic in my past experience. Custom also makes me hope better for the time to come; for, the conduct of this clearing out having so long continued, 'tis to be believed that nature will not alter her course, and that no other worse accident will happen than what I already feel. And besides, the condition of this disease is not unsuitable to my prompt and sudden complexion; when it assaults me gently, I am afraid, for 'tis then for a great while; but it has, naturally, brisk and vigorous excesses; it claws me to purpose for a day or two. My kidneys held out an age without alteration; and I have now almost lived another, since they changed their state; evils have their periods, as well as goods; peradventure, the infirmity draws toward an end. Age weakens the heat of my stomach, and its digestion being less perfect sends this crude matter to my kidneys; why, at a certain revolution, may not the heat of my kidneys be also abated, so that they can no more petrify my phlegm, and nature find out some other way of purgation. Years have evidently helped me to drain certain rheums; and why not these excrements which furnish matter for gravel? But is there anything delightful in comparison of this sudden change, when from an excessive pain, I come, by the voiding of a stone, to recover, as by a flash of lightning, the beautiful light of health, so free and full, as it happens in our sudden and sharpest colics? Is there anything in the pain suffered, that one can counterpoise to the pleasure of so sudden an amendment? Oh, how much does health seem the more pleasant to me, after a sickness so near and so contiguous, that I can distinguish them in the presence of one another, in their greatest show; when they appear in emulation, as if to make head against and dispute it with one another! As the Stoics say that vices are profitably introduced to give value to and to set off

virtue, we can, with better reason and less temerity of conjecture, say that nature has given us pain for the honor and service of pleasure and indolence. When Socrates, after his fetters were knocked off, felt the pleasure of that itching which the weight of them had caused in his legs, he rejoiced to consider the strict alliance between pain and pleasure; how they are linked together by a necessary connection, so that by turns they follow and mutually beget one another; and cried out to the good fellow Æsop, that he ought out of this consideration, to have taken matter for a fine fable.

The worst that I see in other diseases is, that they are not so grievous in their effect, as they are in their issue: a man is a whole year in recovering, and all the while full of weakness and fear. There is so much hazard, and so many steps to arrive at safety, that there is no end on't: before they have unmuffled you of a kerchief, and then of a cap, before they allow you to walk abroad and take the air, to drink wine, to lie with your wife, or eat melons, 'tis odds you relapse into some new distemper. The stone has this privilege, that it carries itself clean off: whereas the other maladies always leave behind them some impression and alteration that render the body subject to a new disease, and lend a hand to one another. Those are excusable that content themselves with possessing us, without extending farther, and introducing their followers; but courteous and kind are those whose passage brings us any profitable issue. Since I have been troubled with the stone, I find myself freed from all other accidents, much more, methinks, than I was before, and have never had any fever since; I argue that the extreme and frequent vomitings that I am subject to, purge me: and, on the other hand, my distastes for this and that, and the strange fasts I am forced to keep, digest my peccant humors, and nature, with those stones, voids whatever there is in me superfluous and hurtful. Let them never tell me that it is a medicine too dear bought: for what avail so many stinking draughts, so many caustics, incisions, sweats, setons, diets, and so many other methods of cure, which often, by reason we are not able to undergo their violence and importunity, bring us to our graves? So that when

I have the stone, I look upon it as physic; when free from it, as an absolute deliverance.

And here is another particular benefit of my disease; which is, that it always plays its game by itself, and lets me play mine, if I have only courage to do it; for, in its greatest fury, I have endured it ten hours together on horseback. Do but endure only; you need no other regimen: play, run, dine, do this and t'other, if you can; your debauch will do you more good than harm; say as much to one that has the pox, the gout, or hernia. The other diseases have more universal obligations; rack our actions after another kind of manner, disturb our whole order, and to their consideration engage the whole state of life: this only pinches the skin; it leaves the understanding and the will wholly at our own disposal, and the tongue, the hands, and the feet; it rather awakens than stupefies you. The soul is struck with the ardor of a fever, overwhelmed with an epilepsy, and displaced by a sharp megrim, and, in short, astounded by all the diseases that hurt the whole mass, and the most noble parts; this never meddles with the soul; if anything goes amiss with her, 'tis her own fault, she betrays, dismounts, and abandons herself. There are none but fools who suffer themselves to be persuaded, that this hard and massive body which is baked in our kidneys is to be dissolved by drinks; wherefore, when it is once stirred, there is nothing to be done but to give it passage; and, for that matter, it will itself make one.

I moreover observe this particular convenience in it, that it is a disease wherein we have little to guess at: we are dispensed from the trouble into which other diseases throw us by the uncertainty of their causes, conditions, and progress; a trouble that is infinitely painful: we have no need of consultations and doctoral interpretations; the senses well enough inform us both what it is and where it is.

By such like arguments, weak and strong, as Cicero with the disease of his old age, I try to rock asleep and amuse my imagination, and to dress its wounds. If I find them worse to-morrow, I will provide new stratagems. That this is true: I am come to that pass of late, that the least motion forces pure blood out of my kidneys:

what of that? I move about, nevertheless, as before, and ride after my hounds with a juvenile and insolent ardor; and hold that I have very good satisfaction for an accident of that importance, when it costs me no more but a dull heaviness and uneasiness in that part; 'tis some great stone that wastes and consumes the substance of my kidneys and my life, which I by little and little evacuate, not without some natural pleasure, as an excrement henceforward superfluous and troublesome. Now if I feel anything stirring, do not fancy that I trouble myself to consult my pulse or my urine, thereby to put myself upon some annoying prevention; I shall soon enough feel the pain, without making it more and longer, by the disease of fear. He who fears he shall suffer, already suffers what he fears. To which may be added, that the doubts and ignorance of those who take upon them to expound the designs of nature and her internal progressions, and the many false prognostics of their art, ought to give us to understand that her ways are inscrutable and utterly unknown; there is great uncertainty, variety, and obscurity in what she either promises or threatens. Old age excepted, which is an indubitable sign of the approach of death, in all other accidents I see few signs of the future, whereon we may ground our divination. I only judge of myself by actual sensation, not by reasoning: to what end, since I am resolved to bring nothing to it but expectation and patience? Will you know how much I get by this? observe those who do otherwise, and who rely upon so many diverse persuasions and counsels; how often the imagination presses upon them, without any bodily pain. I have many times amused myself, being well and in safety, and quite free from these dangerous attacks, in communicating them to the physicians as then beginning to discover themselves in me; I underwent the decree of their dreadful conclusions, being, all the while quite at my ease, and so much the more obliged to the favor of God, and better satisfied of the vanity of this art.

There is nothing that ought so much to be recommended to youth as activity and vigilance: our life is nothing but movement. I bestir myself with great difficulty, and am slow in everything, whether in rising, going to bed, or eating: seven of the clock in the morning is

early for me; and where I rule, I never dine before eleven, nor sup till after six. I formerly attributed the cause of the fevers and other diseases I fell into, to the heaviness that long sleeping had brought upon me; and have ever repented going to sleep again in the morning. Plato is more angry at excess of sleeping, than at excess of drinking. I love to lie hard and alone, even without my wife, as kings do; and well covered with clothes. They never warm my bed, but since I have grown old, they give me at need warm cloths to lay at my feet and stomach. They found fault with the great Scipio, that he was a great sleeper; not, in my opinion, for any other reason, than that men were displeased, that he alone should have nothing in him to be found fault with. If I am anything fastidious in my way of living, 'tis rather in my lying than anything else; but, generally, I give way and accommodate myself, as well as any one, to necessity. Sleeping has taken up a great part of my life, and I yet continue, at the age I now am, to sleep eight or nine hours together. I wean myself to my advantage, from this propension to sloth, and am evidently the better for so doing. I find the change a little hard indeed, but in three days 'tis over; and I see but few who live with less sleep, when need requires, and who more constantly exercise themselves, or to whom long journeys are less troublesome. My body is capable of a firm, but not of a violent or sudden agitation. I evade of late violent exercises, and such as make me sweat, wherein my limbs grow weary before they are hot. I can stand a whole day together, and am never weary of walking: but from my youth, I have ever preferred to ride upon paved roads; on foot, I get up to the breech in dirt; and little fellows as I am are subject in the streets to be elbowed and jostled, for want of presence; I have ever loved to repose myself, whether sitting or lying, with my heels as high or higher than my seat.

There is no profession more pleasant than the military, a profession both noble in its execution (for valor is the stoutest, proudest, and most generous of all virtues), and noble in its cause: there is no utility either more universal or more just, than the protection of the peace and grandeur of one's country. The company of so

many noble, young, and active men delights you: the ordinary sight of so many tragic spectacles; the freedom of the conversation, without art; a masculine and unceremonious way of living, please you; the variety of a thousand several actions; the encouraging harmony of martial music, that ravishes and inflames both your ears and souls; the honor of this occupation, nay, even its hardships and difficulties, which Plato holds so light that, in his Republic, he makes women and children share in them, are delightful to you. You put yourselves voluntarily upon particular exploits and hazards, according as you judge of their luster and importance; and, a volunteer, find even life itself excusably employed,

"Pulchrumque mori succurrit in armis."

To fear common dangers that concern so great a multitude of men; not to dare to do what so many sorts of souls, what a whole people dare, is for a heart that is poor and mean beyond all measure: company encourages even children. If others excel you in knowledge, in gracefulness, in strength, or fortune, you have third causes to blame for that; but to give place to them in stability of mind, you can blame no one for that but yourself. Death is more abject, more languishing and troublesome in bed than in battle; fevers and catarrhs as painful and mortal as a musket-shot. Whoever has fortified himself valiantly to bear the accidents of common life, need not raise his courage to be a soldier. *"Vivere, mi Lucili, militare est."*

I do not remember that I ever had the itch; and yet scratching is one of nature's sweetest gratifications, and nearest at hand; but the smart follows too near. I use it most in my ears, which are often apt to itch.

I came into the world with all my senses entire, even to perfection. My stomach is commodiously good, as also is my head and my breath; and, for the most part, uphold themselves so in the height of fevers. I have passed the age to which some nations, not without reason, have prescribed so just a term of life, that they would not suffer men to exceed it; and yet I have some intermissions, though short and inconstant, so clean and sound as to be

[451]

little inferior to the health and pleasantness of my youth. I do not speak of vigor and sprightliness; 'tis not reason they should follow me beyond their limits:

"Non hoc amplius est liminis, aut aquæ,
    Cœlestis, patiens latus."

My face and eyes presently discover my condition; all my alteration begin there, and appear somewhat worse than they really are; my friends often pity me, before I feel the cause in myself. My looking-glass does not frighten me: for even in my youth it has befallen me more than once to have a scurvy complexion and of ill prognostic, without any great consequence, so that the physicians, not finding any cause within answerable to that outward alteration, attributed it to the mind and to some secret passion that tormented me within; but they were deceived. If my body would govern itself as well, according to my rule, as my mind does, we should move a little more at our ease. My mind was then not only free from trouble, but, moreover, full of joy and satisfaction, as it commonly is, half by its complexion, half by its design:

"Nec vitiant artus ægræ contagia mentis."

I am of the opinion that this temperature of my soul has often raised my body from its lapses; this is often depressed; if the other be not brisk and gay, 'tis at least tranquil and at rest. I had a quartan ague four or five months, that made me look miserably ill; my mind was always, if not calm, yet pleasant. If the pain be without me, the weakness and languor do not much afflict me; I see various corporal faintings, that beget a horror in me but to name, which yet I should less fear than a thousand passions and agitations of the mind that I see about me. I make up my mind no more to run; 'tis enough that I can crawl along; nor do I more complain of the natural decadence that I feel in myself:

"Quis tumidum guttur miratur in Alpibus?"

than I regret that my duration shall not be as long and entire as that of an oak.

I have no reason to complain of my imagination; I have had few thoughts in my life that have so much as broken my sleep, except those of desire, which have awakened without afflicting me. I dream but seldom, and then of chimeras and fantastic things, commonly produced from pleasant thoughts, and rather ridiculous than sad; and I believe it to be true that dreams are faithful interpreters of our inclinations; but there is art required to sort and understand them:

"Res, quæ in vita usurpant homines, cogitant, curant, vident,
Quæque agunt vigilantes, agitantque, ea si cui in somno accidunt,
Minus mirandum est."

Plato moreover says, that 'tis the office of prudence to draw instructions of divination of future things from dreams; I don't know about this, but there are wonderful instances of it that Socrates, Xenophon, and Aristotle, men of irreproachable authority, relate. Historians say that the Atlantes never dream; who also never eat any animal food, which I add, forasmuch as it is, peradventure, the reason why they never dream, for Pythagoras ordered a certain preparation of diet to beget appropriate dreams. Mine are very gentle, without any agitation of body or expression of voice. I have seen several of my time wonderfully disturbed by them. Theon, the philosopher, walked in his sleep, and so did Pericles' servant, and that upon the tiles and top of the house.

I hardly ever choose my dish at table, but take the next at hand, and unwillingly change it for another. A confusion of meats and a clutter of dishes displease me as much as any other confusion; I am easily satisfied with few dishes; and am an enemy to the opinion of Favorinus that in a feast they should snatch from you the meat you like, and set a plate of another sort before you; and that 'tis a pitiful supper, if you do not sate your guests with the rumps of various fowls, the beccafico only deserving to be all eaten. I usually eat salt meats, and yet I love bread that has no salt in it; and my baker never sends up other to my table, contrary to the custom of the country. In my infancy, what they had most to correct in me was the refusal of things that children com-

monly best love, as sugar, sweetmeats, and march-panes. My tutor contended with this aversion to delicate things, as a kind of over-nicety; and indeed 'tis nothing else but a difficulty of taste, in any-thing it applies itself to. Whoever cures a child of an obstinate liking for brown bread, bacon, or garlic, cures him also of pamper-ing his palate. There are some who affect temperance and plainness, by wishing for beef and ham among pheasant and partridge; 'tis all very fine; this is delicacy upon delicacies; 'tis the taste of effemi-nacy that disrelishes ordinary and accustomed things; *"Per quæ luxuria divitiarum tædio ludit."* Not to make good cheer with what another is enjoying, and to be curious in what a man eats, is the essence of this vice:

> *"Si modica coenare times olus omne patella."*

There is, indeed, this difference, that, 'tis better to oblige one's appetite to things that are most easy to be had, but 'tis always vice to oblige one's self: I formerly said a kinsman of mine was over-nice, who, by being in our galleys, had unlearned the use of beds and to undress when he went to sleep.

If I had any sons I should willingly wish them my fortune: the good father that God gave me, who has nothing of me but the acknowledgment of his goodness, but truly 'tis a very hearty one, sent me from my cradle to be brought up in a poor village of his, and there continued me all the while I was at nurse, and still longer, bringing me up to the meanest and the most common way of living: *"Magna pars libertatis est bene moratus venter."* Never take upon yourselves, and much less give up to your wives, the care of their nourishment; leave this to fortune, under popular and natural laws; leave it to custom to train them up to frugality and hardship, that they may rather descend from rigors than mount up to them. This humor of his yet aimed at another end to make me familiar with the people and the condition of men who most need our assistance; considering that I should rather regard them who extend their arms to me, than those who turn their backs upon me; and for this reason it was, that he provided me godfathers of the meanest fortune, to oblige and attach me to them.

Nor has his design succeeded altogether ill: for, whether upon the account of the more honor in such a condescension, or out of a natural compassion that has a very great power over me, I have an inclination toward the meaner sort of people. The faction which I should condemn in our civil wars, I should more sharply condemn, flourishing and successful; it would half reconcile me to it, should I see it miserable and overwhelmed. How much do I admire the generous humor of Chelonis, daughter and wife to kings of Sparta! while her husband, Cleombrotus, in the commotion of her city, had the advantage over Leonidas, her father, she, like a good daughter, stuck close to her father in all his misery and exile, in opposition to the conqueror. But so soon as the chance of war turned, she changed her will with the change of fortune, and bravely turned to her husband's side, whom she accompanied throughout where his ruin carried him; admitting, as it appears to me, no other choice than to cleave to the side that stood most in need of her, and where she could best manifest her compassion. I am naturally more apt to follow the example of Flaminius, who rather gave his assistance to those who had most need of him than to those who had power to do him good, than I do to that of Pyrrhus, who was of an humor to truckle under the great, and to domineer over the poor.

Long sittings at meat both trouble me and do me harm; for, be it for want of moderation, or that I was so accustomed when a child, I eat all the while I sit. Therefore it is that at my own house, though the meals there are of the shortest, I usually sit down a little while after the rest, after the manner of Augustus: but I do not imitate him in rising also before the rest of the company; on the contrary, I love to sit still a long time after, and to hear them talk, provided I am none of the talkers; for I tire and hurt myself with speaking upon a full stomach, as much as I find it pleasant and very wholesome to argue and to strain my voice before dinner.

The ancient Greeks and Romans had more reason than we in sitting apart for eating, which is a principal action of life, if they were not prevented by other extraordinary business, many hours and the greatest part of the night; eating and drinking more delib-

erately than we do, who perform all our actions post-haste; and in extending this natural pleasure to more leisure and better use, intermixing with their meals pleasant and profitable conversation.

They whose concern it is to have a care of me, may very easily hinder me from eating anything they think will do me harm; for in such matters I never covet nor miss anything I do not see; but withal, if it once comes in my sight, 'tis in vain to persuade me to forbear; so that when I design to fast, I must be kept apart from the supper-table, and must have only so much given me, as is required for a prescribed collation; for if I sit down to table, I forget my resolution. When I order my cook to alter the manner of dressing any dish, all my family know what it means, that my stomach is out of order, and that I shall not touch it.

I love to have all meats, that will endure it, very little boiled or roasted, and prefer them very high, and even, as to several, quite gone. Nothing but hardness generally offends me (of any other quality I am as patient and indifferent as any man I have known); so that, contrary to the common humor, even in fish it often happens that I find them both too fresh and too firm: not for want of teeth, which I ever had good, even to excellence, and which age does but now begin to threaten: I have always been used every morning to rub them with a napkin, and before and after dinner. God is favorable to those whom he makes to die by degrees; 'tis the only benefit of old age; the last death will be so much the less painful; it will kill but a quarter of a man or but half a one at most. I have one tooth lately fallen out without drawing and without pain: it was the natural term of its duration; and that part of my being and several others, are already dead, others half dead, of those that were most active, and in highest esteem during my vigorous years; 'tis so I melt and steal away from myself. What a folly it would be in my understanding, to apprehend the height of this fall, already so much advanced, as if it were from the very top! I hope I shall not. I, in truth, receive a principal consolation in meditating my death, that it will be just and natural, and that henceforward I cannot herein either require or hope from destiny any other but unlawful favor. Men make themselves believe that

we formerly had, as greater stature, so, longer lives, but they deceive themselves; and Solon, who was of those elder times, limits the duration of life to threescore and ten years. I, who have so much and so universally adored that ἄριστον μέτρον of ancient times; and who have concluded the most moderate measures to be the most perfect, shall I pretend to an immeasurable and prodigious old age? Whatever happens contrary to the course of nature, may be troublesome; but what comes according to her, should always be pleasant: *"Omnia, quæ secundum naturam fiunt, sunt habenda in bonis."* And so Plato likewise says, that the death which is occasioned by wounds and diseases is violent; but that which comes upon us, old age conducting us to it, is of all others the most easy, and in some sort delicious. *"Vitam adolescentibus vis aufert, senibus maturitas."* Death mixes and confounds itself throughout with life; decay anticipates its hour, and shoulders itself even into the course of our advance. I have portraits of myself taken at five and twenty, and five and thirty years of age; I compare them with that lately drawn; how variously is it no longer me; how much more is my present image unlike the former, than unlike that I shall go out of the world with? It is too much to abuse nature, to make her trot so far that she must be forced to leave us, and abandon our conduct, our eyes, teeth, legs, and all the rest, to the mercy of a foreign and begged assistance, and to resign us into the hands of art, being weary of following us herself.

I am not very fond either of salads or fruits, except melons. My father hated all sorts of sauces; I love them all. Eating too much hurts me; but, as to the quality of what I eat, I do not yet certainly know that any sort of meat disagrees with my stomach; neither have I observed that either full moon or decrease, spring or autumn, have any influence upon me. We have in us notions that are inconstant and for which no reason can be given: for example, I found radishes first grateful to my stomach, since that nauseous, and now again grateful. In several other things, I find my stomach and appetite vary after the same manner; I have changed again and again from white wine to claret, from claret to white.

I am a great lover of fish, and consequently make my fasts

feasts, and feasts fasts: and I believe what some people say, that it is more easy of digestion than flesh. As I make a conscience of eating flesh upon the fish-days, so does my taste make a conscience of mixing fish and flesh; the difference between them seems to me too remote.

From my youth, I have sometimes kept out of the way at meals; either to sharpen my appetite against the next morning (for, as Epicurus fasted and made lean meals to accustom his pleasure to make shift without abundance, I, on the contrary, do it to prepare my pleasure to make better and more cheerful use of abundance); or else I fasted to preserve my vigor for the service of some action of body or mind; for both the one and the other of these is cruelly dulled in me by repletion; and, above all things, I hate that foolish coupling of so healthful and sprightly a goddess with that little belching god, bloated with the fumes of his liquor;—or to cure my sick stomach, or for want of fit company; for I say, as the same Epicurus did, that one is not so much to regard what he eats, as with whom; and I commend Chilo, that he would not engage himself to be at Periander's feast till he first was informed who were to be the other guests; no dish is so acceptable to me, nor no sauce so appetizing, as that which is extracted from society. I think it more wholesome to eat more leisurely and less, and to eat oftener; but I would have appetite and hunger attended to; I should take no pleasure to be fed with three or four pitiful and stinted repasts a day, after a medicinal manner; who will assure me, that, if I have a good appetite in the morning, I shall have the same at supper? But, we old fellows especially, let us take the first opportune time of eating, and leave to almanac makers hopes and prognostics. The utmost fruit of my health is pleasure; let us take hold of the present and known. I avoid the invariable in these laws of fasting; he who would have one form serve him, let him avoid the continuing it; we harden ourselves in it, our strength is there stupefied and laid asleep; six months after, you shall find your stomach so inured to it, that all you have got is the loss of your liberty of doing otherwise but to your prejudice.

I never keep my legs and thighs warmer in winter than in

summer; one simple pair of silk stockings is all. I have suffered myself, for the relief of my colds, to keep my head warmer; and my belly on the account of my colic; my diseases in a few days habituated themselves thereto, and disdained my ordinary provisions; we soon get from a coif to a kerchief over it, from a simple cap to a quilted hat; the trimmings of the doublet must not merely serve for ornament; there must be added a hare's skin or a vulture's skin, and a cap under the hat; follow this gradation, and you will go a very fine way to work. I will do nothing of the sort, and would willingly leave off what I have begun. If you fall into any new inconvenience, all this is labor lost, you are accustomed to it; seek out some other. Thus do they destroy themselves, who submit to be pestered with these enforced and superstitious rules; they must add something more, and something more after that; there is no end on't.

For what concerns our affairs and pleasures, it is much more commodious, as the ancients did, to lose one's dinner, and defer making good cheer till the hour of retirement and repose, without breaking up a day; and so was I formerly used to do. As to health, I since by experience find, on the contrary, that it is better to dine, and that the digestion is better while awake. I am not very used to be thirsty, either well or sick; my mouth is, indeed, apt to be dry, but without thirst; and commonly I never drink but with thirst that is created by eating, and far on in the meal; I drink pretty well for a man of my pitch; in summer, and at a relishing meal, I do not only exceed the limits of Augustus, who drank but thrice, precisely; but not to offend Democritus' rule, who forbade that men should stop at four times as an unlucky number, I proceed at need to the fifth glass, about three half-pints; for the little glasses are my favorites, and I like to drink them off, which other people avoid as an unbecoming thing. I mix my wine sometimes with half, sometimes with the third part water; and when I am at home, by an ancient custom that my father's physician prescribed both to him and himself, they mix that which is designed for me in the buttery, two or three hours before 'tis brought in. 'Tis said, that Cranaus, king of Athens, was the inventor of this custom of dashing wine with water; whether useful or no, I have heard disputed. I think it more decent and

wholesome for children to drink no wine till after sixteen or eighteen years of age. The most usual and common method of living is the most becoming; all particularity, in my opinion, is to be avoided; and I should as much hate a German who mixed water with his wine, as I should a Frenchman who drank it pure. Public usage gives the law in these things.

I fear a fog, and fly from smoke as from the plague; the first repairs I fell upon in my own house, were the chimneys and houses of office, the common and insupportable defects of all old buildings; and among the difficulties of war, I reckon the choking dust they make us ride in a whole day together. I have a free and easy respiration; and my colds for the most part go off without offense to the lungs, and without a cough.

The heat of summer is more an enemy to me than the cold of winter; for, besides the incommodity of heat, less remediable than cold, and besides the force of the sunbeams that strike upon the head, all glittering light offends my eyes, so that I could not now sit at dinner over against a flaming fire.

To dull the whiteness of paper, in those times when I was more wont to read, I laid a piece of glass upon my book, and found my eyes much relieved by it. I am to this hour ignorant of the use of spectacles; and I can see as far as ever I did, or any other. 'Tis true, that in the evening I begin to find a little disturbance and weakness in my sight if I read; an exercise I have always found troublesome, especially by night. Here is one step back and a very manifest one; I shall retire another; from the second to the third, and so to the fourth, so gently, that I shall be stark blind before I shall be sensible of the age and decay of my sight; so artificially do the Fatal sisters untwist our lives. And so I doubt whether my hearing begins to grow thick; and you will see I shall have half lost it, when I shall still lay the fault on the voices of those who speak to me. A man must screw up his soul to a high pitch, to make it sensible how it ebbs away.

My walking is quick and firm; and I know not which of the two, my mind or my body, I have most to do to keep in the same state. That preacher is very much my friend who can oblige my attention

a whole sermon through; in places of ceremony, where every one's countenance is so starched, where I have seen the ladies keep even their eyes so fixed, I could never order it so, that some part or other of me did not lash out; so that though I was seated, I was never settled. As the philosopher Chrysippus' maid said of her master, that he was only drunk in his legs, for it was his custom to be always kicking them about in what place soever he sat; and she said it, when the wine having made all his companions drunk, he found no alteration in himself at all; it may have been said of me from my infancy that I had either folly or quicksilver in my feet, so much stirring and unsettledness there is in them, wherever they are placed.

'Tis indecent, besides the hurt it does to one's health, and even to the pleasure of eating, to eat so greedily as I do; I often bite my tongue, and sometimes my fingers, in my haste. Diogenes meeting a boy eating after that manner, gave his tutor a box on the ear. There were men at Rome that taught people to chew, as well as to walk, with a good grace. I lose thereby the leisure of speaking, which gives great relish to the dinner-table, provided the discourse be suitable, that is, pleasant and short.

There is jealousy and envy among our pleasures; they cross and hinder one another; Alcibiades, a man who well understood how to make good cheer, banished even music from the table, that it might not disturb the entertainment of discourse, for the reason, as Plato tells us, "that it is the custom of ordinary people to call fiddlers and singing men to feasts, for want of good discourse and pleasant talk, with which men of understanding know how to entertain one another." Varro requires all this in entertainments: "Persons of graceful presence and agreeable conversation, who are neither silent nor babblers; neatness and delicacy, both of meat and place; and fair weather." The art of dining well is no slight art, the pleasure not a slight pleasure; neither the greatest captains nor the greatest philosophers have disdained the use or science of eating well. My imagination has delivered three repasts to the custody of my memory, which fortune rendered sovereignly sweet to me, upon several occasions in my more flourishing age; my present state ex-

cludes me; for every one, according to the good temper of body and mind wherein he then finds himself, furnishes for his own share a particular grace and savor. I, who but crawl upon the earth, hate this inhuman wisdom, that will have us despise and hate all culture of the body; I look upon it as an equal injustice to loathe natural pleasures as to be too much in love with them. Xerxes was a coxcombical blockhead who, environed with all human delights, proposed a reward to him who could find out others; but he is not much less so who cuts off any of those pleasures that nature has provided for him. A man should neither pursue nor avoid them, but receive them. I receive them, I confess, a little too warmly and kindly, and easily suffer myself to follow my natural propensions. We have no need to exaggerate their inanity; they themselves will make us sufficiently sensible of it, thanks to our sick wet-blanket mind, that puts us out of taste with them as with itself; it treats both itself and all it receives, one while better, and another worse, according to its insatiable, vagabond, and versatile essence:

"Sincerum est nisi vas, quodcunque infundis, acescit."

I, who boast that I so curiously and particularly embrace the conveniences of life, find them, when I most nearly consider them, very little more than wind. But what? We are all wind throughout; and, moreover, the wind itself, more discreet than we, loves to bluster and shift from corner to corner; and contents itself with its proper offices, without desiring stability and solidity—qualities that nothing belong to it.

The pure pleasures, as well as the pure displeasures, of the imagination, say some, are the greatest, as was expressed by the balance of Critolaus. 'Tis no wonder; it makes them to its own liking, and cuts them out of the whole cloth; of this I every day see notable examples, and, peradventure, to be desired. But I, who am of a mixed and heavy condition, cannot snap so soon at this one simple object, but that I negligently suffer myself to be carried away with the present pleasures of the general human law, intellectually sensible, and sensibly intellectual. The Cyrenaic philosophers will have it that as corporal pains, so corporal pleasures are more

powerful, both as double and as more just. There are some, as Aristotle says, who out of a savage kind of stupidity dislike them; and I know others who out of ambition do the same. Why do they not, moreover, forswear breathing? why do they not live of their own? why not refuse light, because it shines gratis, and costs them neither pains nor invention? Let Mars, Pallas, or Mercury afford them their light by which to see, instead of Venus, Ceres, and Bacchus. Will they not seek the quadrature of the circle, even when on their wives? I hate that we should be enjoined to have our minds in the clouds, when our bodies are at table; I would not have the mind nailed there, nor wallow there; I would have it take place there and sit, but not lie down. Aristippus maintained nothing but the body, as if he had no soul; Zeno stickled only for the soul, as if he had no body; both of them faultily. Pythagoras, they say, followed a philosophy that was all contemplation; Socrates one that was all conduct and action; Plato found a mean between the two; but they only say this for the sake of talking. The true point is found in Socrates; and Plato is much more Socratic than Pythagoric, and it becomes him better. When I dance, I dance; when I sleep, I sleep. Nay, when I walk alone in a beautiful orchard, if my thoughts are some part of the time taken up with foreign occurrences, I some part of the time call them back again to my walk, to the orchard, to the sweetness of the solitude, and to myself.

Nature has with a motherly tenderness observed this, that the actions she has enjoined us for our necessity should be also pleasant to us; and she invites us to them, not only by reason, but also by appetite, and 'tis injustice to infringe her laws. When I see both Cæsar and Alexander in the thickest of their greatest business, so fully enjoy human and corporal pleasures, I do not hold that they slackened their souls, but wound them up higher, by vigor of courage, subjecting these violent employments and laborious thoughts to the ordinary usage of life; wise, had they believed the last was their ordinary, the first their extraordinary vocation. We are great fools. "He has passed over his life in idleness," say we: "I have done nothing to-day." What? have you not lived? that is not only the fundamental, but the most illustrious of all your occupations.

"Had I been put to the management of great affairs, I should have made it seen what I could do." Have you known how to meditate and manage your life, you have performed the greatest work of all. For a man to show and set out himself, nature has no need of fortune; she equally manifests herself in all stages, and behind a curtain as well as without one. Have you known how to regulate your conduct, you have done a great deal more than he who has composed books. Have you known how to take repose, you have done more than he who has taken cities and empires.

The great and glorious masterpiece of man is to know how to live to purpose; all other things, to reign, to lay up treasure, to build, are, at most, but little appendices and props. I delight to see a general of an army, at the foot of a breach he is presently to assault, give himself up entire and free at dinner, to talk and be merry with his friends; to see Brutus, when heaven and earth were conspired against him and the Roman liberty, stealing some hours of the night from his rounds to read and abridge Polybius, in all security. 'Tis for little souls, that truckle under the weight of affairs, not from them to know how clearly to disengage themselves, not to know how to lay them aside and take them up again:

> "O fortes, pejoraque passi
> Mecum sæpe viri! nunc vino pellite curas:
> Cras ingens iterabimus æquor."

Whether it be in jest or earnest, that the theological and Sorbonical wine, and their feasts, are turned into a proverb, I find it reasonable they should dine so much more commodiously and pleasantly, as they have profitably and seriously employed the morning in the exercise of their schools. The conscience of having well spent the other hours, is the just and savory sauce of the dinner-table. The sages lived after that manner; and that inimitable emulation to virtue, which astonishes us both in the one and the other Cato, that humor of theirs, so severe as even to be importunate, gently submits itself and yields to the laws of the human condition, of Venus and Bacchus; according to the precepts of their sect, that require the perfect sage to be as expert and intelligent in the use of natural

pleasures as in all other duties of life: *"Cui cor sapiat, ei et sapiat palatus."*

Relaxation and facility, methinks, wonderfully honor and best become a strong and generous soul. Epaminondas did not think that to take part, and that heartily, in songs and sports and dances with the young men of his city, were things that in any way derogated from the honor of his glorious victories and the perfect purity of manners that was in him. And among so many admirable actions of Scipio, the grandfather, a person worthy to be reputed of a heavenly extraction, there is nothing that gives him a greater grace than to see him carelessly and childishly trifling at gathering and selecting shells, and playing at quoits upon the seashore with Lælius; and, if it was foul weather, amusing and pleasing himself in representing by writing in comedies the meanest and most popular actions of men; or having his head full of that wonderful enterprise of Hannibal and Africa, visiting the schools in Sicily, and attending philosophical lectures, improving himself, to the blind envy of his enemies at Rome. Nor is there anything more remarkable in Socrates than that, old as he was, he found time to make himself taught dancing and playing upon instruments, and thought it time well spent; but this same man was seen in an ecstasy, standing upon his feet a whole day and a night together, in the presence of all the Grecian army, surprised and ravished with some profound thought. He was the first who, among so many valiant men of the army, ran to the relief of Alcibiades, oppressed with the enemy; shielded him with his own body, and disengaged him from the crowd, by absolute force of arms. It was he who, in the Delian battle, raised and saved Xenophon when fallen from his horse; and who, among all the people of Athens, enraged as he was at so unworthy a spectacle, first presented himself to rescue Theramenes, whom the thirty tyrants were hauling to execution by their satellites, and desisted not from his bold enterprise but at the remonstrance of Theramenes himself, though he was only followed by two more in all. He was seen, when courted by a beauty with whom he was in love, to maintain at need a severe abstinence. He was seen ever to go to the wars, and walk upon ice, with bare feet; to wear the same robe winter and

summer; to surpass all his companions in patience of bearing hardships, and to eat no more at a feast than at his own private dinner. He was seen, for seven and twenty years together, to endure hunger, poverty, the indocility of his children, and the claws of his wife, with the same countenance; and, in the end, calumny, tyranny, imprisonment, fetters, and poison. But was this man obliged to drink full bumpers by any rule of civility? he was also the man of the whole army, with whom the advantage in drinking remained. And he never refused to play at cob-nut, nor to ride the hobby-horse with children, and it became him well; for all actions, says philosophy, equally become and equally honor a wise man. We have enough wherewithal to do it, and we ought never to be weary of presenting the image of this great man in all the patterns and forms of perfections. There are very few examples of life, full and pure; and we wrong our teaching every day, to propose to ourselves those that are weak and imperfect, scarce good for any one service, and rather pull us back; corrupters rather than correctors of manners. The people deceive themselves; a man goes much more easily indeed by the ends, where the extremity serves for a bound, a stop, and guide, than by the middle way, large and open; and according to art, more than according to nature: but withal much less nobly and commendably.

Grandeur of soul consists not so much in mounting and in pressing forward, as in knowing how to govern and circumscribe itself; it takes everything for great, that is enough, and demonstrates itself better in moderate than in eminent things. There is nothing so fine and legitimate as well and duly to play the man; nor science so arduous as well and naturally to know how to live this life; and of all the infirmities we have, 'tis the most savage to despise our being.

Whoever has a mind to send his soul abroad, when the body is ill at ease, to preserve it from the contagion, let him, by all means, do it if he can: but, otherwise, let him on the contrary favor and assist it, and not refuse to participate of its natural pleasures with a conjugal complacency, bringing to it, if it be the wiser, moderation, lest by indiscretion they should get confounded with pleasure. Intemperance is the pest of pleasure; and temperance is not its

scourge, but rather its seasoning. Eudoxus, who therein established the sovereign good, and his companions, who set so high a value upon it, tasted it in its most charming sweetness, by the means of temperance, which in them was singular and exemplary.

I enjoin my soul to look upon pain and pleasure with an eye equally regular, *"Eodem enim vitio est effusio animi in lætitia, quo in dolore contractio,"* and equally firm; but the one gayly and the other severely, and, so far as it is able, to be as careful to extinguish the one, as to extend the other. The judging rightly of good brings along with it the judging soundly of evil; pain has something of the inevitable in its tender beginnings, and pleasure something of the evitable in its excessive end. Plato couples them together, and wills that it should be equally the office of fortitude to fight against pain, and against the immoderate and charming blandishments of pleasure; they are two fountains, from which whoever draws, when and as much as he needs, whether city, man, or beast, is very fortunate. The first is to be taken medicinally and upon necessity, and more scantily; the other for thirst, but not to drunkenness. Pain, pleasure, love, and hatred are the first things that a child is sensible of; if, when reason comes, they apply it to themselves, that is virtue.

I have a special nomenclature of my own; I "pass away time," when it is ill and uneasy, but when 'tis good I do not pass it away; "I taste it over again and stick to it;" one must run over the ill, and settle upon the good. This ordinary phrase of pastime, and passing away the time, represents the usage of those wise sort of people who think they cannot do better with their lives than to let them run out and slide away, pass them over, and balk them, and, as much as they can, ignore them, and shun them as a thing of troublesome and contemptible quality; but I know it to be another kind of thing, and find it both valuable and commodious, even in its latest decay, wherein I now enjoy it; and nature has delivered it into our hands in such and so favorable circumstances, that we have only ourselves to blame if it be troublesome to us, or slide unprofitably away: *"Stulti vita ingrata est, trepida est, tota in futurum fertur."* Nevertheless, I compose myself to lose mine without regret; but withal as a thing that is perishable by its condition, not that it troubles or

annoys me. Nor does it properly well become any not to be displeased when they die, excepting such as are pleased to live. There is good husbandry in enjoying it; I enjoy it double to what others do; for the measure of its fruition depends upon the more or less of our application to it. Now especially that I perceive mine to be so short in time, I will extend it in weight; I will stop the promptitude of its flight by the promptitude of my grasp; and by the vigor of using it compensate the speed of its running away; by how much the possession of living is more short, I must make it so much deeper and more full.

Others feel the pleasure of content and prosperity; I feel it too, as well as they, but not as it slides and passes by; one should study, taste, and ruminate upon it, to render condign thanks to Him who grants it to us. They enjoy the other pleasures as they do that of sleep, without knowing it. To the end that even sleep itself should not so stupidly escape from me, I have formerly caused myself to be disturbed in my sleep, so that I might the better and more sensibly relish and taste it. I ponder with myself of content; I do not skim over, but sound it; and I bend my reason, now grown perverse and peevish, to entertain it. Do I find myself in any calm composedness? is there any pleasure that tickles me? I do not suffer it to dally with my senses only, I associate my soul to it too; not there to engage itself, but therein to take delight; not there to lose itself, but to be present there; and I employ it, on its part, to view itself in this prosperous state, to weigh and appreciate its happiness, and to amplify it. It reckons how much it stands indebted to Almighty God that its conscience and the intestine passions are in repose; that it has the body in its natural disposition, orderly and competently enjoying the soft and soothing functions, by which He of His grace is pleased to compensate the sufferings wherewith His justice at His good pleasure chastises us. It reflects how great a benefit it is to be so protected, that, which way soever it turns its eye, the heavens are calm around it. No desire, no fear or doubt, troubles the air; no difficulty, past, present, or to come, that its imagination may not pass over without offense. This consideration takes great luster from the comparison of different conditions; and

therefore it is that I present to my thought, in a thousand aspects, those whom fortune or their own error torments and carries away; and those, who more like to me, so negligently and incuriously receive their good fortune. Those are men who pass away their time, indeed; they pass over the present, and that which they possess, to give themselves up to hope, and for vain shadows and images which fancy puts into their heads:

> "Morte obita quales fama est volitare figuras,
> Aut quæ sopitos deludunt somnia sensus:"

which hasten and prolong their flight, according as they are pursued. The fruit and end of their pursuit is to pursue; as Alexander said, that the end of his labor was to labor:

> "Nil actum credens, cum quid superesset agendum;"

For my part then, I love life, and cultivate it, such as it has pleased God to bestow it upon us. I do not desire it should be without the necessity of eating and drinking; and I should think myself inexcusable to wish it had been twice as long: "*Sapiens divitiarum naturalium quæsitor accerimus:*" nor that we should support ourselves by putting only a little of that drug into our mouths, by which Epimenides took away his appetite, and kept himself alive; nor that we should stupidly beget children with our fingers or heels, but, rather, with reverence be it spoken, that we might voluptuously beget them with our fingers and heels; nor that the body should be without desire, and without titillation. These are ungrateful and wicked complaints. I accept kindly, and with gratitude, what nature has done for me; am well pleased with it, and proud of it. A man does wrong to the great omnipotent Giver of all things, to refuse, annul, or disfigure his gift; all goodness Himself, He has made everything good: "*Omnia quæ secundum naturam sunt, æstimatione digna sunt.*"

Of philosophical opinions, I preferably embrace those that are most solid, that is to say the most human, and most our own: my discourse is, suitable to my manners, low and humble; philosophy plays the child, to my thinking, when it puts itself upon its Ergos,

to preach to us that 'tis a barbarous alliance to marry the divine with the earthly, the reasonable with the unreasonable, the severe with the indulgent, the honest with the dishonest; that pleasure is a brutish quality, unworthy to be tasted by a wise man; that the sole pleasure he extracts from the enjoyment of a fair young wife, is a pleasure of his conscience to perform an action according to order, as to put on his boots for a profitable journey. Oh, that its followers had no more right, nor nerves, nor juice, in getting their wives' maidenhoods, than in its lessons.

That is not what Socrates says, who is its master and ours: he values, as he ought, bodily pleasure; but he prefers that of the mind, as having more force, constancy, facility, variety, and dignity. This, according to him, goes by no means alone—he is not so fantastic—but only it goes first; temperance, with him, is the moderatrix, not the adversary of pleasure. Nature is a gentle guide, but not more sweet and gentle, than prudent and just: *"Intrandum est in rerum naturam, et penitus, quid ea postulet, pervidendum."* I hunt after her foot throughout; we have confounded it with artificial traces; and that academic and peripatetic good, which is, "to live according to it," becomes, by this means, hard to limit and explain; and that of the Stoics, cousin-german to it, which is "to consent to nature." Is it not an error to esteem any actions less worthy, because they are necessary? And yet they will not beat it out of my head, that it is not a very convenient marriage of pleasure with necessity, with which, says an ancient, the gods always conspire. To what end do we dismember by divorce a building united by so close and brotherly a correspondence? Let us, on the contrary, confirm it by mutual offices; let the mind rouse and quicken the heaviness of the body, and the body stay and fix the levity of the soul. *"Qui, velut summum bonum, laudat animæ naturam, et, tanquam malum, naturam carnis accusat, profecto et animam carnaliter appetit, et carnem carnaliter fugit; quoniam id vanitate sentit humana, non veritate divina."* In this present that God has made us, there is nothing unworthy our care; we stand accountable, even to a hair; and 'tis no slight commission to man, to conduct man according to his condition; 'tis express, plain, and the principal injunction of all, and

the Creator has seriously and strictly enjoined it. Authority has alone power to work upon common understandings, and is of more weight in a foreign language; therefore let us again charge with it in this place: *"Stultitiæ proprium quis non dixerit, ignave et contumaciter facere, quæ facienda sunt; et alio corpus impellere, alio animum; distrahique inter diversissimos motus?"* To make this apparent, ask any one, some day, to tell you what whimsies and imaginations he put into his pate, upon the account of which he diverted his thoughts from a good meal, and regrets the time he spends in eating: you will find there is nothing so insipid in all the dishes at your table, as this wise meditation of his (for the most part we had better sleep than wake to the purpose we wake); and that his discourses and notions are not worth the worst mess there. Though they were the ecstasies of Archimedes himself, what then? I do not here speak of, nor mix with the rabble of us ordinary men, and the vanity of the thoughts and desires that divert us, those venerable souls, elevated by the ardor of devotion and religion, to a constant and conscientious meditation of divine things, who, by the energy of vivid and vehement hope, prepossessing the use of the eternal nourishment, the final aim and last step of Christian desires, the sole, constant, and incorruptible pleasure, disdain to apply themselves to our necessitous, fluid and ambiguous conveniences, and easily resign to the body the care and use of sensual and temporal pasture: 'tis a privileged study. Between ourselves, I have ever observed supercelestial opinions and subterranean manners to be of singular accord.

Æsop, that great man, saw his master make water as he walked: "What, then," said he, "must we dung as we run?" Let us manage our time as well as we can, there will yet remain a great deal that will be idle and ill employed. The mind has not other hours enough wherein to do its business, without disassociating itself from the body, in that little space it must have for its necessity. They would put themselves out of themselves, and escape from being men; 'tis folly; instead of transforming themselves into angels, they transform themselves into beasts; instead of elevating, they lay themselves lower. These transcendental humors affright me, like high

and inaccessible cliffs and precipices; and nothing is hard for me to digest in the life of Socrates but his ecstacies and communication with demons; nothing so human in Plato as that for which they say he was called divine; and of our sciences, those seem to be the most terrestrial and low that are highest mounted; and I find nothing so humble and mortal in the life of Alexander, as his fancies about his immortalization. Philotas pleasantly quipped him in his answer: he congratulated him by letter concerning the oracle of Jupiter Hammon, which had placed him among the gods: "Upon thy account, I am glad of it, but the men are to be pitied who are to live with a man, and to obey him, who exceeds and is not contented with the measure of a man." *"Diis te minorem quod geris, imperas."* The pretty inscription wherewith the Athenians honored the entry of Pompey into their city, is conformable to my sense: "By so much thou art a god, as thou confessest thee a man." 'Tis an absolute and, as it were, a divine perfection, for a man to know how loyally to enjoy his being. We seek other conditions, by reason we do not understand the use of our own; and go out of ourselves, because we know not how there to reside. 'Tis to much purpose to go upon stilts, for, when upon stilts, we must yet walk with our legs; and when seated upon the most elevated throne in the world, we are but seated upon our breech. The fairest lives, in my opinion, are those which regularly accommodate themselves to the common and human model; without miracle, without extravagance. Old age stands a little in need of a more gentle treatment. Let us recommend it to God, the protector of health and wisdom, but withal, let it be gay and sociable.

> "Frui paratis et valido mihi
> Latoë, dones, et, precor, integra
> Cum mente; nec turpem senectam
> Degere, nec Cithara carentem."

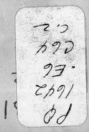